TR

The Demographic Bases of Canadian Society

Warren E. Kalbach, Ph.D. (Wash.),
Department of Sociology, University of Toronto

Wayne W. McVey, M.A.,
Director of the Population Research Laboratory,
Department of Sociology, University of Alberta

D0888168

McGRAW-HILL
COMPANY OF CANADA LIMITED

TORONTO / MONTREAL / NEW YORK / LONDON / SYDNEY
MEXICO / JOHANNESBURG / PANAMA / DÜSSELDORF / SINGAPORE
RIO DE JANEIRO / KUALA LUMPUR / NEW DELHI

To Calvin F. Schmid

THE DEMOGRAPHIC BASES OF CANADIAN SOCIETY

ISBN 0-07-094952-2

12345678910   THB71   0987654321

Printed and bound in Canada

CONTENTS

LIST OF TABLES

LIST OF FIGURE NUMBERS

Preface

This book has a very specific and practical purpose. It provides as simply as possible the basic information about Canada's population; e.g., its growth, distribution, components of change, and characteristics of individuals and families. Anyone interested in obtaining an overall perspective of Canada's population should find this volume of interest whether he be a student of Canada's general history, its geography, or of its social and economic institutions. It is not intended that this book be just a compilation of demographic facts and figures, rather it presents only as much summary data as seems necessary to convey a feeling of knowledgeable familiarity with both the structural aspects of Canadian population and the components of change. Graphic techniques have been utilized wherever it seemed that this form of presentation provided a more efficient means for achieving a reasonable understanding of significant trends and features of a population that are quite often obscured by the publication of large masses of census data.

The book has been prepared primarily for use as a supplemental text in courses where information on the structure, characteristics, and changing nature of Canada's population may have either descriptive or theoretical relevance. Because of practical limitations placed on its length, it is not intended to be the definitive text on Canadian population. The reader may find himself frustrated by the fact that the book is somewhat long on description and short on explanation. Explanations that are offered are often speculative in nature. It is at this point that the experience and theoretical perspective of the instructor must be incorporated to provide more complete explanations of probable causes and the social, economic, and political significance of the characteristics and trends discussed in the following chapters.

Considerable basic data in tabular form have been presented for the convenience of the reader, but caution must be exercised to avoid attributing significance to small differences which may appear in these data. In view of the types of error associated with census enumerations and surveys, the reader will be well advised to keep the emphasis on gross differences and systematic and repetitive patterns. A brief history of data collection in Canada, included in the introduction, provides a basis for the appreciation of the quality and limitations of demographic data. This is followed by the book's two major sections. Chapters 1–6 deal exclusively with population growth, components of growth, internal distribution, and such ascribed characteristics as sex, age, nativity, and ethnic origins which constitute the basic structure. The second section, Chapters 7–13, is concerned with achieved characteristics of the population and changes therein.

To provide an historical perspective, data on the pre-Confederation period have been included in Chapter 1. In order to maintain a proper perspective from Confederation to the present, an attempt has been made to emphasize, wherever data permit, the fundamental regional differentiation that has given Canada its unique demographic character. While such an emphasis highlights the historical bicultural and bilingual features of Canada's population, it also draws attention to the increasingly significant role played by other ethnic origin groups in the settlement and development of Canada's vast territory. Starting with Chapter 6, data and analyses have been arranged wherever possible to correspond with subject matter areas generally found in current texts, such as ethnic and minority groups, marriage and family, education, religion, and labour force. Practical considerations as to the appropriate length for a supplemental text of this kind necessitated the omission of some topics and limited the analyses of many that were included. It is the hope of the authors that their judgment in this respect has not impaired the book's usefulness.

The final product reflects the active interest, participation, and cooperation of a great many people. Major support came from the University of Alberta General Research Fund, the resources of the Population Research Laboratory of the University of Alberta's Department of Sociology, and Erindale College of the University of Toronto. Among those who contributed valuable research, editorial, statistical, and drafting assistance, the following deserve special mention: Donald Demers, Diane Gallagher, Lars Hassbring, Kwai Yiu Ho, Jarmila Horna, Charles S. Lyon, Judith Goldie, and Wayne Miller. Special credit goes to Miss Patricia Dawson who was responsible for the execution of the charts in Chapters 1–6, and to Mrs. Ilze Hobin who developed and delineated the illustrations for the remaining chapters, in addition to organizing many of the required data tables. Mrs. Carol Waugh assisted in the typing of several drafts of the manuscript; and the authors are particularly indebted to Miss Sonia Shaw, Head Secretary of the Department of

Sociology, University of Alberta, for helping to overcome many of the difficulties encountered during the final months of manuscript preparation. The authors, of course, assume full responsibility for inconsistencies between the data presented and the original sources, or errors in their analysis and interpretation.

Warren E. Kalbach
University of Toronto
Wayne W. McVey Jr.
University of Alberta

Introduction

Data Collection in Canada

Canada, like most other countries that have experienced rapid expansion of both population and economic activity, became interested in assessing the dimensions of its domain along with the character of its population and economic activity at a relatively early date. Some 200 years before Confederation, Louis XIV ordered the first census to be taken in New France in order to determine what progress had been made during the half century of expansion following the founding of Quebec. This was followed a year later by a census of cattle, sheep, and farm land under cultivation. During the French regime there were no fewer than 36 censuses of the population of New France. During the latter years of the same period, Nova Scotia, Cape Breton Island, Newfoundland, New Brunswick, and Prince Edward Island conducted some 51 complete censuses and 19 partial censuses.

The quality of statistics declined with the imposition of British control in 1763. While there were censuses in Lower Canada in 1765 and again in 1784 and 1790, it was not until the nineteenth century that real progress was made toward the establishment of a regular decennial census. A landmark of progress was the enactment of the Statistical Act of 1848 providing for the Census of 1851 as well as for the provincial registration of births and deaths. The history of data collection in Canada is the story of the development of more accurate, systematic, and comprehensive data collection procedures to provide the government with the basic facts needed for more rational planning and legislative action. Several semi-official compilations of statistics were produced in the early years of Confederation, culminating in the Act of

1

1879 providing for the Decennial Census of 1881 and the collection, abstraction, tabulation, and publication of "vital, agricultural, commercial, and other statistics." Another significant step forward was taken in 1885 with the passing of an act providing for a census in 1886 of Manitoba, the Northwest Territories, and the District of Keewatin. This was the basis for the establishment of the quinquennial censuses of the Prairie Provinces and the later extension of the quinquennial census to all Canada.

With increasing demand and proliferation of statistical data by increasing numbers of governmental departments, the *ad hoc* basis of organizing for decennial censuses and other data collecting activities became increasingly inadequate. Thus, the establishment of a permanent Census and Statistics Office in 1905 under the Ministry of Agriculture was a significant event in the history of Canadian statistics. Not only could succeeding censuses be conducted more efficiently and accurately with experienced personnel, but greater continuity could be provided in the collection of other data during the intercensal years, as well as improved coordination of data collection activities. Still, there was a lack of overall coordination with other offices, and in 1912 a commission was appointed to investigate and report on a "comprehensive system of general statistics adequate to the necessities of the country and in keeping with the demands of the time."[1] Their extensive recommendations were implemented in 1915 in the creation of the office of Dominion Statistician who was charged with the specific task of organizing a central Canadian statistical office to implement the recommendations of the commission. In 1918, the Dominion Bureau of Statistics was established embodying all previous statistical legislation and expanding its responsibilities to provide the comprehensive system so urgently needed. Its mandate was nothing less than "to collect, abstract, compile and publish statistical information relative to the commercial, industrial, social, economic and general activities and condition of the people" and "to collaborate with all other departments of the government in the compilation and publication of statistical records of administration according to regulations."[2]

One of the more important contributions of this new statistical organization insofar as population data were concerned was the organization of two Dominion-Provincial conferences resulting in the adoption of a bill providing for the uniform collection of birth, marriage, and death records for the whole of Canada. Also, the ground work was laid for securing comprehensive data on the characteristics of immigrants from the Department of Immigration to facilitate comparison and analysis relative to census data. Fluctuations in activity, demands for greater controls over both population and the economy during war, and the increasing complexity of social and economic problems following World War II have increased the need for more detailed and comprehensive data than ever collected before, at both national and international levels. With increasing demands, expansion of the Bureau's staff was inevitable, and in 1943 decisions were made that resulted in the establishment of a Research and Development Division and a sampling organization. The activities of the first led to considerable revision and reorganization and updating of many of the existing statistical series, and the work in sampling led to an amendment of the Statistics Act of 1948 to authorize the collection of official statistics on a sample basis. Additional efforts in recent years have been increasingly centred on the development of more efficient and economical methods of collecting and distributing the basic statistical data which is in demand by business and government at national, provincial, and local levels.

It is important to point out the rather close relationship between perception of social and economic problems and the collection and dissemination of data relevant to these problems. Data on ethnic origin, for example, have been collected for many years in recognition of the cultural diversity of Canada's immigrants and the concern over the relative assimilability of various ethnic groups. At the same time, counterpressures have been developing to eliminate the collection of these data because of its alleged tendency to promote disunity rather than cultural unity and the development of a common Canadian identity. Several provinces have already eliminated ethnic questions from their vital registration forms; and others are moving in this direction on the mistaken assumption that infrequent use of these data in research suggests their general lack of significance, or, perhaps more important, because it is thought that most people find these questions objectionable. However, until it can be shown that ethnic differentials have disappeared from the social and economic characteristics of Canada's population, these data are fundamental for the task of ascertaining the type and extent of problems experienced by the various ethnic groups and their implications for local and federal policy in Canada. Generally, it is hoped that differences will ultimately cease to exist between the various racial and ethnic origin groups in Canada to the extent that they will no longer reflect discriminatory attitudes and practices.

A related problem concerns the state of Canada's knowledge regarding its Native Indian and Eskimo populations. Failure to recognize either the importance or seriousness of their plight has been responsible for the rather inadequate accumulation of data over the years for these two particular populations. Of course, it is true that their combined populations are relatively small and that they have lived in the more remote and inaccessible regions of the country, a fact which has made data collection especially difficult. However, the economic and social development of any population goes hand in hand with the development of adequate statistical systems. The absence of the latter indicates either a low state of development or a lack of concern about the welfare of a particular population, or both. Even though serious problems still exist, the general improvement in quality of Canada's population data and the expanding scope of the government's statistical activities over time reflect the country's rapid social and economic development.

Troublesome by-products of continuing improvement in Canada's data collecting effort are (1) the periodic disruption of historical series, (2) discontinuities created by revision of data collection area boundaries, (3) changes in basic concepts, and (4) updating of specific indicators of social and economic conditions. Increasing awareness of specific problems creates the need for more refined measures and often entails modification of previously used concepts, such as those concerned with employment, occupation, causes of death, definition of household, etc. Such modifications impair the comparability of data over time, but this is an unavoidable consequence of improvement. The problems of trend analysis are often alleviated by providing parallel series of data under both new and old definitions for transitional periods, as has been done with respect to the definition of rural and urban population; but, of course, these efforts are not always completely satisfactory. The student must always be alert for such definitional and procedural changes that might affect the comparability of data and be ready to make allowances for such discontinuities where it is not possible to translate either the original or revised series into comparable form.

The data utilized in the following chapters have been taken, for the most part, from official census and vital statistics tabulations published by the Dominion Bureau of Statistics. No attempts have been made to account for the effects of changes in either definitions or procedures other than calling the fact to the reader's attention. Where possible, the results of special studies have been utilized where such adjustments have already been made. There is a certain parallel between the historical sequence of events associated with the development of an efficient data gathering system and the focusing of a photographic image on the view finder of a single-lens reflex camera. At first, only the major features of the biggest objects are discernible; but with finer focusing, more detail becomes apparent. Beyond this the similarity fades. The camera lens, unlike the data gathering system, records *everything* in its field of vision, whereas the latter must become increasingly proficient in selecting only those data from the total population judged to have the greatest social and economic relevance. There is, however, no built-in guarantee that the data actually collected during any particular census are necessarily the most relevant. The items finally incorporated in the interview or self-enumeration schedules often represent compromises of conflicting interests, expediency, budget considerations, and as such, often fall short of the ideal instrument required for answering the many perplexing questions about our society.

Censuses are basically inventories of defined populations within specified areas at particular moments in time. Registration systems, on the other hand, account for additions and subtractions from populations through births, deaths, immigration, and emigration over specified intervals of time. The Canadian census is designed not only to provide a periodic count of the total resident population living within the politically defined boundaries of the nation, but to assess the demographic, social, and economic character of this population as well. Once every ten years the government carries out a national census, canvassing the entire country and recording the number of inhabitants by their usual place of residence (*de jure* population) and selected social and economic characteristics, as of midnight between May 31st and June 1st (the specified census moment). In addition, there is a quinquennial census five years after the regular decennial census which is much smaller in scope.[3] Both the decennial and quinquennial censuses possess the ideal census attributes: i.e., they achieve *universality* by including all residents within a defined territory of Canada; they are *simultaneous* in that all data gathered refer to one well-defined point in time (midnight between May 31st and June 1st); they possess *regularity* (conducted every ten years); and are legitimatized, being conducted by the elected government.

The vital registration system provides for the continuous registration of all births, deaths, marriages, and divorces as they occur. The registration of vital events in Canada has been the responsibility of the separate provinces and territories, while the federal government has assumed a coordinating function and the responsibility for the compilation and publication of vital statistics. The Dominion-Provincial agreement of 1920 led to uniform standards regarding time limitations in reporting and with respect to the inclusion of specific items. A revised agreement in 1945 established the Vital Statistics Council; and, as a result of its recommendations, uniform national and provincial annual tabulations were established in 1952.[4] However, the standardization achieved relates to a few basic items only and their publication, not to the full content of the registration certificates. The data vary from province to province, and their value for research suffers accordingly.

Vital statistics have been collected and published for all provinces since 1926 and for all territories since 1950. While these data undoubtedly have improved in quality, they still reflect the special problems associated with continuous registration systems. Most important is the problem of under-registration which varies in seriousness from one province to the next. The problem is particularly serious with respect to the recording of infant deaths and to the handling and recording of stillbirths. Then too, as with census enumerations, there are the usual errors in recording such information as the characteristics of parents, the deceased, and cause of death. However, unlike the federally conducted census, there is an inter-provincial variation in the policing and enforcing of vital registration procedures, which introduces another dimension of error with which the student and researcher must contend.

The established procedures for the registration of migrants leave much to be desired. This is especially surprising in view of the continuing concern over the character of immigrants arriving in Canada. Since 1955, both quality and quantity of published data for arriving immigrants have shown marked improvement; but data for emigrants continue to be totally inadequate with little hope for any significant improvement in the near future. For either registration or census data, the basic problem remains to determine standard items of information to be collected and to establish the requisite organization and procedures which will insure reasonably accurate and consistent data. Since the development of more efficient social and political organizations is generally a function of time, a direct relationship tends to exist between the period of data collection and the data's accuracy and completeness. The earlier in time the census or registration data were collected, the more unreliable the results tend to be. It would, of course, be naive to assume either that all early censuses are worthless, or recent ones beyond repute. New France is an example of a population which maintained extremely good records and managed to carry out one of the first modern censuses. On the other hand, the first census of the territories which was conducted at a much later date could not hope to achieve a very high level of quality.

There are many problems associated with census operations, but only a few of the major ones can be mentioned here. Perhaps the greatest problems arise through enumerator fallibility and general lack of experience. Confusion about procedures and definitions is not uncommon, and many people are overlooked during the canvassing operation because of difficulty in locating either atypical housing units or persons with irregular living habits such as apartment dwellers and lodgers in metropolitan areas. The time needed to cover all inhabited areas of Canada and completely enumerate a population of about twenty million presents additional difficulties in the face of considerable population mobility and change. It is easy to incorrectly list infants in the household who were born after the official census date (i.e., after midnight, May 31st), or omit those who had been alive but who had died before the enumerator's arrival. Considering all the potential sources of error, the Dominion Bureau of Statistics should take considerable pride in the quality of the enumerations which they have conducted. However, the important consideration to keep in mind is that no matter how dedicated the personnel may be, no matter how thorough the planning, no matter how efficient the organization, it is practically impossible to execute a perfect census in which every resident of the country is counted once, and once only, and in which all the information required by the census is accurately obtained and processed.

As census procedures are improved, so are the techniques for determining the extent and nature of the errors. This gives rise to the seemingly paradoxical situation wherein census errors *appear* to increase as the census improves. The following statement illustrates both the variety and degree of error associated with modern censuses: "Recent studies conducted by the Dominion Bureau of Statistics have shown that Canadian Censuses, conducted hitherto by the canvasser method, suffer from certain weaknesses—some enumerators' bias; an undercount of 2.5 to 3.0 per cent of the population and up to ten per cent in particular sex-age groups; and a response variance as great as the sampling variance would have been with a 25 per cent sample for characteristics such as education and labour force participation."[5] Similarly, the net undercount of persons in the 1960 U.S. Census has been estimated at 2.3 per cent for the total population and as high as 16.0 per cent for non-white males, 25–44 years of age.[6]

In practice, a *total* enumeration always seems to fall short of its theoretically defined goal, i.e., a complete and accurate count of all residents at their usual place of residence. Even if such a goal were attainable, there are other sources of variability in census results. For example, the actual questions included in any specific enumeration schedule represent only a sample of all possible questions which might have been asked to elicit the desired information. In addition, the responses obtained from a particular respondent about other household members also represent just one sample of many responses had other members of the household been interviewed. It is quite understandable that some errors would be introduced into the data when one respondent is reporting information for others either in his or a neighbouring household. It is more difficult to accept the fact that even when respondents are providing information about themselves, there is apt to be considerable error in their statements regarding their own age, marital status, ethnic origin, income, or other characteristics about which the respondents are assumed to be knowledgeable. There are also serious problems which arise from the respondent's inability to provide answers to certain questions. Many times, the respondent simply does not know, and the nonresponse rate tends to increase as the questions become more difficult and complex. In other cases, enumerators may introduce errors either by not asking a question or failing to record the information when provided by the respondent. Using the recent U.S. census as an example, the nonresponse rate for the question asking for year or decade of birth was just 1.0 per cent. By contrast, the nonresponse rate for the question concerning enrolment in school for persons 5–34 years of age was 8.3 per cent, and for income for persons 14 years of age and over it was 6.2 per cent. For certain areas of Chicago, the nonresponse rate for a majority of the sample items referring to such characteristics as occupation, income, education, employment status, country of birth, number of children ever born, and other similar items was 50 per cent or more.[7]

Opportunities for error present themselves at every step in the complex process of data collection, processing, analysis, and publication. The total error is very simply the sum of (1) coverage error, (2) concept errors, (3) reporting errors, (4) enumerator errors, and (5) processing errors. Among these sources of error, experience has shown that enumerator errors have contributed the lion's share of total error—which is the major argument in support of the use of mail questionnaires and self-enumeration for the 1971 census of Canada. Considering this most recent innovation in census taking procedures, i.e., self-enumeration, it should be patently obvious that the quality of population and vital statistics has been and will continue to be directly related to the educational level of the population and its willingness to cooperate, as well as to the efficiency and dedication of the governmental organizations charged with the responsibility of collecting and processing the data. No census employing self-enumeration techniques could be successful unless there were a high degree of literacy in the population concerned. This is also true of censuses employing more standard canvassing techniques.

Generally speaking, it seems most people everywhere at one time or another have harboured suspicions concerning the government's motives in attempting to collect data on housing, income, marital status, family composition, and similar items. The powers of government to tax, conscript manpower, and to enact restrictive legislation applicable to selected segments of the population have always been viewed with considerable trepidation. Even today, among literate populations of democratic societies, these suspicions and fears linger, handicapping the efforts of "representative" governments to collect the basic facts about the nature of their country's population, its capabilities, and its resources. The formulation of sound policies and programs to deal successfully with pressing social and economic problems of today requires the most relevant, accurate, and complete data; and continued effort in this direction is still urgently needed.

REFERENCES

General Discussions
Hauser, Philip M.: *Population Perspectives,* New Brunswick, N.J., Rutgers University Press, 1960.
Heer, D. M.: *Society and Population,* Englewood Cliffs, N.J., Prentice Hall, 1968.
Wrong, Dennis H.: *Population and Society,* 3rd ed., New York, Random House, 1967.

Issues
Ehrlich, Paul R.: *The Population Bomb.*
Ehrlich, P. R., and A. H. Ehrlich: *Population—Resources—Environment,* San Francisco, W. H. Freeman and Company.

Textbooks
Bogue, Donald J.: *Principles of Demography,* Toronto, John Wiley and Sons, Inc. 1969.

Hauser, P. M. and O. D. Duncan (eds.): *The Study of Population: An Inventory and Appraisal*, Chicago, University of Chicago Press, 1959.
Thomlinson, Ralph: *Population Dynamics: Causes and Consequences of World Demographic Change*. New York, Random House, 1964.
Thompson, W. S. and D. T. Lewis: *Population Problems* (5th edition), New York, McGraw-Hill Book Company, 1965.

Readings
Freedman, Ronald (ed.): *Population: The Vital Revolution*. New York, Doubleday & Co., Inc.
Hauser, Philip M. (ed.): *The Population Dilemma*. Englewood Cliffs, N. J., Prentice-Hall, 1970.
Kammeyer, Kenneth C. (ed.): *Population Studies: Selected Essays and Research*. Chicago, Rand McNally and Company, 1969.
Nam, Charles B. (ed.): *Population and Society: A Textbook of Selected Readings*. New York, Houghton Mifflin, 1968.

Methods
Barclay, George W.: *Techniques of Population Analysis*. New York, John Wiley and Sons, Inc., 1958.
Spiegelman, Mortimer: *Introduction to Demography*. Cambridge, Mass., Harvard University Press, 1968.

Journals
Population Bulletin. Washington, D.C., Population Reference Bureau.

General Data Sources (Annual)
Canada Year Book. Ottawa, The Queen's Printer.
Demographic Year Book. New York, United Nations.

Bibliographic Source
Population Index. Princeton, Office of Population Research, Princeton University and Population Association of America, Inc.

FOOTNOTES

[1]Dominion Bureau of Statistics, *History, Function and Organization*, Ottawa, 1952, p. 9.
[2]*Ibid.*, p. 10.
[3]The decennial census has been taken every ten years since 1851, and quinquennial censuses for Canada every ten years since 1956. Prior to 1956, the quinquennial censuses were limited to the Prairie Provinces, the first being conducted in 1886. The early quinquennial censuses were quite similar to the decennial censuses with respect to the type of data collected, but when they were expanded to include all of Canada, the data were limited to such basic items as place of residence, sex, age, and marital status.
[4]Dominion Bureau of Statistics, *Vital Statistics, 1964*, Ottawa, The Queen's Printer, 1966, p. 3.
[5]E. Yablonski, "The Canadian Test Census Programme, June, 1968," Technical Memorandum. Census Test Series, 14, Census Division, Dominion Bureau of Statistics, June 1968, p. 1.
[6]U. S. Bureau of the Census, *1960 Census of Population and Housing: Procedural History*, Washington, D.C., U. S. Government Printing Office, 1966, pp. 121–122.
[7]U. S. Bureau of Census, *op. cit.*, p. 122.

Population Growth in Canada

The vast area of land stretching from the Arctic to the 49th Parallel and the Great Lakes–St. Lawrence River Seaway, and from the Atlantic to the Pacific Oceans comprising 3,851,809 square miles, has been a challenge of considerable magnitude to man's pioneering spirit. While early man is thought to have crossed into this part of the northern hemisphere from Asia many thousands of years ago, the Indian and Eskimo nomadic populations which have survived are relatively small in numbers and widely dispersed. Official discovery by Europeans of the land that was to become Canada came with the voyage of John Cabot in 1497; but evidence suggests that earlier Viking explorers had already discovered the coast of Newfoundland and European fishermen had been both exploiting the riches of its waters and trading with the natives many years prior to his arrival. From the time Cartier planted the French flag on the Atlantic coast in 1534 and Champlain established settlements at Port Royal in 1605 and Quebec in 1608, the momentum of exploration and settlement by both French and British increased dramatically. While the French were first in time and effort, they ultimately lost political control to the British. However, Canada still retains the unmistakable imprint of both French and British culture.

From a mere handful of settlers in 1608, the initial struggle against a hostile environment plus a continuing flow of immigrants boosted the population to over three million (3,300,000) by the time of Confederation. In 1867, Canada consisted of only four provinces and had a combined area of only one-tenth its current territorial size, being limited primarily to those areas readily accessible from the Gulf of St. Lawrence, the St. Lawrence River, and areas adjacent to the northern shores of the Great Lakes. The westward pressure of new immigrants in search of land, the establishment of the all important rail link with settlements in the prairies and on the West Coast, and a growing awareness of the need to consolidate the vast land under a single political entity brought about stabilized political boundaries just 45 years after Confederation. The early 1900s was the era of large scale immigration and settlement of Western Canada and the last major expansion of Canada's agricultural population. The process of industrialization and urbanization was accelerating, and the basis of the country's economy was undergoing drastic alteration. Unprecedented periods of industrial expansion during the 1920s, World War II and the postwar period, and during most of the 1960s have changed the face of Canada. Just 100 years after Confederation, its population residing in ten provinces and two vast northern territories had reached 20,000,000. The flow of immigrants at mid-century continues to erode the traditionally dominant position of the British origin population, and the shift from agriculture to industry has altered the basic distribution of the population to the point where approximately 70 per cent now reside in urbanized areas.

Pre-Confederation Era

Growth in numbers. In 1608, more than a century after Cabot's first voyage to the New World in 1497, Champlain established the first French post destined to be one of Canada's modern cities. While the original settlement on the site of Quebec City was a highly significant event for the future development of Canada, it fell far short of the dreams of Jacques Cartier who had searched unsuccessfully for the fabled riches of the New World some 67 years earlier. What the royally equipped and financed expedition led by Cartier[1] failed to do was achieved by the somewhat less pretentious activities of French fishermen seeking cod off the Grand Bank. Their contacts with the Indians ultimately led to the establishment of numerous trading posts along the St. Lawrence River and opened the area for more permanent settlement and development.

Early exploration of the New World and settlement by the French were primarily the consequences of political and military concerns, the search for beaver furs, and the Church's interest in the souls of savages. These concerns placed only minor emphasis on the development of a more permanent settlement policy based on large scale migration and agriculture. So, in spite of the fact that France had a population considerably larger and wealthier than that of England, she made little progress towards the establishment of more permanent settlements in the New World. France's preoccupation with Continental matters and continuing conflict with England did not produce a situation conducive to rapid settlement of her New World possessions.

Various individuals and companies were given monopolies of the fur trade at one time or another in return for their promise to settle a certain number of persons per year in the New World. Both fur trading and settlement of population were fraught with many difficulties, and so serious did they become that one company, the Company of One Hundred Associates, surrendered its Charter to Louis XIV in 1663. As a consequence of his attempts to determine the nature of the progress that had been achieved in New France during the half century following the establishment of the first trading post at Quebec, the King's Intendant, Jean Talon, carried out the first systematic census of modern times.[2] The census, conducted on a *de jure* basis,[3] revealed that the Catholic population of New France had increased from 28 in 1608 to 3,215 in 1665.[4] After 97 years of French rule, the population had increased to 69,810.[5]

In 1763, under the terms of the Peace of Paris which marked the end of the Seven Year's War and of hostilities between the French and English, England assumed control over New France.[6] During the preceding century of intermittant conflict and rivalry between these two nations for control of the vast wilderness areas of North America, the population of New France had increased twentyfold. During the same period, the English Colonies experienced the same rate of growth; but their combined population was about 25 times as large, or just over 1,500,000 persons in 1770.[7] The smaller population of New France clearly reflected the greater emphasis placed on fur trading and the establishment of military outposts rather than on more permanent agricultural types of settlement as was the case for the English. In addition, the relatively severe climate of New France was also a significant factor in limiting the size of the population which had managed to establish itself by the year 1765. Estimates of the population of New France for the period 1608 to 1765 are shown in Table 1:1.

Table 1:1

POPULATION OF NEW FRANCE, 1608–1765

Year	Number	Year	Number
1608	28	1698	15,355
1641	240	1706	16,417
1653	2,000	1707	17,204
1665	3,215	1714	18,964
1667	3,918	1720	24,434
1668	6,282	1721	24,951
1681	9,677	1734	37,716
1685	12,263	1739	42,701
1688	11,562	1754	55,009
1692	12,431	1760	70,000
1695	13,639	1765	69,810

SOURCE: *Census of Canada, 1871*, Volume V, pp. 166-171.

Information concerning the characteristics of this early population of New France is somewhat limited, but Langlois provides sufficient information to indicate that at the time of the first census there was a considerable excess of males; i.e., there were approximately 172 males for every 100 females, and 67 per cent of the population was single—a somewhat typical situation for a frontier population. Forty years later the sex ratio (number of males per 100 females) had declined to 109 and by 1765 there were 106 males for every 100 females.[8]

Data on births, deaths, and marriages collected by the French reflect the struggle for existence experienced by the early settlers in their efforts to establish a foothold in the New World.[9] As might be expected, more deaths occurred than births during the earliest years. From 1638, births tended to exceed deaths and natural increase played an increasingly important part in the growth of the population.[10] The number of births and deaths increased along with the growth of population, but deaths fluctuated considerably more than births as a result of epidemics and intermittent hostilities with both the English and Indians. Between the time of the first census and the decade when New France came under British control, death rates varied between 10 and 40 deaths per 1,000 population, but showed signs of a fairly consistent increase throughout the period. Birth rates tended to remain at very high levels, between 50 and 65 births per 1,000 population. With birth rates two to six times larger than death rates, a sizeable rate of growth through natural increase was assured.[11] Prior to 1670, migration appears to have been the most significant factor for growth; however, for the remainder of the French regime, the excess of births over deaths assumed the more important role as the population of Quebec increased from 3,215 in 1665 to approximately 70,000 by 1765, and to over one million (1,111,566) in 1861 just prior to Confederation.[12]

For the growth of the non-French population, immigration has continued to be highly significant. Following the American Revolution, a large scale emigration occurred from the former British Colonies of British subjects still loyal to the Crown (Empire Loyalists). Many moved into the Maritimes and eastern townships, while others settled in Upper Canada. In 1784, the population of Upper Canada was estimated at about 10,000, and by 1824 it had reached approximately 150,000.[13] An additional wave of immigrants came during the post-Napoleonic era when large scale immigration from Europe increased the population of Upper Canada from 150,000 to 950,000 by mid-century.[14]

The need for a large number of censuses conducted in Upper Canada between 1824 and 1842 was reflective of this rapid growth. In 1851, when enumerations were also conducted in Lower Canada, Nova Scotia, New Brunswick, and Prince Edward Island, a sufficient number of censuses had been conducted to provide the first complete enumeration of the organized population that was later to become the Dominion of Canada.[15] The population continued to grow through immigration as well as by an excess of births over deaths, increasing from 2,312,919 in 1851 to 3,090,561 in 1861, just six years prior to Confederation.[16]

One of the unfortunate consequences of British rule was their inability or unwillingness to extend to non-Catholic populations outside Lower Canada the type of data collecting activities in which the French had excelled. Little is known about the specifics of vital events for the populations during this period. However, data for the Catholic population between 1830 and 1860 indicate that death rates declined from 30 to 20 per 1,000 population, birth rates dropped from 60 to 45 per 1,000 population, and marriage rates decreased from approximately 20 to 15 per 1,000. Nevertheless, during the same period, the excess of births over deaths among the predominately Catholic population of Quebec increased the population from 553,000 to 890,000 in 1851, and to 1,112,000 in 1861, or a doubling of the population in just 30 years.

A comparison of population growth and vital events during the French and British regimes is possible in Figure 1:1. Fluctuations in the annual numbers of births, deaths, and marriages were of considerably smaller magnitudes under the British and reflected in part the greater political stability of this period. Also apparent is the generally higher rate of population increase, especially during the latter period between 1765 and 1860. Differences in growth rates for total population and vital events account for the declines in birth and death rates observed during this pre-Confederation period. It should also be pointed out in this connection that the changes in total population not totally explained by differences between births and deaths or error are reflective of net migration. While error components for these data are probably quite large, Figure 1:1 presents one of the best summary pictures of the demographic basis of early Canada that is available.

One of the first estimates for Upper Canada in 1784, as shown in Table 1:2, placed the total population at about 10,000 compared to 113,000 for Quebec. By 1831, Upper Canada's population had increased to 237,000, and at some point between 1844 and 1851, its population surpassed that of Lower Canada. By 1851, Upper Canada reached 952,000, then passed the 1,000,-000 mark the following decade, and reached 1,396,000 in 1861. Lack of adequate data on births, deaths, and immigration for Upper Canada during this period makes it difficult to assess their importance relative to the growth rate which appeared to vary between a low of 3.6 per cent in 1826 to a maximum of 11.4 per cent between 1832 and 1834.[17] Such variation in the rate of growth would appear to reflect variations in mortality as well as fluctuations in the size of successive waves of immigrants. In view of the fact that Quebec's average annual rate of increase during this period appeared to be in the neighbourhood of four per cent,[18] and since Quebec's growth has been attributed primarily to the excess of births over deaths, the high growth rates experienced by Upper Canada during 1828–34, and 1848–51, of over ten per cent must have been due primarily to immigration.[19] Furthermore, the economically prosperous decade of the 1850s appears to have been the last decade of the nineteenth century during which British North America gained more through immigration than it lost by emigration. Between 1851 and 1861, the population of the four provinces that were to join in Confederation increased by 33.6 per cent; but their combined rate of growth dropped to 12.8 per cent during the decade of Confederation, which appears to have been a period of heavy emigration to the United States.[20]

Regional distribution of population. As a result of the general lack of population enumerations, it is somewhat more difficult to describe the broader picture of population distribution in the vast areas of what was ultimately to become present day Canada. The earliest data for any area outside of Quebec and Ontario appear in 1762 for Nova Scotia. Not until 1851 were censuses simultaneously conducted in all areas which were later joined by Confederation. At that time, Ontario, with 41.1 per cent of the total combined population, constituted the largest population, followed by Quebec with 38.5 per cent, Nova Scotia with 12.0 per cent, and New Brunswick with 8.4 per cent. Data in Table 1:3 show that the population of Ontario continued to gain relative to the other three provinces during the 20 years between 1851 and 1871. Quebec's share of the total consistently declined, and the two remaining provinces showed relative declines during the first decade followed by slight increases during the 1861–71 decade.

Population data were also available from an early period for Prince Edward Island. In 1767 its population was reported to be 519. In 1861 it had reached approximately 81,000, and by 1871 it was reported to be 94,021. The settlement of the remaining western and northern areas that would ultimately become part of Canada occurred somewhat later because of the difficulty of finding adequate transportation routes to the Canadian West through the great rocky barrier of Ontario known as the Canadian Shield. In 1831, Manitoba's reported population was 2,390. By 1849, it had increased to almost 5,400. Of the remaining far-flung areas to the west, population growth had been concentrated on the West Coast. British Columbia, under the control of the Hudson's Bay Company since 1670, did not completely become a Crown Colony until 1866 when the mainland joined Vancouver Island under one government. There has not been much agreement as to the correct estimates for the population of British Columbia. However, between 1851 and 1861 there seems to be sufficient evidence to indicate that its population fluctuated considerably as a result of the Fraser River gold discoveries

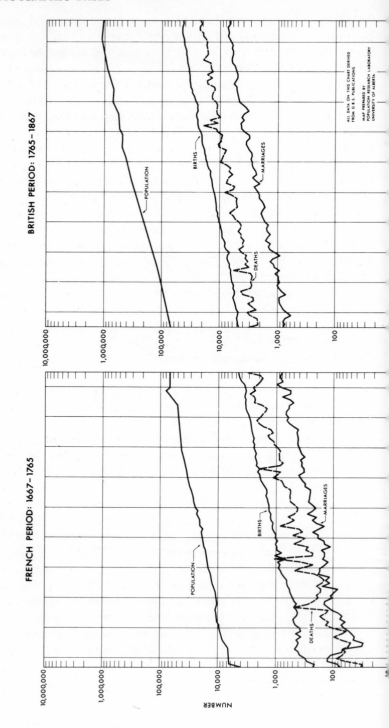

Fig. 1:1

DETERMINANTS OF POPULATION GROWTH
BRITISH AND FRENCH REGIMES
PROVINCE OF QUEBEC, CANADA: 1667 – 1867

Year	Quebec	Ontario	Nova Scotia	New Brunswick	P.E.I.	Manitoba	Terr.	British Columbia	Newfoundland
1765	69,810								
1767			11,779	1,196	519				
1784	113,021	10,000*							
1790	161,311								
1806		70,700*							
1811		77,000*							
1814		95,000*							
1817			81,351						
1822	427,465*								75,094[b]
1824		150,066		74,176					
1825	479,288	157,923							
1827	471,875	177,174	123,630						
1831	553,134	236,702				2,390			
1834		321,145		119,457		3,356			
1836		374,099							
1838		399,422	202,575			3,966			
1840		432,159		156,162		4,704			
1841					47,042				
1842		487,053							
1843						5,143			
1844	697,084								
1845						4,871			52,064
1846									
1848		725,879			62,678				
1849						5,391			
1851	890,261	952,004	276,854	193,800					
1857							5,700[a]	55,000[a]	
1861	1,111,566	1,396,091	330,857	252,047	80,857		6,691[a]	51,524[a]	124,288[b]
1869									146,536
1871	1,191,516	1,620,851	387,800	285,594	94,021	25,228	48,000[a]	36,247	

SOURCE: *Census of Canada, 1871,* Vol. I and IV; also, *1906 Atlas of Canada,* Plates 52 and 53. *Census of Canada, 1941,* Vol. I, Table I, p. 5. The *1906 Atlas of Canada* gives the population of the Alberta, Assiniboia, and Saskatchewan Districts as 18,000 in 1871, and 30,000 for the remaining territories.
[a] *Canada Yearbook, 1950,* Ottawa, 1950, p. 173 (Table 23).
* Estimates.

in 1856, and that in 1861, after the "gold rush", its population was estimated to be 52,000. In the same year, the Territories were estimated to contain approximately 7,000 inhabitants. Considering the vast extent of the Canadian West and its underdeveloped state in conjunction with the difficulties of transportation, the possibility that these estimates are too low is readily apparent. Estimates of the size of undercount vary from 30,000 to 100,000 for the Indian population in these western areas for 1851 and 1861, and a more realistic estimate for the combined populations of British Columbia and the Territories might be closer to 95,000 than the 59,000 suggested above.[21] Canada as it was at the time of Confederation in 1867 is shown in Figure 1:2. The 1967 boundaries are also shown for each of the provinces and territories as are their respective dates of Confederation.

One Hundred Years of Population Growth, 1867–1967

Growth in numbers. It is difficult to pinpoint the specific factors precipitating the act of Confederation in 1867. Major influences would certainly include the common British allegiance that had survived the American Revolution, and the gradual extension of communication throughout British North America. However, it is doubtful that these alone would have brought about this union without a simultaneous improvement in educational levels, the emergence of exceptional leadership, visions of westward expansion, a common and persistent fear concerning the intentions of their neighbour to the south, and the support of the British government for a larger and more viable union among its North American Colonies.[22] The struggle to establish a

Table 1:3

PERCENTAGE DISTRIBUTION OF THE POPULATION
OF CANADA BY PROVINCE, 1851–1871

Area	Year		
	1851	1861	1871
Ontario	41.1	45.2	46.5
Quebec	38.5	36.0	34.2
Nova Scotia	12.0	10.7	11.1
New Brunswick	8.4	8.1	8.2
Total: Per Cent	100.0	100.0	100.0
Number	2,312,919	3,090,561	3,485,761

SOURCE: Table 1:2.

Fig. 1:2

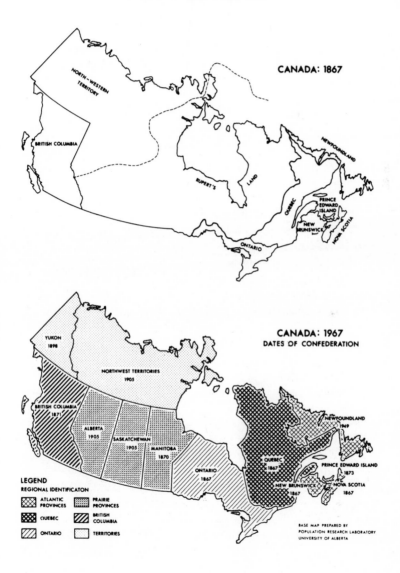

HISTORICAL MAP
CANADA: 1867 AND 1967

CANADA: 1867

CANADA: 1967
DATES OF CONFEDERATION

LEGEND
REGIONAL IDENTIFICATON

BASE MAP PREPARED BY
POPULATION RESEARCH LABORATORY
UNIVERSITY OF ALBERTA

larger political union during the uncertainties of this crucial period is reflected in its population growth. The total combined population of the original four provinces of Confederation during the 1861–71 decade increased by only 12.8 per cent, reaching 3,485,761 in 1871 compared to a 14.2 per cent increase for the total population of British North America (excluding Newfoundland). The relatively slower rate for the original four provinces continued throughout the remaining decades of the nineteenth century.

Just three years after Confederation, the Hudson's Bay Company territories of Rupert's Land and the North-Western Territory were transferred to the new Dominion, and the "postage stamp" Province of Manitoba was established.[23] Originally only about half the size of New Brunswick, Manitoba accounted for 25,228 of Canada's population in 1871. Another 36,247 was added in 1871 when British Columbia joined Confederation after receiving assurances that it would ultimately be linked with the rest of Canada by means of a transcontinental railroad. Canada's population in 1871 now totalled 3,595,236. Remaining outside of the Dominion were an estimated 94,000 inhabitants of Prince Edward Island, plus an additional 150,000 Newfoundlanders.

In 1873, almost 100,000 people living on Prince Edward Island were added to the population of Canada; and, in 1880, the remaining and practically uninhabited British territory within the Arctic Archipelago came under Canada's administrative jurisdiction. Two years later, the districts of Assiniboia, Saskatchewan, Athabasca, and Alberta were created within the area encompassed by its territories. Rapid growth resulting from the penetration of the west by the Canadian Pacific Railway and the settlement of the prairies during the next 20 years boosted the population to a point slightly in excess of 164,000. In 1905, the Provinces of Alberta and Saskatchewan were established.

Increases in the population of Canada as it expanded between 1867 and 1901 (shown in Table 1:4) contrast with the population growth for the four combined original provinces. With the exception of the 1871–81 decade, rates of growth for the original provinces tended to decline between 1851 and 1901 and were consistently lower than the rate of growth for Canada as a whole after 1861. This is true whether all the population in the areas yet to be joined to the Dominion are included or just those populations which actually were a part of the Dominion at each of the census years.

Following the census of 1901, large scale immigration of the foreign born combined with a favourable natural increase revived Canada's growth rate and almost doubled the total population from 5,371,315 in 1901 to 10,376,-786 in 1931. The greatest percentage increase (34.2 per cent) occurred during the 1901–11 decade, followed in 1911–21 by an increase of 21.9 per cent and by a considerably lower rate of 18.1 per cent during the pre-depres-

Table 1:4

POPULATION AND PERCENTAGE INCREASE BY DECADE FOR CANADA'S FOUR ORIGINAL PROVINCES, THE DOMINION OF CANADA AND BRITISH NORTH AMERICA, 1851–1901

Year	Four Original Provinces		Dominion of Canada		British North America	
	Number	Per Cent Increase	Number	Per Cent Increase	Number	Per Cent Increase
1851	2,312,919	—	—	—	2,546,530[c]	—
1861	3,090,561	33.6	—	—	3,361,337[c]	32.0
1871	3,485,761	12.8	3,595,236[a]	—	3,841,566[c]	14.3
1881	4,047,754	16.1	4,324,810[b]	20.3	4,511,357[c]	17.4
1891	4,374,515	8.1	4,833,239[b]	11.8	5,035,279	11.6
1901	4,622,539	5.7	5,371,315[b]	11.1	5,592,299	11.1

SOURCE: *Census of Canada, 1871*, Vol. I and IV; *Census of Canada, 1951*, Table 1:1; *Canada Year Book, 1950*, p. 173 (Table 23).
[a] Includes all of British North America except Prince Edward Island and Newfoundland.
[b] Excludes only Newfoundland.
[c] Totals for Newfoundland included in the total for British North America for 1851, 1861, 1871, and 1881 are estimates derived by linear interpolation using totals for the years 1836, 1857, 1869, 1874, and 1884 published by the Newfoundland government.

sion decade. The lowest rate of growth occurred during the depression years. The increase of 1,129,869 between 1931 and 1941 amounted to only 10.9 per cent for the entire decade. A marked increase in both fertility level and immigration during the 1941–51 decade of rapid economic development boosted the growth rate to 18.6 per cent. Newfoundland's decision to join the Confederation in 1949 contributed to the overall increase of 21.8 per cent in Canada's population over the 1941 total of 11,506,655. Continuing high fertility and increasing numbers of immigrants pushed Canada's total to 18,238,247 in 1961, an increase of 30.2 per cent above the 1951 total. The growth of Canada's population during the 100-year period, 1861–1961, reflecting historical variations in fertility, mortality, and immigration, is presented in Figure 1:3.

Regional distribution of population. Between 1861 and 1901, the four original provinces of Confederation retained their rank order position in terms of size; i.e., Ontario remained the largest, closely followed by Quebec, while Nova Scotia and New Brunswick remained third and fourth respectively. Growth curves for Ontario and Quebec, shown in Figure 1:3, exhibit marked similarity to each other as do those for Nova Scotia and New Brunswick throughout the entire 100 years. However, their rank order positions were altered by the rapidly growing populations of the Prairie Provinces and British Columbia during the 1901–11 decade of heavy immigration and rapid settlement in the West. A continuation of heavy immigration in the years just preceding World War I boosted the populations of Saskatchewan, Manitoba, Alberta, and British Columbia into third, fourth, fifth, and sixth positions respectively, followed by Nova Scotia, New Brunswick, Newfoundland, Prince Edward Island, and the Territories as may be seen in Figure 1:3.

The relative rates of growth can be determined in Figure 1:3 by directly comparing the slopes of the various growth curves. The decade of Canada's most rapid growth during the 100 years is easily discernible, as are the areas primarily responsible, i.e., Manitoba, Saskatchewan, Alberta, and British Columbia. Decennial rates of growth for these provinces were 80.0, 439.5, 412.6, and 119.7 per cent respectively, compared to the growth rate of 34.2 per cent for Canada during 1901–11. Quebec's population increased more rapidly than Ontario's during the decade (1910–11) with an increase of 21.6 per cent compared to 15.8 per cent for the latter. Quebec had the larger increase during each decade between 1891 and 1951. Between 1951 and 1961, as a result of heavy immigration destined for Ontario, Quebec's growth rate of 29.7 per cent was exceeded by Ontario with 35.6 per cent.

Growth curves for the western provinces reveal significant population shifts which have occurred since Alberta and Saskatchewan became separate provinces in 1905. Population growth in Manitoba began slowing down noticeably after 1911, almost coming to a complete standstill during the

Fig. 1:3

POPULATION GROWTH
CANADA: 1861–1961

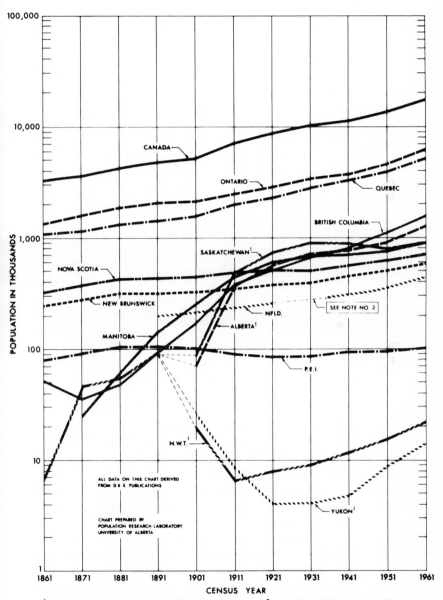

100,000

10,000

CANADA

ONTARIO

QUEBEC

BRITISH COLUMBIA

SASKATCHEWAN[1]

NOVA SCOTIA

NEW BRUNSWICK

SEE NOTE NO. 2

NFLD.

ALBERTA[1]

MANITOBA

1,000

100

P.E.I.

N.W.T.[1]

ALL DATA ON THIS CHART DERIVED
FROM D.B.S PUBLICATIONS

CHART PREPARED BY
POPULATION RESEARCH LABORATORY
UNIVERSITY OF ALBERTA

YUKON[1]

10

1

POPULATION IN THOUSANDS

1861   1871   1881   1891   1901   1911   1921   1931   1941   1951   1961

CENSUS YEAR

[1]ALBERTA, SASKATCHEWAN AND YUKON WERE ENUMERATED WITH
THE NORTHWEST TERRITORIES IN THE CENSUSES OF 1871 TO 1901
AND ARE INDICATED SEPARATELY COMMENCING WITH 1901 FIGURES.

[2]PRIOR TO 1951 CENSUSES WERE CONDUCTED BY THE
NEWFOUNDLAND GOVERNMENT. THESE POPULATION
FIGURES ARE USED IN THIS CHART.

depression decade before beginning to rise again during the post-World War II period. Saskatchewan's growth rate skyrocketed past that of Manitoba, reaching its peak population in 1931. Not until the 1951–61 decade did it again achieve a positive rate of growth; but even then, only one other area, Prince Edward Island, experienced a lower growth rate. Alberta's growth was also phenomenal during the 1901–11 period, and its population exceeded that of both Newfoundland and New Brunswick by the end of the decade. While Alberta's growth rate declined following World War I, its growth was still sufficient for it to pass Nova Scotia and British Columbia during the 1921–31 decade, and it passed Saskatchewan during the first post-World War II decade. Its rate of growth of 41.8 per cent during the 1951–61 decade was exceeded only by that of the Yukon and Northwest Territories, and in 1961 it was the fourth largest province following Ontario, Quebec, and British Columbia. The provinces with the highest percentage increases are shown in Table 1:5 for each decade between 1851 and 1961 compared to percentage increases for Canada.

Regional population growth is illustrated in Figure 1:4. It is quite clear that population growth in the Prairie Provinces between 1921 and 1951 slackened considerably relative to other major regions. Only as a conse-

Table 1:5

PROVINCES WITH THE DECADE'S HIGHEST PERCENTAGE
POPULATION INCREASE, AND PERCENTAGE INCREASE
BY DECADE, CANADA: 1851–1961

Decade	Province With Highest Increase	Percentage Increase	Percentage Increase for Canada
1851–1861	Ontario	46.6	32.6
1861–1871	Nova Scotia	17.2	14.2
1871–1881	Manitoba	146.8	17.2
1881–1891	Manitoba	145.0	11.8
1891–1901	British Columbia	82.0	11.1
1901–1911	Saskatchewan	439.5	34.2
1911–1921	Alberta	57.2	21.9
1921–1931	British Columbia	32.4	18.1
1931–1941	N.W. Territories	29.1[a]	10.9
1941–1951	Yukon	85.1[b]	18.6[d]
1951–1961	Yukon	60.8[c]	30.2[e]

[a] British Columbia was second highest with 17.8 per cent.
[b] British Columbia was second highest with 42.5 per cent.
[c] Northwest Territories and Alberta were second and third highest with 43.7 and 41.8 per cent respectively.
[d] Excluding Newfoundland in 1951.
[e] Including Newfoundland in 1951 and 1961.

quence of the gains experienced by Alberta during the most recent decade
was it possible for the region to make a sizeable recovery. From an overall
perspective, the Western regions of Canada, i.e., British Columbia and the
Prairie Provinces, dominated the growth picture during the years between
1871 and 1931. Since the onset of the Great Depression, the relatively small
population of the Far North (Yukon and Northwest Territories) has shown
the largest relative gains, closely followed by British Columbia. During the
most recent 1951–61 decade, Ontario's growth rate approached that of
British Columbia, reaching 35.6 per cent compared to 39.8 per cent for the
latter. Considering that Ontario's population of 4,597,542 in 1951 was
almost four times the size of that of British Columbia, Ontario's growth rate

Fig. 1:4   POPULATION GROWTH BY REGION
                         CANADA: 1871–1961

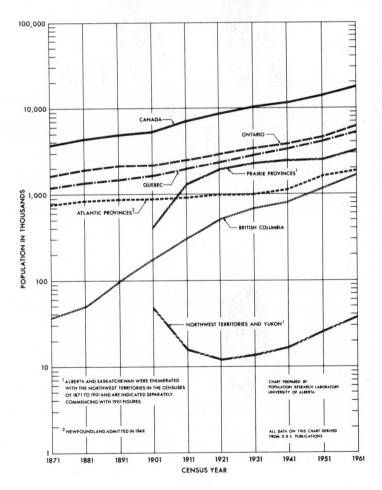

Fig. 1:5

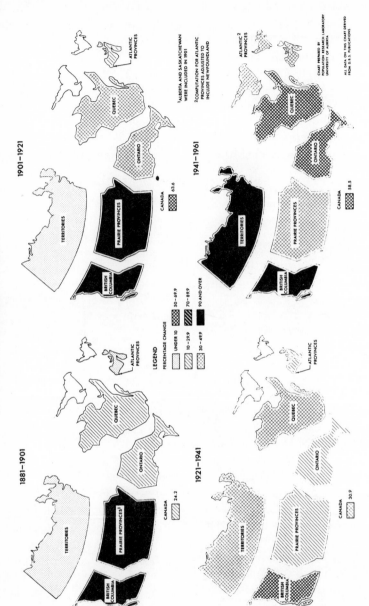

POPULATION CHANGE BY REGION
CANADA: 1901, 1921, 1941 AND 1961

becomes very impressive.[24] Population change for Canada's regions by 20-year periods between 1881 and 1961 is illustrated in Figure 1:5. The more rapid growth which has occurred in the Western regions is as clearly visible from 1881 to 1921 as it is during the 20-year period from 1921 to 1941 for British Columbia, a period when a major economic depression slowed population growth considerably. Again, the resurgence of growth was greatest in the less populated Western and Northern regions during the post-World War II period, but significant rates of increase were also observed for the larger population concentrations in Ontario and Quebec.

The importance of these regional growth patterns through time lies in their net effects on the regional distribution of population. It is only logical to expect that during the period in which the vast Canadian West and North were being opened for settlement, the demographic balance which existed at the time of Confederation would change as new waves of immigrants sought the free land and opportunities of the frontier along with many of those who had formerly resided in the older provinces and British Colonies. Figure 1:6 shows this shift very clearly. In 1861 Ontario had the largest proportion of the population, or 43.2 per cent, followed by Quebec with 34.4 per cent.[25] The Maritime Provinces (not including Newfoundland) accounted for most of the remaining population, i.e., 21.9 per cent. The populations of each of these three major regions, while increasing significantly in numbers during the century under consideration, have actually experienced declines in their proportionate share of the total population. Quebec's percentage of the total declined consistently until 1921 when it reached 26.9 per cent, then increased in 1941 to 29.0 per cent where it has remained relatively constant during the post-World War II period. Ontario's share actually increased to 44.6 per cent in 1881 before beginning its long decline to 32.8 per cent in 1951. However, during the 1951–61 decade, its proportion of the total increased slightly to 34.2 per cent. The Maritime Provinces declined steadily to 9.8 per cent in 1941. When Newfoundland joined the Confederation, it boosted the proportion for the combined Atlantic Provinces to 11.6 per cent in 1951. By 1961, their proportion had declined slightly to 10.4 per cent.

By way of contrast, since the time British Columbia joined the Confederation in 1871, its population steadily increased its proportionate share from 1.0 per cent to 8.9 per cent. The Northwest Territories experienced early declines, partly through loss of territory and population as new provinces were carved out of their domain and partly because of actual loss of population due to unstable economic conditions. Subsequent to 1931, when it had reached its minimum of 0.1 per cent of the total population, high rates of growth doubled its proportionate share to 0.2 per cent. The pattern for the Prairie Provinces was similar to that of Ontario but somewhat more extreme. Beginning in 1901, just before Alberta and Saskatchewan were established

Fig. 1:6

POPULATION TRENDS BY REGION
CANADA: 1861–1961

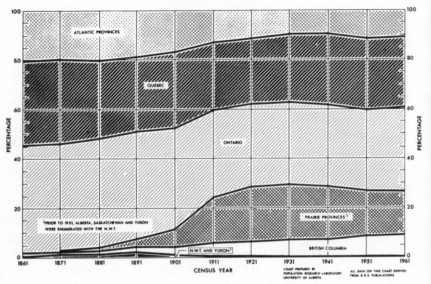

as separate provinces, their population, along with that of Manitoba, constituted 7.8 per cent of the total. Under the impact of heavy immigration, their proportion more than doubled in one decade to 18.4 per cent and increased to 22.3 per cent in 1921. By 1931, the Prairie Provinces reached their peak (22.7 per cent) and then gradually declined until 1961 at which time they comprised 17.4 per cent of Canada's population.

A continuation of population trends apparent in Figure 1:6, along with many of the complex social and economic trends observed during the post-World War II period, seems quite probable. The Atlantic and Prairie Provinces' share of Canada's total population will continue to decline while the remaining regions will continue to increase. The forecast made by the Royal Commission on Canada's Economic Prospects indicates that this trend in the regional distribution of Canada's population should continue at least until 1980.[26]

REFERENCES

Dominion Bureau of Statistics: *1961 Census of Canada. General Review: Growth of Population in Canada*. Vol. 7: 1–10, Ottawa, The Queen's Printer, 1965.

Keyfitz, Nathan: "The Growth of Canadian Population" in B. R. Blishen, *et al.*, *Canadian Society: Sociological Perspectives*. Toronto, Macmillan of Canada, 1968.

Keyfitz, Nathan: "The Changing Canadian Population". *Population Studies*. Vol. 4(1): 47–63 (June 1950).

Sametz, Z. W.: "The People" in P. Camu, E. P. Weeks and Z. W. Sametz. *Economic Geography of Canada*. Toronto, Macmillan, 1965.

Urquhart, M. C. and K. Buckley: *Historical Statistics of Canada*. Toronto, The Macmillan Company, 1965.

FOOTNOTES

[1]Samuel E. Morrison, *The Oxford History of the American People*, New York, Oxford University Press, 1965, pp. 39–42.

[2]Dominion Bureau of Statistics, *Dominion Bureau of Statistics: History, Function, Organization*, Ottawa, Queen's Printer and Controller of Stationery, 1958, p. 7.

[3]A census conducted on a *de jure* basis enumerates the population where they usually live rather than where they happen to be at the time of the census as is the case of censuses conducted on a *de facto* basis.

[4]Georges Langlois, *Histoire de la Population Canadienne Française*, Appendice II, Montreal, Editions: Albert Levesque, 1934, pp. 75–76; and, Canada, *Census of 1871, Volume V*, Ottawa, Department of Agriculture, p. 166.

[5]*Ibid.*

[6]For a brief and interesting history of New France from its early origins to Montcalm's defeat by Wolfe on the Plains of Abraham, see Samuel E. Morrison, *op. cit.*, pp. 39–170.

[7]Michel Brunet, *La Presence Anglaise et les Canadiens*, études sur l'histoire la pensée des 2 Canadas, Montreal: Beauchemin, 1958, pp. 27–32.

[8]Georges Langlois, *op. cit.*, p. 244 (Appendix II).

[9]*Census of 1871, Volume V*, Ottawa, Department of Agriculture, pp. 166–170; J. Henripin, *La Population Canadienne an Dieput de XVIII Siecle*, Paris, Pressas Universitaires de France, 1954, p. 119; and G. Langlois, *op. cit.*, p. 262 (Appendice VII).

[10]Dominion Bureau of Statistics, *op. cit.*

[11]G. Langlois, *op. cit.*, p. 262 (Appendix VII).

[12]G. Langlois, *op. cit.*, p. 267 (Appendix X).

[13]*Atlas of Canada*, 1906, Department of the Interior, Plates Number 51 and 52; and, *Census of Canada, 1871*, Vol. I and IV.

[14]*Ibid.*

[15]Dominion Bureau of Statistics, *op. cit.*

[16]1851 and 1861 totals are for the combined populations of Upper Canada (Canada West), Lower Canada (Canada East), Nova Scotia, and New Brunswick.

[17]*1851 Census of Canada*, Vol. I, p. xv.

[18]Estimate based on data for Quebec presented in Table 1:2.

[19]This would be the case assuming mortality to be approximately the same and that fertility in Upper Canada was probably not any higher than that of the Catholic population in Lower Canada. Also, it has been estimated by the Dominion Bureau of Statistics that 800,000 left Britain for North America between 1815 and 1850. See Dominion Bureau of Statistics, *Canada, One Hundred, 1867–1967*, Ottawa, Queen's Printer and Controller of Stationery, 1967, p. 73.

[20]See the analysis by Duncan McDougall, "Immigration Into Canada, 1851–1921," *Canadian Journal of Economics and Political Science,* Vol. XXVII, No. 2, May, 1961, p. 172; and Zenon Sametz in P. Camu, E. P. Weeks, and Z. W. Sametz, *Economic Geography of Canada,* 1964, pp. 58–59.

[21]For an excellent discussion and appraisal of early estimates see M. C. Urquhart, and K. Buckley, *Historical Statistics of Canada,* Toronto, The Macmillan Company of Canada Ltd., 1965, pp. 3–4. As Urquhart and Buckley point out, Eskimos were not enumerated in these early censuses and no estimates of their numbers are included in these figures.

[22]Dominion Bureau of Statistics, *op. cit.,* pp. 15–19.

[23]The number and size of administrative districts within the Territories were changed several times after their acquisition and the present boundaries of Manitoba were not finally established until 1912. At the same time, substantial areas were also added to Ontario and Quebec. While these areas did not contain large numbers of persons, almost all the population decline for the Territories shown in Figure 1:3 can be attributed to these boundary changes.

[24]High rates of population growth are significant indicators of favourable social, economic, and political conditions. However, the reader must remember that high rates of growth are more easily achieved by small populations as compared to larger populations. In other words, while a very high rate of growth for a relatively small population is a significant event, a somewhat lower rate for a much larger population would probably have greater economic, political, and social significance.

[25]Percentages based on the total population of British North American excluding Newfoundland.

[26]Royal Commission on Canada's Economic Prospects, *Output, Labour, and Capital in the Canadian Economy,* Ottawa, Queen's Printer and Controller of Stationery, 1955, p. 180 (Table 4.20).

Components of Growth

Changes in Canada's population are a function of three basic components—migration, mortality, and fertility. Each of these exerts an independent effect on growth, as well as producing interactional effects which are consequences of their relative magnitudes, and the internal age-sex structure. Their independent contributions to population change are summarized in the following "bookkeeping" equation:

$$P_2 = P_1 + \text{Births} - \text{Deaths} + \text{Immigration} - \text{Emigration}$$

Where
P_1 = Population enumerated at time 1
P_2 = Population enumerated at time 2
and
births, deaths, immigration, and emigration
refer to the number of events occurring
during the time interval $t_1 - t_2$.

This chapter examines each of the basic components in turn and assesses their relative significance for population growth in Canada following Confederation.

Migration
The migration factor in population change consists of two major components, immigration and emigration, and its significance generally is a function of their relative sizes. Yet, even when a large immigration is perfectly balanced

31

by an equally large emigration so that the net contribution is zero, it would be erroneous to assume that such a situation might necessarily have the same significance as the case where both immigration and emigration were zero. To the extent that immigrants differed from emigrants in terms of their age, sex, ethnic, or any other characteristic, a major shift in the overall character of the population could occur even though the net numerical gain or loss might be insignificant. Obviously, a total absence of migration in both directions would not produce the same effect. In reality, net migrations close to zero (either positive or negative) seldom are the result of a complete cessation of movement. They are instead, the consequence of complex countermovements of populations which have remarkable sensitivity to real or anticipated changes in the economic, social, and political climate.

Variations in immigration. The great migrations of Europeans to North America, after the original exploration and settlement, were highly significant for the development of Canada's population. Between 1867 and 1967, more than 8,000,000 immigrants arrived in Canada; and, while all who arrived did not remain, this influx of immigrants has been a vital factor in the growth and development of the country. The level of immigration fluctuated considerably during this period reaching a maximum of approximately 400,000 during the immediate pre-World War I period (1913) as a result of Sifton's vigorous immigration policies and extensive publicity aimed primarily at the land-hungry peasants of Europe. The lure of the New World faded considerably during the Great Depression, and in 1935 only 11,277 immigrants were recorded. However, with an end of hostilities in World War II and the rapid economic development during the post-war years combined with occasional political upheavals in Europe, immigration recovered rapidly, reaching peaks second only to those of the pre-World War I years.

Data in Table 2:1 clearly reveal these significant peaks and valleys of immigration which followed the initial flurry of migration occasioned by the construction of the Canadian Pacific Railway, circa 1883, and the subsequent opening of the Canadian West.

Fluctuations in immigration are the consequence of many interrelated factors among which the actual economic and political conditions of the sending and receiving countries are extremely important. In addition, the perception of opportunity in the country of destination, the degree of active encouragement of immigrants in the form of travel and settlement assistance by the receiving country, varying restrictions imposed to regulate the classes of admissible immigrants, as well as the degree of freedom to emigrate granted by the countries of origin are all relevant factors in accounting for variations in the ebb and flow of migrants. This is partly observable in Figure 2:1 in which a few selected events of significance are identified in relation to variations in the composition of immigration by area of origin. Note, for example, the increase in proportion of immigrants of origins other than the

Table 2:1

IMMIGRATION TO CANADA BY CALENDAR YEAR, 1867–1969

Year	Number	Year	Number	Year	Number
1867	10,666				
1868	12,765				
1869	18,630				
1870	24,706	1910	286,839	1950	73,912
1871	27,773	1911	331,288	1951	194,391
1872	36,578	1912	375,756	1952	164,498
1873	50,050	1913	400,870	1953	168,868
1874	39,373	1914	150,484	1954	154,227
1875	27,382	1915	36,665	1955	109,946
1876	25,633	1916	55,914	1956	164,857
1877	27,082	1917	72,910	1957	282,164
1878	29,807	1918	41,845	1958	124,851
1879	40,492	1919	107,698	1959	106,928
1880	38,505	1920	138,824	1960	104,111
1881	47,991	1921	91,728	1961	71,689
1882	112,458	1922	64,224	1962	74,586
1883	133,624	1923	133,729	1963	93,151
1884	103,824	1924	124,164	1964	112,606
1885	79,169	1925	84,907	1965	146,758
1886	69,152	1926	135,982	1966	194,743
1887	84,526	1927	158,886	1967	222,876
1888	88,766	1928	166,783	1968	183,974
1889	91,600	1929	164,993	1969	161,531
1890	75,067	1930	104,806		
1891	82,165	1931	27,530		
1892	30,996	1932	20,591		
1893	29,633	1933	14,382		
1894	20,829	1934	12,476		
1895	18,790	1935	11,277		
1896	16,835	1936	11,643		
1897	21,716	1937	15,101		
1898	31,900	1938	17,244		
1899	44,543	1939	16,994		
1900	41,681	1940	11,324		
1901	55,747	1941	9,329		
1902	89,102	1942	7,576		
1903	138,660	1943	8,504		
1904	131,252	1944	12,801		
1905	141,465	1945	22,722		
1906	211,653	1946	71,719		
1907	272,409	1947	64,127		
1908	143,326	1948	125,414		
1909	173,694	1949	95,217		

SOURCE: Canada Immigration Division, Department of Manpower and Immigration, *1969 Immigration Statistics: Canada*, Ottawa, 1970, Table 2, p. 4.

United States and United Kingdom at the time of the Hungarian revolt during the latter part of the 1951–61 decade.

Perhaps a better means of evaluating the significance of immigration is to examine totals by decades in relation to the average size of the resident population for that decade. During 1901–11, the total influx of immigrants amounted to 1,500,000, or 24.6 per cent of the average population of Canada during that decade. By this criterion, immigration amounting to 17.5 per cent during the 1911–21 decade was the next most significant, followed by 1881–91 with 14.9 per cent. By contrast, immigration during the post-World War II period, 1951–61, amounted to only 9.6 per cent. For the entire 15 post-war years, the 2,000,000 immigrants amounted to 13.6 per cent of Canada's average population. While in absolute numbers of immigrants the 1951–61 decade ranked second only to the 1901–11 decade (relative to the size of Canada's resident population), it ranked only fifth among all decades since Confederation. Immigration as a percentage of the nation's average population is presented for all decades starting with 1851–61 in Table 2:2.

At no time since 1867 has the contribution of net migration comprised more than half of the decade's change in population. The largest proportion of the observed total change for any specific decade occurred during 1901–11 when the gain through net migration accounted for 44.0 per cent of the decade's growth. The second highest contribution occurred during 1951–61 when 25.5 per cent of the decade's growth was attributable to net migration. The only other periods during which migration made a positive contribution were 1911–21, 1921–31, and 1941–51. During these particular decades, the proportions of the total increase attributable to net migration were 19.6, 14.5,

Fig. 2:1

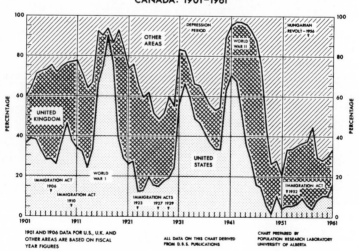

IMMIGRATION BY AREA OF ORIGIN
CANADA: 1901–1961

Table 2:2

TOTAL DECADE IMMIGRATION AS A PERCENTAGE OF THE AVERAGE POPULATION, CANADA, 1851–1861 TO 1951–1961

Intercensal Decade	Decade Immigration as a Percentage of Average Population	Average Population[a]
1851–1861	12.3	2,832,965
1861–1871	7.5	3,459,445
1871–1881	8.7	4,007,034
1881–1891	14.9	4,579,024
1891–1901	4.9	5,102,277
1901–1911	24.6	6,288,979
1911–1921	17.5	7,997,296
1921–1931	12.5	9,582,367
1931–1941	1.4	10,941,720
1941–1951	4.4	12,577,334[b]
1951–1961	9.6	16,123,838[c]

SOURCE: Data based on estimates of immigration presented in P. Camu, E. P. Weeks, and Z. W. Sametz, *Economic Geography of Canada*, Toronto, Macmillan, 1964, Table 3:1, p. 59; and, population totals in *1951 Census of Canada*, Vol. I, Table 6; and *1961 Census of Canada*, Bulletin 1.1-10, Ottawa, The Queen's Printer, 1963, Table 6.
[a] Arithmetic mean of the two successive census populations.
[b] Excludes Newfoundland in 1951.
[c] Includes Newfoundland in 1951 and 1961.

and 7.2 per cent respectively. Maximum losses, where emigration exceeded immigration by 100,000 or more, occurred during three of the last four decades of the nineteenth century. Easy access to Canada's West had not yet been achieved, and a depressed economy made the opportunities for employment and free land in the United States relatively more attractive.[1]

Areas of origin. During the immediate post-Confederation period, the bulk of immigrants came from the United States and United Kingdom. For example, between 1881 and 1891, the proportion reported originating from the United States varied between 45.5 and 75.5 per cent, while that from the United Kingdom accounted for an additional 21.2 to 36.8 per cent. Not until 1927 did the proportion of immigrants from other areas briefly comprise more than half of all the immigrants. Again, during the post-World War II period, the character of immigration changed from its historical antecedents, but this time in a more drastic fashion. In 1951, 71.7 per cent of all immigrant arrivals reported originating in areas other than the United States and United Kingdom.[2]

Fig. 2:2

NUMBER OF IMMIGRANTS
BY AREA OF ORIGIN
CANADA: 1901–1961

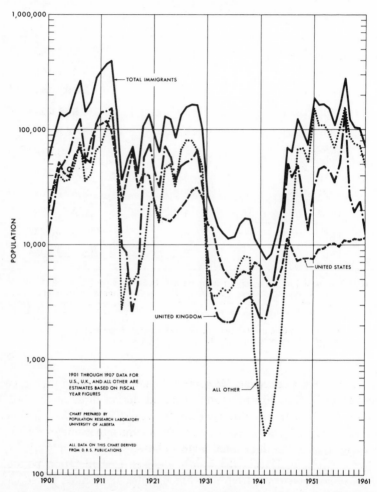

Immigrant arrivals by year and area of origin are shown in Figure 2:2, whereas the proportional composition of the immigrant stream was depicted in Figure 2:1. It is interesting to note the variations in character of these immigrants in relation to the occurrence of important economic, political, and social events. Maximum proportions of immigrants from the United States, exceeding 75 per cent of all arriving immigrants, occurred during World War I, World War II, and the Great Depression. Increased economic and political opportunities provided by Canada's earlier involvement in World War I attracted many from the United States at a time when other potential immigrants were barred because of increased war-time restrictions designed to prevent the landing of aliens from enemy countries. The depression of the 1930s virtually halted the immigration of all but the most favoured categories of immigrants, as did the restrictions imposed during World War II.

Immigrants from the United Kingdom comprised more than half of all arrivals during the two years immediately following World War I, as well as in 1923, and again during the immediate post-World War II years, 1944–47. Only after 1947 did the "other" origins dominate the composition of immigrant arrivals. Obviously, wars and economic depressions have been key events relative to changes in composition of immigration. Also interesting, in this regard, was the timing of the various immigration acts in relation to the arrival of immigrants from areas of origin other than the United Kingdom and the United States. The early immigration acts beginning in 1869, and again in 1906, were primarily concerned with the more general aspects of regulation of immigration for the purpose of preventing the entry of mentally retarded or ill, those with infectious diseases, criminals, those likely to become public charges, and others defined as undesirable.[3]

Amendments in 1908 were made whose primary objectives were the prohibition of East Indian immigrants and restriction of entry to very limited numbers and classes of Chinese and Japanese immigrants. After the end of World War I when the proportion of immigrants from "other" areas of origin began to increase rapidly, so did attempts to control the quality and character of immigration. Generally speaking, agricultural workers and domestics were encouraged to immigrate to Canada, as well as the wives and children under 18 of anyone already a legal resident of Canada. However, the only persons able to enter Canada with a minimum of red tape were those who belonged to the preferred groups; i.e., United States citizens and British subjects by reason of birth or naturalization in Great Britain or Ireland, Newfoundland, New Zealand, Australia, and the Union of South Africa. Increased restrictions were imposed on Chinese immigration and, by 1920, Japanese immigrants were limited to 150 per year. In 1929, just prior to the depression and perhaps in anticipation of it, legislation was passed to prevent importation of any labour that would displace Canadian workers. By 1931, immigration was restricted to certain classes of British subjects and United States citizens, wives and unmarried children under 18, or fiancé(e)s of a legal resident in Canada, and agriculturalists having sufficient means to farm in Canada. By 1939, and the outbreak of World War II, all enemy aliens were denied entry. Not until 1952 were the last of the remaining restrictions prohibiting entry to enemy aliens finally revoked by Order in Council, P.C. 3689. During the immediate post-World War II period, the rapid increase in immigrants from sources other than the United Kingdom and United States was facilitated by special efforts to aid in the settlement of refugees and displaced persons, and to find the labour needed by the rapidly expanding economy.

One extremely important aspect concerning the character of immigration remains obscured because of the broad origin categories used in the preceding discussion. For this reason, special mention must be made of French immigrants. The French are most conspicuous by their absence, a fact all the more surprising in view of the important role which they played in the original settlement of New France. While direct evidence is lacking in statistics covering the early years of Confederation, immigration data from 1926 to 1961 indicate that the proportions of annual immigrant arrivals who were of French ethnic origin were exceedingly small. In 1926, they constituted only 2.1 per cent of all arrivals, and in 1961 the proportion was just 3.1 per cent. For the entire period, their proportion exceeded 10.0 per cent only twice (1931 and 1932), and in these particular years there is reason to believe that the immigrants of French origin were returning to Canada from the United States rather than emigrating from France.[4]

Data on birthplace of the foreign-born resident in Canada at the time of the various censuses starting as early as 1871 also emphasize the relative insignificance of immigration from France. Just four years after Confederation, only 0.5 per cent of the foreign-born population had been born in France. This proportion increased to 1.1 per cent in 1901 and 1911, declining to 0.7 per cent in 1931 and 1941, and then increased to 1.3 per cent in 1961.[5] Compared to the 83.6 per cent in 1871 who had been born in the United Kingdom, France as a source of immigrants was totally insignificant. The proportion born in the United Kingdom has dropped rapidly and continuously, reaching 34.1 per cent in 1961; but this has been the consequence of increasing numbers settling in Canada from birth places other than France or the United States.

Age and sex characteristics of immigrants. The data available suggest that early immigrants were predominantly younger adults, particularly those traveling great distances. High sex ratios observed among older foreign-born populations in Canada also suggest that early immigration was composed, to a great majority, of young adult males who seemed particularly suited for the hard life of a frontier-type society. However, the dominance of the young adult male has not been consistent. During the early years of the French regime, there was evidence that the excessive numbers of males in relation to females gave way to a more equitable distribution as early as 1719. Even more recently, data on immigration during the depression and war years, from 1933 to 1946, indicate that immigrants were predominantly females. It is quite clear that the occurrence of wars, revolutions, religious persecutions, economic booms, and recessions have affected the character of Canada's immigration in unique ways. The age-sex character of immigration, in turn, determines the significance of its contribution for population growth. Obviously, an influx of elderly dependents would make a relatively short term contribution to growth since the high mortality level associated with older ages would quickly reduce this component to zero. On the other hand, immigration of young married adults would add a far greater number of person-years[6] as well as contributing to overall growth through their continuing fertility.

Data from 1933 to 1961 show the impact that a major depression and war can have on age and sex characteristics of immigrants. The large number of women and children significantly reduced both the sex ratio and median age far below their general level for this period. Shortly after the war, the sex ratio rose rapidly and males again predominated until 1958 when the sex ratio fell to 94.4 and another cycle of excess female immigrants began. The average age of immigrants between 1933 and 1961 was approximately 25 years; but, in 1940 and 1947 the median age reached 28.6 and 28.3 respectively, with an abrupt drop to 22.7 years in 1946 caused by the arrival of married dependents and children of World War II veterans.[7]

In order to illustrate more clearly the age and sex selectivity of migration, estimates of net migration by broad age groups for males and females are shown for the 1951–61 decade in Table 2:3. Note that net migration for all ages combined was higher for males than females during this period, and that the highest rates for both males and females occurred for those who were 20–34 years of age in 1951. The more detailed calculations upon which these rates were based indicate that the higher rates actually occurred in the 20–24 year age group and were 196 and 138 per 1,000 mid-decade population for males and females respectively. The next highest rates were observed for the 15–19 year age group and were 158 for males and 131 for females.

Table 2:3

ESTIMATES OF NET-INTERCENSAL MIGRATION[a] BY SEX
AND AGE GROUPS, CANADA, 1951–1961

Age of Cohort in 1951	Males	Females
0– 9	34.4	33.7
10–19	94.8	103.7
20–34	154.1	107.9
35–49	51.3	31.0
50–64	33.7	27.7
65+	22.0	16.0
Total:	75.8	61.6

SOURCE: W. E. Kalbach, The Impact of Post-war Immigration on Canadian Population, 1961 Census Monograph, Ottawa, The Queen's Printer, 1970, Table 3.9, p. 117.
a Net migrants per 1,000 mid-decade population.

Emigration

The extent and nature of emigration from Canada during the century follow-ing Confederation has been a subject of considerable conjecture. The basis for such uncertainty lies in the government's failure to systematically collect data for persons leaving Canada to establish residence elsewhere,[8] and also in certain weaknesses in birth and death statistics collected during the late nineteenth and twentieth centuries. In the absence of specific data, emigration can only be estimated by indirect means. A common estimating procedure has been the "residual method" which compares the population as recorded in each decennial census with the population that would be ex-pected in view of known immigration and the excess of births over deaths. The "residual" or difference between the known population and the "ex-pected" would be the estimated emigration. This is, of course, made possible through a variation of the basic demographic equation referred to earlier:

$$\text{Emigration} = P_1 + (\text{Births} - \text{Deaths}) + \text{Immigration} - P_2$$

Major attempts to estimate emigration for various periods during the 100 years following 1851 have been made by Keyfitz, McDougall, Ryder, Sametz, and others.[9] Because of questions regarding the completeness and quality of data on immigration, fertility, and mortality, especially during the early decades, the estimates vary considerably from one another depending upon the particular assumptions employed regarding the nature of the presumed errors and the procedures used in correcting for these errors. Table 2:4 presents data on immigration, emigration, and net migration in terms of the range of estimates found in the four major studies mentioned above.

Although the individual estimates vary considerably, it is important to note that they are consistent with respect to the direction of net migration; i.e., they are all in agreement as to the periods during which immigration exceeded emigration and vice versa. Thus, it may be noted that the 1851–61 decade just prior to Confederation was the last decade of the nineteenth century during which the gain through immigration was sufficiently large to com-pensate for losses through emigration. Not until the record influx of migrants during the early twentieth century did immigration significantly exceed those emigrating to the United States, back to Europe, or elsewhere. Gains through net migration were gradually reduced in succeeding decades until the Great Depression when the volume of gross movement reached an all time low and the level of emigration again exceeded that of immigration. During the post-war decades, levels of emigration again increased but not as rapidly as im-migration, and the latter again contributed significantly to the growth of Canada's population. According to Sametz, the amount of immigration during the 1951–61 decade was only slightly less than that which occurred

Table 2:4

MAXIMUM AND MINIMUM ESTIMATES OF IMMIGRATION,
EMIGRATION, AND NET MIGRATION FOR CANADA, 1851–1961,
REPORTED BY FOUR MAJOR STUDIES[a]

Decade	Immigration	Emigration	Net Migration[b]
	(Estimates in 1,000s)		
1851–1861	209– 486	86– 332	+(123–180)
1861–1871	187– 266	370– 436	–(150–191)
1871–1881	253– 353	293– 440	–(40– 85)
1881–1891	448– 903	602–1110	–(150–205)
1891–1901	249– 326	364– 510	–(115–181)
1901–1911	1111–1782	317–1067	+(715–810)
1911–1921	1373–1592	1067–1380	+(233–310)
1921–1931	1195–1204	967–1174	+(103–230)
1931–1941	150– 151	240– 353	–(90–202)
1941–1951	548– 568	370– 437	+(131–180)
1951–1961	1540	460	+(1080)

[a] N. Keyfitz, "The Growth of Canadian Population", *Population Studies*, IV (June, 1950), pp. 47-63. D. M. McDougall, "Immigration Into Canada, 1851–1920", *Canadian Journal of Economics and Political Science*, XXVII, No. 2, May, 1961, pp. 162-175. N. B. Ryder, "Components of Canadian Population Growth", *Population Index*, XX, No. 2, 1954, pp. 71-80. P. Camu, E. P. Weeks, and Z. W. Sametz, *Economic Geography of Canada*, Toronto, Macmillan, 1964, pp. 56-64.
[b] Estimates in this column are not derived directly from the data presented in the adjacent columns. Therefore, maximum and minimum estimates of net migration will not necessarily correspond to the differences between extreme estimates of immigration and emigration. This is so because the maximum or minimum estimates for immigration and emigration do not necessarily come from the same study.

during the 1901–11 decade; yet net migration was one-third higher. Obviously this was possible only because of decreased emigration which was estimated to be only two-thirds the size of what it had been at the beginning of the twentieth century.[10] These trends and changes in the relative levels of immigration and emigration are clearly illustrated in Figure 2:3.

The emigration of both native born and foreign born from Canada to the United States has always been a concern. Emigration of native born has been perceived as a "brain drain" while emigration of foreign born suggests that Canada serves only as a temporary base for immigrants primarily interested in migrating to the United States. Certainly the major part of the European migration to the New World has been directed to the United States and the evidence for the period following Confederation suggests that many residents of Canada did in fact move on to the United States or elsewhere. However, the relatively small net loss through migration during the depression years of the 1930s represented a different kind of movement in which people appeared

Fig. 2:3

NET MIGRATION
CANADA: 1851–1961

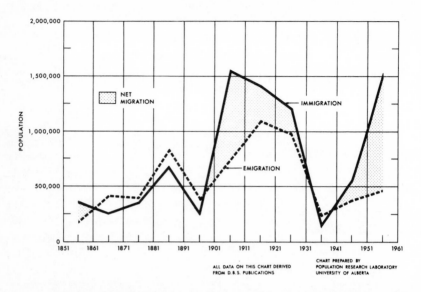

ALL DATA ON THIS CHART DERIVED
FROM D.B.S. PUBLICATIONS

CHART PREPARED BY
POPULATION RESEARCH LABORATORY
UNIVERSITY OF ALBERTA

to be returning to their previous places of residence as a means of coping with the extremely difficult economic situation of the Great Depression. The number of emigrants leaving for the United States dropped from 924,515 during the 1921–31 decade to 108,527 for the depression decade and the total for Canadian-born white population resident in the United States declined by 234,393 during the same period.[11] Further, it has been estimated that the actual number of Canadian born returning to Canada from the United States exceeded the number moving to the United States during this decade by over 100,000.[12] A relatively small emigration in comparison to immigration during the post-war period is also evident in data presented in Table 2:5 which show that the number of Canadian born in the United States declined by an additional 49,557 between 1941 and 1950 and by another 42,056 during the 1951–61 decade. The 952,506 Canadian born residing in the United States in 1960 represented the lowest number since 1900. This reduction in resident Canadian-born population in the United States could only occur if the combined effect of mortality and return migration of Canadian born to Canada exceeded their emigration to the United States. The fact that the total number continued to decline even though the number of immigrants from Canada during the 1951–61 decade was more than twice the number in 1941–51 (378,000 vs. 172,000) suggests that the increase in volume of return migration must have been proportionately greater.[13]

Even though the evidence suggests that emigration has decreased in significance for Canada during the post-World War II period, it is important to recognize the two-way nature of population movement in the modern world. Too often, the fact is overlooked that periods of heavy immigration are also likely to be periods of heavy emigration. This was certainly the case for

Table 2:5

NUMBER OF CANADIAN-BORN WHITE POPULATION RESIDENT IN THE UNITED STATES, 1900 TO 1960 AND IMMIGRATION TO THE UNITED STATES FROM CANADA, 1901–1960

Year	Total Canadian-born White Population[a]	Total Immigration[b] in Decade[c]
1900	1,172,860	—
1910	1,196,070	179,226
1920	1,117,878	742,185
1930	1,278,512	924,515
1940	1,044,119	108,527
1950	994,562	171,718
1960	938,866[d]	377,952[e]

SOURCE: Dominion Bureau of Statistics, *The Canadian-born in the United States*, Reference Paper No. 71, Ottawa, The Queen's Printer, 1956, pp. 4-5, Tables 1 and 2.
[a] Persons born in Newfoundland are included in totals for 1900, 1950, and 1960.
[b] Immigrants from Newfoundland included in totals for each decade.
[c] For decade prior to year indicated, i.e., 1901–1910, 1911–1920, etc.
[d] U.S. Bureau of the Census, *U.S. Census of the Population: 1960, Vol. I. Characteristics of the Population*, Part I. United States Summary, Washington, D.C., U.S. Government Printing Office, 1964, Table 163, pp.1-367.
[e] U.S. Bureau of the Census, *Statistical Abstracts of the United States: 1968*, (89th edition), Washington, D.C., U.S. Government Printing Office, 1968, Table No. 127, p. 92.

Canada between 1901 and 1930. In addition, return migration appears to vary considerably with country of origin. A recent study tentatively estimated that during the post-World War II period about 40 per cent of those immigrating to Canada from the United States returned, compared to 30 per cent and 20 per cent for Britain and other countries respectively.[14]

A further concern over the consequences of excessive emigration is the possible loss of trained manpower or "brain drain." A recent investigation of professional and skilled manpower emigration showed that actual losses to the United States were more than offset by the net results of the total international movements of professional and skilled workers. In other words, while Canada did lose professional and skilled manpower to the United States and United Kingdom, these losses were more than made up by the number of professional and skilled workers immigrating to Canada from all sources (including those from the United States and United Kingdom).[15]

While the loss of skilled manpower trained in Canada or elsewhere can have serious consequences for economic growth, the problem is not quite as serious as it may seem at first glance, especially with respect to the immigrant who does not remain permanently in Canada. Immigrants who contribute their labour for even part of a decade before returning home or moving on to other destinations do make a positive contribution to the economic development of the country in which they have worked. The cumulative total of person-years of life, representing the number of years each immigrant lives and works in Canada before emigrating, should be considered in any accounting system. The total contribution by immigrants could represent a significant proportion of the total investment of manhours of labour in any country experiencing relatively large turnovers in population caused by high levels of immigration and emigration.

Mortality

The continuous struggle of man to improve his environment, and hence his chances of survival, are most apparent in the examination of his mortality record through time. His consciousness and concern about death is reflected in the increasing care with which he collects detailed information on frequency, timing, and causes of death. His achievements in the struggle for survival are reflected in declining mortality and increasing life expectancy.

Mortality levels since Confederation. As is generally the case, the number of deaths tend to increase with increasing size of population, but at a somewhat slower pace if the standard of living is improving. At no time since 1867 have mortality levels exceeded those reported for the Catholic population during the 1750–60 decade. In fact, mortality levels declined consistently throughout the century; and by 1867, mortality levels in the Catholic population as measured by a crude death rate of 20.9 deaths per 1,000 population were just 50 per cent of what they had been 100 years earlier.[16] By 1920, the crude death rate had fallen to 17.5[17] and since then consistently decreased to a level of 6.8 deaths per 1,000 population in 1964. The same trend has been evident for the total population of Canada with death rates declining by 28.3 per cent to a low of 7.4 in 1968 from a level of 10.6 in 1921.[18] The trend in crude death rates for the period 1921–61 is shown in Figure 2:4.

There are certain difficulties inherent in the study of vital events, such as mortality, by means of crude rates. Since the crude mortality rate relates the number of deaths to the total population, variations in the proportionate size of certain age groups with high or low mortality risks can actually produce variations in the crude death rate even when mortality has remained constant for the age groups in question. For example, just increasing the size of one high risk population, e.g., the population over 65 years of age, relative to the other age groups will tend to increase the number of deaths (because there

Fig. 2:4

DEATH RATES BY SEX
CANADA: 1921–1961

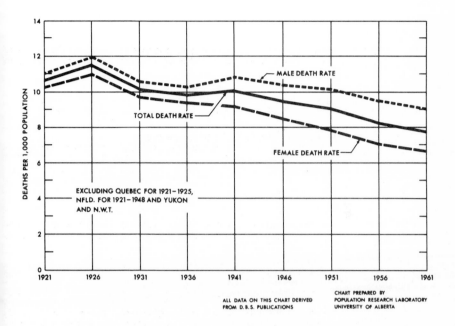

EXCLUDING QUEBEC FOR 1921–1925, NFLD. FOR 1921–1948 AND YUKON AND N.W.T.

MALE DEATH RATE

TOTAL DEATH RATE

FEMALE DEATH RATE

DEATHS PER 1,000 POPULATION

ALL DATA ON THIS CHART DERIVED FROM D.B.S. PUBLICATIONS

CHART PREPARED BY POPULATION RESEARCH LABORATORY UNIVERSITY OF ALBERTA

are larger numbers exposed to the higher risk of dying) and to raise the crude mortality rate to a higher level than it would have been otherwise. Since crude rates can be affected by such changes in the internal distribution of age and sex groups, standardized rates are better indicators of actual changes in mortality conditions.[19] For Canada, the standardized mortality rate for males and females combined was 12.9 in 1921 and 7.1 in 1968, a decline of 45.0 per cent for the 48-year period.[20] Crude and standardized death rates for the years 1921 to 1968 are shown in Table 2:6.

Levels of mortality for Canada's population have been relatively low in comparison with other countries having predominantly European populations. The Netherlands is the only country since 1931 to consistently experience mortality rates lower than those of Canada, but since 1960 Canada's mortality has been the lowest. During 1935–39, Canada's average death rate was 19.7 per cent lower than that of the United Kingdom and 35.6 per cent lower in 1966. Compared to the United States' white population, Canada's crude death rates were 7.6 per cent and 20.0 per cent lower for the same two periods respectively.[21] In the absence of more detailed information, crude mortality rates provide a rough estimation of relative mortality conditions. However, it must be kept in mind that lower mortality rates for one country

Table 2:6

CRUDE AND STANDARDIZED DEATH RATES BY SEX, CANADA: 1921–1968 (per 1,000 live births)

Year	Total Deaths	Male² Death Rates	Female² Death Rates	Death Rates Both Sexes	Standardized² Male Death Rates	Standardized² Female Death Rates	Both Sexes
1968	153,196	8.6	6.2	7.4	8.7	5.6	7.1
1967	150,283	8.6	6.1	7.4	8.7	5.6	7.1
1966	149,863	8.7	6.2	7.5	8.8	5.7	7.2
1965	148,939	8.8	6.3	7.6	8.8	5.9	7.3
1964	145,850	8.8	6.3	7.6	8.8	5.9	7.3
1963	147,367	9.0	6.5	7.8	9.0	6.2	7.6
1962	143,699	8.9	6.5	7.7	8.9	6.2	7.6
1961	140,985	9.0	6.5	7.7	9.0	6.3	7.6
1960	139,693	9.0	6.6	7.8	9.1	6.4	7.8
1959	139,913	9.2	6.8	8.0	9.3	6.7	8.0
1958	135,201	9.1	6.7	7.9	9.3	6.6	8.0
1957	136,579	9.5	6.9	8.2	9.6	6.9	8.3
1956	131,961	9.4	7.0	8.2	9.4	7.0	8.2
1955	128,476	9.4	6.9	8.2	9.4	6.9	8.2
1954	124,855	9.3	7.0	8.2	9.3	7.0	8.2
1953	127,791	9.8	7.4	8.6	9.8	7.5	8.6
1952	126,385	10.0	7.5	8.7	9.9	7.6	8.8
1951	125,823	10.1	7.8	9.0	10.0	8.0	9.0
1950	124,220	10.1	7.9	9.1	10.1	8.1	9.1
1949	124,567	10.3	8.1	9.2	10.3	8.3	9.4
1948	122,974	10.4	8.3	9.3	10.4	8.5	9.5
1947	121,503	10.4	8.3	9.4	10.6	8.7	9.7
1946	118,785	10.3	8.4	9.4	10.7	9.0	9.9
1945	117,325	10.3	8.5	9.4	10.9	9.2	9.3
1944	120,393	10.5	8.9	9.7	11.3	9.7	10.5
1943	122,640	10.9	9.2	10.1	11.8	10.1	11.0
1942	117,110	10.6	8.8	9.7	11.6	9.8	10.7

Table 2:6—concluded

CRUDE AND STANDARDIZED DEATH RATES BY SEX, CANADA: 1921–1968 (per 1,000 live births)

Year	Total Deaths	Male[2] Death Rates	Female[2] Death Rates	Death Rates Both Sexes	Standardized[2] Male Death Rates	Standardized[2] Female Death Rates	Both Sexes
1940	114,717	10.5	9.0	9.8	11.8	10.2	11.0
1939	112,729	10.4	9.0	9.7	11.8	10.4	11.1
1938	110,647	10.3	8.9	9.6	11.8	10.4	11.1
1937	118,019	10.9	9.7	10.3	12.7	11.4	12.1
1936	111,111	10.2	9.3	9.8	12.0	11.0	11.5
1935	109,724	10.2	9.2	9.7	12.1	11.0	11.6
1934	105,277	10.0	8.9	9.5	11.9	10.8	11.4
1933	105,603	10.0	9.2	9.6	12.0	11.2	11.6
1932	108,161	10.3	9.5	9.9	12.5	11.6	12.1
1931	108,446	10.5	9.6	10.1	12.7	11.7	12.2
1930	113,283	11.2	10.2	10.7	13.5	12.4	13.0
1929	117,622	11.8	10.8	11.3	14.3	13.3	13.8
1928	113,176	11.6	10.6	11.1	14.0	13.0	13.5
1927	109,104	11.4	10.4	10.9	13.8	12.7	13.3
1926	111,055	11.9	10.9	11.4	14.3	13.4	13.9
1925	102,528	10.3	9.5	9.9	12.5	11.7	12.1
1924	102,820	10.3	9.6	10.0	12.6	11.9	12.2
1923	108,858[1]	11.0	10.4	10.7	13.5	12.9	13.2
1922	106,068[1]	11.0	10.3	10.6	13.4	12.6	13.0
1921	104,531[1]	10.9	10.2	10.6	13.3	12.4	12.9

SOURCE: Dominion Bureau of Statistics, *Vital Statistics, 1962,* and *1968,* Ottawa, The Queen's Printer, Tables D5, D6.
[1] Excluding Yukon and Northwest Territories.
[2] Excluding Quebec for 1921–25, Newfoundland for 1921–48, and Yukon and Northwest Territories for 1921–49. Standardized to Canada's 1956 Census population.

relative to those of another such as Canada may reflect a more favourable age-sex distribution, i.e., a population with larger proportions in those particular age and sex groups for which mortality is especially low, rather than more favourable mortality conditions *per se*.

Sex and age differentials in mortality. The declining trend in mortality rates for the population as a whole between 1921 and 1961, depicted in Figure 2:4, has been experienced by both male and female populations, but with two major differences: (1) mortality rates for males have been consistently higher throughout the period, and (2) mortality rates for females have decreased more rapidly than those for males. Standardized mortality rates for males and females (Table 2:6) reveal that in 1921 the male mortality rate of 13.3 deaths per 1,000 population was only 7.3 per cent higher than the female rate of 12.4. By 1968, the rate for males of 8.7 was 55.4 per cent higher than the rate of 5.6 for females. The ratios of male to female death rates for the entire period show this increasing divergence very clearly.

The consistently high sex ratios at birth combined with significantly higher infant and fetal mortality rates for males suggests a greater biological susceptibility on the part of males to the forces of mortality. However, the validity of this explanation for the increasing divergence by sex is less certain. Part of this trend has been explained in terms of the greater benefit accruing to females from recent reductions in certain causes of deaths, e.g., those associated with childbearing and tuberculosis, and because of increasing mortality to males due to accidents, heart disease, and cancer.[22] There is also an indication of a greater health consciousness on the part of females which leads to a greater utilization of health and medical facilities apart from those visits related to their unique childbearing function.[23] Regardless of which factors have causal primacy, it is obvious that they have contributed disproportionately more to the decline in mortality for females.

The age-specific death rates for 1921 and 1961, presented in Figure 2:5, show very clearly those ages for which major improvements have been achieved. The greatest absolute reduction in mortality rates has occurred in the first year of life. The average infant mortality for 1921–25 was 99 deaths per 1,000 live births, while in 1961 it was only 27.2. By 1968, it had declined to 20.8, a level representing an overall decline of 79.0 per cent. The second largest absolute reduction in mortality was experienced by those 70–74 years of age. Their rates declined from 54.9 in 1921 to 43.9 in 1961 and 40.5 in 1968, or a relative decline of 26.2 per cent for the entire period. At the same time, the absolute reduction in mortality for the 10–14 year olds, who consistently have had the lowest mortality rate of any age group, was only 1.6 percentage points, representing a decline from just 2.0 to 0.4 deaths per 1,000 population.

Fig. 2:5

AGE-SPECIFIC DEATH RATES
CANADA: 1921 AND 1961

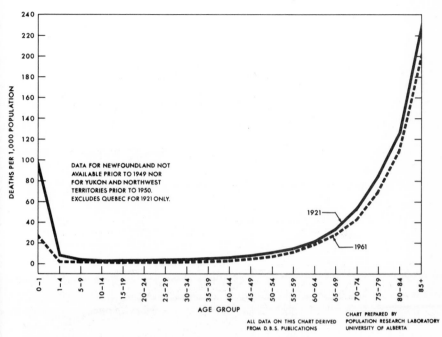

DATA FOR NEWFOUNDLAND NOT
AVAILABLE PRIOR TO 1949 NOR
FOR YUKON AND NORTHWEST
TERRITORIES PRIOR TO 1950.
EXCLUDES QUEBEC FOR 1921 ONLY.

ALL DATA ON THIS CHART DERIVED
FROM D.B.S. PUBLICATIONS

CHART PREPARED BY
POPULATION RESEARCH LABORATORY
UNIVERSITY OF ALBERTA

Mortality trends for specific age groups from 1921 to 1961 are illustrated in Figure 2:6. It is readily apparent that, while mortality conditions have improved throughout the entire age range, the degree of improvement varies considerably from younger to older age groups. For those 60 years of age and older, very little improvement can be noted. The rate of improvement increases as one progresses to younger age groups. However, the rate of decline in mortality for those under one year of age has not been as great as for the other groups under 15 years of age.

In view of infant mortality's importance as an indirect indicator of standard of living and in terms of its role with respect to major improvements in life expectancy, mortality rates for ages under one year are shown in Figure 2:7 for 1931 through 1961. As might be expected, mortality has continued to be highest during the first week of life. The perinatal death rate[24] which was 65 per 1,000 total live births in 1921 declined to 59 in 1931, 28 in 1961, and 24 by 1968. Note also that neonatal rates[25] were somewhat lower and have experienced a corresponding decline during this period. However, post-neonatal mortality rates[26] broke sharply with the trend for neonatal rates after 1941, dropping from 30 deaths per 1,000 live births to 9.2 in 1961. It would appear that the slower rate of improvement in survival for the first days of life

Fig. 2:6   MORTALITY TRENDS BY SELECTED AGES
                        CANADA: 1921–1961

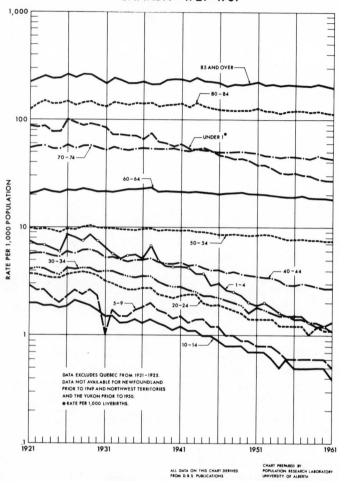

reflects the higher proportion of deaths due to causes associated with foetal development, intra-uterine environment, and the birth process. In 1968, immaturity, postnatal asphyxia, injuries at birth, and congenital malformations accounted for 71.6 per cent of all neonatal deaths.[27] By way of contrast, the major causes of death during the post-neonatal period were infectious and respiratory diseases, malformations, accidents, and constitutional disorders. Some of these causes, e.g., infectious and respiratory diseases, are more amenable to control than are such causes as immaturity and congenital malformations which are among the major causes of neonatal mortality.

Previously it was shown (Figure 2:4) that while both male and female mortality rates have been declining those for females have declined more

Fig. 2:7   INFANT MORTALITY TRENDS
                      CANADA: 1931-1961

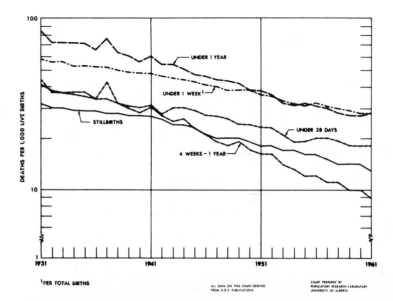

rapidly during the period 1921–68. However, the increasing differential between male and female mortality rates has not been occurring uniformly
throughout the age distribution. The ratio of male to female mortality rates
has changed very little for those under one year of age and for those 85 years
and over. Of the remaining age groups, those between 10 and 30, and especially the 20–24 year olds, showed the most rapid increase in the ratio of
male to female mortality. During the period 1926–30, male mortality exceeded female mortality by approximately 30 per cent. By 1951, and after a
long period of declining mortality, the rate for males was 90 per cent higher,
and by 1961 it was 183 per cent higher. Outside the age group 10–29, the
only other ages showing a rapid increase in male-female mortality ratios were
those 55–59 and 60–64 years, but here the excess male mortality during the
1926–30 period only increased from 16.8 and 14.8 per cent for the two age
groups respectively to 90.0 and 87.5 per cent respectively in 1961. Thus, the
overall trend toward divergence is the result of two rather distinct and separate changes affecting two separate segments of the total age distribution.

   A similar analysis of trends in the United States has indicated that the
increase in the sex mortality ratios for the younger age groups was a function
of declines in specific causes of mortality having particular relevance for
women, e.g., childbearing and tuberculosis, and relatively greater increases
in accidental deaths for males—particularly motor vehicle accidents. For the

older age groups, the primary factor responsible for the increasing sex mortality ratios was found to be an increase in heart disease and malignant neoplasms in general and specifically among males at a time when female mortality from these causes actually declined.[28] While it is not certain that the same factors can provide an explanation for similar trends in sex-age differentials in Canada, the trends are sufficiently similar to those in the United States to suggest their relevance for the Canadian experience.

Expectation of life. Life tables are very useful devices for summarizing the effects of a given set of mortality conditions existing at a particular point in time upon a given population. Very simply, the life table is an hypothetical model of a population which indicates, among other things, how many years (on the average) individuals of a particular birth cohort will live if they

Fig. 2:8

**LIFE EXPECTANCY
SELECTED AGES BY SEX
CANADA: 1931–1961**

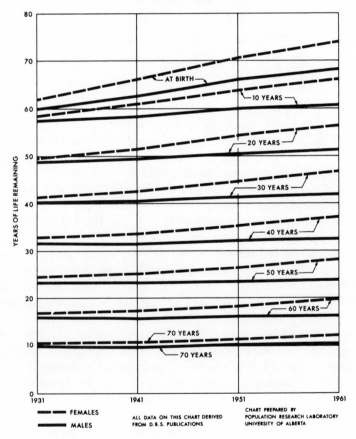

experience a given set of age and sex mortality rates during the course of their life time. For example, data in Figure 2:8 which have been obtained from four life tables indicate that individuals of the cohort born in 1931 (experiencing throughout their life time the mortality conditions existing in Canada as of 1931) could expect to live, on the average, 60.0 years if they were males and 62.1 years if they were females. Those surviving to age ten could expect to live another 58.0 and 58.7 years; those living to age 20 could expect an additional 49.1 and 49.8 years for males and females respectively; and so on, until those still living 70 years after their birth could expect an additional 10.1 and 10.6 years depending upon their particular sex.

Comparisons of life expectancies for specific ages through successive periods of time are presented in Figure 2:8. The relative improvement which has been accomplished is a direct reflection of improvements in living standards and the success which has been achieved in reducing mortality from specific causes through implementation and expansion of public health services and improved medical technology. As may be noted in Figure 2:8, expectancy of life has increased for each of the selected age groups but with greater increases having been realized for the younger ages. In addition, the increases have been greater for females than males at all age levels, a fact consistent with the previously observed trends in mortality sex differentials. Life expectancies by age and sex are presented in Table 2:7 for the years 1931, 1941, 1951, and 1961. It should be kept in mind, when examining these data, that, in reality, mortality conditions existing at each age level for a specific year do not remain constant. By the time survivors of a particular birth cohort (born in 1931) reach the age of 30 years, for example, mortality conditions will generally be improved over what they were 30 years earlier. To the extent that this continues to be true, life expectancies in terms of years of life remaining will tend to understate the "actual" number of years remaining for the individual as he successfully survives to older ages.[29] Nevertheless, life table data present the best overall picture of mortality and consequences of changing mortality patterns for the longevity of Canada's population that is available. The gain in life expectancy at birth over the 30-year period 1931–61, was 13.9 per cent for males and 19.4 per cent for females. At age 20, the gains were 5.1 and 13.8 per cent and at age 40 just 3.1 and 13.4 per cent for males and females respectively. For men 60 years of age, the percentage gain was just 2.7, while for women it was 16.0 per cent.

Major causes of death. As mortality rates have declined and sex mortality ratios increased since the 1920s, the major causes of death have also changed. Deaths due to influenza, bronchitis, and pneumonia, which constituted the second highest cause of death during the 1926–30 period, declined from a level of 134.0 deaths per 100,000 population to just 34.2 in 1964, an overall decline of 74.5 per cent. The first and third ranked causes of death during 1926–30, cardiovascular-renal disease[30] and cancer,[31] increased by 38.3 and

Table 2:7 LIFE EXPECTANCY BY AGE AND SEX: 1931, 1941, 1951, 1956, AND 1961, CANADA

Age	1931 Males	1931 Females	1941 Males	1941 Females	1951 Males	1951 Females	1956 Males	1956 Females	1961 Males	1961 Females
At Birth	60.00	62.10	62.96	66.30	66.33	70.83	67.61	72.92	68.35	74.17
1 Year	64.69	65.71	66.14	68.73	68.33	72.33	69.04	73.99	69.50	74.98
2 Years	64.46	65.42	65.62	68.16	67.56	71.55	68.21	73.15	68.63	74.11
3 Years	63.84	64.75	64.88	67.38	66.68	70.66	67.31	72.24	67.71	73.18
4 Years	63.11	63.99	64.07	66.56	65.79	69.74	66.38	71.31	66.78	72.23
5 Years	62.30	63.17	63.22	65.69	64.86	68.80	65.45	70.35	65.83	71.27
10 Years	57.96	58.72	58.70	61.08	60.15	64.02	60.67	65.51	61.02	66.41
15 Years	53.41	54.15	54.06	56.36	55.39	59.19	55.86	60.64	56.20	61.51
20 Years	49.05	49.76	49.57	51.76	50.76	54.41	51.19	55.80	51.51	56.65
25 Years	44.83	45.54	45.18	47.26	46.20	49.67	46.61	50.97	46.91	51.80
30 Years	40.55	41.38	40.73	42.81	41.60	44.94	41.98	46.17	42.24	46.98
35 Years	36.23	37.19	36.26	38.37	37.00	40.24	37.34	41.40	37.56	42.18
40 Years	31.98	33.02	31.87	33.99	32.45	35.63	32.74	36.69	32.96	37.45
45 Years	27.79	28.87	27.60	29.67	28.05	31.14	28.28	32.09	28.49	32.82
50 Years	23.72	24.79	23.49	25.46	23.88	26.80	24.04	27.65	24.25	28.33
55 Years	19.88	20.84	19.64	21.42	20.02	22.61	20.12	23.38	20.30	24.01
60 Years	16.29	17.15	16.06	17.62	16.49	18.64	16.54	19.34	16.73	19.90
65 Years	12.98	13.72	12.81	14.08	13.31	14.97	13.36	15.60	13.53	16.07
70 Years	10.06	10.63	9.94	10.93	10.41	11.62	10.51	12.17	10.67	12.58
75 Years	7.57	7.98	7.48	8.19	7.89	8.73	7.98	9.15	8.21	9.48
80 Years	5.61	5.92	5.54	6.03	5.84	6.38	5.89	6.75	6.14	6.90
85 Years	4.10	4.38	4.05	4.35	4.27	4.57	4.27	4.97	4.46	4.89
90 Years	2.97	3.24	2.93	3.13	3.10	3.24	3.07	3.67	3.16	3.39
95 Years	2.14	2.40	2.09	2.26	2.24	2.27	2.18	2.74	2.20	2.32
100 Years	1.53	1.77	1.46	1.64	1.60	1.59	1.52	2.05	1.49	1.56

SOURCE: Dominion Bureau of Statistics, Vital Statistics, 1967, Ottawa, The Queen's Printer, 1969, Table L.1, p. 214.

51.5 per cent respectively during the same period with cancer becoming the second major cause of death during the 1930s. Mortality rates from these two causes were 369.2 and 137.9 deaths per 100,000 population respectively in 1968. The death rate for accidents remained fairly consistent throughout the period at close to 55 deaths per 100,000, but it still managed to replace tuberculosis as the fourth most important cause of death by the early 1940s. Deaths from tuberculosis had dropped to insignificant levels by 1968 with a death rate of only 2.7 per 100,000 population compared to 80.3 for the earlier period.[32]

The increase in deaths from cardiovascular-renal diseases and cancer has been due in part to the relatively successful control of infectious diseases, to the rapid growth of population in the older age groups, and to improved diagnosis which has tended to reduce the number of deaths attributed to senility or to other ill-defined and unknown causes. Herein also lies the key to the expectation that further reductions in mortality for Canada's population will not be very great and will be achieved very slowly compared to the rapid gains resulting from the effective control of infectious and communicable diseases in the past. Recent analyses concerned with the determination of gains in expectation of life at birth which may be expected as a consequence of the elimination of specific causes of death in the United States have shown that significant but relatively small increases in life expectancy will be achieved only if efforts are successful in reducing death rates due to malignant neoplasms or cardiovascular-renal diseases. For example, success in the former would add an estimated 2.27 years to life expectancy at birth while the elimination of arteriosclerotic heart disease (including coronary disease) would add an estimated 3.98 years. By way of contrast, the complete elimination of influenza and pneumonia (except of the newborn) would add only 0.53 years while the elimination of fatalities due to motor vehicle accidents would add only 0.55 years to life expectancy at birth.[33] The reason why these additions to life expectancy at birth are so low is that improvements in mortality merely enable the population to survive until they are affected by a new set of mortality causes.

Fertility

Of the three basic demographic components, fertility has been most significant for understanding Canada's growth since 1867. The slower decline of mortality in recent times and the decrease in magnitude of net migration in relation to total population have increased the importance of fertility's contribution to total growth. Not only does it contribute directly to population size, but variations in fertility also have profound effects on a population's age-sex structure, its rate of aging or "younging," and changes in the ratios of economically active persons to both young and old dependents.

Levels of fertility. Early records pertaining to New France have shown that fertility among the Catholic population was very high. As early as 1660–70, fertility was estimated to have been as high as 60 births per 1,000 population. Fertility fluctuated considerably during the early period of settlement and not until after the 1830–40 decade did there appear to be any consistent tendency for fertility to decline. Official national figures were not collected on an annual basis until 1921, so that estimates of fertility have to be based on studies of early Canadian census data. The estimates of average annual

Table 2:8

ESTIMATED CRUDE FERTILITY RATES, CANADA
1851–1861 TO 1911–1921

Intercensal Period	Estimated Average Annual Number of Births per 1,000 Population
1851–1861	45
1861–1871	40
1871–1881	37
1881–1891	34
1891–1901	30
1901–1911	31
1911–1921	29

SOURCE: Dominion Bureau of Statistics, *Canada Year Book, 1967,* Ottawa, The Queen's Printer, 1967, p. 241.

crude birth rates in Table 2:8 show a fairly rapid and consistent decline up to the 1891–1901 decade just prior to the onset of the great immigrations of the early twentieth century.

Birth rates, as well as number of births, continued to decline until 1937 at which point the 227,869 live births represented a fertility rate of 20.1 births per 1,000 total population. In the face of impending war in Europe and economic revival at home, the trend, both in numbers and rates, reversed. By 1942, the number of births (281,569) had exceeded the number born during 1921; but because of increasing population size, the crude fertility rate did not approach the level of the 1921–25 period until 1946 when the rate climbed to 27.2 and then to its post-war peak of 28.9 in 1947. The number of births did not exceed the peak of 1947 until 1951, but then it continued to rise to an all time high of 479,275 in 1959. However, since 1954, when the crude birth rate was 28.5, fertility has declined and in 1961 the rate had reached 26.1 and by 1968 it dropped to an all-time low of 17.6. The number of live births and births per 1,000 population for the years 1921 to 1968 are shown in Table 2:9.

Trends in fertility levels for provinces generally have followed the long term trends for the country as a whole. However, as Figure 2:9 illustrates,

NUMBER OF LIVE BIRTHS AND CRUDE BIRTH RATES, CANADA, 1921–1968

Year	Number of Live Births	Crude Birth Rates	Year	Number of Live Births	Crude Birth Rates
1921	264,879	29.3	1951	381,092	27.2
1922	259,825	28.3	1952	403,559	27.9
1923	247,404	26.7	1953	417,884	28.1
1924	251,351	26.7	1954	436,198	28.5
1925	249,365	26.1	1955	442,937	28.2
1926	240,015	24.7	1956	450,739	28.0
1927	241,149	24.3	1957	469,093	28.2
1928	243,616	24.1	1958	470,118	27.5
1929	242,226	23.5	1959	479,275	27.4
1930	250,335	23.9	1960	478,551	26.8
1931	247,205	23.2	1961	475,700	26.1
1932	242,698	22.5	1962	469,693	25.3
1933	229,791	21.0	1963	465,767	24.6
1934	228,296	20.7	1964	452,915	23.5
1935	228,396	20.5	1965	418,595	21.3
1936	227,980	20.3	1966	387,710	19.4
1937	227,869	20.1	1967	370,894	18.2
1938	237,091	20.7	1968	364,310	17.6
1939	237,991	20.6			
1940	252,577	21.6			
1941	263,993	22.4			
1942	281,569	23.5			
1943	292,943	24.2			
1944	293,967	24.0			
1945	300,587	24.3			
1946	343,504	27.2			
1947	372,589	28.9			
1948	359,860	27.3			
1949	367,092	27.3			
1950	372,009	27.1			

SOURCE: Dominion Bureau of Statistics, *Vital Statistics*, *1958*, *1964*, and *1968*, Ottawa, The Queen's Printer.

the range in levels of fertility for the various regions was considerably higher in 1921 than in 1961. For those provinces shown, there has been a significant convergence during the 40 years since 1921. Data for all provinces show that Quebec had higher crude rates up to 1936, at which time it was exceeded by Newfoundland. Since 1937, Quebec's rates have also been exceeded by New Brunswick's, and since 1953 by Alberta's. Of all the provinces, Newfoundland has maintained the highest fertility rate since entering Confederation, and in 1968, its crude rate was 25.3 births per 1,000 population compared to 17.6 for all areas combined. World War II contributed additional changes, and in 1945 the Northwest Territories' birth rate of 42.6 exceeded all others. During the post-war period, it has continued to exhibit the highest fertility as well as showing increases at a time when crude rates for all other areas were decreasing. Its crude rate of 49.7 in 1960 is something of a national record for Canada in recent times. Also indicative of the high fertility levels among Native Indian and Eskimo populations is the fact that in 1949 and subsequent years the fertility level in the Yukon exceeded all other provinces, being second only to the Northwest Territories. While these rates are highly indicative of social conditions in the North, their significance is considerably attenuated insofar as the growth of Canada's total population is concerned because of their relatively small populations.

Fig. 2:9

**FERTILITY TRENDS
CANADA AND SELECTED PROVINCES: 1921–1961**

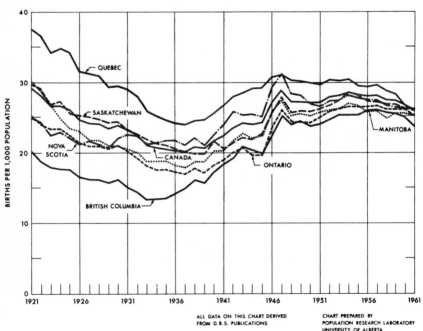

ALL DATA ON THIS CHART DERIVED
FROM D.B.S. PUBLICATIONS

CHART PREPARED BY
POPULATION RESEARCH LABORATORY
UNIVERSITY OF ALBERTA

Of greater significance at this point is the cumulative effect of regional fertility for Canada's growth relative to that of other countries. Since 1921, levels of fertility have been consistently higher than those of the United States, but have paralleled to a remarkable extent the annual variations in crude rates for the United States. Furthermore, levels of fertility in North America have tended to exceed those of Western Europe and have been unique with respect to the duration of the post-World War II "baby boom." During 1950–54 and 1955–59, Canada's average birth rates of 27.7 and 27.8 births per 1,000 population were higher than those for any of the major countries in Europe, and the European populations of Oceania in addition to the United States. They were exceeded only by Poland and Yugoslavia during the 1950–54 period. The decline since 1954 from 28.5 to 19.6 in 1965 placed the level of fertility in Canada only slightly lower than that of Ireland (21.6), Northern Ireland (22.5), New Zealand (22.5), and Yugoslavia (20.2).[34]

Fertility differentials. The reversal of the long term decline in fertility after 1937 appears to have been the result of increasing fertility rates among the younger women. Figure 2:10 shows that fertility declines between 1921 and 1937 were characteristic of all women 15–49 years of age. After 1937, reversals occurred in each of the three youngest age groups with the most rapid increase taking place in the 15–19 year age group, followed by the 20–24 and 25–29 year old women. The trend reversal for those 30–34 years of age was somewhat delayed and did not become apparent until 1940. For the three oldest groups, the overall trend for 40 years was one of continuing decline. There were, however, slight increases between 1941 and 1946 for those 35–39 and 40–44 years of age. For the oldest group, fertility has continued to decline significantly since 1927.

During this period, the peak age for childbearing among Canadian women shifted toward the younger age groups. Women 25–29 years of age had the highest fertility rate of any age group from 1921 until 1954 when they were surpassed by women aged 20–24 years. The rates for 30–34 year old women had been second highest between 1926 and 1939 after which they were also bypassed by the more rapidly increasing fertility of the 20–24 year olds. While fertility for the youngest women, 15–19, exceeded only that of the oldest age group for the entire 40-year period, their rapidly increasing fertility after 1936 placed them above those 40–44 years of age in 1943, and after 1945 the gap between these two groups increased rapidly. However, before 1961, signs of a downtrend had already begun to appear among the younger women. The three youngest age groups actually reached their maximum levels of fertility in 1959 with rates of 60.4, 233.8, and 226.7 respectively. The 30–34 year olds had reached their peak in 1954 and showed consistent declines in the following years.[35]

Unlike crude birth rates, age-specific rates are not significantly affected by changes in the age-sex structure. However, they are affected by changes in

Fig. 2:10

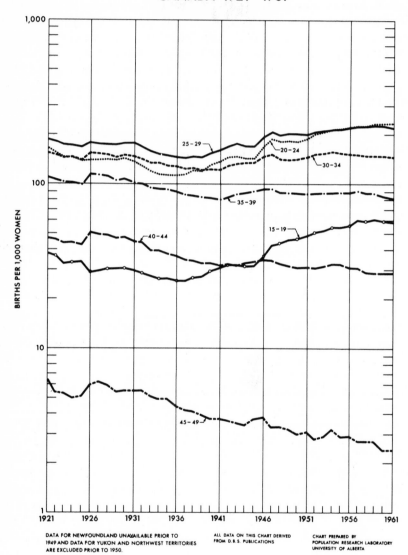

FERTILITY TRENDS
BIRTH RATES BY AGE
CANADA: 1921−1961

DATA FOR NEWFOUNDLAND UNAVAILABLE PRIOR TO
1949 AND DATA FOR YUKON AND NORTHWEST TERRITORIES
ARE EXCLUDED PRIOR TO 1950.

ALL DATA ON THIS CHART DERIVED
FROM D.B.S. PUBLICATIONS

CHART PREPARED BY
POPULATION RESEARCH LABORATORY
UNIVERSITY OF ALBERTA

age at marriage, proportions married, timing of first child, spacing of subsequent children, as well as by changing attitudes towards ideal family size, family planning, and availability of inexpensive, reliable, and acceptable means of contraception. The gradual decline in average age at marriage of single persons between 1940 and 1968 from 24.4 to 22.6 years for brides and from 27.7 to 25.0 years for bridegrooms would explain in part the increases in fertility among younger age groups.[36] Such declines would tend to increase the proportion married and those exposed to the risk of pregnancy. The proportion of women 15–19 who were married did increase from 2.7 per cent in 1931 to 3.0 per cent in 1941, and to 4.9 per cent in 1961.

The effect on age-specific fertility of the relatively small proportion of married females 15–19 years of age can be observed by a comparison of Figure 2:10 with data in Table 2:10 which presents age-specific marital fertility rates for Canada, 1931 to 1966. Note that the trends through time for each of the age groups of married women are roughly similar to the age-specific rates illustrated in Figure 2:10. Both measures of fertility show the same general effects of the depression era for all age groups as well as post-war recoveries to levels higher than 1931 for those under 30 years of age. Similarly, the two age groups over 40 years show consistent declines. However, the most significant difference between the two sets of data is the consistent negative relationship between age and marital-specific fertility for all time periods. Married women 15–19 years of age have had the highest fertility of any group, while each successively older age group has been consistently lower. Each of the five youngest groups of married women also show evidence of new and increasingly rapid declines in fertility after the post-war peaks in 1956, suggestive of future declines in completed fertility and family size.

Table 2:10

AGE-SPECIFIC MARITAL FERTILITY RATES, CANADA: 1931 TO 1966

Year	15-19	20-24	25-29	30-34	35-39	40-44	45-49	15-49
1931	485.0	357.6	257.7	180.9	123.1	52.5	6.5	160.9
1941	453.1	340.2	237.8	158.3	99.1	38.9	4.5	149.3
1951	498.5	350.4	248.1	168.7	100.6	36.6	3.7	158.9
1956	551.5	381.7	265.6	169.8	101.0	35.6	3.4	162.6
1961	541.2	374.4	255.6	161.4	89.9	32.1	2.8	152.9
1966	465.8	280.2	187.3	112.5	62.5	21.0	2.0	112.4

SOURCE: Dominion Bureau of Statistics, *Vital Statistics, 1966*, Ottawa, The Queen's Printer, 1968, p. 74.

Other measures of Canadian fertility. Total fertility rates calculated on the basis of age-specific rates indicate the total number of births which 1,000 women would have during their childbearing years, assuming that they experienced no mortality during this period and that the specific fertility rates characteristic of each age group would not change. The advantage of total fertility rates is that they provide a single summary measure which, unlike crude rates, is unaffected by a particular age distribution. Total fertility rates

Table 2:11

TOTAL FERTILITY RATES,[a] CANADA: 1921–1968

Year	Total Fertility Rate	Year	Total Fertility Rate
1921	3,536	1946	3,374
1922	3,402	1947	3,595
1923	3,234	1948	3,441
1924	3,221	1949[b]	3,456
1925	3,132	1950	3,455
1926	3,357	1951	3,503
1927	3,319	1952	3,641
1928	3,294	1953	3,721
1929	3,217	1954	3,828
1930	3,282	1955	3,831
1931	3,200	1956	3,858
1932	3,084	1957	3,925
1933	2,864	1958	3,880
1934	2,803	1959	3,935
1935	2,755	1960	3,895
1936	2,696	1961	3,840
1937	2,646	1962	3,756
1938	2,701	1963	3,669
1939	2,654	1964	3,502
1940	2,766	1965	3,145
1941	2,832	1966	2,812
1942	2,964	1967	2,586
1943	3,041	1968	2,441
1944	3,010		
1945	3,018		

SOURCE: Dominion Bureau of Statistics, *Vital Statistics, 1950, 1962,* and *1968,* Ottawa, The Queen's Printer.
[a] Data for Newfoundland not available.
[b] Yukon and Northwest Territories excluded prior to 1950.

for Canada presented in Table 2:11 show that, with the fertility levels existing in 1959, 1,000 women passing through the childbearing ages would have 3,935 children, or each woman would have on the average 3.9 children.

While this was the highest total fertility rate for the 1921–68 period, the rate dropped rapidly, reaching record lows in 1967 and 1968.

Another measure, the gross reproduction rate, can be derived from the total fertility rate and represents the average number of female infants that would be born to each woman living through the childbearing years if the age-specific fertility rates for a particular year remained unchanged. The gross reproduction rate provides a crude replacement index whereby rates below 1.0 indicate that, under prevailing fertility levels, women passing through their reproductive cycle are failing to have sufficient children to replace themselves even if the cohort of women experience no losses through mortality. Gross reproduction rates for Canada reveal that its reproduction level has never fallen below the minimum replacement level, i.e., below 1.0 since 1926–30, the earliest period for which data are available.[37] Even during the low point of the depression years, the gross reproduction rate was 1.286. It subsequently rose to record peaks of 1.907 and 1.915 in 1957 and 1959 respectively, before commencing its rapid decline during the 1960s. While gross reproduction rates have always been among the highest achieved by any of the industrialized countries of the world, the precipitous drop of the past decade may alter its relative position in the near future.

Several words of caution are necessary at this point regarding the interpretation of the gross reproduction rate (GRR). Unlike the net reproduction rate, it tends to overestimate fertility in that the mortality experience of the cohort of women is assumed to be zero. Perhaps of more importance is the fact that the gross reproduction rate shares an important weakness with the net reproduction rate. Both show a cross-sectional picture of fertility in that they reflect the cumulative fertility experience of women of different age groups (and birth cohorts) at a given point in time. For this reason, it is possible for both gross and net reproduction rates, under certain circumstances, to imply a level of total completed fertility considerably in excess of the actual experience of any known cohort of women who have completed their fertility, or of expected levels of completed fertility for women who have not yet finished their childbearing. This is especially likely to happen when women in both younger and older age groups are experiencing above average fertility during the same period of time. Since it is highly unlikely that the age-specific fertility rates existing during a given year will actually continue unchanged, the gross reproduction rate (as well as the net reproduction rate) is not always a good predictor of future fertility. For this reason, more attention has been directed in recent years to the analysis of cumulative fertility rates.

Cumulative fertility rates provide information on the total number of infants born to women ever married. For women 50 years of age and over, cumulative rates provide measures of completed fertility (family size); and trend analysis for cohorts of women born in different years provide an excellent basis for estimating future trends in completed fertility. Cumulative rates by age of mother in 1961 are shown in Table 2:12. Those women who were 50 years of age and over at the time of the census represent cohorts which have completed their fertility, and for these women a decline in family size is quite apparent. Completed fertility for those 50–54 years of age was 3,154 per 1,000 women compared to 4,038 for those 65 years and over. The change in completed fertility between the 60–64 and 50–54 year old cohorts represents a decline of 13.6 per cent in just ten years.

Table 2:12

NUMBER OF CHILDREN BORN PER 1,000 WOMEN EVER MARRIED BY AGE OF MOTHER, CANADA, 1961

Age of Mother	Year of Birth	Births per 1,000 Women Ever Married
65+	Prior to 1896	4,038
60–64	1897–1901	3,650
55–59	1902–1906	3,385
50–54	1907–1911	3,154
45–49	1912–1916	3,110
40–44	1917–1921	3,231
35–39	1922–1926	3,102
30–34	1927–1931	2,775
25–29	1932–1936	2,178
20–24	1937–1941	1,327
15–19	1942–1946	735

SOURCE: Dominion Bureau of Statistics, *1961 Census of Canada*, Bulletin 4.1-8, Ottawa, The Queen's Printer, 1966, Table H.1.

While cumulative fertility for those 45–49 was lower than for the 50–54 year age group, it is quite possible that completed fertility for the former will exceed 3,154 and hence reverse the earlier downward trend in completed fertility size. Even if it does not, the cohort born during 1917–21, i.e., women 40–44 years of age in 1961, has already exceeded the completed fertility of the next older cohort of women born during 1907–11, and their completed fertility will undoubtedly be somewhat higher. It is also quite probable that family size will continue to increase as several of the younger cohorts complete their childbearing years. A more detailed analysis of similar data for the United States has shown that completed fertility reached its minimum level (2,230) with the cohort of women born in 1909, and increases in completed fertility are now expected to continue in each successive cohort up to the cohorts born in 1940. Projections for the 1936–40 and 1941–45 cohorts made by the U.S. Bureau of Census are 3,200–3,500 and 3,000–3,500 respectively.[38] The 1941–45 cohort (those 19–23 years of age by the end of 1963) had born slightly under 700 births per 1,000 women compared to the

735 births reported for the slightly younger Canadian cohort born during the 1942–46 period.

Relative Significance of Migration, Mortality and Fertility

At the time of Confederation, the number of births appeared to have exceeded the number of deaths by a ratio of about two to one. Data for the Province of Quebec indicated that its ratio was slightly higher than that for Canada, being 2.1 compared to 1.9, circa 1860–70.[39] The ratio of births to deaths for Canada continued at about the same level throughout the last 30 years of the nineteenth century. During the first decade of the twentieth century, with the onset of the great migrations from Europe, the ratio increased to 2.4; and in the 1911–21 decade it reached 2.6 before dropping to 2.3 during 1921–31, and to 2.1 during the depression decade. The post-World War II revival of immigration combined with the post-depression era rise in fertility to increase the ratio of births to deaths to 2.7 during the 1941–51 decade. Between 1951 and 1961, the ratio of births to deaths reached an unprecedented record high of 3.4, representing 4,470,000 births and 1,320,000 deaths for a total natural increase of 3,150,000.

The trends in number of births relative to deaths and natural increase are shown in Figure 2:11 for single years from 1921 to 1961. The largest natural increase occurred in 1959 when 339,362 more births than deaths were recorded. However, the greatest rate of natural increase (the excess of births relative to the total population) occurred in 1954 when it reached 20.3 per 1,000 population. Since 1954, the rate has declined and the absolute number of births in excess of deaths began its decline after 1959. By 1968, the annual excess of births had declined to 211,100 and the rate of natural increase to 10.2 per 1,000 population, its lowest level since 1937.

During the 100 years following 1861, the population of Canada increased from 3,229,633 to 18,238,247, an increase of 15,008,614. Approximately 13 million of this total increment was accounted for by the excess of births over deaths. In other words, close to 87 per cent of the total growth during this period was attributable to this source while the balance of slightly more than 2,000,000 was the direct consequence of net migration. There is some variation in the estimates of net migration because of difficulties in estimating deaths during the earlier periods. Even so, taking this margin of possible error into account increases the estimates of net migration's contribution from 13.4 to 15.7 per cent at the most. All estimates tend to underestimate the total contribution of net migration in that births occurring in Canada to foreign-born parents are counted as part of the native born's natural increase. In 1931, for example, 26.3 per cent of all live births were to foreign-born women. Their proportion of total live births declined consistently, reaching a minimum of 9.3 per cent in 1945. By 1947, the proportion had increased to

Fig. 2:11

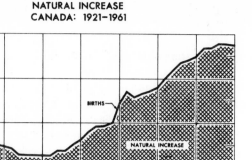

NATURAL INCREASE
CANADA: 1921–1961

BIRTHS

NATURAL INCREASE

DEATHS

1921   1926   1931   1936   1941   1946   1951   1956   1961
DATA EXCLUDED FOR YUKON AND
NORTHWEST TERRITORIES FROM   ALL DATA ON THIS CHART DERIVED   CHART PREPARED BY
1921 TO 1923 INCLUSIVE.   FROM D.B.S. PUBLICATIONS   POPULATION RESEARCH LABORATORY
                                                                                UNIVERSITY OF ALBERTA

11.5 per cent and it remained close to 10.0 per cent up to 1951. Estimates for 1961 place the proportion of births to foreign-born women at approximately 11.4 per cent.[40] By the same line of reasoning, it is apparent that immigrants also contribute to the number of deaths, hence have their own component of the natural increase. Because of their higher average age, their contribution to deaths is proportionately higher than for births. Assuming that the foreign born are subjected to approximately the same levels of mortality as the native born, it has been estimated that their proportion of total deaths varied from 25.6 in 1941 to 31.1 per cent in 1961. Their natural increase, i.e., excess of births over deaths, was estimated to have varied from zero in 1941–42 to 3,000 in 1951–52, and 10,000 in 1961–62.[41]

In a comparison of 30 different countries, Canada ranked fifth in terms of its rate of natural increase behind Venezuela, Mexico, Chile and Peru. Its relatively high position was due to its extremely favourable crude death rate of 7.6 which placed it fourth in rank order behind the U.S.S.R., Japan, and Venezuela, and also to its relatively high birth rate of 23.5 which ranked eighth behind such countries as Ireland, Italy, and the birth registration area of India.[42]

The patterns of change in Canada's vital rates have been very similar to those of the United States. The long term decline in fertility and reversal towards the end of the depression ending in the post-war peak of 1948 and the high plateau which lasted most of the 1950–60 decade closely paralleled the experience of the United States. The primary difference was Canada's consistently higher level of fertility. Mortality in Canada showed the same overall decline as in the United States but at a consistently lower level, thus producing, in combination with higher levels of fertility, a much higher natural increase for Canada. In 1964, for example, the United States ranked considerably lower than Canada with a rate of natural increase of 11.6 per 1,000 population compared to 15.9 for Canada. Both had rates in 1964 higher than such countries as England and Wales with 7.1, France with 7.3, Italy and Ireland with 11.1, and Japan with 10.8, even though fertility had been declining since 1954 in Canada. The length of the post-war baby boom in Canada and the United States surprised many of the experts, but whatever the reasons for this phenomenon might have been, they affected both Canada and the United States in much the same way. Variations in the volume of immigration have been very much the same for the two countries and though the United States has consistently attracted the larger share, the size of immigration to Canada relative to its total population has been proportionately larger than that for the United States. During the 1960–70 decade, both countries adopted a skill criterion for the admission of immigrants, so that trends relative to each other in the future should not be much different than they have been in the past. Whether or not the differential in natural increase will continue into the future will depend on the future course of mortality and fertility in the two countries. It seems reasonable to expect that as Canada becomes more similar to the United States, relative to its degree of urbanization and industrialization, it will become even more similar with respect to its balance of births and deaths.

REFERENCES

Camu, P., E. P. Weeks, and Z. W. Sametz: *Economic Geography of Canada.* Toronto, Macmillan, 1964.

Dominion Bureau of Statistics: *1961 Census of Canada. General Review: Fertility Trends in Canada.* Vol 7:2–2, Ottawa, The Queen's Printer, 1963.

George, M. V.: *Mortality Trends in Canada, 1926–1965.* Technical Memorandum (General Series) No. 20. Census Division, Dominion Bureau of Statistics, Ottawa, 1967.

Henripin, J. A.: *Tendances et facteurs de la Fecondité au Canada.* 1961 Census Monograph, Dominion Bureau of Statistics, Ottawa, The Queen's Printer, 1968.

Kalbach, W. E.: *The Impact of Immigration on Canada's Population.* 1961 Census Monograph, Dominion Bureau of Statistics, Ottawa, The Queen's Printer, 1970.

Richmond, A. H.: *Post-War Immigrants in Canada.* Toronto, University of Toronto Press, 1967.

Ryder, N. B.: "Components of Canadian Population Growth" in *Population Index,* Vol. XX, No. 2 (1954) pp. 71-81.

FOOTNOTES

[1]Net out-migrations for 1861–71, 1881–91, and 1891–1901 were approximately 33, 29, and 24 per cent of the total increases for these decades respectively, based on estimates of births, deaths, immigration and emigration reported in P. Camu, E. P. Weeks, and Z. W. Sametz, *Economic Geography of Canada,* Toronto, Macmillan of Canada, 1964, Table 3:1.

[2]Data based on immigration statistics collected by the Immigration Division, Department of Manpower and Immigration (formerly the Department of Citizenship and Immigration) and published in the *Canada Year Books.*

[3]For a more detailed discussion of the history of immigration legislation, see Dominion Bureau of Statistics, *Canada Year Book, 1957–58,* Ottawa, Queen's Printer, 1958, pp. 154–170.

[4]Data on characteristics of arriving immigrants are published regularly in the *Canada Year Book.* Also, see the annual reports of the Immigration Division, Department of Manpower and Immigration (formerly the Department of Citizenship and Immigration).

[5]Dominion Bureau of Statistics, *1961 Census of Canada,* Bulletin 7:1–7, Ottawa, The Queen's Printer, 1965, Table 1, p. 7–27.

[6]The total person-years contributed by a given group of immigrants would be the sum of the number of years lived by each immigrant.

[7]Statistics Section, Department of Citizenship and Immigration, now Canada's Immigration Division, Department of Manpower and Immigration.

[8]The major sources for emigration data have been the immigration and census records of other countries, chiefly those of the United Kingdom and the United States.

[9]N. Keyfitz, "The Growth of Canadian Population," *Population Studies,* IV (June, 1950), pp. 47–63. D. M. McDougall, "Immigration into Canada, 1851–1920," *Canadian Journal of Economics and Political Science,* Vol. XXVII, No. 2, May, 1961, pp. 162–175. N. B. Ryder, "Components of Canadian Population Growth," *Population Index,* XX, No. 2 (1954), pp. 71–80. P. Camu, E. P. Weeks, and Z. W. Sametz, *Economic Geography of Canada,* Toronto, Macmillan of Canada, 1964, pp. 56–64.

[10]P. Camu, E. P. Weeks, and Z. W. Sametz, *op. cit.,* p. 59.

[11]Dominion Bureau of Statistics, *The Canadian-born in the United States,* Reference Paper No. 71, Ottawa, The Queen's Printer, 1956, Tables 1 and 2.

[12]N. Keyfitz, *op. cit.* See also Dominion Bureau of Statistics, *op. cit.,* p. 4.

[13]Dominion Bureau of Statistics, *op. cit.,* pp. 3–5. U.S. Bureau of the Census, *U.S. Census of Population 1960, Subject Reports, Nativity and Parentage,* U.S. Government Printing Office, Washington, D.C.; and U.S. Bureau of the Census, *Statistical Abstract of the United States, 1966,* Washington, D.C., U.S. Government Printing Office, 1966, Table No. 125, p. 94.

[14]Anthony H. Richmond, *Post-war Immigrants in Canada,* Toronto, University of Toronto Press, 1967, p. 229.

[15]L. Parai, *Immigration and Emigration of Professional and Skilled Manpower During the Post-war Period,* Special Study No. 1, Economic Council of Canada, Ottawa, The Queen's Printer, 1965, pp. 1–4.

[16]*D'après les Annuaires de Québec,* 1916, p. 125. Also, these data may be found in Georges Langlois, *Histoire de la Population Canadienne Française,* Montréal Editions, Albert Levesque, 1934, Appendix VII, p. 262.

[17]Georges Langlois, *op. cit.,* Appendix VIII, p. 263; and *D'après les Annuaires de Québec,* 1914.

[18]Excludes Quebec, Newfoundland and Northwest Territories in 1921 but not in 1964. Dominion Bureau of Statistics, *Vital Statistics,* 1962, Table D6, pp. 132–37, and 1968, Table D1.

[19]Standardized or age-adjusted rates indicate what the overall death rate would have been each year had the age-sex composition of the population remained constant over the entire period from 1921 to 1964. The standardized rates shown in Table

2:6 were standardized to the 1956 Census population of Canada.

[20]Standardized rates excluded Newfoundland, Quebec, Yukon, and Northwestern Territories in 1921 but include them in 1961.

[21]Based on data published by the United Nations Statistical Office and the United States National Office of Vital Statistics presented in *Population Index*, Vol. 22, No. 3, July, 1956, Table 2, pp. 247–48; and Vol. 33, No. 3, July–September, 1967, Table 2, pp. 496–498.

[22]P. E. Enterline, "Causes of Death Responsible for Recent Increases in Sex Mortality Differentials in the United States," *Milbank Memorial Fund Quarterly*, Vol. XXXIX, No. 2, April, 1961, pp. 312–328.

[23]Dominion Bureau of Statistics and Department of National Health and Welfare, *Illness and Health Care in Canada: Canadian Sickness Survey, 1950–51*, Ottawa, The Queen's Printer, July, 1960, p. 48.

[24]A measure of mortality covering both foetal deaths and deaths to infants occurring during the first week of life.

[25]Deaths to infants occurring between 7 and 28 days after birth.

[26]Deaths to infants occurring from four weeks to one year after birth.

[27]Dominion Bureau of Statistics, *Vital Statistics, 1964* and *1968*, Ottawa, The Queen's Printer, 1966, p. 31, and 1969, Table K.

[28]P. E. Enterline, *op. cit.*, pp. 312–328.

[29]Cohort life tables are the only ones which take these temporal improvements in mortality conditions into account. However, they have the disadvantage accruing from the fact that cohort tables based on actual experience can not be completed until after all members of the original cohort have died. Projections as to the future course of mortality for present cohorts must depend upon the extrapolation of changes observed for completed cohorts through time.

[30]Includes: diseases of the heart (including rheumatic fever) and arteries, intracranial lesions, chronic nephritis.

[31]Includes: Hodgkins disease, leukemia and aleukemia.

[32]Dominion Bureau of Statistics, *Vital Statistics, 1964* and *1968*, Ottawa, The Queen's Printer, 1966, and 1969, Table G and Table D8.

[33]United States Department of Health, Education, and Welfare, *Life Tables: 1959–61*, Vol. 1, No. 6, Table C, p. 8.

[34]*Population Index*, Vol. 33, No. 3, 1967, Table 1, pp. 494–496.

[35]For 1921–1925 see *Vital Statistics, 1950*, Table 6, p. 21. For 1926–1936 see *Vital Statistics, 1962*, Table B6, p. 101, and for 1936–1964 see *Vital Statistics, 1964*, Table B6, p. 72.

[36]Dominion Bureau of Statistics, *Vital Statistics, 1968*, Ottawa, The Queen's Printer, 1969, Table M3, p. 205.

[37]Dominion Bureau of Statistics, *Vital Statistics, 1964*, Ottawa, The Queen's Printer, 1966, Table B6, p. 72.

[38]U.S. Department of Health, Education, and Welfare, *Natality Statistics Analysis, United States, 1964*, Public Health Service Publication No. 1000, Series 21, No. 11, Washington, D.C., U.S. Government Printing Office, February, 1967.

[39]*Census of Canada, 1871*, Table II, pp. 166–171; P. Camu, E. P. Weeks, and Z. W. Sametz, *Economic Geography of Canada*, Toronto, Macmillan, 1964, Table 3:1.

[40]W. E. Kalbach, *The Impact of Post-war Immigration on Canadian Population*, 1961 Census Monograph, Dominion Bureau of Statistics, Ottawa, The Queen's Printer, 1970, Table 3:6.

[41]Kalbach, *op. cit.*, Table 3:8.

[42]Dominion Bureau of Statistics, *Vital Statistics, 1964*, Ottawa, The Queen's Printer, 1966, Table SI, p. 42.

The Changing Internal Distribution

The major features of Canada's population growth and distribution during the 100 years following Confederation were described in Chapter 1. The original settlement patterns had already given Quebec and Ontario an early advantage over the rest of Canada with respect to their numerical size and rate of growth. They have continued to maintain their dominant position through the years even though each constituted a smaller proportion of the total population in 1966 than they had in 1861. This general trend was previously illustrated in Figure 1:6. However, as may be seen in Table 3:1, this occurred even though their populations experienced continuous growth throughout the entire period. It is also noteworthy that both Quebec and Ontario were able to maintain their demographic dominance during a period of radical economic transformation.

The Agricultural-Industrial Transition

At the time of Confederation, more people were concerned with farming than any other occupation. Eighty per cent of the population was classified as rural in 1871 and slightly more than 36,000,000 acres were reported in farmland. Almost half, or 49 per cent, of all the gainfully employed workers in Ontario were farmers, as were 47 per cent in Quebec.[1] As the Prairies were opened for settlement and development, the acreage of farmland increased tremendously. By 1961, 136,500,000 acres had been added to the area in farms, with most of this expansion occurring between 1870 and the beginning of the depression in 1931.[2]

This agricultural development and increased activity in the Prairies was of

70

utmost importance to the development of Canada's economy. Yet, even during this period, two notable trends were occurring which were highly indicative of the basic transformation taking place. First, the average size of farms was increasing rapidly. In 1871, the average area per farm was 97.9 acres. By 1961, the average acreage had increased to 358.8, somewhat more than three and a half times larger than it had been in 1871. In terms of improved farm land, the expansion was still greater.[3] The second significant trend was to be seen in the declining proportion of the labour force in agricultural occupations. In 1901, just prior to the establishment of Alberta and Saskatchewan, 718,281 or 40.3 per cent of the labour force were in agricultural occupations. While the actual numbers continued to increase until 1931, their proportion of the labour force showed a consistent decline, reaching 28.6 per cent in 1931. After 1931, numbers as well as proportion declined, and by 1961 there were fewer persons in agricultural occupations than there had been in 1901. The 648,910 persons working in agricultural jobs constituted only 10.0 per cent of Canada's labour force in 1961. These changes are summarized in Table 3:2.

It is quite clear that other sectors of the economy were growing much more rapidly than agriculture. Centres of industrial activity were becoming more attractive to the marginal farmers as well as to the sons and daughters of the more successful agriculturalists. With so much land available, it is understandable that the government was somewhat slow in reducing its efforts to attract immigrants who were willing to farm or work as farm labourers.

However, the increasing size of farms and efficiency of agriculture simply meant that fewer workers were needed to produce more food. The newly arrived immigrant, settling on marginal types of farm land and trying to win his own homestead, must have found it increasingly difficult to be competitive. Undoubtedly, his strength to resist the allure of increasingly attractive economic opportunities so near at hand in the urban centres must have quickly weakened. The difficulties of land settlement are evident in the rather high failure rate associated with homesteading. Homestead entries up to 1927 represented 98,997,800 acres of land. Of this total, only 59,777,460 acres were actually disposed of by 1930 with the difference representing homestead failures.[4]

One other basic condition of Canadian economic life must be mentioned in order to more clearly understand its demographic history. Canadian development has always been highly dependent upon outside capital, hence its prosperity and growth have tended to reflect the health of outside economies. The early development of transportation networks in Canada, e.g., canals, roads, and railways, so necessary for its settlement and access to its resources, was financed primarily by British and United States capital. Similarly, the increased demands for resources and manufactured products stimulated by two world wars could be met rapidly only through the assistance

Table 3:1

NUMERICAL AND PERCENTAGE DISTRIBUTION, CANADA AND ALL PROVINCES, 1861-1966

Area	1861[1] Number	Per Cent	1871[4] Number	Per Cent	1881[4] Number	Per Cent	1891[4] Number	Per Cent
Canada	3,229,633	100.0	3,689,257	100.0	4,324,810	100.0	4,833,239	100.0
Newfoundland	—	—	—	—	—	—	—	—
Prince Edward Island	80,857	2.5	94,021	2.6	108,891	2.5	109,078	2.3
Nova Scotia	330,857	10.2	387,800	10.5	440,572	10.2	450,396	9.3
New Brunswick	252,047	7.8	285,594	7.7	321,233	7.4	321,263	6.7
Quebec	1,111,566	34.4	1,191,516	32.3	1,359,027	31.4	1,488,535	30.8
Ontario	1,396,091	43.2	1,620,851	43.9	1,926,922	44.6	2,114,321	43.7
Manitoba	[2]	—	25,228	0.7	62,260	1.4	152,506	3.2
Saskatchewan	[2]	—	[2]	—	[2]	—	[2]	—
Alberta	[2]	—	[2]	—	[2]	—	[2]	—
British Columbia	51,524[3]	1.6	36,247	1.0	49,459	1.1	98,173	2.0
Yukon	—	—	—	—	—	—	—	—
Northwest Territories	6,691[3]	0.2	48,000	1.3	56,446	1.3	98,967	2.1

Area	1901[4] Number	Per Cent	1911[4] Number	Per Cent	1921[4] Number	Per Cent	1931[4] Number	Per Cent
Canada	5,371,315	100.0	7,206,643	100.0	8,787,949[5]	100.0	10,376,786	100.0
Newfoundland[7]	—	—	—	—	—	—	—	—
Prince Edward Island	103,259	1.9	93,728	1.3	88,615	1.0	88,038	0.9
Nova Scotia	459,574	8.6	492,338	6.8	523,837	6.0	512,846	4.9
New Brunswick	331,120	6.2	351,889	4.9	387,876	4.4	408,219	3.9
Quebec	1,648,898	30.7	2,005,776	27.8	2,360,510[6]	26.9	2,874,662	27.7
Ontario	2,182,947	40.6	2,527,292	35.1	2,933,662	33.4	3,431,683	33.1
Manitoba	255,211	4.8	461,394	6.4	610,118	6.9	700,139	6.8
Saskatchewan	91,279	1.7	492,432	6.8	757,510	8.6	921,785	8.9
Alberta	73,022	1.4	374,295	5.2	588,454	6.7	731,605	7.1
British Columbia	178,657	3.3	392,480	5.5	524,582	6.0	694,263	6.7
Yukon	27,219	0.5	8,512	0.1	4,157	0.1	4,230	0.08
Northwest Territories	20,129	0.4	6,507	0.1	8,143	0.1	9,316	0.1

NUMERICAL AND PERCENTAGE DISTRIBUTION, CANADA AND ALL PROVINCES, 1861–1966

Area	1941[4] Number	Per Cent	1951[4] Number	Per Cent	1961 Number	Per Cent	1966 Number	Per Cent
Canada	11,506,655	100.0	14,009,429	100.0	18,238,247	100.0	20,014,880	100.0
Newfoundland[7]	—	—	361,416	2.6	457,853	2.5	493,396	2.5
Prince Edward Island	95,047	0.8	98,429	0.7	104,629	0.6	108,535	0.5
Nova Scotia	577,962	5.0	642,584	4.6	737,007	4.0	756,039	3.8
New Brunswick	457,401	4.0	515,697	3.7	597,936	3.3	616,788	3.1
Quebec	3,331,882	29.0	4,055,681	29.0	5,259,211	28.8	5,780,845	28.9
Ontario	3,787,655	32.9	4,597,542	32.8	6,236,092	34.2	6,960,870	34.8
Manitoba	729,744	6.3	776,541	5.5	921,686	5.1	963,066	4.8
Saskatchewan	895,992	7.8	831,728	5.9	925,181	5.1	955,344	4.8
Alberta	796,169	6.9	939,501	6.7	1,331,944	7.3	1,463,203	7.3
British Columbia	817,861	7.1	1,165,210	8.3	1,629,082	8.9	1,873,674	9.4
Yukon	4,914	0.0[8]	9,096	0.1	14,628	0.1	14,382	0.1
Northwest Territories	12,028	0.1	16,004	0.1	22,998	0.1	28,738	0.1

1836	75,094
1857	124,288
1869	146,536
1874	161,374
1884	197,335
1891	202,040
1901	220,984
1911	242,619
1921	263,033
1935	289,588
1945	321,819

SOURCE: *1951 Census of Canada, Volume I, Population: General Characteristics, Table 6; and 1966 Census of Canada, Bulletin 1: 1-10*, Ottawa, The Queen's Printer, 1963, Table 6; *and 1966 Census of Canada, Vol. 1 (1-2)*, Ottawa, The Queen's Printer, 1967.

1 Dominion Bureau of Statistics, *1951 Census of Canada, Vol. X*, Table 1. Also available in M. C. Urquhart and K. A. H. Buckley, *Historical Statistics of Canada*, Toronto, The Macmillan Co. of Canada, Ltd., 1965, p. 14, Table A2-14.

2 Included with Northwest Territories.

3 Ambiguities and under-enumeration.

4 *Census of Canada, 1951*, Table 1:1.

5 Included 485 members of the Royal Canadian Navy whose province of residence was not known.

6 The population of Northwest River Arm and Rigolet on Hamilton Inlet was deducted from Quebec, as these parts were awarded to Newfoundland by decision of the judicial committee of the Privy Council, March 1, 1927.

7 Newfoundland was included in the Census of Canada for the first time in 1951, following union with Canada in 1949. Earlier censuses taken by the Newfoundland government showed the following totals.

8 Less than 0.1 per cent.

SOURCE: *1951 Census of Canada*, Table 1:1. Also available in *Canada Year Book, 1950*, pp. 171-5.

Table 3:2

NUMBER AND PERCENTAGE OF THE LABOUR FORCE[a] IN AGRICULTURAL OCCUPATIONS, CANADA, 1901–1961

Year	Number	Per Cent
1901	718,281	40.3
1911	928,336	34.4
1921	1,025,358	32.6
1931	1,118,342	28.6
1941[c]	1,074,904	25.7
1951[d]	826,093	15.7
1961[d]	648,910	10.0

SOURCE: Dominion Bureau of Statistics, *Canada, One Hundred Years, 1867–1967*, Ottawa, The Queen's Printer, 1967, p. 281.
[a] In 1901, the labour force population was 10 years of age and over. All other years, it was 15 years of age and over.
[b] Not including Yukon and Northwest Territories.
[c] Not including persons on active service on June 2, 1941.
[d] Including Newfoundland.

provided by the injections of large amounts of foreign capital. The net result of this financial assistance was that industrialization and urbanization of Canada's population could and did proceed much more rapidly than would have been the case had it relied upon its own resources alone. These events, of course, had considerable significance for changes in the distribution of population in Canada during the period under consideration.[5] It is against this background of economic development that the following discussion examines variations in regional growth and assesses the relative significance of migration and natural increase for these changes.

Components of Regional Population Changes

It is obvious that if levels of mortality and fertility were uniform throughout Canada, and arriving immigrants as well as native born did not move from their original place of residence, the only cause of changes in regional distributions of the population would be shifts in the destination of immigrant streams. It is equally obvious that neither immigrants nor native born have shown any overwhelming inclination to remain permanently attached to their original community of settlement or birth. As far as immigrants were concerned, conditions at their destination were not always what they had been led to expect. On the other hand, there was equally little assurance that the native born would find the same opportunities that originally attracted their immigrant parents to a particular locality. Even when the opportunities were sufficiently strong to hold the original immigrants throughout their working years, there was no automatic process by which their natural increase could be kept in line with economic development. Quite to the contrary, rates of natural increase have shown a distressing tendency to be highest in just those areas experiencing the least economic growth. As a consequence of this tendency towards higher fertility in the lesser developed areas, demographic pressures build up which can be relieved only through a reduction in fertility, an increase in mortality, an out-migration of surplus population, or by greater economic development to provide additional jobs.

Differences in levels of mortality and fertility throughout Canada have been sufficient to produce differences in regional growth rates and changes in the regional distribution of population. These are apart from any shifts in the area of destination of arriving immigrants or a shifting of the native born through internal migration. Natural increase is the basic component of regional growth to which is added or subtracted the effects of net migration. As will be shown, high rates of natural increase in some areas often have been offset by high rates of out-migration; and, in others, relatively small excesses of births have been reinforced by high rates of in-migration. In addition to these compensating effects, migration patterns have been observed of a reinforcing nature, i.e., large net in-migrations reinforcing high rates of natural increase in some areas, while in other areas, large out-migrations have occurred with low rates of natural increase to produce significant population declines.

Natural increase for Canada as a whole during the 40-year period between 1921 and 1961 has been depicted in Figure 2:11. The primary concern of the following sections is (1) to examine the extent to which Canada's regions departed from this general pattern, and (2) to determine the degree to which regional patterns of net migration have reinforced or compensated for these regional imbalances. Attention is then directed to the relative contribution made by these two components to the rural-urban shift and increasing urbanization of Canada's population.

The Natural Increase Component of Regional Change

The quickest way to demonstrate the potential contribution of natural increase to a region's population would be to assume a condition of zero net migration and calculate future population as a consequence of the excess number of births over deaths. For purposes of illustration, this has been done for several provinces for the period 1936–64. The results are shown in Table 3:3 along with estimates of the actual population.

Note that for either Newfoundland or Saskatchewan, the population which would have resulted from natural increase alone between 1936 and 1961 exceeded the actual enumerated population in 1961. In the case of Saskatchewan, the population would have been at least 40.9 per cent greater, whereas for Newfoundland it would have been only 9.0 per cent larger. By way of contrast, Ontario's population would have been 16.4 per cent smaller and

Table 3:3

COMPARISON OF CENSUS POPULATIONS WITH ESTIMATES
OF GROWTH DUE TO NATURAL INCREASE ONLY,
SELECTED PROVINCES, CANADA, 1936–1961
(in 1,000s)

Population and Estimates	Nfld.	Ont.	Sask.	B.C.
Est. Population June 1, 1936	292	3,606	931	745
Est. Population June 1, 1961 based on natural increase alone (zero net migration)	499	5,215	1,303	1,112
Census Population June 1, 1961	458	6,236	925	1,629
Census Population, 1961, minus estimate based on natural increase alone	−41	+1,021	−378	+517

SOURCE: Dominion Bureau of Statistics, *Vital Statistics, 1964*, Ottawa, The Queen's Printer, 1966, Table S2, S5.

British Columbia's 31.7 per cent smaller had the source of growth been limited to natural increase of the original residents.[6] Thus the effect of natural increase on a province's growth can be highly significant either by retaining its own excess of births over deaths or by attracting this excess from other areas. A province's retaining power, insofar as its population is concerned, would appear to depend upon its rate of economic growth. Where the latter exceeds its rate of population growth (in the labour force ages) from the natural increase of earlier years, a province would have to rely on in-migration to supply the additional manpower it needs. Where population growth exceeds the rate of economic development, then the reverse process, out-migration, must operate if unemployment and a declining standard of living are to be avoided. Since natural increase is a composite of two other factors, each will be discussed before examining regional trends and differentials representing their combined effect.

Regional variations in mortality. The general long term decline in mortality discussed in Chapter 2 for Canada as a whole has been shared by all the regional populations, even though mortality levels have shown distinctive regional differences. Using life expectancy at birth as a summary measure of mortality conditions throughout the age range, regional comparisons, as well as analyses of trends through time, can be made for any given date for which life tables are available. Life expectancies at birth for both males and females for census years since 1931 are shown in Table 3:4.

Quebec has the somewhat dubious distinction of having the lowest life expectancies (at birth) for both males and females for each of the census years shown. By contrast, the highest life expectancies have been found most

Table 3:4

AVERAGE LIFE EXPECTANCY (YEARS) AT BIRTH BY SEX
FOR CANADA'S REGIONS, 1931-1961

Area	1931		1941		1951		1961	
	Male	Female	Male	Female	Male	Female	Male	Female
Canada	60.0	62.1	63.0	66.3	66.3	70.8	68.4	74.2
Atlantic Provinces	60.2	61.9	61.7	64.6	66.6	70.5	68.6	73.9
Quebec	56.2	57.8	60.2	63.1	64.4	68.6	67.3	72.8
Ontario	61.3	63.9	64.6	68.4	66.9	71.9	68.3	74.4
Prairie Provinces	63.5	65.5	65.4	68.2	68.4	72.3	69.8	75.7
British Columbia	62.2	65.3	63.7	69.0	66.7	72.4	68.9	75.4

SOURCE: Dominion Bureau of Statistics, *Vital Statistics, 1964*, Ottawa, The Queen's Printer, 1966, Table L2, p. 212.

consistently in the Prairie Provinces. Over the entire 30-year period, there is evidence of some convergence between regions. This, no doubt, reflects the fact that Quebec, with the lowest life expectancy at birth, has shown the most rapid improvement during these years. The increase for males and females in Quebec was 19.8 and 26.0 per cent respectively. By way of contrast, the increase for the Prairie Provinces was 9.9 per cent for males and 15.6 per cent for females.

Crude death rates exhibited the same general decline during the 1931–61 period. However, there are more irregularities in crude death rates than in life expectancy data (at birth) since the former are affected by changes in the age composition of the population, in addition to changes in actual mortality conditions. For this reason, Quebec did not have the highest mortality rates as might be expected on the basis of life expectancy data. The Atlantic Provinces tended to have higher crude death rates during the earlier years, followed by British Columbia. Ontario and Quebec had similar crude rates up to 1942, but Quebec's rate subsequently declined more rapidly. Death rates for the Prairie Provinces were consistently lowest prior to 1946, but since that time Quebec's rate has tended to be lower than that of Manitoba's and lower than Saskatchewan's since 1955. Again, as was the case for life expectancy data, there is evidence of a decrease in regional differentials during this period.[7]

Regional variations in fertility. Regional variations in fertility, as measured by the crude fertility rate, were partially illustrated in Figure 2:9. Like crude mortality rates, the crude birth rate is similarly affected by variations in the age-sex structure and may not reflect true differences in actual reproductive behaviour. For this reason, when the requisite data are available, it is more useful to use other measures such as total fertility rates, gross reproduction rates, or cumulative fertility rates to provide a measure of fertility behaviour free of the obtrusive effect of the age-sex structure.

The gross reproduction rates presented in Table 3:5 indicate the number of female births each woman would have during her reproductive years if she experienced the age-specific fertility rates existing at a particular point in time. For example, if the women of Prince Edward Island experienced the age-specific fertility rates for that province in 1961 throughout their child-bearing years, each woman could expect to bear on the average 2.4 female children (or a total of 4.9 children as indicated by the total fertility rate).[8]

As one might expect, the gross reproduction rates for the provinces reflect the same general trend characteristic of the crude rates in Figure 2:9. There are rapid decreases during the pre-depression period, reaching minimum levels during 1936–41 before the post-war resurgence and the attainment of new peaks in fertility, circa 1956–61, followed again by sharp declines. Convergence is still evident for this period, but perhaps not as apparent as in the case of the crude birth rates.

Three provinces, British Columbia, Ontario, and Manitoba, have experienced consistently low fertility as measured by gross reproduction rates. Saskatchewan, Alberta, and New Brunswick, on the other hand, have had consistently high gross reproduction rates. Quebec's fertility experience has been somewhat unique in that it has dropped from the highest level in 1926 (GRR = 2.08) to the lowest in 1966 (GRR = 1.28). Prince Edward Island's experience was just the reverse. In 1926, its GRR of 1.90 was just slightly higher than that for Canada as a whole, while in 1961 it had increased to 2.36, the highest for any of the provinces. Even after the general decline between 1961 and 1966, Prince Edward Island still maintained its position relative to the other provinces.[9]

Regional variations in natural increase. It is clear from the preceding sections that there have been and continue to be significant differences in the mortality and fertility levels experienced by the regional populations of Canada. Measures of life expectancy and reproductive replacement have provided the data to substantiate these differences. However, the relative differences between these levels of vital events are not the only factors affecting the actual excess of births over deaths, i.e., natural increase. The age-sex distributions of these populations are of utmost importance. For example, two regions might have equivalent mortality conditions for each age and sex group; but, if one region has a disproportionate number of its population in the age group with minimal mortality risk, it will not contribute as many deaths as another region. The implications of this are quite clear. When considering natural increase in relation to the regional distribution of population, the

Table 3:5

TOTAL FERTILITY AND GROSS REPRODUCTION RATES FOR CANADA AND PROVINCES, 1931–1966

Area	Total Fertility Rates					Gross Reproduction Rates				
	1931	1941	1951	1961	1966	1931	1941	1951	1961	1966
Canada	2,937a	2,832	3,503	3,840	2,812	1,432a	1,377	1,701	1,868	1,369
Prince Edward Island	3,521	3,228	4,189	4,881	3,578	1,652	1,530	2,020	2,355	1,724
Nova Scotia	3,397	3,097	3,682	4,159	3,150	1,663	1,521	1,781	2,021	1,523
New Brunswick	3,990	3,688	4,378	4,543	3,312	1,941	1,825	2,147	2,210	1,606
Quebec	4,001	3,389	3,775	3,700	2,646	1,940	1,645	1,834	1,787	1,284
Ontario	2,648	2,403	3,222	3,742	2,790	1,285	1,164	1,560	1,824	1,361
Manitoba	2,815	2,506	3,302	3,936	2,944	1,394	1,218	1,584	1,922	1,438
Saskatchewan	3,478	2,809	3,590	4,221	3,284	1,694	1,368	1,756	2,055	1,588
Alberta	3,377	2,833	3,721	4,267	3,066	1,627	1,379	1,825	2,087	1,506
British Columbia	2,171	2,305	3,201	3,785	2,659	1,054	1,125	1,557	1,852	1,299
Yukon	—	—	5,019	5,376	3,626	—	—	2,480	2,640	1,808
Northwest Territories	—	—	6,159	7,189	6,154	—	—	3,150	3,521	2,987

SOURCE: Dominion Bureau of Statistics, *Vital Statistics, 1964*, Ottawa, The Queen's Printer, 1966, Table B6; and *Vital Statistics, 1966*, Ottawa, The Queen's Printer, 1968, Table B6.
a Average of 1931–1935.

Table 3:6

RATES OF NATURAL INCREASE, CANADA AND PROVINCES, 1936–1968 (Rates per 1,000 population)

Year	Canada	Nfld.	P.E.I.	N.S.	N.B.	Quebec	Ontario	Manitoba	Sask.	Alberta	B.C.	Yukon	N.W.T.
1936	10.4	12.2	10.3	10.8	13.2	14.0	6.9	9.4	13.7	12.4	4.5	-8.8	4.7
1937	9.7	11.5	10.2	10.0	11.8	12.8	6.3	9.5	12.7	12.4	4.4	0.4	5.8
1938	11.0	12.7	10.0	11.1	14.8	14.4	7.9	10.5	13.2	12.8	6.5	2.6	4.0
1939	10.9	15.8	10.5	9.8	13.8	14.4	7.2	10.2	13.2	13.6	6.1	-3.8	3.3
1940	11.8	14.5	10.9	11.6	14.9	15.6	8.0	11.6	14.3	14.1	6.9	5.6	4.4
1941	12.3	14.8	9.7	12.1	15.5	16.5	8.7	11.4	13.4	13.7	8.0	1.0	0.7
1942	13.7	16.3	13.0	15.1	16.2	18.0	10.0	12.7	14.1	15.8	9.1	-2.4	12.3
1943	14.1	16.9	13.9	14.7	17.7	18.5	10.2	13.0	14.2	16.3	9.8	-4.2	8.3
1944	14.2	17.1	14.9	15.3	18.1	19.3	9.7	12.8	14.0	16.2	10.0	7.2	-2.8
1945	14.8	24.5	14.8	16.0	18.9	19.9	9.8	13.4	15.0	16.7	9.6	7.2	2.8
1946	17.8	26.1	20.4	19.6	23.8	21.4	14.1	16.9	18.0	19.4	12.4	8.3	15.4
1947	19.5	27.6	20.9	21.5	26.5	22.0	16.1	18.4	20.0	22.0	15.0	18.4	15.6
1948	18.0	24.8	21.1	18.7	24.7	21.4	14.5	16.4	17.9	20.0	13.5	20.3	17.2
1949	18.0	27.3	20.3	18.7	23.2	21.3	14.4	16.4	18.1	20.2	14.3	27.8	13.2
1950	18.0	28.5	20.7	17.6	22.4	21.6	14.5	16.5	18.4	20.6	13.6	27.1	18.1
1951	18.2	24.2	17.9	17.6	21.8	21.2	15.4	17.0	18.4	21.2	14.1	28.6	22.8
1952	19.2	26.2	17.8	18.7	22.9	21.9	16.6	17.8	18.9	22.4	14.8	32.9	18.8
1953	19.5	26.3	17.9	18.8	22.2	22.1	17.1	17.6	19.7	23.4	15.6	29.7	23.9
1954	20.3	27.2	17.4	19.6	22.9	22.8	17.9	18.8	21.4	24.7	15.8	34.0	22.4
1955	20.0	28.4	18.8	19.1	22.3	22.0	17.9	18.5	20.6	24.2	15.9	41.1	26.8
1956	19.8	27.6	17.4	19.2	21.5	21.8	17.9	17.5	19.7	24.2	16.3	33.0	26.0
1957	20.0	28.6	17.7	19.1	22.1	22.1	18.1	17.4	19.5	23.6	16.8	33.4	30.3
1958	19.6	27.1	16.3	18.1	20.8	21.5	17.8	16.6	19.5	23.7	16.8	29.3	30.6
1959	19.4	26.4	16.9	17.6	20.1	21.1	17.8	17.3	19.1	23.7	16.4	34.5	33.3
1960	19.0	27.2	17.2	17.9	19.8	20.0	17.7	17.4	18.8	23.3	15.8	31.5	35.5

Table 3:6—concluded

RATES OF NATURAL INCREASE, CANADA AND PROVINCES, 1936–1968 (Rates per 1,000 population)

Year	Canada	Nfld.	P.E.I.	N.S.	N.B.	Quebec	Ontario	Manitoba	Sask.	Alberta	B.C.	Yukon	N.W.T.
1961	18.4	27.5	17.8	18.0	19.8	19.1	17.1	17.3	18.2	22.5	14.9	31.7	37.2
1962	17.6	25.4	16.3	17.5	19.3	18.2	16.4	16.5	17.6	21.5	14.0	31.5	33.0
1963	16.8	25.7	18.2	16.8	18.0	17.4	15.6	15.6	17.2	20.7	13.3	27.9	34.5
1964	15.9	24.1	16.0	15.8	17.3	16.7	15.1	14.6	16.3	18.7	11.4	28.5	38.9
1965	13.7	23.6	13.6	13.5	15.3	14.4	12.9	12.7	13.8	15.9	9.9	23.5	36.8
1966	11.9	22.3	10.6	11.5	12.9	12.3	11.2	10.5	12.1	14.3	8.6	20.0	32.3
1967	10.8	19.5	9.3	10.1	12.0	10.7	10.1	9.9	11.0	14.2	8.6	20.8	34.2
1968	10.2	19.1	10.1	9.4	10.7	9.6	9.7	9.8	11.2	13.3	8.4	19.1	34.5

SOURCE: Dominion Bureau of Statistics, Vital Statistics, 1964, and 1968, Ottawa, The Queen's Printer, 1966 and 1970, Table S5.

focus is on the actual number of deaths and births generated by regional levels of mortality and fertility acting upon existing age-sex structures. The rate at which the excess of births over deaths is added to the base population is a crucial factor, and the difference between the crude birth and death rates is the crude rate of natural increase.

Since the birth rate is both the larger and more variable of the two vital components comprising the rate of natural increase, its influence is more readily detectable. The rate of natural increase for Canada reached its lowest point of 9.7 per 1,000 in 1937 before beginning its World War II recovery. Reflecting the post World War II baby boom, the rate of natural increase reached a peak of 19.5 per 1,000 in 1947; but by 1954, even this was exceeded as Canada experienced even higher levels of fertility. However, not all regions experienced their peak rates at the same time. For example, the 1947 peak was most pronounced in the Atlantic Provinces, while for the remaining provinces, the peak rates occurred between 1954 and 1957. During the 1960s, the trend everywhere in Canada has been downward.

The five provinces with the highest rates of natural increase throughout most of the period following the mid-depression years were Newfoundland, New Brunswick, Quebec, Saskatchewan, and Alberta. Ontario, Manitoba, and British Columbia, on the other hand, tended to have the lowest rates throughout this same period, with the remaining provinces, Nova Scotia and Prince Edward Island, holding intermediate positions to these extremes, as may be seen in Table 3:6. Three eastern provinces and two western provinces tended to generate the greatest excesses of births over deaths in relation to their population size. The extent to which their own economic and cultural development was sufficient to retain this potential growth or to attract the surplus population from other areas can only be determined by examining the estimates of net migration for these areas during this particular period.

Migration

One of the most direct means available to an individual for coping with inequities between the size of the labour force population in any area and the number of opportunities for earning a livelihood is migration. In any new and developing country such as Canada, physical mobility of the population is anything but unusual. In reality, not everyone can move; but many have and will continue to do so in their search for better jobs, better education, or better climate. Canada is a product of immigration; but even as late as the twentieth century, it had one of the highest rates of net immigration of any country in the world. Yet this is only part of the picture. According to estimates made by Isabel Anderson for the period 1921 to 1960, Canada's internal net movement was more than twice as large as the net movement into Canada during the same period.[10]

Information on migration during the 1956–61 period indicated that 45.4 per cent of the population had been living in a different residence in 1961 than they had been in 1956. In this connection, it should be noted that most recent analyses of migration data have indicated that the preponderance of moves tends to be over relatively short distances, and the experience of Canada has been no exception. The 1961 Census revealed that only 3.1 per cent had been living abroad while the remaining 42.3 per cent changed residences within Canada. Not all of this movement was equally significant for changes in the regional distribution of the population. Of those who had been living elsewhere in Canada, 91.8 per cent did not cross provincial boundaries and would not have contributed to changes in the provincial populations. However, 40.4 per cent of these intra-provincial movers did move from one municipality to another, and a good share of these movers contributed to the rural-urban shift during this period.[11] It is well to keep in mind that the significance of any population movement for population re-distribution is totally dependent upon both the definition of areas and the specific boundaries being utilized in a given analysis. Since the immediate concern here is with changes in distribution by provinces, the 469,915 resident immigrants who had been living abroad in 1956 had roughly the same potential for effecting the provincial redistribution of populations as did the 532,674 internal migrants who crossed provincial boundaries during the same period.

Figure 3:1 shows the proportion of the total population five years of age and over for each province who were movers within Canada, as well as the proportion of movers for each mobility type during the five-year period, 1956–61. Somewhat more than half or 59.9 per cent of all movers within Canada were local movers (i.e., within the same municipality), while slightly less than one-third (32.0 per cent) moved only within provinces and 8.1 per cent moved between provinces. Provincial deviations from these norms for Canada are clearly evident in Figure 3:1. Not shown are the 470,000 who moved from abroad, but 91 per cent of these settled in the four provinces, Ontario (253,000), Quebec (83,000), British Columbia (54,000), and Alberta (38,000).[12]

Estimates of net migration. In most analyses of net migration, no distinction is made between the native born moving within Canada and the foreign born arriving as an immigrant. The natural increase of the province or region during a specified time period is added to the population existing at the beginning of the period, and the total is compared with the count or estimate of population at the end of the period. The difference provides an estimate of the net migration and the sign indicates whether it is a net gain or loss. Because it is generally not possible to separate out births and deaths to migrants from the natural increase, it is not a precise method of estimation. In addition, it is worth remembering that the estimated net migration cannot

Fig. 3:1

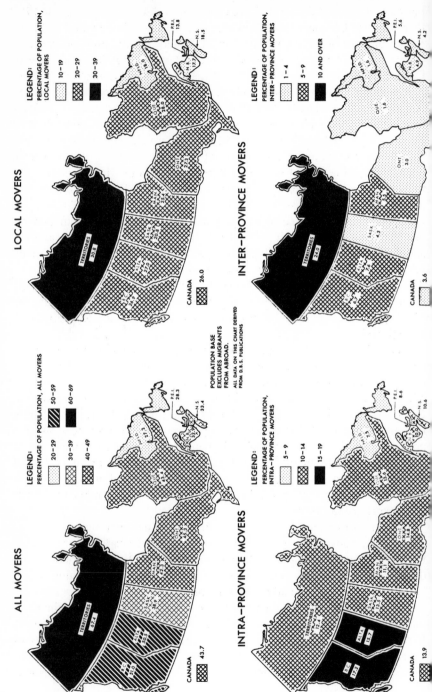

POPULATION MOBILITY BY TYPE
CANADA: 1956–1961

be relied upon to provide any accurate measure of the *gross* movement of population. This is very clearly illustrated in Table 3:7. Note the contrast between Quebec and British Columbia. In the former, a gross movement of 178,322 was required to produce a net out-immigration of 1,584, while in British Columbia a somewhat larger gross movement of 193,518 produced a net in-migration of 82,498. Ontario's gross movement of 324,502 was considerably larger than that experienced by British Columbia, yet its net in-migration of 77,484 was slightly smaller.

Estimates of net migration for the population ten years of age and over by decades from 1881 to 1921 by Keyfitz and from 1921 to 1961 by Anderson are quite revealing as to the nature and direction of population movement.[13] For every decade, the Maritime Provinces as well as Quebec showed net losses due to an excess of out-migration over in-migration with Quebec contributing the most out-migrants by far of any province during this period.[14] This pattern continued in the Maritimes during the entire post-World War II period as well. Data for Newfoundland for the 1951–61 decade show a net loss due to migration consistent with the pattern for the region as a whole.

Between 1881 and 1901, Ontario showed sizeable net out-migrations; but, since 1901, there have been consistent net in-migrations for each decade. British Columbia has been the only province to experience net in-migration during each of the decades since 1881. Since 1931, the Yukon and Northwest

Table 3:7

NET CHANGE THROUGH MIGRATION FOR PROVINCES SHOWING GROSS MOVEMENT, TOTAL IN-MIGRANTS AND OUT-MIGRANTS, CANADA, 1931–1941

Province	Net Change through Migration	Gross Movement	Total In-Migration	Total Out-Migration
Prince Edward Island	−2,672	8,820	3,074	5,746
Nova Scotia	+7,848	47,444	27,646	19,798
New Brunswick	−10,177	43,279	16,551	26,280
Quebec	−1,584	178,322	88,369	89,953
Ontario	+77,484	324,502	200,993	123,509
Manitoba	−48,478	143,620	47,571	96,049
Saskatchewan	−157,545	218,863	30,659	188,204
Alberta	−41,841	149,709	53,934	95,775
British Columbia	+82,498	193,518	138,008	55,510

SOURCE: Dominion Bureau of Statistics, *Eighth Census of Canada, 1941*, "Interprovincial Migration in Canada 1931–1941." Population: No. M-1, p. 4.

Territories have also showed small but consistent numbers of net in-migration.

The Prairies experienced their largest net influx of migrants during the 1901–11 decade. However, by the 1921–31 decade, Manitoba showed a net out-migration, and during the depression decade, all the Prairie Provinces were showing net losses. Not until 1951–61 did the Prairies again show a net in-migration, but this was due solely to the experience of Alberta. Net migration for each of the provinces by decades between 1921 and 1961 is shown in Figure 3:2.

Table 3:8

NATURAL INCREASE AND ESTIMATED NET MIGRATION BY DECADES FOR CANADA'S PROVINCES, 1921–1931, 1931–1941, 1941–1951, AND 1951–1961

(in 1,000s)

Province	1921–1931[a]		1931–1941[a]		1941–1951[a]		1951–1961[a]	
	Nat. Inc.	Net Mig.	Nat. Inc.	Net Mig.	Nat. Inc.	Net Mig.	Nat. Inc.	Net Mig.
Newfoundland	—	—	—	—	—	—	111	−14
Prince Edward Island	8	−9	10	−2	16	−13	18	−11
Nova Scotia	51	−62	57	+8	104	−39	128	−35
New Brunswick	57	−37	59	−10	100	−41	119	−37
Quebec	496	+17	459	−1	736	−12	998	+205
Ontario	343	+154	278	+78	505	+305	953	+685
Manitoba	99	−9	78	−48	108	−62	150	−4
Saskatchewan	153	+11	132	−158	135	−199	172	−79
Alberta	105	+40	106	−42	150	−7	265	+128
British Columbia	48	+121	41	+83	116	+231	224	+240
Yukon and Northwest Territories	—	—	1	+3	3	+4	9	+3

SOURCE: Based on births and deaths by Province on a census-year basis. See Dominion Bureau of Statistics, Census Division, Technical Memorandum (General Series No. 14), Ottawa, January 20, 1967; Tables I and IV; and, annual estimates of population in Dominion Bureau of Statistics, *Estimated Population of Canada by Province at June 1, 1962*, Catalogue No. 91-201 (annual), Ottawa, Queen's Printer, 1962, Table 1.
[a] June 1 to May 31.

Data in Table 3:8 present natural increase and estimates of net migration for the decades since June 1, 1921, while Table 3:9 presents rates.

The most apparent aspect of these data is that the relationship between natural increase and net migration varies considerably from one province to

Fig. 3:2

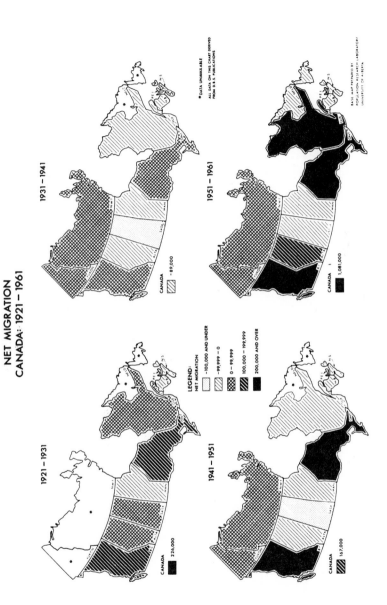

NET MIGRATION
CANADA: 1921 – 1961

Table 3:9

AVERAGE ANNUAL RATES OF NATURAL INCREASE AND NET MIGRATION BY DECADES FOR PROVINCES, CANADA, 1921–1931, 1931–1941, 1941–1951, 1951–1961

Province	1921–1931		1931–1941		1941–1951		1951–1961	
	Nat. Inc.	Net Mig.	Nat. Inc.	Net Mig.	Nat. Inc.	Net Mig.	Nat. Inc.	Net Mig.
Newfoundland	—	—	—	—	—	—	26.7	−3.4
Prince Edward Island	9.2	−10.3	9.7	−2.2	17.0	−13.8	18.1	−11.1
Nova Scotia	9.9	−12.0	10.5	+1.5	17.1	−6.4	18.6	−5.0
New Brunswick	14.4	−9.3	13.6	−2.3	20.9	−8.6	21.4	−6.7
Quebec	19.1	+0.6	14.8	−0.0[a]	20.3	−0.3	21.6	+4.4
Ontario	10.9	+4.9	7.7	+2.2	12.3	+7.4	17.6	+12.7
Manitoba	15.5	−1.4	11.0	−6.8	14.8	−8.5	17.6	−0.5
Saskatchewan	18.6	+1.3	14.2	−17.0	16.2	−23.9	19.5	−9.0
Alberta	17.1	+6.6	13.7	−5.4	18.7	−0.9	23.6	+11.4
British Columbia	7.9	+20.0	5.5	+11.1	11.6	+23.0	16.0	+17.2
Yukon and Northwest Territories	—	—	6.2	+18.8	12.5	+16.7	29.0	+9.7

SOURCE: Same as Table 3:8.   [a]Less than 0.05 per cent.

another, and there is no consistent tendency for provinces with high natural increase rates to experience net out-migration, or vice versa. Rates of natural increase for the Atlantic Provinces increased over the 40-year period while migration operated to siphon off the surplus. Quebec produced the largest excess of births over deaths, both in absolute as well as relative terms; yet, average rates of net migration by decades (either positive or negative) were relatively insignificant. Its net in-migration of 205,000 during the 1951–61 decade, representing a rate of 4.4 per 1,000 population, was the most substantial during the entire 40-year period.

The combined Prairie Provinces had rates of natural increase fairly comparable on the average to the Maritime Provinces over the same period, yet their net migration varied considerably from one to another. Of the three, Manitoba and Saskatchewan were most similar in that both experienced losses through migration during every decade except 1921–31 when Saskatchewan last showed a net gain of 11,000 through migration. Subsequently, it has experienced the largest absolute net losses of any province. Alberta's experience has been more mixed, and its experience during the 1951–61 decade is perhaps unique among the provinces in having combined a relatively high average annual rate of net in-migration of 41.4 per 1,000 with an extremely high rate of natural increase of 23.6 per 1,000 population.

Ontario and British Columbia are perhaps the best examples of rapidly growing industrialized urban populations. Their rates of natural increase have been consistently low while simultaneously experiencing net in-migrations every decade. In fact, British Columbia had the highest average net in-migration rates of any province for each of the four decades between 1921 and 1961.

In terms of absolute numbers of both natural increase and net migration, the Territories were relatively unimportant. However, in relative terms, their average rate of natural increase rose steadily from the depression decade to reach a level higher than that of any province during 1951–61. On the other hand, while its average rate of net in-migration of 18.8 was the highest anywhere in Canada during the depression decade, it declined until it reached a level of 9.7 per 1,000 during the 1951–61 decade, and was exceeded only by British Columbia, Alberta, and Ontario.

Migration of the native-born and foreign-born populations. The following estimates of provincial net migration make no distinction between those net migrants who were native born and those who were foreign born, or whether they came from other provinces or abroad. Some idea of the relative contributions made by these two components and the differences, if any, in their net patterns of movement can be obtained from census data. For example, on June 1, 1961, 1,892,052 or 12.3 per cent of all native born were enumerated in provinces other than their province of birth. Of course, these data do not reveal the extent of movement between birth and the time of the 1961 Census. However, they do show the net effect of all native-born movers who crossed provincial boundaries. The same is true for the foreign born enumerated in Canada on June 1, 1961. Whether they moved (and crossed a provincial boundary) subsequent to their arrival or not, they are all originally migrants from abroad and their distribution as of the census date shows the net effect of their total movement since their date of entry. Like the native born living in a province other than province of birth, they would appear in estimates of net migration whenever their place of residence at one census was in a different province than that reported in the preceding census.

On June 1, 1961, there were 2,844,263 foreign born in Canada or 50.3 per cent more than the number of native-born migrants. Distributions by province of residence are given in Table 3:10. If all areas were equally attractive to the migrant, each would attract one-eleventh or 9.1 per cent of the total. Clearly, this is not the case, nor are they distributed in relation to the relative sizes of the respective provinces. As of 1961, Ontario was by far the

Table 3:10

NUMBER OF NATIVE-BORN[a] AND FOREIGN-BORN MIGRANTS
BY PROVINCE OF RESIDENCE, CANADA, 1961

Province	Native Born, Born Elsewhere in Canada	Foreign Born	Per Cent Native Born, Born Elsewhere	Per Cent Foreign Born
Newfoundland	9,783	6,269	0.5	0.2
Prince Edward Island	8,017	2,992	0.4	0.1
Nova Scotia	74,108	34,168	3.9	1.2
New Brunswick	56,284	23,283	3.0	0.8
Quebec	223,183	388,449	11.8	13.7
Ontario	577,647	1,353,157	30.5	47.6
Manitoba	118,830	169,998	6.3	6.0
Saskatchewan	110,972	149,389	5.9	5.2
Alberta	255,161	288,749	13.5	10.1
British Columbia	445,111	423,132	23.5	14.9
Yukon and Northwest Territories	12,956	4,677	0.7	0.2
Total	1,892,052	2,844,263	100.0	100.0

SOURCE: Dominion Bureau of Statistics, *1961 Census of Canada*, Bulletin 7: 1-7, Ottawa, The Queen's Printer, 1965, Table 4.
[a] Native-born migrants are defined here as resident native-born population born elsewhere in Canada.

most attractive to native and foreign born alike. While the rank order of preference, based on the proportions in each area is very close to being the same for each group, there are significant differences in the relative drawing power of the different areas. For example, 47.6 per cent of all foreign born were residing in Ontario compared to only 30.5 per cent of the native-born migrants. While British Columbia ranked second for each group, a much larger proportion of the native-born migrants located in this province, 23.5 per cent, compared to 14.9 per cent for the foreign born. Quebec ranked third for the foreign born but only fourth for native born, being edged out in this instance by Alberta. For the foreign born, both Ontario and Quebec together accounted for almost two-thirds, or 61.3 per cent, compared to just 42.3 per cent of the native-born migrants.

For the native born, this pattern of relative attractiveness has appeared only recently, i.e., since World War II. Earlier, each of the Prairie Provinces drew more of the native-born migrants, while Quebec drew considerably less. This is clearly illustrated in Figure 3:3. Again, the pattern over time has been

Fig. 3:3

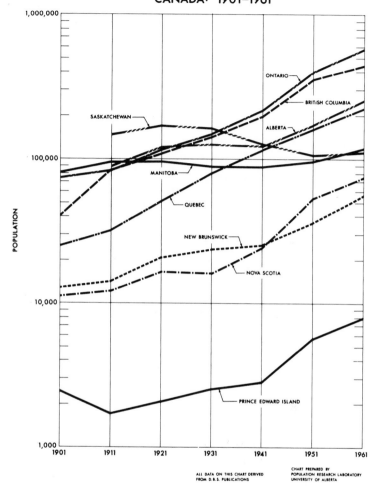

RESIDENT NATIVE–BORN POPULATION
BORN ELSEWHERE
CANADA: 1901–1961

quite similar for the foreign born; however, Ontario and British Columbia's relatively greater attractiveness extended over a much longer period, 1911 to 1961. In 1911 and 1921, each of the Prairie Provinces had attracted and held more than Quebec. Between 1931 and 1941, only Saskatchewan and Alberta had larger numbers of foreign born and by 1951, only Alberta. During the 1951–61 decade, Quebec's foreign born increased much more rapidly than did Alberta's to place it in third position behind Ontario and British Columbia, as may be seen in Figure 3:4. Of course, on a regional basis, the combined Prairie Provinces declined from a position of dominance during the 1911–31 period, but maintained their position second to Ontario during the 1941–61 period.

Fig. 3:4

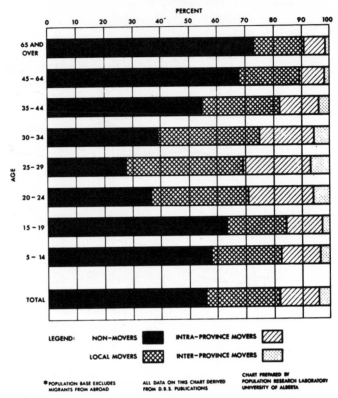

MOBILITY STATUS BY AGE
POPULATION FIVE YEARS OF AGE AND OVER*
CANADA: 1961

Destination of arriving immigrants and residence of the foreign-born population. There may be some doubts as to the accuracy or usefulness of data relating to the "intended" destination of immigrants arriving in Canada. However, the veracity of the immigrant's statement has not been questioned so much as the effects of subsequent changes in plans once the immigrant has arrived at his intended destination. Interestingly, there is a considerable degree of similarity between the distribution of the foreign-born population by residence and by intended destination. Quebec, in 1961, ranked second to Ontario as the most important destination, as it has in every period since 1931, and British Columbia ranked third. The most amazing aspect of the distribution of intended destinations shown in Table 3:11 is the consistency of the rank orders for the 35 years for which data are available. In addition, the increases in the proportion intending to settle in Ontario and Quebec have reflected the shift in the economic base of Canada and have paralleled declines in the proportions intending to settle in the Prairie and Atlantic

Table 3:11

INTENDED DESTINATION OF ARRIVING IMMIGRANTS FOR SELECTED PERIODS, 1931–1941 TO 1961–1966

Province	Period				
	1931–1941	1941–1951	1951–1956	1956–1961	1961–1966
Newfoundland	—	—	0.3	0.2	0.4
Prince Edward Island	0.5	0.4	0.1	0.1	0.1
Nova Scotia	5.6	3.9	1.4	1.1	1.2
New Brunswick	2.8	2.0	0.6	0.6	0.8
Quebec	19.7	17.3	21.0	21.1	22.8
Ontario	41.8	49.7	53.2	52.8	53.3
Manitoba	5.9	5.4	4.7	3.9	2.9
Saskatchewan	4.5	4.0	2.3	1.7	1.7
Alberta	8.1	7.6	7.7	6.9	5.5
British Columbia	11.1	9.8	8.6	11.5	11.3
Yukon and Northwest Territories	0.1	0.0	0.1	0.1	0.1
Total: Per Cent	100.1	100.1	100.0	100.0	100.1
Number	149,479	547,838	783,161	759,692	538,554

SOURCE: Department of Manpower and Immigration, *Immigration Statistics* (Annual Reports), Ottawa. Prior to 1966, annual immigration statistics were published by the Department of Citizenship and Immigration.

Provinces. British Columbia has maintained a relatively stable position, reflecting perhaps its consistent attraction for migrants over the years.

Direct comparisons between intended destination of arriving immigrants and the residential pattern of all foreign born are meaningful only in the grossest sense, since the former reflects the attractiveness as perceived by new arrivals unaffected by subsequent experiences with reality and additional moves which are reflected in the data for resident foreign born. Data on province of residence in 1961 for immigrants who arrived during the 1956–61 period are available and are directly comparable with destination data for those arriving during the same period of years as shown in Table 3:12. Note first that not all who arrived during this period remained at the time of the census. Of the original 759,942 some 123,750 left Canada or died, leaving 635,942 to be counted as residents in 1961. The distribution represents the net surviving immigrants, and their distribution pattern is very similar to the distribution of intended destinations. Also note that for every province and territory shown, the difference is insignificant except for Quebec, Ontario,

Table 3:12

PERCENTAGE DISTRIBUTION BY PROVINCE OF INTENDED DESTINATION
OF IMMIGRANTS ARRIVING IN CANADA 1956–1961, AND RESIDENCE
IN 1961 OF THOSE ARRIVING IN 1956–1961

Province	Intended Destination of Immigrants arriving 1956–1961	Residence in 1961 of those arriving during 1956–1961
Newfoundland	0.2	0.3
Prince Edward Island	0.1	0.1
Nova Scotia	1.1	1.0
New Brunswick	0.6	0.7
Quebec	21.1	19.1
Ontario	52.8	53.6
Manitoba	3.9	4.0
Saskatchewan	1.7	1.8
Alberta	6.9	7.5
British Columbia	11.5	11.7
Yukon and Northwest Territories	0.1	0.2
Total: Per Cent	100.0	100.0
Number	759,692	635,942

SOURCE: Table 3:11, and Dominion Bureau of Statistics, *1961 Census of Canada*, Bulletin
1: 3-11, Ottawa, The Queen's Printer, 1964, Tables 125, 126.

and Alberta. While 21.1 per 100 immigrants arriving during the 1956–61
period originally intended to settle in Quebec, only 19.1 were found to be
residents in 1961. Most of this difference is accounted for by the net gains
exhibited by Ontario and Alberta. For the remaining areas, with the exception of British Columbia, the change in percentage points was 0.1 or less.
Quebec's cultural character may provide some unexpected difficulties for
non-French-speaking immigrants and a plausible explanation for the observed shift. Evidence on this, however, is scarce and inconclusive.

Urbanization of the Population

Up to this point, the emphasis has been on regional or provincial patterns of
population distribution and change without comment as to the actual character of the area of origin or settlement within the provinces. However,
implicit in the data showing the declining attraction of the Prairie and Atlantic

Provinces, and the increasing drawing power of Ontario, Quebec, and British Columbia, is the fact of industrialization and urbanization. In addition, Figure 3:1 has shown that the greatest volume of movement tends to be either local or intra-provincial in nature, with inter-provincial migrants accounting for only 3.6 per cent of the total resident population. While either of the latter types of mobility can involve rural-to-urban as well as urban-to-urban movement, the following section deals predominantly with the rural-urban movement.[15]

Rural-Urban Migration

Even before Confederation, the population of British North America had achieved a level of urbanization higher than the world average with an estimated seven per cent residing in cities of 20,000 population and over.[16] In terms of the broader definition of "urban" population, urbanization in Canada, subsequent to 1851, has continued at an average decennial rate of increase of 34 per cent, but with considerable fluctuation from one decade to the next.[17] Regardless of the particular index of urbanization used, the overall urban growth pattern remains. Between 1871 and 1901, the proportion of population residing in incorporated cities, towns, and villages increased from 18.3 to 34.9 per cent during a period which witnessed a decline in the average decade rate of urban growth.[18] However, with the large influx of immigrants during the 1901–11 decade, the urban proportion jumped from 34.9 to 41.8 per cent, the highest rate of increase for any decade between Confederation and 1961. Paradoxically, the rapid settlement of the Prairies during this decade also produced the largest increase in rural population since Confederation, although its proportion of the total declined from 65.1 to 58.2 per cent. While the urban population increased from 1.9 to 3.0 million under the stimulus provided by the development of Canada's wheat economy, the rural population also increased rapidly as it grew from 3.5 to 4.2 million. Even so, its rate of growth was only about one-third the rate experienced by the urban population.

Using incorporated places to delineate the population, Canada reached an even balance between rural and urban during the depression decade. On the other hand, if the 1961 definition of urban population is used, the balance between rural and urban was reached during the preceding decade.[19] Additional impetus was given to the industrialization of Canada by World War II, and the post-war economic boom boosted the urban population to 69.6 per cent of the total in 1961, and 73.6 per cent in 1966.[20]

Data for 1966, in Table 3:13, illustrate how unevenly urbanization has proceeded throughout Canada. Ontario's population was the most urbanized with 80.4 per cent, followed by Quebec and British Columbia with 78.3 and 75.3 per cent respectively. Manitoba, Alberta, Nova Scotia, Newfoundland,

Table 3:13

NUMBER AND PER CENT OF THE POPULATION, RURAL AND URBAN
FOR CANADA AND PROVINCES, 1966

Province	Total Population	Rural		Urban	
		Number	Per Cent	Number	Per Cent
Canada	20,014,880	5,288,121	26.4	14,726,759	73.6
Newfoundland	493,396	226,707	45.9	266,689	54.1
Prince Edward Island	108,535	68,788	63.4	39,747	36.6
Nova Scotia	756,039	317,132	41.9	438,907	58.1
New Brunswick	616,788	304,563	49.4	312,225	50.6
Quebec	5,780,845	1,255,731	21.7	4,525,114	78.3
Ontario	6,960,870	1,367,430	19.6	5,593,440	80.4
Manitoba	963,066	317,018	32.9	646,048	67.1
Saskatchewan	955,344	487,017	51.0	468,327	49.0
Alberta	1,463,203	455,796	31.2	1,007,407	68.8
British Columbia	1,873,674	463,181	24.7	1,410,493	75.3
Yukon	14,382	7,554	52.5	6,828	47.5
Northwest Territories	28,738	17,204	59.9	11,534	40.1

SOURCE: Dominion Bureau of Statistics, *1966 Census of Canada*, Vol. 1 (1-8), Ottawa, The Queen's Printer, 1968, Table 13.

and New Brunswick populations were more than 50 per cent urban, while the least urban were Prince Edward Island, the Yukon, Northwest Territories, and Saskatchewan. Probably more revealing of the total impact of urbanization is the proportion of population classified as rural farm, i.e., the population living on a farm of one acre or more with sales of agricultural products amounting to $50 or more during the preceding years. By this definition, only 9.6 per cent of the total population was truly "rural" in 1966. The most rural populations were to be found in Saskatchewan, with 29.3 per cent rural-farm and Prince Edward Island, with 28.4 per cent. Provinces and territories are listed in Table 3:14 by rank order of their proportions classified as rural-farm in 1966.

Character of Recent Migration Streams

Data on migration for the five-year period preceding June 1, 1961, show that rural-urban movement of the population is still taking place. Of the migrants

Table 3:14

RANK ORDER OF PROVINCES BY PROPORTION OF THEIR POPULATIONS CLASSIFIED AS RURAL-FARM IN THE 1966 CENSUS OF CANADA

Rank	Province	Per Cent Rural-farm
1.	Saskatchewan	29.3
2.	Prince Edward Island	28.4
3.	Alberta	19.0
4.	Manitoba	16.6
5.	Quebec	8.5
6.	New Brunswick	8.4
7.	Ontario	6.9
8.	Nova Scotia	6.0
9.	British Columbia	4.5
10.	Newfoundland	1.7
11.	Yukon	0.4
12.	Northwest Territories	0.1

SOURCE: Dominion Bureau of Statistics, *1966 Census of Canada*, Vol. 1 (1-8), Ottawa, The Queen's Printer, 1968, Table 13.

living in Canada five years prior to the census, 538,154 had moved to a more urban location, i.e., from rural farm or rural non-farm to urban areas, or from farm to non-farm areas. However, a surprising number, almost 500,000 persons, moved to a more rural area leaving a net movement (in an urban direction) of only 43,420. The largest number of migrants, 1,500,000, moved from one urban area to another. While it is not possible to determine how many of these moved from a smaller to a larger urban place, such moves probably exceeded those from larger to smaller or between places of the same size. As may be seen in Table 3:15, relatively small numbers were involved in moves between rural non-farm areas and between farms.

An additional net migration of 469,915 (comprised of immigrants still residing in Canada as of June 1, 1961, who had been living abroad in 1956) contributed considerably more residents to urban areas than to either of the two types of rural areas. Almost 90 per cent of those living abroad settled in urban areas in contrast to 8.2 and 2.1 per cent in rural non-farm and farm areas respectively. Since the type of locality from which these immigrants came is unknown, it is not possible to determine the type of movement as was

Table 3:15

NUMBER OF INTERNAL MIGRANTS BY TYPE OF MOVEMENT,
CANADA, 1956–1961

Type of Internal Migration	Number
Rural to Urban:	*538,154*
non-farm to urban	141,507
farm to urban	244,278
farm to non-farm	152,369
Urban to Rural:	*494,734*
urban to rural non-farm	371,711
urban to rural farm	75,075
non-farm to farm	47,948
Circular Movement:	*1,552,521*
urban to urban	1,467,326
rural non-farm to rural non-farm	65,287
farm to farm	19,908
Total	2,585,409

SOURCE: Dominion Bureau of Statistics, *1961 Census of Canada*, Bulletin 4:1-9, Ottawa, The Queen's Printer, 1965, Tables 12 and 13.

possible with the Canadian internal migration data. However, it is quite likely that a good deal of this represents movement from less to more urban areas.

One other important aspect of internal migration must be pointed out. Migration between municipalities was not the dominant type of movement between 1956 and 1961, since it constituted only 40.4 per cent of all changes of residence, or less than half of all moves. Local movement, i.e., moves made within the same municipality, constituted 59.6 per cent of all moves during this period. Of all moves between different municipalities, the largest proportion (79.7 per cent) was intra-provincial and only 20.3 per cent represented movement across provincial boundaries. For the latter group, moves between contiguous provinces constituted the somewhat larger share, being 10.7 per cent compared to 9.6 per cent for moves involving non-contiguous provinces. In other words, most changes of residence were made within municipalities or between municipalities in the same province.[21]

Emergence of Metropolitan Centres

Urbanization has proceeded more rapidly than the preceding analysis suggests. It is highly doubtful that the boundaries of incorporated cities, towns, and villages were any more successful in containing the actual limits of the expanding community during the early 1900s than they generally are today. Where urban aggregates began to form, the unincorporated areas adjacent to the central cities, as well as satellite towns and villages, have shown a tendency to grow more rapidly than the core city. The five cities in 1901 with populations of 50,000 and over undoubtedly experienced considerable growth in unincorporated areas adjacent to their municipal boundaries. Not only did the number of such urban centres increase during the 1901–21 period, but so did their size and the extent of their suburban sprawl. Since new growth tended to occur on the periphery of the built-up areas, the suburban areas grew more rapidly than the central cities. Even during the depression decade, when levels of economic activity were low, population growth tended to be more rapid in adjacent unincorporated areas and in satellite towns than in the central cities of these urban aggregates.[22]

To the extent that the concept "urban" intended to include the population living under urban conditions, the census definition became increasingly inadequate. Even the Census Metropolitan Areas, first established in 1931, included just the incorporated cities, towns, and villages within each metropolitan area. For the 1951 Census of Canada, the entire metropolitan area for those cities having built-up suburbs surrounding the core city was included as urban. In addition, unincorporated places of 1,000 or more were classified as urban while incorporated places of less than 1,000 were excluded. The result of this definitional change was to increase the urban population 8.7 per cent more than it would have been under the old definition.[23] Definitional changes were made again in 1956 and in 1961 for the purpose of sharpening the urban definition to include those populations living in the heavily built-up areas outside the corporate boundaries and functionally related to the core city.

As previously mentioned, the Dominion Bureau of Statistics first gave official recognition to the phenomenon of metropolitanization in the 1931 census. However, the emergence of large urban cities surrounded by densely populated unincorporated areas and satellite communities had occurred much earlier. As early as 1901, there were two such centres, Montreal and Toronto, each with over 200,000 population; and three additional centres, Quebec City, Ottawa, and Hamilton, had already exceeded 50,000 population. After the heavy immigration of the 1901–11 period and the initial settlement of the Prairie Provinces, two more cities exceeded the 50,000 mark. Winnipeg reached 136,035 and Vancouver, 100,401. By 1921, all of the ten largest cities of the 1960s, as well as Halifax, had passed 50,000.

Growth curves for the ten largest cities are shown in Figure 3:5 for the period 1901 to 1961. The rapid increase in urban population during the 1901–11 decade is readily apparent for the total urban population as well as most of these ten largest cities. The prairie centres of Winnipeg, Calgary, and Edmonton experienced extremely rapid growth; and the increases for both Montreal and Toronto were fairly substantial. Growth rates declined in following decades reaching minimal levels during the depression years. The

Fig. 3:5

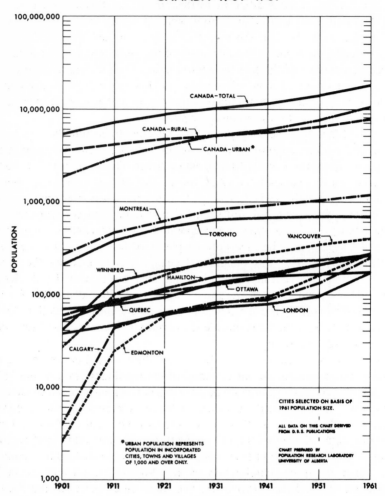

**POPULATION TRENDS
TEN LARGEST CITIES
CANADA: 1901–1961**

resurgence of the economy as a result of World War II and post-war growth of industry are both reflected in the increased urban growth rates for most of these major urban centres following 1941. However, the City of Toronto actually suffered a population decline during the 1951–61 decade, and the other cities would have shown larger rates of increase had they been more successful in annexing their rapidly growing suburbs.

Recognition of metropolitan areas as significant statistical units may have been somewhat slow in arriving, but by 1941, 12 such areas were officially recognized. Three more were added in 1951, and by 1961 the number had increased to 17. These 17 metropolitan areas comprised somewhat over 8,000,000 persons or 45 per cent of Canada's total population on June 1, 1961. The distribution of metropolitan areas by size in 1961 is illustrated in Figure 3:6. For comparison, these same 17 urban centres are shown as they were 60 years earlier to emphasize the very significant growth which has occurred.[24]

Two additional and important aspects of metropolitanization need to be mentioned: the increasingly rapid rate of growth and the distribution of this growth within the metropolitan area. During the post-World War II period, the rate of growth of metropolitan area population was phenomenal. In 1941, the 12 metropolitan areas contained approximately one-third of the total population of Canada. By 1951, the combined 15 metropolitan areas accounted for 37.6 per cent; and in 1961, the 17 metropolitan areas comprised 44.8 per cent. During the latter decade, the population in these areas increased by 2,527,000 and almost half of this growth was accounted for by Montreal and Toronto. As may be seen in Table 3:16, the highest growth rates were experienced by Calgary (96 per cent) and Edmonton (91 per cent), while the lowest rates occurred in Windsor (18 per cent) and Saint John (22 per cent). Continuing development of Alberta's oil resources accounted for much of the growth in the two western centres, while some

Table 3:16

TOTAL POPULATION AND PERCENTAGE INCREASE FOR CANADA'S CENSUS, METROPOLITAN AREAS, 1951–1961

Metropolitan Areas	Population		Percentage Increase
	1951	1961	
All Metropolitan Areas	5,637,075	8,163,986	44.8
Calgary	142,315	279,062	96.1
Edmonton	176,782	337,568	91.0
Halifax	133,931	183,946	37.3
Hamilton	280,293	395,189	41.0
Kitchener	107,474	154,864	44.1
London	128,977	181,283	40.6
Montreal	1,471,851	2,109,509	43.3
Ottawa	292,476	429,750	46.9
Quebec	276,242	357,568	29.4
Saint John (New Brunswick)	78,337	95,563	22.0
St. John's (Newfoundland)	68,620	90,838	32.4
Sudbury	73,826	110,694	49.9
Toronto	1,210,353	1,824,481	50.7
Vancouver	561,960	790,165	40.6
Victoria	113,207	154,152	36.2
Windsor	163,618	193,365	18.2
Winnipeg	356,813	475,989	33.4

SOURCE: Dominion Bureau of Statistics, *1961 Census of Canada*, Bulletin 7:1-2, Ottawa, The Queen's Printer, 1963, Table VIII, p. 15.

Fig. 3:6

METROPOLITAN POPULATION
CANADA: 1901 AND 1961

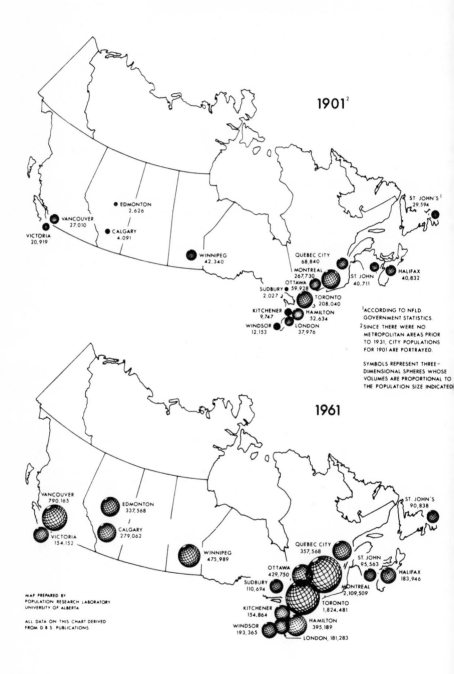

1901[2]

EDMONTON 2,626
VANCOUVER 27,010
VICTORIA 20,919
CALGARY 4,091
WINNIPEG 42,340
ST. JOHN'S[1] 29,594
QUEBEC CITY 68,840
MONTREAL 267,730
OTTAWA 59,928
SUDBURY 2,027
ST. JOHN 40,711
HALIFAX 40,832
TORONTO 208,040
KITCHENER 9,747
HAMILTON 52,634
WINDSOR 12,153
LONDON 37,976

[1] ACCORDING TO NFLD. GOVERNMENT STATISTICS.
[2] SINCE THERE WERE NO METROPOLITAN AREAS PRIOR TO 1931, CITY POPULATIONS FOR 1901 ARE PORTRAYED.

SYMBOLS REPRESENT THREE-DIMENSIONAL SPHERES WHOSE VOLUMES ARE PROPORTIONAL TO THE POPULATION SIZE INDICATED

1961

VANCOUVER 790,165
EDMONTON 337,568
VICTORIA 154,152
CALGARY 279,062
WINNIPEG 475,989
ST. JOHN'S 90,838
QUEBEC CITY 357,568
OTTAWA 429,750
SUDBURY 110,694
ST. JOHN 95,563
HALIFAX 183,946
MONTREAL 2,109,509
KITCHENER 154,864
TORONTO 1,824,481
WINDSOR 193,365
HAMILTON 395,189
LONDON, 181,283

MAP PREPARED BY POPULATION RESEARCH LABORATORY UNIVERSITY OF ALBERTA

ALL DATA ON THIS CHART DERIVED FROM D B S PUBLICATIONS

slackening in automobile manufacturing appeared to account for the low growth in the Windsor area.

The impressive growth rate of 45 per cent for all metropolitan areas combined during the 1951–61 decade obscures rather significant variations in the drawing power of individual metropolitan centres. Toronto's "attractiveness" for foreign-born immigrants is beyond question. Over one-fourth (26.9 per cent) of all post-World War II immigrants still residing in Canada at the time of the 1961 Census were living in Toronto, with 14.2 per cent in Montreal, and 6.6 per cent in Vancouver. These three centres combined accounted for just less than half of all foreign born in Canada.[25]

The degree of concentration exhibited by native-born migrants was not nearly so great. The same three metropolitan areas accounted for only 27.4 per cent of all native-born migrants with Vancouver having the largest proportion (11.5 per cent) followed by Toronto and Montreal with 8.9 and 7.0 per cent respectively. If the proportion of native-born inter-provincial migrants among the total native born is used as a measure of the metropolitan area's attractiveness, the greater drawing power of the western centres for native born becomes evident. The metropolitan area of Vancouver with 38.7 per cent of its native-born population classified as migrants (from other provinces) would rank first, followed by Victoria with 38.0 per cent, and Calgary and Edmonton with 36.1 and 26.2 per cent respectively. By way of contrast, only 13.8 per cent of Toronto's and 7.4 per cent Montreal's metropolitan areas native-born populations were classified as inter-provincial migrants.[26]

The metropolitan areas vary in yet another way with respect to their attractiveness for the native-born population. Partly due to their particular location, and partly due to the differences in types of urban amenities and opportunities, the sources of native-born migrants vary considerably for each of the centres. Kasahara's "index of attractiveness" based on province of birth data showed that Toronto possessed the greatest "attractiveness" or ability to draw from all provinces, followed closely by Vancouver, with Montreal third. Toronto's attraction was more widespread than any other metropolitan area, being greatest for migrants from the Atlantic Provinces, Quebec, and British Columbia. Vancouver drew most extensively from the Prairie Provinces while Montreal drew primarily from Ontario and New Brunswick. Metropolitan areas with the lowest attractiveness for migrants born outside their respective provinces were St. John's and Quebec City.[27]

The rapid growth for metropolitan areas in general has not been evenly distributed between the central cities and their suburbs. As urban aggregates have grown, the central cities have found it increasingly difficult to encompass all of their functionally related population within their legally defined boundaries through the normal annexation process. In many cases, populations locating in suburban areas have done so deliberately as a means of escaping greater land costs, congestion, and taxes associated with the central city. It is hardly surprising to find suburban residents resisting the increasing threat to their political autonomy implicit in the city's attempt to annex adjacent built-up areas. Whatever the specific reasons for their resistance might be, the results have been essentially the same. The central city's growth tends to slow down as its vacant land is occupied and its efforts fail to obtain new land for expansion. Growth can only continue at a rapid rate in the suburbs, and as more and more land in the central city is taken over by business and industry, the central city soon reaches the point where it actually begins to lose population as the metropolitan area continues to grow. Two of the 17 metropolitan areas, Toronto and Windsor, actually experienced population declines within the city proper during the 1951–61 decade. The net result of these differential growth rates was that the suburban proportion of the metropolitan areas increased from about one-quarter in 1941 to 45.3 per cent in 1961.[28]

When city governments have been more successful in their annexation efforts or showed initial foresight by establishing their boundaries to allow for future expansion, the proportion of the population residing in suburban areas tends to be considerably smaller. For example, in 1961, only 6.5 per cent of London's metropolitan area population resided outside the city

Table 3:17

PER CENT OF METROPOLITAN AREA POPULATION IN CENTRAL CITY AND SUBURBAN AREAS, CANADA'S METROPOLITAN AREAS, 1961

Metropolitan Area	Per Cent of Metropolitan Area	
	Central City	Suburbs
All Metropolitan Areas	54.7	45.3
Calgary	89.5	10.5
Edmonton	83.3	16.7
Halifax	50.3	49.7
Hamilton	69.3	30.7
Kitchener	48.1	51.9
London	93.5	6.5
Montreal	56.5	43.5
Ottawa	62.4	37.6
Quebec	48.1	51.9
Saint John	57.7	42.3
St. John's	70.1	29.9
Sudbury	72.4	27.6
Toronto	36.9	63.1
Vancouver	48.7	51.3
Victoria	35.6	64.4
Windsor	59.1	40.9
Winnipeg	55.8	44.2

SOURCE: Dominion Bureau of Statistics, *1961 Census of Canada*, Bulletin 7:1-2, Ottawa, The Queen's Printer, 1963, Table VII, p. 14.

proper, and only 10.5 per cent for Edmonton. Some cities like Regina and Saskatoon were so successful in this respect that they had insufficient suburban populations to qualify as metropolitan areas.[29] The distribution of population between central cities and suburbs for each of Canada's metropolitan areas is shown in Table 3:17.

Demographic sources of metropolitan growth. As with urban growth in general, migration and natural increase are the two major sources of metropolitan growth.[30] Historically, and with respect to the rural-urban movement of population in particular, the rural areas with their higher fertility levels have been regarded as the nation's nursery, producing the surplus population required for the maintenance and continued growth of the urban centres. Census data as early as 1921 do show that Canada's urban populations have never matched the fertility of the rural population.[31] Yet, it is not possible to say with any certainty that migration has been the relatively more important of these two components for growth in the larger urban centres since 1921. Stone's analysis of urban change during the 1951–61 decade has shown that the relative contributions of the two to urban growth were quite similar for urban places 5,000 or more in population, but that this varied considerably by region and urban size group. For urban size groups under 30,000 in each region, natural increase tended to be more important in accounting for the decennial rate of change, while in the largest size groups the direct effect of net migration exceeded that of natural increase.[32]

Both region and size appear to be significant factors in explaining the relative importance of natural increase and net migration for growth in Canada's 15 metropolitan areas during this same period. As Table 3:18 indicates, these two sources contributed almost identical numbers to the combined populations of Canada's metropolitan areas. However, for individual metropolitan areas their significance varies radically. Net migration exceeded natural increase in Calgary, Edmonton, London, Ottawa, Toronto, Vancouver, and Victoria. In the case of Calgary and Edmonton, high levels of growth due to both net migration and natural increase illustrate the way in which net in-migration can have a double effect by contributing to natural increase when migrants include disproportionate numbers of young married couples in the high fertility age groups. For the metropolitan areas of the Atlantic Provinces, as well as the Quebec and Windsor metropolitan areas, net migration was of little significance. For Windsor, only its natural increase kept it from experiencing a population decline in the face of a net out-migration of −1.9 per cent for the 1951–61 decade.

Internal Differentiation of Metropolitan Area Populations

From its early beginnings as a predominantly rural society comprised of relatively scattered, isolated, and autonomous communities, Canada has ex-

Table 3:18

COMPONENTS OF POPULATION GROWTH IN CENSUS METROPOLITAN AREAS, 1951–1961

Metropolitan Areas	Natural Increase[b]	Net Migration	Per Cent of 1951 Population	
			Nat. Increase	Net Migration
Metropolitan Area[a]	1,082,433	1,097,933	20.6	20.9
Calgary	48,487	88,337	34.5	62.8
Edmonton	70,646	82,957	40.7	47.7
Halifax	32,960	17,055	24.6	12.7
Hamilton	58,951	51,617	21.6	19.0
London	24,649	27,657	19.1	21.4
Montreal	285,572	224,197	20.5	16.1
Ottawa	67,227	70,047	23.0	23.9
Quebec	56,627	24,308	20.6	8.8
Saint John	14,572	2,654	18.6	3.4
St. John's	19,680	2,026	29.2	3.0
Toronto	209,577	291,740	18.8	26.1
Vancouver	87,001	141,204	15.5	25.1
Victoria	11,434	21,531	10.6	19.9
Windsor	32,885	–3,138	20.1	–1.9
Winnipeg	62,165	55,741	17.6	15.7

SOURCE: Dominion Bureau of Statistics, *1961 Census of Canada*, Bulletin 7:1-2, Ottawa, The Queen's Printer, 1963, Table X, p. 2-19.
a Areas as defined for the 1956 Census.
b Estimated for a few small fringe parts of metropolitan areas.

perienced a basic transformation as a consequence of the development of industry and concomitant improvements in its transportation and communication networks. With growth in size and heterogeneity of population and industrialization has come an increasingly complex division of labour and a greater degree of inter-dependence. Not only is this true at the individual and community level, but also in a regional and national sense. The growth, emergence, and recognition of regional centres of dominance are reflections of differentiation and specialization at this level. Since references already have been made to the broad aspects of regional distribution and population growth, this section will deal specifically with some of the recent and more apparent differentiations which have occurred within metropolitan area populations. Suburbs begin to grow at more rapid rates than their central cities as the latter becomes increasingly filled up with population and non-residential land uses. For metropolitan areas as a whole, migration tends to be more important than natural increase for population growth. But what is their relative importance with respect to central cities as compared to their respective suburbs? Of the two major sub-areas, the suburbs grew more rapidly during the 1951–61 decade. The population for all 17 metropolitan area suburbs combined increased by 97.0 per cent from 1,653,361 to 3,256,756, compared to 16.0 per cent for the combined central cities. The relative contributions made by natural increase and net migration during the 1951–61 decade are shown in Table 3:19. The central cities (combined) grew only because natural increase exceeded their losses through net out-migration. On the other hand, for the combined suburban populations, a large net in-migration added to a relatively large natural increase to produce an increment approximately three times as large as that experienced by the central cities. Net migration accounted for 71 per cent of the total increase of 1,603,395 recorded for the 1951–61 decade, while natural increase accounted for just 29 per cent.

Table 3:19

COMPONENTS OF POPULATION GROWTH FOR CENTRAL CITIES AND SUBURBS FOR ALL METROPOLITAN AREAS COMBINED, 1951–1961

Metropolitan Area[a]	Natural Increase[b]	Net Migration	Per Cent of 1951 Population	
			Natural Increase	Net Migration
Central cities	619,977	− 43,006	17.2	− 1.2
Suburbs	462,456	1,140,939	28.0	69.0

SOURCE: Dominion Bureau of Statistics, *1961 Census of Canada*, Bulletin 7:1-2, Ottawa, The Queen's Printer, 1963, Table X, p. 2-19.
[a] Areas defined for the 1956 Census of Canada.
[b] Estimated for a few small fringe parts of metropolitan areas.

Fig. 3:7

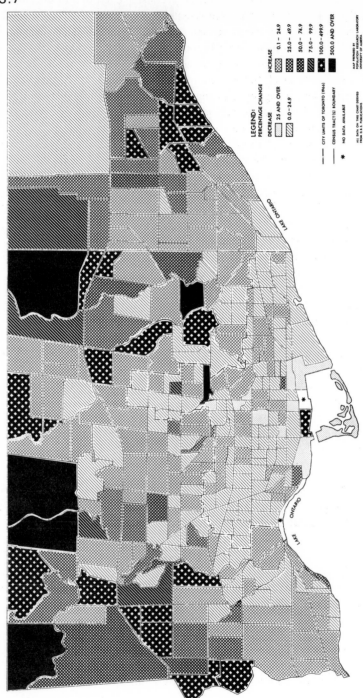

POPULATION CHANGE
TORONTO METROPOLITAN AREA: 1961-1966

There were, of course, variations from this general pattern for a number of metropolitan areas, specifically with reference to the central cities. Calgary, Edmonton, Hamilton, Ottawa, and Vancouver were the only central cities which did not experience a net out-migration during this period. However, in not one case did the gain from net in-migration exceed their gain from natural increase.[33] Of the three cities showing the highest net in-migration, Calgary and Edmonton could attribute their favourable showing to the existence of large areas of underdeveloped land, whereas Ottawa's position was in large part due to a significant extension of its city boundaries just prior to the 1951 Census.

Toronto exemplified the plight of the large central city of a rapidly growing metropolitan area which has been unsuccessful in its attempts to adjust its boundaries to incorporate a greater proportion of its functionally related population. Its net loss through migration of −82,590 exceeded its natural increase of 79,243 to produce an actual loss in population of −3,347 over the decennial period 1951–61.[34] This tendency to lose population in the central city while the suburbs expand at an explosive rate is clearly evident in Figure 3:7 which shows population change by census tracts within the Toronto Metropolitan Area for the 1961–66 period. At the end of this period, the City of Toronto's share of the total metropolitan area population had dropped to 30.8 per cent from 36.9 per cent in 1961.[35] Note also that there are numerous deviant cases of population change for census tracts both inside and outside the central city. Construction of high density housing obviously contributes to popplation increase for some areas, while changes in land use can produce opposite effects outside the central city as well as within its boundaries.

Future Trends

Chapter 1 concluded with the statement that Canada as a whole would continue to show strong growth, but that the Prairie and Atlantic Provinces were expected to increase at somewhat lower rates while British Columbia, Ontario, and Quebec increased their respective shares of the population through 1980. Chapter 3 has provided additional evidence for this trend in its analysis of the rural-urban movement of population in Canada. In addition, the increasing concentration of Canada's population in a relatively few large metropolitan centres is patently clear. Between 1951 and 1961, 60 per cent of the total population increase for Canada occurred in the 1961 metropolitan areas as a result of the 45 per cent increase experienced by these combined populations themselves during the same period. Close to half of this combined growth occurred in the two largest metropolitan areas, Toronto and Montreal. The somewhat lower, but still remarkably high rate of growth of 27 per cent experienced by the 12 census metropolitan areas (as defined in the 1941

Census) reveals the rather amazing dimensions of the metropolitan explosion in Canada during the 1951–61 decade.

In 1961, approximately 70 per cent of Canada's population was classified as urban and 45 per cent lived in its 17 metropolitan areas. In 1941, somewhat more than half of the population was classified as urban with about one-third of the population residing in its 12 metropolitan areas.[36] It is somewhat difficult to say how much further Canada's urbanization will proceed. According to Kingsley Davis' research on urbanization trends throughout the world, the rate of urbanization tends to slow down after passing the 50 per cent point; and, by the time urbanization reaches 75 per cent, its growth curve may be expected to either have flattened out or declined.[37] According to the United Nations, the United States, like Canada, had approximately 70 per cent of its population living in urban areas in 1960.[38] However, a considerably larger percentage of its population, i.e., 63 per cent versus 45 per cent for Canada, was contained in its 212 Standard Metropolitan Statistical Areas.[39] Perhaps of more relevance here is the fact that the percentage increase in the population of U.S. metropolitan areas during the 1950–60 decade was considerably lower than that for Canada during the 1951–61 period. In addition, the percentage increase for the United States during 1960–68 was only 12.9 per cent for an annual average increase of only 1.5 per cent compared to 2.4 per cent per year for the 1950–60 inter-censal decade.[40] To the extent that the U.S. experience may be reflective of a more advanced stage of industrialization and technological development, it may very well provide a clue to Canada's future course of metropolitan development. Regional growth differentials, coupled with the very high metropolitan area growth rate of the 1951–61 decade, suggest a continuation of urbanization throughout the 1961–71 inter-censal decade and into the 1970s at a somewhat diminished rate. Results of the 1966 Census of Canada have already shown a decline in the rate of growth for Canada's 17 major metropolitan areas. The percentage increase between 1961 and 1966 was just 15.0 per cent compared to increases of 20.0 and 20.7 per cent for the 1956–61 and 1951–56 periods respectively.[41]

REFERENCES

Anderson, Isabel B.: *Internal Migration in Canada, 1921–1961*. Economic Council of Canada, Staff Study 13. Ottawa, The Queen's Printer, 1966.
Dominion Bureau of Statistics: *1961 Census of Canada. General Review: Internal Migration*. Bulletin 7:1–3, Ottawa, The Queen's Printer, 1970.
Dominion Bureau of Statistics: *1961 Census of Canada. General Review: Rural and Urban Population*. Bulletin 7:1–2, Ottawa, The Queen's Printer, 1963.

George, M. V.: *Internal Migration in Canada: Demographic Analyses.* 1961 Census Monograph, Dominion Bureau of Statistics. Ottawa, The Queen's Printer, 1970.
Kasahara, Yoshiko: "A Profile of Canada's Metropolitan Centers," *Queen's Quarterly,* LXX (Autumn 1963).
Lithwick, N. H., and G. Paquet: *Urban Studies: Canadian Perspective.* Toronto, Methuen, 1968.
Simmons, J. and R. Simmons: *Urban Canada.* Toronto, The Copp Clark Publishing Co., 1969.
Stone, Leroy O.: *Migration in Canada: Regional Aspects.* 1961 Census Monograph, Dominion Bureau of Statistics. Ottawa, The Queen's Printer, 1969.
Stone, Leroy O.: *Urban Development in Canada.* 1961 Census Monograph, Dominion Bureau of Statistics, Ottawa, The Queen's Printer, 1967.

FOOTNOTES

[1]Dominion Bureau of Statistics, *Canada, One Hundred, 1867–1967.* Ottawa, The Queen's Printer, 1967, p. 104.
[2]*Ibid.,* pp. 104–106.
[3]*Ibid.,* p. 107.
[4]*Ibid.,* p. 106.
[5]*Ibid.,* pp. 317–328.
[6]The actual differences would have been greater than those shown. In the two former cases, migrants who would have stayed under conditions of zero migration would have contributed an additional excess of births over deaths; whereas, in the latter two cases, some of the recorded natural increase was contributed by the net in-migrants.
[7]Dominion Bureau of Statistics, *Vital Statistics, 1964,* Ottawa, The Queen's Printer, 1966, Table D1, p. 94.
[8]Replacement needs would require that each woman replace herself with one female infant. The gross reproduction rate is only a crude replacement index in that it does not take into consideration the possible losses in the original cohort of women due to mortality from birth to the end of their childbearing years. The net reproduction rate overcomes this deficiency by taking mortality into account, but such data are not readily available in published form for Canada.
[9]Similar data are not available for Newfoundland. Its crude death rates for the 1936–64 period have been consistently higher than those of the other provinces. Data have not been included for either the Yukon or the Northwest Territories, but available data indicate very high fertility in these areas. For example, in 1961, the crude birth rates were 38.1 and 48.6 per 1000 population respectively. Gross reproduction rates were 2.64 and 3.52. Total fertility rates: 5.38 and 7.19. Dominion Bureau of Statistics, *Vital Statistics, 1964,* Ottawa, The Queen's Printer, 1966, Tables B1 and B6.
[10]Isabel B. Anderson, *Internal Migration in Canada, 1921–1961,* Economic Council of Canada Staff Study No. 13, Ottawa, The Queen's Printer, March, 1966, pp. 15–17.
[11]Dominion Bureau of Statistics, *1961 Census of Canada,* Bulletin 4:1–9, Ottawa, The Queen's Printer, 1965, Table 11.
[12]*Ibid.*
[13]Nathan Keyfitz, "The Growth of Canadian Population," *Population Studies,* Vol. IV, No. 1, June, 1950, pp. 52–55; Isabel B. Anderson, *op. cit.*
[14]Nova Scotia was the one exception during the depression decade of 1931–41 when it experienced a net in-migration of just 2,000.
[15]The definitions of urban and rural populations used by the Canadian government have changed a number of times in recent years. For the period preceding the 1951 Census, the urban population was defined to include all populations residing in places which under the municipal acts of the provinces were incorporated as cities, towns, or villages. All populations residing outside these urban communities were classified as rural. Changes in definition in 1951, 1956, and 1961 were made to encompass

more of the population living under urban conditions. For example, in 1951 incorporated cities, towns or villages under 1,000 population were excluded while unincorporated places of 1,000 or more were included. In addition, the whole metropolitan area of larger cities having built up suburbs adjacent to the core city were included. Subsequent changes in 1956 and 1961 were designed to improve the measurement of populations living in urbanized areas surrounding the larger cities and towns. For a more detailed discussion of definitional changes and their implications, see: Dominion Bureau of Statistics, *1961 Census of Canada*, Bulletin 7:1–2, Catalogue 99-512, Ottawa, The Queen's Printer, pp. 1–3.

[16]Leroy O. Stone, *Urban Development in Canada*, 1961 Census Monograph, Ottawa, The Queen's Printer, 1967, pp. 14–15.

[17]Based on the analysis of the population of incorporated cities, towns, and villages of 1,000 and over from 1851 to 1911, and from 1921 to 1961 on estimates of urban population (based on the 1961 Census definition) made by Leroy Stone, *op. cit.*, pp. 26–36.

[18]*Ibid.*, Table 2.2, p. 29.

[19]*Ibid.*, p. 29.

[20]Dominion Bureau of Statistics, *1961 Census of Canada*, Bulletin 7:1–2, Ottawa, The Queen's Printer, 1963, Table II, p. 4; and *1966 Census of Canada*, Vol. I (1–8), Ottawa, The Queen's Printer, 1968, Table 13.

[21]Dominion Bureau of Statistics, *1961 Census of Canada*, Bulletin 4:1–9, Ottawa, The Queen's Printer, 1965, Table II, p. 11–1.

[22]Enid Charles, *The Changing Size of the Family in Canada*, Census Monograph No. 1 (1941 Census of Canada), Ottawa, The King's Printer, 1948, pp. 146–47.

[23]Dominion Bureau of Statistics, *1961 Census of Canada*, Bulletin 7:1–2, Ottawa, The Queen's Printer, 1963, p. 1.

[24]As metropolitan areas were not established as early as 1901, the sizes depicted are for the central cities only. Since the suburban development was relatively small at that time, relatively little distortion has been introduced.

[25]Dominion Bureau of Statistics, *1961 Census of Canada*, Bulletin 1:2–8, Ottawa, The Queen's Printer, 1963, Tables 58 and 61.

[26]Based on data in Dominion Bureau of Statistics, *1961 Census of Canada*, Bulletin, 1:2–7, Ottawa, The Queen's Printer, 1963, Table 53.

[27]Yoshiko Kasahara, "A Profile of Canada's Metropolitan Centers." *Queen's Quarterly*, LXX (Autumn, 1963).

[28]Dominion Bureau of Statistics, *1961 Census of Canada*, Bulletin 7:1–2, Ottawa, The Queen's Printer, 1963, Table VIII, p. 15.

[29]Dominion Bureau of Statistics, *op. cit.*

[30]Changes in boundaries of metropolitan areas, caused both by growth and definitional changes are a contributive source of change in metropolitan area populations. However, compared to natural increase and net migration, this source is relatively insignificant. For a discussion of the relative importance of the demographic components of recent urban population increase, see Leroy O. Stone, *Urban Development in Canada*, Ottawa, The Queen's Printer, 1967, pp. 90–98.

[31]Jacques Henripin, *Tendances et facteurs de la fécundité au Canada*, Ottawa, Imprimeur de la Reine, 1968, Tableau 4.2.

[32]Leroy O. Stone, *op. cit.*

[33]Dominion Bureau of Statistics, *1961 Census of Canada*, Bulletin 7:1–2, Ottawa, The Queen's Printer, 1963, Table X, p. 2–19.

[34]*Ibid.*

[35]Dominion Bureau of Statistics, *1966 Census of Canada*, Vol. 1 (1–7), Ottawa, The Queen's Printer, 1967, Table 11.

[36]In the 1941 Census of Canada, only the population in incorporated cities, towns, and villages of 1,000 population or more was classified as urban. In 1941, the urban population amounted to 5,853,603 or 50.9 per cent of the total.

[37]Kingsley Davis, "The Urbanization of the Human Population," *Scientific American*, September, 1965, Vol. 213, No. 3, p. 44.

[38]United Nations, *1963 Demographic Year Book,* Table 5; also, U.S. Bureau of the Census, *Statistical Abstract of the United States, 1969* (90th edition), Washington, D.C., U.S. Government Printing Office, 1969, Table No. 15.

[39]U.S. Bureau of the Census, *Statistical Abstract of the United States, 1968,* Washington, D.C., U.S. Government Printing Office, 1968, Table No. 17, p. 18.

[40]U.S. Bureau of the Census, "Population Characteristics", Series P-20, No. 181, April 21, 1969, Current Population Reports, Washington, D.C., U.S. Government Printing Office, Table A.

[41]Dominion Bureau of Statistics, *1961 Census of Canada,* Bulletin 7:1-2. Ottawa, The Queen's Printer, 1963, Table VIII; and *1966 Census of Canada,* Vol. 1 (1–7) Ottawa, The Queen's Printer, 1967, Table 11.

Age and Sex Structure

The most fundamental aspect of population is its age and sex composition. This is partly because, at any given moment in time, its age-sex structure is the consequence of earlier fertility, mortality, and migration experience, and partly because its structure simultaneously is a determinant of future trends in fertility, mortality, and migration. For example, if a large proportion of the female population were in the childbearing ages, and assuming that there were no deficiency in the number of males in the relevant age groups, larger number of births and higher birth rates could be expected than if a smaller proportion were in the fertile years. Deficits of males through excessive war-time mortality or emigration would naturally affect marriage patterns as well as subsequent fertility. Thus, age-sex composition is both a consequence of and determinant of demographic processes. In addition, the relative size of the various age and sex groups has considerable significance for a population's productivity, standard of living, cost of educational and welfare programs, degree of racial and ethnic integration, and the achievement of national social and economic goals in general.

Sex Composition

The relative numbers of males and females in any population are determined by (1) the cumulative and combined effects of the sex ratio at birth, (2) ratio of males to females among both immigrants and emigrants, and (3) sex differentials in mortality. Chapter 2 has already illustrated how the first two factors have tended to contribute an excess of males. Mortality, however, has consistently and increasingly operated to reduce the excess of

Fig. 4:1

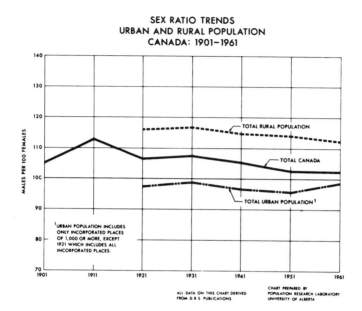

SEX RATIO TRENDS
URBAN AND RURAL POPULATION
CANADA: 1901–1961

males found at birth and among Canada's early immigrants. Since 1881, the greatest excess of males was recorded in the 1911 Census of Canada when 112.9 males were enumerated for every 100 females. Subsequently, the ratio of males to females steadily declined for the country as a whole until 1966, when there were only 100.9 males for every 100 females. An excess of males is still to be found in both the Prairies, where the lure of free land drew them during the early twentieth century, and the rural populations in general, as may be seen in Figure 4:1. In contrast, Canada's urban population has exhibited sex ratios below 100, but note how heavy urban-oriented immigration during the 1951–61 decade reversed a 20-year decline and increased the sex ratio from a low of 95.8 (males per 100 females) in 1951, to 98.2 in 1961. By 1966, it had dropped slightly to 97.8.

The tendency for rural populations to have an excess of males and the long term decline in sex ratios which has been occurring throughout most of Canada are reflected in the regional data appearing in Table 4:1. The more rural regions continue to have higher sex ratios than either of the two provinces with the highest concentrations of metropolitan area populations. Canada's "frontier" is still to be found in the West and North, but in 1966, only the North retained any semblance of an excess of males, the traditional hallmark of the frontier.

The technological revolution in agriculture and industry has contributed

Table 4:1

SEX RATIOS BY REGIONS FOR CANADA: 1901, 1961, AND 1966

Region	Year		
	1901	1961	1966
Atlantic	103.3	103.5[a]	102.1[a]
Quebec	100.0	100.2	99.7
Ontario	101.0	101.1	99.9
Prairies	120.1	106.2	103.5
British Columbia	177.0	103.6	102.5
Territories	236.1	126.3	118.3
Canada	105.0	102.2	100.9

SOURCE: Dominion Bureau of Statistics, *1961 Census of Canada*, Bulletin 1:2-2, Ottawa, The Queen's Printer, 1962, Table 20-1; *1966 Census of Canada*, Vol. 1 (1-8), Ottawa, The Queen's Printer, 1968.
[a] Includes Newfoundland.

to an increasing concentration of population in urban centres. The higher productivity of farms with its concomitant decline in workers created a surplus population in the rural areas which has been attracted in increasing numbers to the rapidly expanding service and production centres where new employment opportunities were to be found. This has been amply demonstrated by the data on urbanization presented in Chapter 3. What remains to be shown, in greater detail, is the extent of sex selectivity in the urbanward movement. This has already been suggested by the data in Table 4:1, but is more clearly evident in Table 4:2, which shows a fairly consistent decline in the number of males per 100 females as one moves from rural-farm population to increasingly larger urban centres. This is precisely what one would expect to find if women were more inclined than men to move from rural areas or from smaller to larger urban places. The more "urban" areas, i.e., the cities of 100,000 or more, have the fewest males relative to their female populations.

Age Composition

Like individuals, aggregate populations may be thought of as being young, mature, or aged; but, unlike them, a population can attenuate or reverse its aging process by increasing its reproductivity, or by rejuvenation through immigration. Declining fertility has contributed significantly to the long-term aging of Canada's population. In 1881, the median age was 20.1 years compared to 25.6 years today.[1] It is significant that the largest increase for any decade occurred during the depression years of lowest fertility when the median age increased from 24.7 years in 1931 to 27.0 in 1941. The impact of heavy immigration at about the time of the 1911 Census was reflected in

Table 4:2

SEX RATIOS FOR RURAL FARM, RURAL NON-FARM, AND URBAN PLACES BY SIZE, CANADA, 1966

Locality	Sex Ratio
Rural Farm	115.1
Rural Non-farm	107.4
Urban:	
1,000– 2,499	101.0
2,500– 4,999	100.0
5,000– 9,999	100.2
10,000–29,999	98.3
30,000–99,999	98.0
100,000 and over	97.1
Canada	100.9

SOURCE: Dominion Bureau of Statistics, *1966 Census of Canada*, Vol. 1 (1-8), Ottawa, The Queen's Printer, 1968.

an attenuation of the aging process; and, more significantly, the resurgence of both fertility and migration after World War II actually reversed this aging trend. The decline in median age since 1951 may be seen in Table 4:3.

A more detailed picture of trends in the age structure may be obtained from Figure 4:2. From 1901 to 1951, proportions in the broad age groups 30 years of age and over increased noticeably while an overall decrease occurred for the two major aged groups under 15 years up to 1941. Subsequently, the resurgence in fertility reversed the trend for the youngest two age groups enabling them to regain in 20 years what they had lost in the previous 40 years. Of the older groups, i.e., 30 years and over, only the 45–64 year age group showed a decline in their relative proportion of the population from 1941 to 1961. The young adults, 15–29 years of age, experienced the

Table 4:3

MEDIAN AGE OF THE POPULATION, CANADA: 1881–1966

Year	Median Age[a]	Year	Median Age[a]
1881	20.1	1941	27.0
1891	21.4	1951	27.8
1901	22.7	1956	27.4
1911	23.8	1961	26.5
1921	23.9	1966	25.6
1931	24.7		

SOURCE: Dominion Bureau of Statistics, *1961 Census of Canada*, Bulletin 7:1-4, Ottawa, The Queen's Printer, 1964, Table IV; *1966 Census of Canada*, Vol. 1 (1-11), Ottawa, The Queen's Printer, 1968.
[a] Excludes Newfoundland.

largest decline in proportion, dropping from 27.1 per cent in 1941 to 20.9 in 1961. Very clearly, the decline in median age after 1951 was due to the increase in the proportion of the population under 15 years from 30.4 to 34.0 per cent. The absolute numbers of all age groups increased between 1951 and 1961, but the relative increase was greatest for those under 15 years of age. By 1966, the effects of declining fertility were becoming visible in the age structure, as the proportion under 15 years declined slightly from 34.0 to 33.0 per cent.

Fig. 4:2

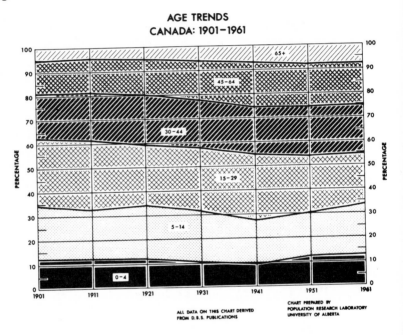

AGE TRENDS
CANADA: 1901–1961

ALL DATA ON THIS CHART DERIVED FROM D.B.S. PUBLICATIONS

CHART PREPARED BY POPULATION RESEARCH LABORATORY UNIVERSITY OF ALBERTA

Age and Sex Composition

Sex ratios by age group. For the total population, males have outnumbered females at every census since Confederation. This was also true for every age group during the early twentieth century. However, as early as the Census of 1901, Ontario and Quebec had deficiencies of males in the young adult age groups (20–34 years) with Quebec and the Atlantic Provinces also showing sex ratios of under 100 for some of the older ages. On the other hand, the Prairies, British Columbia, and Canada's North showed large excesses of males relative to females in every age group 15 years of age and over.

The decline in total sex ratios since 1921 has been the consequence of declines in the age groups 30 years and over as the excess males of the bi

Fig. 4:3

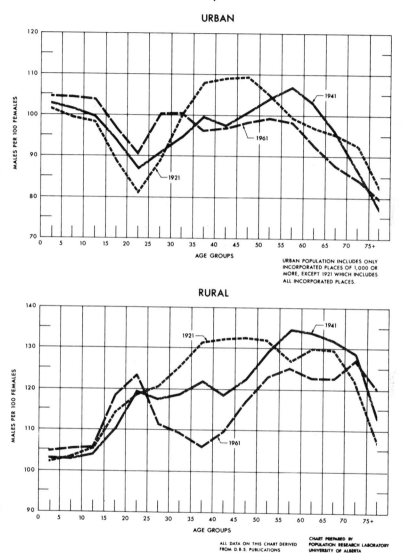

SEX RATIO TRENDS
URBAN AND RURAL POPULATION
CANADA: 1921, 1941 AND 1961

URBAN

URBAN POPULATION INCLUDES ONLY
INCORPORATED PLACES OF 1,000 OR
MORE, EXCEPT 1921 WHICH INCLUDES
ALL INCORPORATED PLACES.

RURAL

ALL DATA ON THIS CHART DERIVED
FROM D.B.S. PUBLICATIONS

CHART PREPARED BY
POPULATION RESEARCH LABORATORY
UNIVERSITY OF ALBERTA

immigrations, circa 1911, have aged and died. This is apparent for both rural and urban populations in Figure 4:3. There are, however, two major contrasts. First, the sex ratios for any rural age group have yet to decline below 100, but by 1961 all urban age groups 35 years and over had dropped below this point of parity. Second, the sex ratios for rural and urban populations between 10 and 30 years are roughly mirror images of each other. The deficiency of males, visible in all three distributions of urban populations for 1921, 1941, and 1961, reflects the urbanward movement of young adult females. Some of this, however, may reflect some underenumeration of highly mobile urban males. Since the sex ratio for the combined urban and rural population of males in the 20–24 year age group is also below 100, a fact inconsistent with the sex ratios for adjacent age groups, there is the additional possibility of a significant loss through emigration. Another anomaly in the 1961 distribution may be observed for the 35–39 year age group. Undoubtedly, the sex ratio for this group would have been higher had it not been for the high male mortality associated with World War II. Beyond 40 years of age sex ratios may be expected to decline through the normal aging process, and as the mortality experiences of women become increasingly favourable compared to those for men.

The changing age-sex structure. Both the long term aging trend and recent rejuvenation of the population are visible in a comparison of the age-sex

Fig. 4:4

AGE AND SEX COMPOSITION
CANADA: 1901, 1921, 1941, 1961

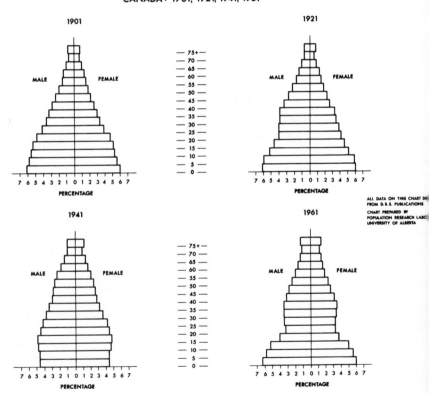

pyramids for 1901, 1921, 1941, and 1961, presented in Figure 4:4. The relatively symmetrical shape of the 1901 population pyramid becomes progressively distorted by heavy immigration of males and the bulge is still apparent in 1921, starting with the 25–29 year age group. By 1941, a further distortion appears in the truncation of lower age groups reflecting the minimal fertility, and to a lesser extent low immigration, during the 1930s. Post-World War II revival of fertility and immigration, combined with the normal aging of the deficient birth cohorts of the depression years, produced a "pinched-waist" effect in the population pyramid for 1961. As fertility again

Fig. 4:5   COMPARISON OF AGE AND SEX DISTRIBUTIONS
CENSUS AND STATIONARY POPULATIONS
CANADA: 1961 AND 1930-32

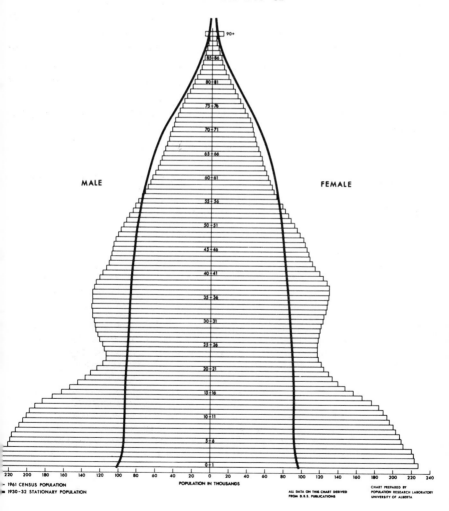

- 1961 CENSUS POPULATION
- 1930-32 STATIONARY POPULATION

POPULATION IN THOUSANDS

ALL DATA ON THIS CHART DERIVED
FROM D.B.S. PUBLICATIONS

CHART PREPARED BY
POPULATION RESEARCH LABORATORY
UNIVERSITY OF ALBERTA

declines, another narrowing of the pyramid's base will occur and the smaller cohorts will begin to move up through the age structure following the post-World War II baby boom bulge.

At this point it might be helpful to compare Canada's population in 1961 with a theoretical population that might have developed had the mortality conditions of the early 1930s continued indefinitely, net migration stabilized at zero, and fertility declined to the point where the number of births equalled the number of deaths. During the depression years, this type of population (i.e., stationary population) had more than theoretical interest as there was considerable concern over the possibility that Canada's population just might stop growing. Had this been the case and the above conditions had both developed and continued indefinitely, Canada's population would have ultimately taken on the appearance of the distribution of the hypothetical population shown in Figure 4:5. By superimposing the actual distribution of age and sex groups in 1961 over this "stationary" population, the cumulative effects of Canada's changing mortality, fertility, and migration experience can be more easily discerned. It is evident that the effects of immigration during the early 1900s have not yet passed completely through the system; and the reduced depression-year cohorts between 20 and 30 years of age are moving up through the age structure in advance of the relatively large cohorts of post-war births.

Rural-urban contrasts. Age and sex distributions for rural and urban populations in 1961 differed significantly in three respects. The first and most apparent distinction in Figure 4:6 is the larger proportion of both males and

Fig. 4:6

**AGE AND SEX COMPOSITION
URBAN AND RURAL POPULATION
CANADA: 1961**

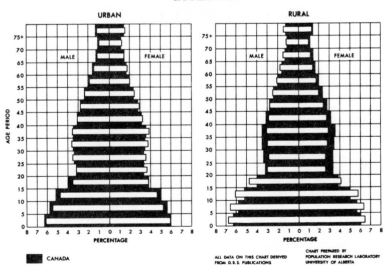

females in the age groups under 20 years residing in rural areas. Second is the relatively smaller proportions in the young labour force, ages 20–44 years, to be found in the rural population; and, third is the proportionately greater numbers of rural males in the age groups beyond 50 years in contrast to the excess of females in all age groups over 20 years which is found in urban areas. Urban population in general had relatively fewer under 20 years, more of the young labour force, and more women over 20 years than did the rural population in 1961, reflecting the fertility, mortality, and migration differentials previously described in Chapters 2 and 3.

Regional variations. Regional differences in the age-sex structure can be observed in Figure 4:7 and tend to reflect the rural-urban differences mentioned above. As might be expected, relative excesses of younger people under 20 years of age are found in the Atlantic Provinces and Quebec, and age groups under ten years in the Territories. Associated with these relatively large numbers of young people are deficiencies in proportions of the population in the older age groups, especially in the Territories. Conversely, where

Fig. 4:7

AGE AND SEX COMPOSITION
BY REGION
CANADA: 1961

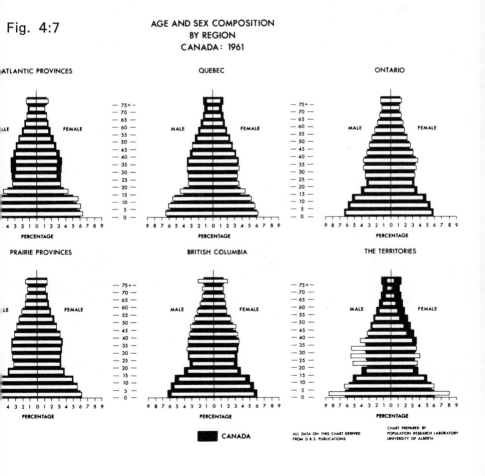

Fig. 4:8

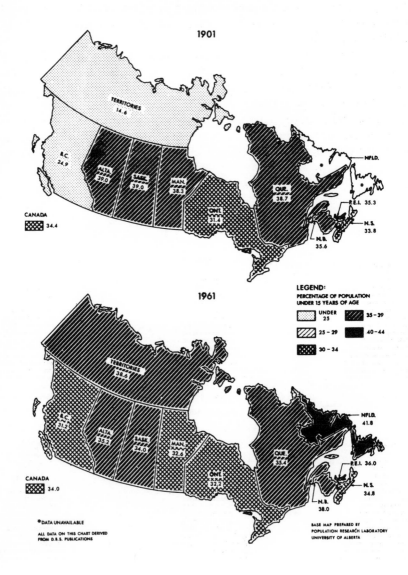

POPULATION UNDER 15 YEARS OF AGE
CANADA: 1901 AND 1961

Fig. 4:9

POPULATION 65 YEARS OF AGE AND OVER
CANADA: 1901 AND 1961

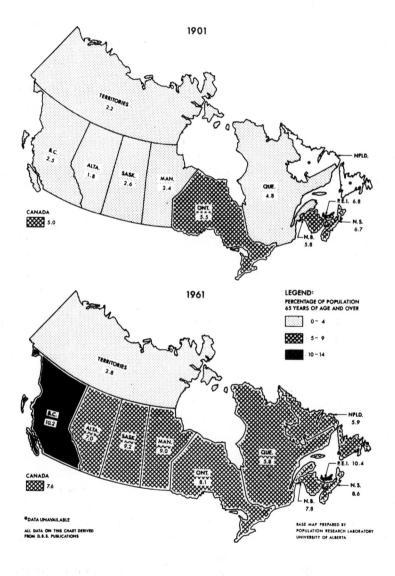

1901

1961

LEGEND:
PERCENTAGE OF POPULATION
65 YEARS OF AGE AND OVER

0 – 4

5 – 9

10 – 14

*DATA UNAVAILABLE

ALL DATA ON THIS CHART DERIVED
FROM D.B.S. PUBLICATIONS

BASE MAP PREPARED BY
POPULATION RESEARCH LABORATORY
UNIVERSITY OF ALBERTA

there are fewer young people relative to the distribution for Canada as a whole, e.g., Ontario and British Columbia, there tend to be larger than normal proportions of population in the older ages as well as the labour force age group. British Columbia is notable in this respect for its retirement population plus its older labour force population 40 years of age and over. Territorial population represents the opposite extreme of the continuum with respect to both young and old age groups, and its disproportionately high concentration of males in the young labour force ages between 20 and 40 years of age. While they also have large excesses of males in all age groups over 40 years, their size relative to the age and sex groups for Canada as a whole is not great.

Geographical shifts in relative distributions of the aged and young for provinces and territories between 1901 and 1961 are shown in Figures 4:8 and 4:9. With the exception of New Brunswick, Nova Scotia, and Prince Edward Island, all of which tended to remain the same, provinces with the highest proportions of population under 15 years of age experienced declines, while those with lower proportions increased over the 60-year period. Thus, the proportions under 15 years of age have become more uniform as fertility levels in all areas of the country have tended to converge.

The pattern of change for the older population is somewhat different. All of the provinces in 1961 showed higher proportions 65 years of age and over than in 1901 with the Territories being the only exception. Prince Edward Island still had the largest proportion of older population in 1961 with 10.4 per cent, but three western provinces had higher proportions than Nova Scotia which had ranked second in 1901. Percentage distribution for selected age groups for provinces and territories are presented in Table 4:4 for the years 1901 and 1961.

Changes in the dependent populations. Social, economic, and political consequences of changes in distributions by age and sex are extremely complex; but the most apparent are to be found in the relationship between size of the dependent populations and the labour force ages. Relatively large proportions in the labour force group compared to the dependent age groups would make the maintenance of a given standard of living or an increase much easier to achieve; however, the reverse situation would create heavier economic burdens for those who are economically active. Again, if the increasing dependent population were primarily an older population, greater conservatism could be expected in politics, economic policies, and other institutional sectors of society. On the other hand, a more rapid growth of the younger population would tend to place more emphasis on youth, i.e., its culture and values, and social change.

Canada's population 65 years of age and over has steadily increased from 4.1 per cent in 1881 to 7.7 per cent in 1966. During the same period, the

Table 4:4

PERCENTAGE DISTRIBUTION OF THE POPULATION BY BROAD AGE GROUPS, FOR CANADA AND PROVINCES, 1901 AND 1961

1901

Age Group	Canada	Nfld.	P.E.I.	N.S.	N.B.	Que.	Ont.	Man.	Sask.	Alta.	B.C.	Yukon & N.W.T.
0–14	34.4		35.3	33.8	35.6	38.7	31.4	38.3	39.0	39.0	24.9	14.6
15–44	46.7		42.4	44.1	44.1	43.5	48.1	48.3	47.5	48.5	59.2	69.9
45–64	13.9		15.5	15.3	14.5	13.0	15.0	11.0	10.9	10.7	13.4	13.3
65+	5.0		6.8	6.7	5.8	4.8	5.5	2.4	2.6	1.8	2.5	2.2
Total: Per Cent	100.0	100.0	100.0	100.0	100.0	100.0	100.0	100.0	100.0	100.0	100.0	100.0
Number (in 1,000s)	5,371		103	460	331	1,649	2,183	255	91	73	179	47

1961

Age Group	Canada	Nfld.	P.E.I.	N.S.	N.B.	Que.	Ont.	Man.	Sask.	Alta.	B.C.	Yukon & N.W.T.
0–14	34.0	41.8	36.0	34.8	38.0	35.4	32.2	32.6	34.0	35.2	31.3	38.6
15–44	41.1	38.3	36.0	39.4	38.2	42.6	41.3	39.9	39.0	41.6	39.6	46.5
45–64	17.4	14.0	17.5	17.2	16.0	16.2	18.4	18.5	17.8	16.2	18.9	11.9
65+	7.6	5.9	10.4	8.6	7.8	5.8	8.1	9.0	9.2	7.0	10.2	2.8
Total: Per Cent	100.0	100.0	100.0	100.0	100.0	100.0	100.0	100.0	100.0	100.0	100.0	100.0
Number (in 1,000s)	18,238	458	105	737	598	5,259	6,236	922	925	1,332	1,629	38

SOURCE: Dominion Bureau of Statistics, *1961 Census of Canada*, Bulletin 7:1-4, Ottawa, The Queen's Printer, 1964, Table 2.

Table 4:5

YOUNG, OLD, AND TOTAL DEPENDENCY RATIOS, CANADA: 1881–1966[a]

Year	Young Dependency Ratio (0-14)÷(15-64)	Old Dependency Ratio (65+)÷(15-64)	Total Dependency Ratio [(0-14)+(65+)]÷(15-64)
1881	67.7	7.2	74.9
1891	61.5	7.7	69.2
1901	56.8	8.3	65.1
1911	52.9	7.5	60.3
1921	56.6	7.9	64.4
1931	50.3	8.8	59.2
1941	42.4	10.2	52.6
1951	48.5 (49.0)[b]	12.5 (12.5)[b]	61.0 (61.5)[b]
1961	57.6 (58.1)[b]	13.1 (13.1)[b]	70.7 (71.2)[b]
1966	55.0 (55.5)[b]	13.0 (13.0)[b]	68.0 (68.4)[b]

SOURCE: Dominion Bureau of Statistics, *1961 Census of Canada*, Bulletin 7:1-4, Ottawa, The Queen's Printer, 1964; *1966 Census of Canada*, Vol. 1 (1-10), Ottawa, The Queen's Printer, 1968.
[a] Excludes Newfoundland in 1951, 1961, and 1966.
[b] Includes Newfoundland.

proportion under 15 years declined from 38.7 to a low of 27.8 per cent in 1941 before post-war fertility reversed the trend and pushed the proportion back up to 33.0 per cent in 1966. Together, these two dependent groups constituted 40.7 per cent of Canada's total population. More meaningful is the dependency ratio which relates the dependent population to the more economically active age group 15–64 years, rather than to the total population. Such ratios are presented in Table 4:5. These data indicate that the total dependency burden was lowest in Canada in 1941 at the end of the depression era, and relatively high during the post-World War II period at a time when economic activity and productivity were also high.

Dependency ratios based on Canada's total population obscure one very important problem. When these ratios are calculated for rural and urban populations, it becomes apparent that the areas having the highest "young" dependency ratios are the rural areas which are least industrialized and tend to have the smallest tax base. In 1966, the dependency ratio for Canada's combined rural population was 81.5 compared to 64.2 for its urban population. Within rural areas, the rural non-farm population had the highest dependency ratios as may be seen in Table 4:6. This population, with its abundance of children, tends to be located in the newly developing suburbs outside the established urban centres where new and relatively inexpensive housing is in greatest supply, and the need for new and extended institutional facilities and services is greatest. Again, the lack of industry in these areas tends to shift most the tax burden required to provide these services to a relatively small proportion of economically active persons.

Table 4:6

DEPENDENCY RATIOS FOR RURAL AND URBAN POPULATIONS,
CANADA: 1966

Locality	Young Dependency Ratios	Old Dependency Ratios	Total Dependency Ratios
Urban	51.7	12.5	64.2
Rural	67.2	14.3	81.5
Rural farm	64.4	11.2	75.6
Rural non-farm	68.8	16.2	85.0
Canada	55.5	13.0	68.4

SOURCE: Dominion Bureau of Statistics, *1966 Census of Canada*, Vol. 1 (1-10), Ottawa, The Queen's Printer, 1968.

Aging of the population. In discussing "aging", attention is generally focused on changes which have been occurring in the older population, i.e., those 65 years of age and over. The number of persons 65 years of age and over increased from approximately 178,000 in 1881 to 1,540,000 in 1966. However, growth in absolute numbers, while important in itself, does not take into consideration changes occurring in other age groups which determine whether or not the population as a whole is growing younger or older. Declining mortality, coupled with immigration during the pre-World War II years, contributed to increasing proportions of older persons as did declining fertility. A resumption of immigration of young adults following World War II combined with the post-war baby boom to arrest the aging process as the median age declined from 27.8 years in 1951 to 25.6 years in 1966, and the proportion 65 years and over declined from 7.8 per cent to 7.7.

The United Nations uses the proportion 65 years of age and over as an index of aging, classifying populations as young, mature, or aged depending upon their proportion in this age group.[2] A population is classified as "young" if the proportion is under 4 per cent, as "mature" if between 4 and 8 per cent, and "aged" if 8 per cent or over. Using this criterion, Canada has shifted from an *early mature* population in 1881 when 4.1 per cent of its population was 65 years of age and over, to a *late mature* population in 1966 when this group constituted 7.7 per cent of the total. During this same period, the female population made the transition from a young to an aged population increasing from 3.9 per cent 65 years and over in 1881 to 8.3 per cent in 1966. Further improvements in mortality will no doubt contribute to a further aging of the population, but far more important will be a continuation of the decline in total fertility which began after the post-war peak was achieved in 1959.

REFERENCES

Dominion Bureau of Statistics: *1961 Census of Canada. General Review: Age and Sex Composition*. Bulletin 7:1–4, Ottawa, The Queen's Printer, 1964.

Riley, Matilda W. and Anne Foner: *Aging and Society. Vol. One: An Inventory of Research Findings*. New York, Russell Sage Foundation, 1968.

United Nations, Department of Economic and Social Affairs: *The Aging of Populations and its Economic and Social Implications*, New York, United Nations, 1956.

FOOTNOTES

[1]Excluding Newfoundland.

[2]United Nations, *The Aging of Populations and the Economic and Social Implications*, New York, United Nations, 1956, p. 7.

Native- and Foreign-Born Populations

The North American wilderness that is now Canada was inhabited by an estimated 200,000 Native Indians when the Europeans first began their invasion. In the early years, migration from Europe had to exceed the heavy losses through mortality or the first settlements would have died out before the early settlers could establish a permanent foothold. In spite of the physical hardships, epidemics, and periodic shortages of food, the balance was clearly in favour of the Europeans for they continued to increase in numbers and expand their bridgeheads in the New World. Their presence, as well as their activities, exposed the Native Indians to diseases against which they had little immunity, contributed to the scarcity of their natural food supply, and otherwise generated excess mortality by involving them in sporadic hostilities. While the European settlements continued to grow through a combination of immigration and high fertility, the Indians were increasingly threatened with extinction. The full tragedy of the Native Indian in Canada is almost obscured by the observation that as late as the mid-twentieth century there were fewer Indians than when the white man had first arrived. However, their numbers had begun to increase during the 1930s and by 1961 the census reported 220,121 Native Indians and Eskimos living in Canada. In 1965, their annual rate of increase was estimated to be over three per cent.[1] Ironically, it was the white man's medicine that probably saved them from extinction while at the same time confronting them with new problems arising from their phenomenal growth rate. In spite of this demographic revival, they constituted only 1.2 per cent of Canada's population in 1961. Because of their relatively small numbers, the Native Indian and Eskimo populations are not treated separately in this chapter. Most will be included in the larger category of "native born" which includes all persons born in Canada. All those born outside Canada, regardless of the nativity of their parents, are treated as part of the foreign-born population.

Once the European immigrant had become established in Canada, the native-born component of the population, i.e., persons born in Canada, tended to grow at a faster rate by means of natural increase than the foreign-born population which could increase only as long as immigration exceeded losses through mortality. As early as 1851, the native-born population was more than four times as large as the foreign born; and just four years after Confederation they were approximately five times as large—partly as a result of considerable emigration by foreign born to the United States during the preceding decade. This tendency for the native born to increase at a faster rate reduced the proportion of foreign-born population to a low of 12.9 per cent by 1901. However, the record immigration of the 1901–11 decade boosted their proportion to 22.0 per cent in 1911 and slightly higher for the following two decades, as may be seen in Figure 5:1. The depression decade reversed this trend and the number of foreign born actually decreased from 2,308,000 to 2,019,000. Even though the aftermath of World War II produced a slight increase in foreign born by 1951, it took the heavy immigration of the 1951–61 decade to again produce a significant increase in their rate of

Fig. 5:1

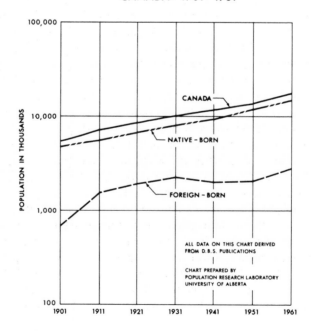

POPULATION TRENDS
NATIVE AND FOREIGN BORN
CANADA: 1901–1961

Table 5:1

GROWTH OF FOREIGN- AND NATIVE-BORN
POPULATION, CANADA, 1851–1961

Year	Total	Foreign Born	Native Born	Per Cent Foreign Born
1851	2,436,000	460,000	1,976,000	18.9
1861	3,230,000	683,000	2,547,000	21.1
1871	3,605,000	602,000	3,003,000	16.7
1881	4,325,000	603,000	3,722,000	13.9
1891	4,833,000	644,000	4,189,000	13.3
1901	5,371,000	700,000	4,672,000	13.0
1911	7,207,000	1,587,000	5,620,000	22.0
1921	8,788,000	1,956,000	6,832,000	22.3
1931	10,377,000	2,308,000	8,069,000	22.2
1941	11,507,000	2,019,000	9,488,000	17.5
1951	14,009,000	2,060,000	11,950,000	14.7
1961	18,238,000	2,844,000	15,394,000	15.6

SOURCE: Dominion Bureau of Statistics, Censuses of Canada, 1851 to 1961.
Note: All figures rounded to the nearest 1,000.

growth. Data in Table 5:1 show that there was just one other period prior to the depression of the 1930s during which the number of foreign born actually declined. This seems to have been the consequence of considerable emigration to the United States which occurred during the economically and politically unsettled decade of Confederation.

The foreign born constituted 15.6 per cent of the population in 1961; but even though the Immigration Act of 1962 removed most of the ethnic and racial restrictions, it is doubtful that immigration will ever again produce the relative increase in foreign born that it did during the 1901–11 decade. The foreign-born population will continue to grow only to the extent that Canada is successful in attracting sufficient numbers of skilled workers and their families to offset losses through emigration and mortality. Past experience would indicate that this situation will be possible only as long as Canada's economy continues to show healthy growth.

Sex Ratios

The source of Canada's relatively high sex ratios, previously discussed in

Fig. 5:2

**SEX RATIO TRENDS
NATIVE AND FOREIGN BORN
CANADA: 1901–1961**

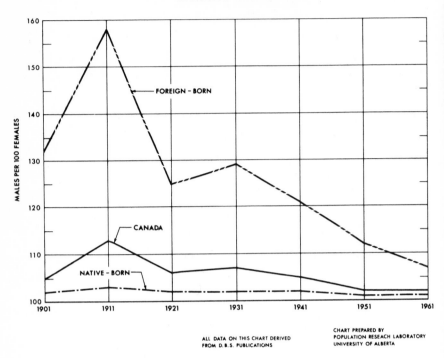

ALL DATA ON THIS CHART DERIVED
FROM D.B.S. PUBLICATIONS

CHART PREPARED BY
POPULATION RESEACH LABORATORY
UNIVERSITY OF ALBERTA

Chapter 4, is clearly evident in Figure 5:2. The heavy immigration of foreign born during the early twentieth century had the excess of males typical of long distance migrations. Since the sex ratios for native born changed very little during this 60-year period, most of the variation observed in the total population was due to changes in the distribution of males and females among the foreign born. Immigration during the 1901–11 decade boosted the sex ratio of resident foreign born from 132 in 1901 to 158 in 1911. Thereafter, it decreased rather rapidly, reaching a low of 107 in 1961. Changes in mortality increasingly favoured the longer survival of women; and other changes occurred to make the social, psychological, and economic costs of traveling long distances less of an obstacle for women.

An approximation of the extent of differences in sex ratios of immigrants over time and by place of origin can be obtained by looking at sex ratios of the most recent immigrants still resident in Canada at the time of any specific census. To illustrate, data are presented in Table 5:2 for foreign-born residents of Canada in 1931 and 1961 who had immigrated to this country during the preceding decades. The temporal decline in excess males is apparent during this 30-year period, but more interesting is the variation exhibited by

Table 5:2

SEX RATIOS FOR IMMIGRANTS OF THE 1921–1931 DECADE AT
THE 1931 CENSUS AND FOR THE 1951–1961 DECADE AT THE
1961 CENSUS BY SELECTED BIRTHPLACES, CANADA

Birthplace	Sex Ratio for Immigrants, 1921–1931a at 1931 Census	Sex Ratio for Immigrants, 1951–1961a at 1961 Census
Total	133	109
United Kingdom	114	97
Other Commonwealth Countries	97	105
United States	98	90
European countries	169	116
Austria	172	107
Czechoslovakia	317	128
Finland	155	100
France	97	107
Germany	181	106
Italy	138	117
Netherlands	190	116
Poland	149	114
Scandinavian countries	268	129
U.S.S.R.	113	113
Other	200	127
Asiatic countries	180	99
China	700	98
Japan	85	61
Other	87	110
Other countries	110	100

SOURCE: Dominion Bureau of Statistics, *1961 Census of Canada,* Bulletin 7:1-7, Ottawa,
The Queen's Printer, 1965, Table VI. page 7-14.
a Includes the first five months only of 1931 and 1961.

country of birth. Those with the highest sex ratios were those born in China,
700 males per 100 females, followed by Czechoslovakia with 317, Scandinavian countries with 268, and the residual category of "other European"
countries with a sex ratio of 200. Both the Netherlands and Germany also
had high sex ratios of 190 and 181 respectively, compared to the average of
133 for all birthplaces combined. By 1960, most of these had declined
significantly, but Scandinavians and Czechoslovaks were still highest with
sex ratios of 129 and 128 respectively, again followed by "other European"
with 127. The extreme excess of males among Chinese immigrants had given
way to a deficiency of males as the older surviving coolie labourers who had
worked at building the railroads died and the younger immigrants, who had
become established, were able to bring their wives and other dependents to
Canada. Sex ratios for those born in the United Kingdom declined from 114

to 97, while the deficiency of males among immigrants from the United States in 1931 continued to increase with ratios dropping from 98 to 90 by 1961. Changes in the sex ratios of immigrants from these two latter sources were particularly important insofar as they had supplied the major proportion of immigrants arriving in Canada for many years.

Age Structure

The foreign-born population ages rather quickly if the flow of immigrants is either stopped or significantly reduced. Since the offspring of foreign born are by definition native born, a continuing flow of immigrants is the only means of assuring that losses in the younger age groups through the normal aging process will be replaced. The population age-sex structure depicted in Figure 5:3 clearly shows the impact of variations in immigration and emigration on the age-sex distribution of foreign born. Note, for example, the heavy concentration in 1921 of males in the working force ages over 25 years resulting from heavy immigration during the two preceding decades. With virtual cessation of immigration in the 1930s, the proportion of foreign born below age 30 in 1941 was relatively insignificant. The impact of post-war immigration on the age-sex structure of the foreign born is again easily visible in 1961 as the influx of young immigrants increased the proportions in the young adult ages at the expense of the older age-sex groups.

Shifts in the age structure for both native- and foreign-born populations

Fig. 5:3

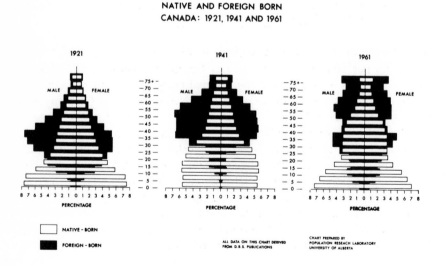

AGE AND SEX COMPOSITION
NATIVE AND FOREIGN BORN
CANADA: 1921, 1941 AND 1961

Table 5:3

MEDIAN AGE OF FOREIGN- AND NATIVE-BORN POPULATIONS, CANADA, 1921–1961[a]

Year	Foreign Born	Native Born	Total
1921	34.7	19.4	23.9
1931	38.6	19.8	24.7
1941	46.5	22.8	27.0
1951	50.2	23.9	27.7
1961	44.8	22.2	26.3

SOURCE: Censuses of Canada, 1921 to 1961.
[a] Includes Newfoundland in 1951 and 1961.

shown in Figure 5:3 are summarized in Table 5:3 which gives median ages by decades from 1921 to 1961. The foreign born "aged" by 11.8 years between 1921 and 1941, a period including the minimal migration of the depression, and "younged" to the extent of 1.7 years as a result of heavy post-war immigration. The native born also aged, but as a consequence of declining fertility rather than immigration. Not until the end of the 1951–61 decade did high post-war fertility offset this trend and produce a decline in the median age. However, the native-born population also showed a net aging over the entire 40-year period as their median age increased by 2.8 years.

Being a simple summary measure, the median fails to reveal some of the significant changes occurring within the age distribution during this period. Data presented in Table 5:4 for broad age groups allow a more precise determination of these internal changes, particularly those relating to the young and old labour force age groups. Since 1921, the proportion of native born in the young labour force, i.e., those 15–44 years of age, has never been less than 40.3 per cent nor more than 47.6 per cent, and in 1961 was not much different than in 1921. Similarly, the proportion in the older working ages, 45–64 years, changed very little during this same period, increasing from 13.4 to 14.9 per cent. In contrast, the foreign born in the 15–44 year age group comprised 64.4 per cent of the total in 1921, but had declined by almost one-half to 33.1 per cent in 1951 as a result of minimal immigration during the depression years. Revival of immigration during the 1951–61 decade and the influx of young working-age adults reversed this decline by boosting their proportion to 40.9 per cent by 1961. Also interesting is the fact that the older age group increased from 20.5 per cent in 1921 until it actually exceeded the proportion in the 15–44 year age group, reaching 43.0 per cent by 1951. Only the heavy immigration of younger working-age adults during the 1951–61 decade managed to reduce this proportion to 30.7 per cent. As for the retirement-age population, both native and foreign born

Table 5:4

PERCENTAGE AGE DISTRIBUTIONS FOR NATIVE- AND FOREIGN-BORN POPULATIONS, CANADA, 1921–1961

Age Group	1921	1931	1941	1951	1961
Native Born					
Under 15	41.5	38.8	33.2	34.8	38.5
15–44	40.3	42.6	47.6	46.1	41.1
45–64	13.4	13.4	13.7	13.4	14.9
65 and over	4.6	5.2	5.6	5.8	5.5
Total	100.0	100.0	100.0	100.0	100.0
Foreign Born					
Under 15	9.5	6.6	2.5	4.7	9.5
15–44	64.4	58.3	44.0	33.1	40.9
45–64	20.5	28.4	41.7	43.0	30.7
65 and over	5.5	6.7	11.8	19.2	19.0
Total	100.0	100.0	100.0	100.0	100.0

SOURCE: Dominion Bureau of Statistics, *1961 Census of Canada*, Bulletin 7:1-7, Ottawa, The Queen's Printer, 1965, Table VIII, p. 7-16.

experienced relative increases in population 65 years and over. However, the increase for the foreign born was far more significant. If the high level of immigration during the 1951–61 decade is not maintained during the next decade or two, a heavier concentration of the foreign born can be expected in the older age groups as the resident population continues to age.

Age distributions for foreign born by place of birth also show significant variations for the selected birthplaces shown in Table 5:5. These variations reflect both differences in period of maximum immigration and age at which migration tends to occur from particular geographic regions. Thus, if the period of heaviest immigration for a particular group occurred during the early twentieth century, it will tend to have larger proportions among the older age groups than will those foreign born from another area whose migration has been primarily a post-World War II phenomenon. Foreign populations born in the United Kingdom, United States, and Scandinavia are representative of the former while those born in Germany and Italy are more representative of the latter situation. For the U.S.S.R., the high proportion over 45 years of age reflects both a diminution of earlier immigration plus a rather high age for immigrants following World War II as many established professional people fled their homeland as political refugees. The very high proportion from "other countries" below the age of 15 years suggests that those coming from areas outside Europe, Asia, Commonwealth countries, and the United States tended to be almost as fertile as native-born Canadians. The proportion of this group 65 years of age and over, as well as for those

Table 5:5

PERCENTAGE AGE DISTRIBUTION FOR FOREIGN-BORN POPULATIONS
BY SELECTED BIRTHPLACES, CANADA, 1961

Birthplace	Age				
	Total	0–14	15–44	45–64	65+
United Kingdom and Commonwealth	100.0	7.3	32.7	32.8	27.2
United States	100.0	9.4	27.3	39.3	24.0
Europe	100.0	10.6	49.0	28.1	12.3
Germany	100.0	20.7	59.5	15.4	4.4
Italy	100.0	16.1	61.8	16.6	5.7
Poland	100.0	1.8	41.1	43.8	13.3
Scandinavia	100.0	9.0	30.6	34.1	26.3
U.S.S.R.	100.0	0.3	30.9	44.3	24.6
Other	100.0	11.0	50.5	26.5	11.9
Asia	100.0	10.5	42.0	25.9	21.7
Other Countries	100.0	32.9	50.6	12.3	4.0

SOURCE: Dominion Bureau of Statistics, *1961 Census of Canada*, Bulletin 7:1-7, Ottawa, The Queen's Printer, 1965, Table IX, p. 7-17.

born in Germany and Italy, will increase if their volume of immigration declines or the age of more recent immigrants from these areas increases; and it may well do so if the foreign born from these areas begin to bring their older parents and relatives to Canada.

Regional Variations from 1901 to 1961

Native-born and foreign-born populations have had significantly different regional distributions and patterns of change between 1901 and 1961. Perhaps the most striking feature of the distribution of native born has been the similarity in Ontario and Quebec's proportionate share since 1911. In 1901, Ontario possessed a slight edge over Quebec with 39.8 per cent compared to 33.4 per cent for Quebec. This difference gradually declined until 1931, after which their proportions have remained approximately equal. The other notable aspect of the data in Table 5:6 is the decline in the Maritime Provinces' share of Canada's native born as a result of out-migration and increase for both British Columbia and the Prairie Provinces. Whereas British Columbia's share of native born increased consistently throughout this period, the Prairie Provinces reached their peak in 1931 and thereafter have suffered losses through out-migration to the more rapidly industrializing areas. Prior to 1921, the Maritime Provinces actually had exceeded the Prairie Provinces; but by the time of the 1921 Census the shift of native born to the West had

Table 5:6   POPULATION OF CANADA BY NATIVITY AND REGIONS, 1901 TO 1961

Nativity and Region	1901	1911	1921	1931	1941	1951[a]	1961[a]
Native Born							
Atlantic Provinces	18.1	15.7	13.7	11.6	11.2	13.1	11.9
Quebec	33.4	33.0	31.8	32.5	32.8	32.0	31.6
Ontario	39.8	35.9	33.5	32.6	32.2	31.4	31.7
Prairie Provinces	6.0	12.0	17.0	18.5	18.2	16.4	16.7
British Columbia	2.1	3.0	3.9	4.6	5.4	6.9	7.8
Yukon and N.W.T.	0.6	0.4	0.1	0.2	0.2	0.2	0.2
Total:							
Per Cent	100.0	100.0	100.0	100.0	100.0	100.0	100.0
Number (1,000s)	4,672	5,620	6,832	8,069	9,488	11,950	15,394
Foreign Born							
Atlantic Provinces	6.7	3.6	3.4	3.0	3.2	2.7	2.3
Quebec	12.7	9.2	9.7	10.9	11.1	11.1	13.6
Ontario	46.3	32.0	32.8	34.9	36.3	41.2	47.6
Prairie Provinces	20.3	40.8	40.7	37.3	34.2	28.4	21.4
British Columbia	11.3	14.1	13.3	13.8	15.1	16.5	14.9
Yukon and N.W.T.	2.7	0.3	0.1	0.1	0.1	0.1	0.2
Total:							
Per Cent	100.0	100.0	100.0	100.0	100.0	100.0	100.0
Number (1,000s)	700	1,587	1,956	2,308	2,019	2,060	2,844

SOURCE: Dominion Bureau of Statistics, Censuses of Canada, 1901 to 1961.
[a] Includes Newfoundland in 1951 and 1961.

brought about a significant change in their pattern of distribution. By 1961, Canada's West had almost one-quarter of the native born compared to just under twelve per cent for the three original Maritime Provinces.

For the foreign born, the most important trend has been the decline from the dominant position of the Prairie Provinces in 1911 during the peak of the agricultural development of the West, and the ascendency of Ontario as the area of residence for almost half of all foreign born as it became the focal point of industrialization during the post-World War II period. In 1911, 55.2 per cent of all foreign born were located in the West and North with just under one-third in Ontario. By 1941, Ontario, with 36.3 per cent, exceeded the proportion in the Prairies, but not until 1961 did its share of foreign born exceed the combined proportions living in the West and North. The only other region showing a consistent increase in its share of foreign born since 1911 was Quebec. As may be seen in Table 5:6, the proportion for Quebec increased from 9.2 to 13.6 per cent in 1961. It would seem quite likely that if the 1951–61 trend were to continue, Quebec's proportion of foreign born would soon surpass that of British Columbia. These trends are summarized in Figure 5:4.

The proportionate distribution of population by region is not the only criterion of significance. For example, two regions may have approximately the same proportionate share of total foreign born, as was the case for Ontario

Fig. 5:4

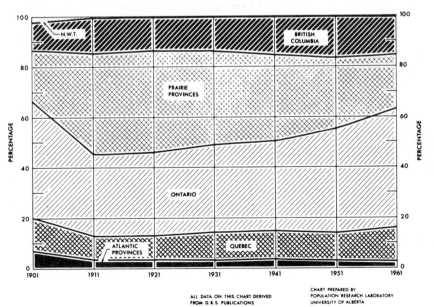

FOREIGN BORN POPULATION
BY REGION, CANADA: 1901 – 1961

ALL DATA ON THIS CHART DERIVED
FROM D.B.S. PUBLICATIONS

CHART PREPARED BY
POPULATION RESEARCH LABORATORY
UNIVERSITY OF ALBERTA

and the Prairie Provinces in 1941; yet the foreign born in one region may constitute a significantly smaller proportion of its total population than the other. As an illustration, Ontario actually had more foreign born than the Prairie Provinces in 1941 and again in 1951, as may be seen in Table 5:7. However, the foreign born constituted only 19.4 and 18.5 per cent of its population compared to 28.5 and 22.9 per cent of the total Prairie population for these same two years. In other words, while numerically larger, the foreign born in Ontario represented a significantly smaller share of their regional population than was the case in the Prairies. The proportion of foreign born in Ontario's population did not actually exceed the proportion for the Prairies until 1961 when it reached 21.7 per cent as compared to 19.1 per cent for the latter. Nevertheless, there have always been enough foreign born in Ontario to create a demand for special ethnic institutions even though their cultural impact on the total population might not have been as great as in the Prairies. Shifts in concentration of foreign born relative to their total regional populations at four different periods in time between 1901 and 1961 may be seen in Figure 5:5. The most apparent feature is the decline in the heavy concentrations of foreign born found in Canada's West and the Yukon which occurred as the primary receiving area for immigrants and internal migrants shifted to the industrial areas of Ontario. The contrast between 1901 and 1961 is most striking.

The rate of growth of foreign born for the major regions, like that for Canada, has not been constant over time. From the decade growth rates presented in Table 5:8, it may be seen that the maximum growth experienced by Canada during the 1901–11 decade was due to settlement of the Prairies and the Far West. During the following decade, the Prairies increased at about the same rate as for Canada as a whole; but, from that point on, its growth rate was less favourable as population growth responded more directly to the rate of industrial growth in Ontario and Quebec and economic development in the North.

The economic depression of the 1930s hit the foreign-born populations in all areas, but hardest in the Prairies and Quebec. Both the Prairie and Maritime regions continued to lose population during the 1941–51 decade, possibly as a result of the urban-centred economic boom triggered by World War II. Growth rates since 1941 show very clearly why Ontario has become the primary region of residence for the foreign born, and Quebec's rapid increase during 1951–61 suggests why Quebec may easily surpass British Columbia in number of foreign born by 1971, or soon after.

Table 5:7
NUMBER OF FOREIGN BORN AND PERCENTAGE OF THE POPULATION FOREIGN BORN, CANADA'S REGIONS, 1901–1961

Region	1901	1911	1921	1931	1941	1951	1961
				(Number[b])			
Atlantic Provinces[a]	46,600	57,200	67,300	69,000	63,800	55,000	66,700
Quebec	88,700	146,500	188,600	251,700	223,900	228,900	388,400
Ontario	324,200	507,800	641,700	804,300	733,300	850,000	1,353,200
Prairie Provinces	141,800	646,900	795,400	860,900	690,900	584,200	608,100
British Columbia	79,000	223,200	260,500	319,500	304,700	339,200	423,100
Territories	19,200	5,400	1,800	2,100	2,200	2,700	4,700
			(Per Cent of Regional Population)				
Atlantic Provinces[a]	5.2	6.1	6.7	6.8	5.6	3.4	3.5
Quebec	5.4	7.3	8.0	8.8	6.7	5.6	7.4
Ontario	14.8	20.1	22.0	23.4	19.4	18.5	21.7
Prairie Provinces	24.2	48.9	20.7	36.6	28.5	22.9	19.1
British Columbia	44.2	56.9	49.7	46.0	37.3	29.1	26.0
Territories	36.5	20.0	14.5	15.1	13.3	10.6	12.4

SOURCE: Dominion Bureau of Statistics, Censuses of Canada, 1901 to 1961.
a Includes Newfoundland in 1951 and 1961.
b All figures rounded to the nearest 100.

Fig. 5:5

FOREIGN BORN POPULATION BY PROVINCE
CANADA: 1901, 1921, 1941 AND 1961

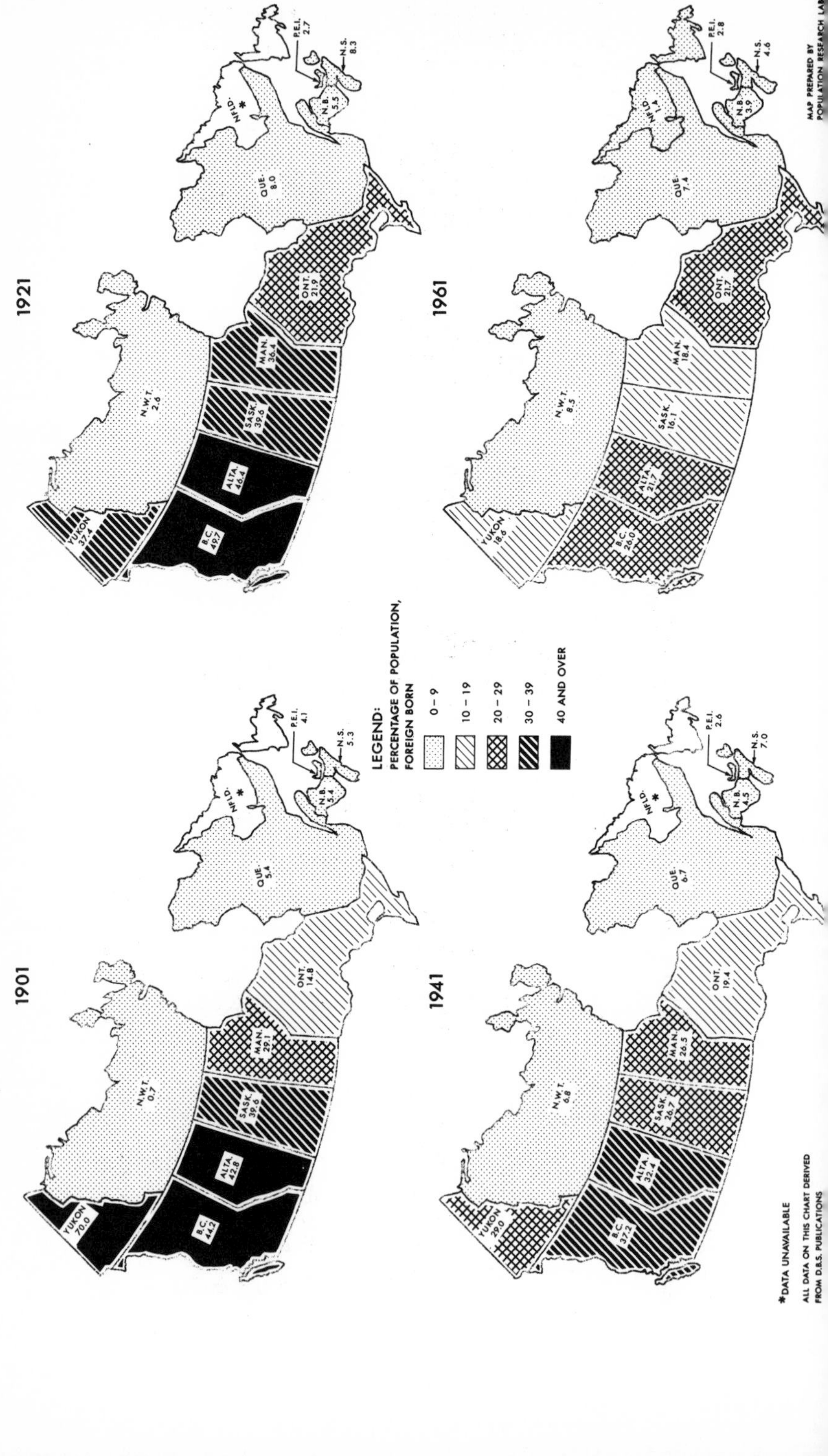

1901

1921

1941

1961

LEGEND:
PERCENTAGE OF POPULATION,
FOREIGN BORN

0 – 9

10 – 19

20 – 29

30 – 39

40 AND OVER

MAP PREPARED BY
POPULATION RESEARCH LABORATORY

*DATA UNAVAILABLE

ALL DATA ON THIS CHART DERIVED
FROM D.B.S. PUBLICATIONS

Table 5:8

PERCENTAGE INCREASE IN FOREIGN BORN BY DECADES
FOR CANADA AND REGIONS, 1901–1961

Region	Decade					
	1901–1911	1911–1921	1921–1931	1931–1941	1941–1951	1951–1961
Canada	126.9	23.2	18.0	−12.5	2.0[a]	38.1[a]
Atlantic Provinces	22.7	17.8	2.5	−7.6	−13.8[a]	21.4[a]
Quebec	65.2	28.7	33.5	−11.0	2.2	69.7
Ontario	56.7	26.4	25.3	−8.8	15.9	59.2
Prairie Provinces	356.3	23.0	8.2	−19.8	−15.4	4.1
British Columbia	182.3	16.8	22.6	−4.6	11.3	24.8
Territories	−72.0	−67.2	19.7	6.4	19.0	75.0

SOURCE: Dominion Bureau of Statistics, Censuses of Canada, 1901 to 1961.
[a] Includes Newfoundland. Excluding Newfoundland, percentage increases are 1.8 and 38.0 for Canada in 1941–51 and 1951–61 respectively. For Atlantic Provinces, percentage increases are −19.8 and 18.2 for 1941–51 and 1951–61 respectively.

Rural-urban Distribution

The settlement of agricultural lands in the West, involving the disproportionate numbers of foreign born that it did, suggests that the foreign-born population would be heavily concentrated in rural areas. Perhaps this was true for the earlier decades following Confederation and the first two decades of the twentieth century, when 62.5 per cent of the total population in 1901, and 54.6 per cent in 1911, were still living outside incorporated areas. However, by 1921, when data showing nativity of the population by rural and urban areas were published, 56.4 per cent of the foreign born were already living in urban areas compared to 47.6 per cent of native born. Between 1921 and 1941, the proportion of foreign born residing in urban places increased and continued to exceed the proportions of native born similarly classified, as may be seen in Table 5:9. Definitional changes made in 1951 and 1961 do not invalidate native- and foreign-born comparisons for these years, and the data show that not only was a greater share of the foreign born to be found in urban areas during the more recent periods, but that the differences in percentage points has been increasing. According to the 1961 Census definition, 81.4 per cent of the foreign born were urban compared to just slightly more than two-thirds of the native born.

Evidence of the greater tendency among the most recent immigrants to settle in urban areas is also found by comparing the residence of those foreign born who immigrated to Canada during the five years preceding a given

Table 5:9

PER CENT URBAN[a] FOR FOREIGN- AND NATIVE-BORN POPULATIONS
IN CANADA, 1921–1961

Year	Foreign Born	Native Born	Total
1921	56.4	47.6	49.5
1931	59.9	52.0	53.7
1941	60.5	53.0	54.3
1951	71.0	60.0	61.6
1961	81.4	67.5	69.6

SOURCE: Dominion Bureau of Statistics, Censuses of Canada, 1921 to 1961.
    [a] See the discussion of definitional changes in Chapter 3, Footnote 15.

census with the total foreign born. For example, in 1941, 62.0 per cent of the most recent immigrants were living in urban areas compared to 60.5 per cent for the total foreign born. In 1951 and 1961, the percentages were 73.9 and 89.2 per cent compared to 71.0 and 81.4 per cent for total foreign born respectively. Again, the differences are greater as one proceeds from 1941 to 1961. It would appear that the most recent foreign-born immigrant is able to respond more quickly to new employment opportunities resulting from continuing urbanization and industrialization than is the native born with an established residence in Canada. By virtue of being foreign born and a recent immigrant, the move to Canada was most likely directly influenced by current economic conditions. The "intended" destination would then tend to reflect the immigrant's perception of the areas with the greatest economic opportunities. That the immigrant's greatest opportunities now lie in the largest urban centres seems apparent from an examination of Table 5:10 if one concedes that his area of residence reflects "perceived" opportunities and that the latter are not much different from "real" opportunities. Sixty-eight per cent of all post-war immigrants were living in urban centres of 100,000 or more compared to 61.1 per cent for all foreign born and 40.2 per cent of the native born.

As in the past, both the sensitivity of immigration policy to changing economic conditions along with its implementation will continue to play a significant role in the selection of immigrants with skills most in demand by the economy. As long as immigration is used as an instant source of specialized labour for a highly urbanized and industrialized society, a greater concentration of immigrants in urban areas can be expected in the future. Perhaps this discussion might raise the question as to why the government has not encouraged the movement of native born (as well as the foreign born from abroad) from economically depressed regions to the rapidly developing areas within Canada. Of course, this would require much more than the

Table 5:10

PERCENTAGE DISTRIBUTION OF NATIVE AND FOREIGN-BORN POPULATION BY TYPE OF RURAL AND URBAN RESIDENCE, CANADA, 1961

Locality	Total	Native Born	Foreign Born	
			Total	Post-war Immigrants
Rural Farm	11.4	12.1	7.3	4.6
Rural Non-Farm	19.0	20.4	11.3	9.0
Urban under 10,000	11.1	11.8	7.5	6.2
10,000–29,999	5.8	6.0	4.3	3.7
30,000–99,999	9.3	9.5	8.5	8.4
100,000 and over	43.4	40.2	61.1	68.1
Total: Per Cent	100.0	100.0	100.0	100.0
Number (in 1,000s)	18,238	15,394	2,844	1,507

SOURCE: Dominion Bureau of Statistics, *1961 Census of Canada*, Bulletin 1:2-7, Ottawa, The Queen's Printer, 1963, Table 50, p. 50-1; and Bulletin 7:1-7, Ottawa, The Queen's Printer, 1965, Table X, p. 7-18.

provision of assistance with transportation costs that many foreign immigrants have received. The native born would probably need considerable retraining to acquire those particular skills in demand, as well as increased incentives to encourage the native born to migrate.

REFERENCES

Dominion Bureau of Statistics: *1961 Census of Canada. General Review: Native and Foreign Born Populations.* Bulletin 7:1–7. Ottawa, The Queen's Printer, 1965.

Hurd, W. B.: *Ethnic Origin and Nativity of the Canadian People.* 1941 Census Monograph. Ottawa, The Queen's Printer, 1965.

Kalbach, W. E.: *The Impact of Immigration on Canada's Population.* 1961 Census Monograph. Ottawa, The Queen's Printer, 1970.

FOOTNOTES

[1]Dominion Bureau of Statistics, *1967 Canada Year Book*, Table 14, p. 197.

Ethnicity and Race

An understanding of Canada's culture and its uniqueness as a society must be sought in the cultural heritage of its founders and their descendants, as well as in the contributions made by the thousands of immigrants who followed and joined the struggle to tame a vast and formidable environment. Historically, Canada has been bicultural and bilingual, a fact of life representing an early accommodation between the entrenched French and the politically-dominant British. Had immigration continued to draw only from these two primary cultural pools, the complexion of Canadian society would perhaps be somewhat simpler than it now appears.

Migrant streams from countries of diverse cultures are rapidly approaching a size which might conceivably challenge the long established primacy of biculturalism. Canada's policy has traditionally been oriented towards encouraging the migration of those people who are most similar to resident Canadians and who would have the least difficulty in adapting to its climate and to its established customs, institutions, and value systems. This steadfast resolve not to alter the cultural balance of power has weakened as the demand for workers has exceeded the available supply in the preferred countries, and as more of the discriminatory aspects of immigration policy have been eliminated.

Thus, the analysis of the changing ethnic or cultural origins of Canada's population has always enjoyed a high priority notwithstanding the fact that such analyses are fraught with many difficulties. While cultural heritage is reflected in the country of birth or national origin of the arriving immigrant, it is obviously much more than this. Religion and race, as well as country of last permanent residence, can be at least of equal or greater relevance. Certainly, no one single characteristic can provide a complete picture. This complexity is reflected in the fact that the decennial censuses of Canada have continued to employ a number of questions to obtain information about the cultural background of its people. One question in particular has been used with varying success through the years; and, while it has lacked consistency in application, the basic procedures appear to have been good enough to permit a rough but adequate delineation of the basic ethnic structure and its evolution through time.[1] The following discussion is based on the ethnic or cultural group questions which have been used in the censuses of Canada. Other aspects of ethnic identity have already been discussed in the preceding chapter, and the religious dimension will be the subject of the following chapter.

Canada's Two Founding Peoples

The period of early exploration, trading, and settlement in North America by the French, and the ultimate winning of political control by the British after the Seven Year's War, has been covered briefly in Chapter 2. It is perhaps sufficient at this point to remind the reader that when the British became politically dominant, the majority of people living in New France were not English speaking. The relatively few English-speaking persons were located primarily in Nova Scotia, and not until the emigration of the British Empire Loyalists from the American Colonies did the British origin population develop an adequate demographic basis for future expansion. During the nineteenth century, growth through the combined effects of immigration and natural increase was sufficient to overtake the population of French origins.[2] Just four years after Confederation, there were 2,111,000 of British origin compared to 1,083,000 of French origin, constituting 60.5 and 31.1 per cent respectively of the combined populations of the four original provinces. It must be remembered that the British origin group does not possess the same degree of homogeneity as the French, and that its internal structure has not remained constant. Until 1901, the Irish constituted the largest component of the British Isles origins, followed by the English and Scottish. By 1921, the Irish were exceeded in numbers by both English and Scottish, as may be seen in Table 6:1.

Growth trends for the British, French, and all other origins combined are graphically summarized in Figure 6:1. The rate of growth for those of French origins, dependent primarily on natural increase, has been remarkably steady during the entire 60-year period. On the other hand, as the increase in British origins has been dependent primarily on immigration, their rate of growth has varied considerably in response to changing economic conditions. It is clear that if the British and French origin groups had been the only constituent parts of the total, the French origin component would have increased

Table 6:1

POPULATION OF BRITISH ISLES, FRENCH AND OTHER ORIGINS, CANADA, 1871, 1881, AND 1901–1961

Ethnic Group	1871[a]	1881	1901	1911	1921	1931	1941	1951	1961
					(1,000s)[c]				
British Isles	2,111	2,549	3,063	3,999	4,869	5,381	5,716	6,710	7,997
English	706	881	1,261	1,871	2,545	2,741	2,968	3,630	4,195
Irish	846	957	989	1,075	1,108	1,231	1,268	1,440	1,753
Scottish	550	700	800	1,027	1,174	1,346	1,404	1,547	1,902
Other	8	10	13	26	42	62	76	92	146
French	1,083	1,299	1,649	2,062	2,453	2,928	3,483	4,319	5,540
Other	292	477	659	1,146	1,466	2,068	2,308	2,981	4,702
Total[b]	3,486	4,325	5,371	7,207	8,788	10,377	11,507	14,009	18,238
					(Per Cent)				
British Isles	60.5	58.9	57.0	55.5	55.4	51.9	49.7	47.9	43.8
English	20.3	20.4	23.5	26.0	29.0	26.4	25.8	25.9	23.0
Irish	24.3	22.1	18.4	14.9	12.6	11.9	11.0	10.3	9.6
Scottish	15.8	16.2	14.9	14.2	13.4	13.0	12.2	11.0	10.4
Other	0.2	0.2	0.2	0.4	0.5	0.6	0.7	0.7	0.8
French	31.1	30.0	30.7	28.6	27.9	28.2	30.3	30.8	30.4
Other	8.4	11.0	12.2	15.9	16.7	19.9	20.0	21.2	25.8
Total	100.0	100.0	100.0	100.0	100.0	100.0	100.0	99.9	100.0

SOURCE: Dominion Bureau of Statistics, *1961 Census of Canada*, Bulletin 7:1-6, Ottawa, The Queen's Printer, 1966, Table I, and Table 1.
  [a] Four original provinces only.
  [b] Exclusive of Newfoundland prior to 1951.
  [c] Numbers rounded to the nearest 1,000. Sums of individual entries may not equal totals shown.

much more than it actually did relative to the British. It is equally clear that the key to the changing ethnic composition in Canada now lies in the changes occurring in the combined "other origins" group. For the period depicted in Figure 6:1, the proportion of British has steadily declined from 57.0 to 43.8 per cent. The French have remained relatively stationary during this period, varying between 30.8 and 27.9 per cent, only because their rate of growth closely approximated that for "other" origins. The decline exhibited by British origins was to a considerable extent the result of low rates of growth for both Scottish and Irish. However, since 1921 even those of English origin have experienced rates of growth below those for Canada as a whole.

Fig. 6:1

POPULATION TRENDS
BRITISH AND FRENCH ORIGINS
CANADA: 1901–1961

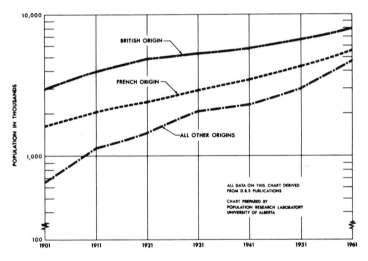

The Other Ethnic and Racial Groups of Canada

In 1871, only 8.4 per cent of the total population or 292,300 were neither of British nor French origins. Almost all, or 203,000, were of German origin, with 30,000 reported as from The Netherlands. Native Indians and Eskimos combined were somewhat more numerous than Negroes, with 23,000 compared to 21,500 for the latter; but there may well be reasonable doubt about the accuracy of the total count for these two groups considering the vastness of the territory they occupied and the difficulties of transportation and communication in these areas. Historical data for other ethnic groups presented in Figure 6:2 show that the Germans have continued to be the next largest

Fig. 6:2

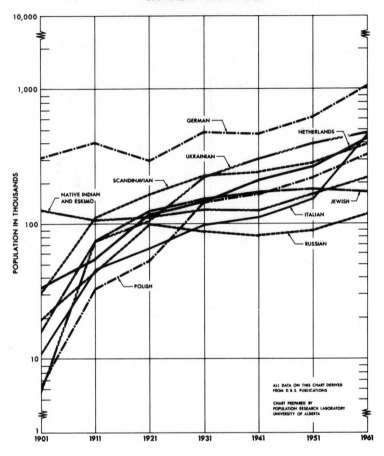

POPULATION TRENDS
SELECTED ETHNIC ORIGINS
CANADA: 1901–1961

group throughout the entire period following the turn of the twentieth
century.

With the exception of Russian origins since 1921, and Jewish since 1941,
most European origins shown in Figure 6:2 have exhibited rapid growth in
numbers over the entire period. The very rapid increases during the 1901–11
decade declined during the subsequent decade for every group except Netherlands and Russian. During the pre-depression decade, Polish, Ukrainian, and
Italians all showed increased growth rates in comparison to the preceding
decade. As would be expected, most all groups experienced declines in
growth rates during the depression years, the only exception being those of
Netherlands origin. In this particular case, it is suspected that the rather

unusual increase was not independent of the decline in numbers stating their origin as German during the 1931–41 decade when it was increasingly unpopular to be "German". Most likely, many of those reporting themselves as Netherlander in 1941 had previously reported themselves as German.

Growth rates increased again during the post-World War II period for all except Ukrainians and Jewish. For the former, it was perhaps a reflection, in part, of the increase in aging of their population mainly due to a complete halt in immigration. For the latter, some loss seems attributable to changes in instructions to enumerators which placed additional emphasis on language as a means of ascertaining ethnic background. Thus, many who thought of themselves as Jewish, but who spoke Russian, Polish, or some other language, might have been classified as Russian, Polish, or some other origin rather than Jewish. Among the major ethnic groups shown in Figure 6:2, the most spectacular growth was recorded during the 1951–61 decade by those of Italian origin who exceeded all but the Ukranians and Germans in size by the end of the decade. By 1971, the population of Italian origin should be fourth in size. Minor ethnic groups which experienced higher percentage increases during the 1951–61 decade than the Italians, according to census reports, were the Austrians (230.5 per cent), Greek (304.4 per cent), and Yugoslavs (220.4 per cent).[3]

The percentage increase for "other European" origins by decades since 1941 has exceeded that of either the French or British. A continuation of this trend will certainly produce a change in the demographic position of the French in Canada during the 1970s. On the other hand, since the basis of growth for French Canada lies almost entirely in its natural increase, it may more easily maintain its present relative position than any of the other origins which have been more dependent upon continuing immigration to produce significant growth rates. Populations for ethnic groups within the "other origins" category of Table 6:1 are presented in Table 6:2 for the period 1901 to 1961. Again, caution is advised when making comparisons by decades between specific ethnic groups within this general "other European" category. The considerable decline in Germans between 1911 and 1921, and again between 1931 and 1941, suggests a reluctance on the part of many to identify themselves as German so soon after World War I and during World War II. The gain of some 70,000 Austrians during the 1951–61 decade exceeds any estimate of expected increase based on immigration and natural increase data and is thought to reflect some confusion in distinguishing between Austrians and Ukrainian ethnic origins during the 1961 Census.[4]

Native- and Foreign-born Components of Ethnic Groups

Eighty-four per cent of the total Canadian population was classified as native born at the time of the 1961 Census. Since the proportion native born is

Table 6:2

POPULATION BY ETHNIC ORIGINS OTHER THAN BRITISH ISLES AND FRENCH FOR CANADA: 1871, 1881, AND 1901–1961

(1,000s)

Ethnic Group	1871	1881	1901	1911	1921	1931	1941	1951	1961
Other European	240	299	458	945	1,247	1,825	2,044	2,554	4,117
Austrian, n.o.s.	—	—	11	44	108	49	38	32	107
Belgian	—	—	3	10	20	28	30	35	61
Czech and Slovak	—	—	—	—	9	30	43	64	73
Finnish[a]	—	—	3	16	21	44	42	44	59
German	203	254	311	403	295	474	465	620	1,050
Greek	—	—	—	4	6	9	12	14	56
Hungarian[b]	—	—	2	12	13	41	55	60	126
Italian	1	2	11	46	67	98	113	152	450
Jewish	—	1	16	76	126	157	170	182	173
Lithuanian	—	—	—	—	2	6	8	16	28
Netherlands	30	30	34	56	118	149	213	264	430
Polish	—	—	6	34	53	146	167	220	324
Roumanian[c]	—	—	—	6	13	29	25	24	44
Russian[d]	1	1	20	44	100	88	84	91	119
Scandinavian	2	5	31	113	167	228	245	283	387
Ukrainian	—	—	6	75	107	225	306	395	473
Yugoslavic	—	—	—	7	4	16	21	21	69
Other	4	6	5	7	18	9	10	36	88
Asiatic	—	4	24	43	66	85	74	73	122
Chinese	—	4	17	28	40	47	35	33	58
Japanese	—	—	5	9	16	23	23	22	29
Other	—	—	2	6	10	15	16	19	34
Other	52	174	177	158	153	158	190	354	463

SOURCE: Dominion Bureau of Statistics, 1961 Census of Canada, Bulletin 7:1-6, Ottawa, The Queen's Printer, 1966, Table 1.
a Includes Estonian prior to 1951.
b Includes Lithuanian and Moravian in 1901 and 1911.
c Includes Bulgarian in 1901 and 1911.

affected by the relative sizes of contributions made by immigration and natural increase, there is considerable variation from one ethnic group to another. The French origin group, which has gained primarily through natural increase, has had the highest proportions of native born. In 1921, 97.0 per cent of the French origin population was native born and the proportion had increased to 98.4 by 1961. For those of British origin, 74.1 per cent were native born in 1921; but, as immigration has become relatively less important, this proportion increased to 85.6 per cent in 1961. As might be expected, other ethnic groups which were predominant during earlier migrations to Canada, or whose recent immigration has been reduced to extremely low levels, would also tend to have high proportions of native born. Thus, the Germans have 72.6 per cent native born; Scandinavians have 72.9 per cent; Russians have 72.9 per cent; and Ukrainians have 76.7 per cent. For the Japanese, whose immigration virtually ceased during World War II and whose subsequent immigration has been relatively small, the native born constitute 78.2 per cent of their total. This stands in considerable contrast to those of Chinese origins whose native born comprise only 39.5 per cent of their total—a reflection of their heavy post-World War II immigration. Other groups with less than half of their numbers native born in 1961 were Hungarians (43.1 per cent), Italian (41.1 per cent), and "other Europeans" (42.5 per cent), all of whom experienced significant growth during the 1951–61 decade. As this information is important for assessing the significance of other characteristics, e.g., educational attainment, family size, housing, the proportions of foreign born for major ethnic origins are presented in Table 6:3.

Ethnic origin by place of birth. Generally speaking, there is a close correspondence between one's country of birth and ethnic origin. For example, in the 1961 Census 97.2 per cent of those reporting being born in the United Kingdom were of British Isles origins, and 96.8 per cent of those born in European countries were of European origins, etc. However, for those born in the United States the situation is somewhat different in that "American" is not an acceptable ethnic category within the meaning of the concept as used in the censuses of Canada.[5] In the case of those born in the United States, it is difficult to understand the significance of these immigrants' contribution to Canada's ethnic composition. Their ethnic or cultural origins, as defined by the census, must be examined separately while, at the same time, keeping in mind that in 1961 they constituted just under ten per cent of the foreign born residing in Canada.

It is apparent in Table 6:4 that Americans of British origin were a significant component of immigration from the United States. It is interesting to note that during a period when the proportion of all foreign born reporting British origins has declined sharply, their proportion among immigrants from the United States following World War II was higher than it was among pre-

Table 6:3

PERCENTAGE NON-CANADIAN BORN, BY MAJOR ETHNIC GROUPS
FOR CANADA,[a] 1921–1961

Ethnic Group	1921	1931	1941	1951	1961
British Isles	25.9	25.1	20.2	16.1	14.4
French	3.0	2.6	2.2	1.6	1.6
Other European	44.2	44.7	36.2	33.7	37.1
Austrian, n.o.s.	47.9	46.3	39.5	35.9	41.0
Czech and Slovak	56.0	72.2	61.4	55.5	45.9
Finnish	63.0	71.8	59.9	50.1	48.9
German	28.3	30.5	24.2	20.9	27.4
Hungarian	50.0	72.2	58.0	51.5	56.9
Italian	57.0	46.9	38.5	41.0	58.9
Jewish	59.7	56.2	49.0	43.0	37.8
Netherlands	17.2	20.1	16.0	24.9	36.2
Polish	48.2	53.0	42.1	44.4	39.9
Russian	50.4	46.0	38.2	33.7	27.1
Scandinavian	62.4	56.4	43.7	33.8	27.1
Ukrainian	45.8	43.0	34.8	30.4	23.3
Other	—[b]	60.0	50.3	55.7	57.5
Asiatic	86.8	71.2	58.5	47.7	46.0
Chinese	92.5	88.4	80.2	69.4	60.5
Japanese	72.7	51.5	39.0	27.3	21.8
Other	—[b]	48.2	40.1	33.4	41.9
Other and Not Stated	22.6	4.0	3.0	5.3	4.8

SOURCE: Dominion Bureau of Statistics, *1961 Census of Canada*, Bulletin 7:1-6, Ottawa,
    The Queen's Printer, 1966.
    [a] Exclusive of Newfoundland in censuses prior to 1951.
    [b] Included with "Other and Not Stated."

war immigrants. With respect to the decline in proportion of French origins
from 18.0 per cent for pre-war immigrants, to 9.6 per cent among post-war
immigrants, it should be pointed out that the United States still retained its
position as the major source for French-origin immigrants. Even though the
volume of immigration from the United States declined significantly between
1901 and 1961, its ethnic composition has tended to reinforce and slow the
decline in relative size of both British and French origin groups among the
foreign born.

Regional Distribution of Ethnic Groups

British and French ethnic origins. The two founding ethnic groups are shown
as proportions of provincial totals in Figure 6:3 for both 1901 and 1961. It
is apparent that over the 60-year period, those of British origins have become

Table 6:4

PERCENTAGE DISTRIBUTION OF THE POPULATION BY MAJOR ETHNIC GROUPS, FOR TOTAL FOREIGN BORN AND THOSE BORN IN THE UNITED STATES, BY PERIOD OF IMMIGRATION, CANADA, 1961

Ethnic Group	Total Foreign Born		Born in the United States	
	Pre-War Immigrants	Post-War Immigrants	Pre-War Immigrants	Post-War Immigrants
British Isles	54.1	28.2	45.9	49.9
French	3.8	2.5	18.0	9.6
Other European	39.7	66.2	32.8	33.5
Asiatic	1.6	2.2	0.1	0.8
Other[a]	0.8	0.9	3.2	6.2
Total:				
Per cent	100.0	100.0	100.0	100.0
Number	1,337,146	1,507,116	213,881	70,027

SOURCE: Dominion Bureau of Statistics, *1961 Census of Canada*, Bulletin 7:1-6, Ottawa, The Queen's Printer, 1966, Table VII; and W. E. Kalbach, *The Impact of Immigration on Canada's Population*, Ottawa, The Queen's Printer, 1970, Table 4:4.
[a] Includes Native Indian and Eskimo and those whose origins were not stated.

more evenly dispersed, increasing where their proportions were low and decreasing where they were high. The only exceptions were in Quebec where they declined from 17.6 to 10.8 per cent, and in the Atlantic Provinces where in spite of relative declines their concentration is still extremely high. West of Quebec, even though the proportions of British have remained quite large, they constituted a majority only in Ontario and British Columbia.

Unlike the British, the pattern of concentration of French Canadians has remained virtually unchanged during the same period while increasing their proportionate share of the population everywhere except in Alberta. The pattern for French Canadians emphasizes again the strategic importance of fertility for maintaining their demographic position. For the British, it has had importance only in Newfoundland, Prince Edward Island, and Nova Scotia. Throughout the rest of Canada, the demographic stance of those of British origins will continue to be affected primarily by the ethnic mix of both internal and international migration. Of 5,500,000 French Canadians enumerated in 1961, approximately 4,250,000 were living in Quebec where they constituted 80.6 per cent of the population. Sixty years earlier, there were just under 1,333,000 living in Quebec; but they still constituted 80.2 per cent of the total, indicating that the growth of the non-French Canadian population in this province almost kept pace with the dominant ethnic group during this period. The next largest number of French Canadians, in 1961, was found in Ontario (648,000), followed by New Brunswick (232,000). How-

Fig. 6:3

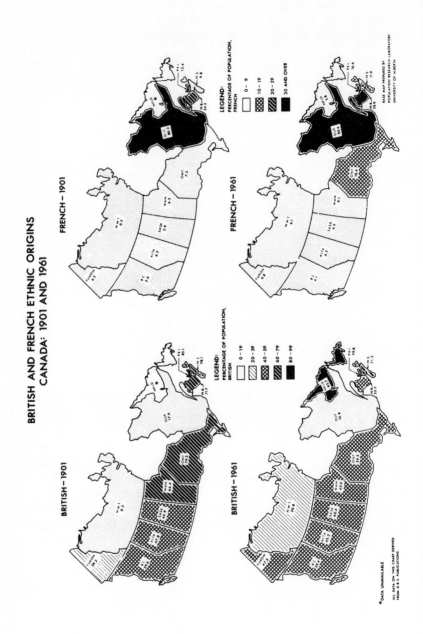

BRITISH AND FRENCH ETHNIC ORIGINS
CANADA: 1901 AND 1961

ever, in relative terms, they constituted only 10.4 per cent of Ontario's population compared to 38.8 per cent for New Brunswick.

Other origins. The remaining European origins, Asiatics, and a residual category of "other and not stated" comprise the balance of the population. Of these, the Europeans, i.e., those of other than British and French origins, constituting 22.6 per cent of Canada's total in 1961, were the most significant component. Above average proportions of "other Europeans" were found in Ontario, the Prairie Provinces, British Columbia, and the Yukon where the lure of free land, gold, and job opportunities have beckoned in turn to the arriving immigrant. As might be expected, the largest concentrations of Asiatics were still to be found in British Columbia and Alberta where they had originally come to help push the railroads through the Rockies; and the residual category, consisting mainly of Native Indians and Eskimos, were heavily concentrated in the Northwest Territories and the Yukon. All of the provinces west of Quebec, as well as Nova Scotia, had above average proportions of these native populations that still reside primarily in those marginal areas of little interest to the average white man.

Percentage distributions by ethnic origins for Canada and provinces presented in Table 6:5, provide more detailed information for the "other Europeans". From these data certain significant deviations may be observed. For example, the Germans are present in above average proportions in Nova Scotia in addition to those areas already mentioned as having significant concentrations of "other Europeans". The Italians, for another, are most heavily concentrated in Ontario's industrial areas while the Jews in Quebec comprise the second largest relative concentration outside the province of Manitoba with percentages for these two provinces being 1.4 and 2.1 respectively. However, in terms of numbers, most of the Jewish population was located in the urban centres of Quebec (75,000), followed by Ontario (65,000), while Manitoba (19,000) had the third largest number. Outside of the areas west of Quebec, those of Netherlands origin were found in significant concentration only in Nova Scotia, while Ukrainians had their largest concentration in Manitoba. In the Prairie Provinces, Germans and Ukrainians ranked second and third respectively after British origins, both numerically and relatively. In British Columbia, the Scandinavians ranked third following the British and Germans.

Variations within regional patterns. Data for provinces are useful in delineating the general patterns of ethnic distributions, but in certain instances the picture tends to be distorted because of the general arbitrariness of political boundaries. In other cases, the degree of existing cultural diversity is obscured because the areas used for analyses are too big, thus failing to detect many of the existing ethnic communities. As an example of the first situation, the previous analysis revealed a concentration of French Canadians in Quebec, but failed to show the significant spillover into adjacent areas in

Table 6:5

PERCENTAGE DISTRIBUTION OF THE POPULATION BY ETHNIC GROUP FOR CANADA AND PROVINCES, 1961

Ethnic Group	Canada	Nfld.	P.E.I.	N.S.	N.B.	Que.	Ont.	Man.	Sask.	Alta.	B.C.	Yukon	N.W.T
British Isles	43.8	93.7	79.8	71.3	55.2	10.8	59.5	43.0	40.4	45.2	59.4	47.5	20.8
French	30.4	3.8	16.6	11.9	38.8	80.6	10.4	9.1	6.5	6.3	4.1	6.8	6.1
Other European	22.6	1.1	2.7	12.9	4.4	7.6	26.5	43.5	48.7	44.4	29.9	27.1	11.8
German	5.8	0.4	0.6	6.2	1.2	0.8	6.4	10.0	17.1	13.8	7.3	7.5	3.1
Italian	2.5	0.1	0.1	0.5	0.2	2.1	4.4	0.7	0.3	1.1	2.4	1.4	0.6
Jewish	1.0	—	—	0.2	0.1	1.4	1.0	2.1	0.2	0.3	0.3	—	—
Netherlands	2.4	0.1	1.2	3.4	1.3	0.2	3.1	5.2	3.2	4.2	3.7	2.4	0.8
Polish	1.8	0.1	0.1	0.4	0.1	0.6	2.4	4.8	3.1	3.0	1.5	1.6	0.7
Russian	0.7	—	—	0.1	0.1	0.3	0.5	0.9	2.4	1.3	1.7	0.7	0.2
Scandinavian	2.1	0.3	0.4	0.8	0.8	0.2	1.0	4.1	7.3	7.2	5.9	5.3	2.5
Ukrainian	2.6	—	0.1	0.2	0.1	0.3	2.1	11.4	8.5	8.0	2.2	2.4	1.6
Other	3.9	0.2	0.2	1.0	0.4	1.8	5.6	4.4	6.5	5.4	4.9	5.9	2.2
Asiatic	0.7	0.2	0.3	0.4	0.2	0.3	0.6	0.5	0.5	0.9	2.5	1.0	0.3
Other and not stated	2.5	1.2	0.5	3.5	1.4	0.7	3.0	4.0	3.9	3.3	4.1	17.6	61.0

SOURCE: Dominion Bureau of Statistics, *1961 Census of Canada*, Bulletin 7:1-6, Ottawa, The Queen's Printer, 1966, Table IV.

—Less than 0.05 per cent.

both Ontario and New Brunswick. In three of the four Ontario counties located in the fork of the Ottawa and St. Lawrence Rivers, more than half of the population were of French origins. Similarly, the northwestern area of New Brunswick contained three counties with proportions of French varying between 68 and 94 per cent. In addition, data for the latter province obscure a rather significant concentration of French on the east coast in Kent County where those of French origin comprise 82 per cent of the population. Similar analysis of data by census divisions reveals high concentrations of French on the northeast and southwest coasts of Nova Scotia, while in the West, significant concentrations of French are found in southwestern Manitoba and northeastern Alberta.

For the other European origins, as has already been mentioned, most were located in the West. The Germans were heavily concentrated in the areas of Alberta and Saskatchewan adjacent to their common border in the south, with additional concentrations in the Okanagan Lake area of south-central British Columbia and south-central Manitoba along the Red River. Other significant settlements of Germans are found in the Waterloo area of Ontario and the southeastern section of Nova Scotia. The pattern for Netherlands origin is quite similar to that of the Germans, while the Scandinavians have no significant concentrations anywhere east of Ontario. The only areas west of the Lakehead that do not have concentrations of Scandinavians significantly above the average for Canada as a whole are two census divisions in south-central Manitoba and six census divisions in the southwest portion of the same province.

While both Ukrainians and Russians are concentrated in Western Canada, the Ukrainians have perhaps the more interesting distribution. Their areas of greatest concentration form a very distinct band running northwest from the Lakehead, across the centre of the southern half of Manitoba into central Saskatchewan, and the central eastern half of Alberta. For the Russians, the areas containing the largest concentrations were west of Manitoba in the same general areas of German settlement.

Of those ethnic groups predominant in post-World War II immigration, the Italians are perhaps more representative of recent locational trends reflecting post-war industrialization in Canada. They have concentrated primarily in urban and industrial areas. East of Toronto, the only area of concentration is in Montreal. In Ontario, they are heavily concentrated in Toronto, Hamilton, and Windsor in the south, and Sault Ste. Marie and the mining areas to the north. In the West, concentrations are to be found in the coal mining area of southwestern Alberta, in southeastern British Columbia and the mining areas along the coast north of Vancouver. These are the areas that, with few exceptions, have experienced the greatest need for labourers, craftsmen, and other industrial workers associated with construction, heavy manufacturing, and mining activities; and these have been the areas which have attracted the largest share of the skilled, semi-skilled, and unskilled workers who have comprised post-war immigration.

Rural-urban Distribution

It has already been shown that urbanization did not proceed uniformly throughout the country, and that the foreign born have responded more directly to changing economic conditions than have the native born. Similar variations can be observed amongst ethnic populations in Canada which have differed in the timing of immigration to this country and consequently differ significantly with respect to settlement patterns, age, sex structure, and nativity.

Of the two founding peoples, those of British origins have continued to be more urbanized than the French. From Figure 6:4, it is clear that, while both have become more urbanized, the difference between them was less in 1961 than at the beginning of the twentieth century. With 71.2 per cent of those of British origins living in urban areas in 1961, they were somewhat more urbanized than the population as a whole. On the other hand, those of French origins, with 68.2 per cent residing in urban areas, were somewhat below the 69.6 per cent for all ethnic groups combined.

Data in Figure 6:5 clearly show that the most highly urbanized of all ethnic groups were the Jews and the Italians. By way of contrast, only 55.6 per cent of Netherlanders were found in urban areas. The most rural, i.e., the Native Indians and Eskimos, had only 12.9 per cent living in urban areas. However, a closer look at the data; presented in Table 6:6, which distinguishes between

Fig. 6:4

**URBAN TRENDS
SELECTED ETHNIC ORIGINS
CANADA: 1901–1961**

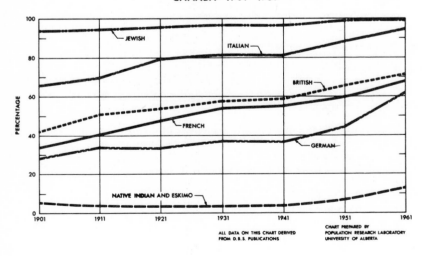

ALL DATA ON THIS CHART DERIVED
FROM D.B.S. PUBLICATIONS

CHART PREPARED BY
POPULATION RESEARCH LABORATORY
UNIVERSITY OF ALBERTA

Fig. 6:5

**RURAL—URBAN DISTRIBUTION
SELECTED ETHNIC ORIGINS
CANADA: 1961**

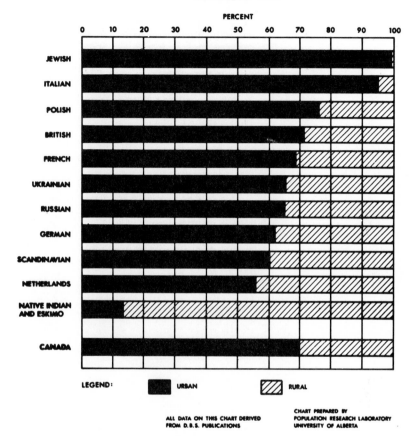

LEGEND: ■ URBAN   ▨ RURAL

ALL DATA ON THIS CHART DERIVED
FROM D.B.S. PUBLICATIONS

CHART PREPARED BY
POPULATION RESEARCH LABORATORY
UNIVERSITY OF ALBERTA

those living on rural farms and rural non-farms, reveals that the Netherlanders are actually the most rural in that they have the largest per cent living
on farms (22.1), closely followed by Ukrainians (20.9), Germans (19.4),
Scandinavians (18.6) and Russian (17.0). Thus, information on the basis
of the simple urban-rural dichotomy fails to reveal the particular ethnic
population most directly associated with farming as a source of income. The
category including Native Indians and Eskimos, while ranking lowest in terms
of non-urban residence, had slightly less than half (45.9 per cent) living in
rural non-farm areas.

Urban size groups. Generally, those with the larger proportions residing
in urban areas tended to have above average concentrations in the larger
urban centres of 100,000 and over. Of all the major ethnic groups, neither
the British, French, Netherlanders, nor Scandinavians exceeded the 62.4 per

Table 6:6

PERCENTAGE DISTRIBUTION OF THE POPULATION OF SPECIFIED ETHNIC GROUPS, BY RURAL FARM, RURAL NON-FARM AND URBAN, CANADA: 1961

Ethnic Group	Canada	RURAL			URBAN	URBAN SIZE GROUP		
		Total	Rural Farm	Rural Non-Farm		Total	100,000 and over	Under 100,000
British	100.0	28.8	9.4	19.4	71.2	100.0	61.2	38.8
French	100.0	31.8	12.2	19.6	68.2	100.0	58.1	41.9
Other European	100.0	29.7	15.0	14.6	70.3	100.0	69.6	30.4
German	100.0	38.2	19.4	18.8	61.8	100.0	63.2	36.8
Italian	100.0	5.3	1.2	4.1	94.7	100.0	77.4	22.6
Jewish	100.0	1.2	0.3	0.9	98.8	100.0	95.5	4.5
Netherlands	100.0	44.4	22.1	22.3	55.6	100.0	57.1	42.9
Polish	100.0	24.0	13.0	11.0	76.0	100.0	72.3	27.7
Russian	100.0	34.9	17.0	17.9	65.1	100.0	71.0	29.0
Scandinavian	100.0	40.1	18.6	21.5	59.9	100.0	59.1	40.9
Ukrainian	100.0	34.8	20.9	13.9	65.2	100.0	67.1	32.9
Other	100.0	23.3	11.5	11.8	76.7	100.0	72.8	27.2
Asiatic	100.0	10.7	2.9	7.8	89.3	100.0	76.1	23.9
Other and not stated[a]	100.0	51.3	5.4	45.9	48.7	100.0	64.7	35.3
Total	100.0	30.4	11.4	19.0	69.6	100.0	62.4	37.6

SOURCE: Dominion Bureau of Statistics, *1961 Census of Canada*, Bulletin 7:1.6, Ottawa, The Queen's Printer, 1966, Table V and Table VI.
[a] Includes Native Indians and Eskimos which comprise slightly more than half of residual category.

cent for all groups combined. On the other hand, 95.5 per cent of the Jewish origin group, and 77.4 per cent of Italians living in urban areas, lived in urban places of 100,000 or more; and approximately three-fourths of both groups were located in the two metropolitan areas of Toronto and Montreal.[6]

Three groups, in particular, have tended to concentrate heavily in the metropolitan areas. In 1941, Asiatics, Italians, and Jews had 57.8, 61.0, and 89.9 per cent of their populations, respectively, living in metropolitan areas. By 1961, the percentages for these groups had increased to 68.6, 75.2, and 94.0 per cent, respectively, while those of Polish origins, passed the 50 per cent mark as did the residual "other" European category which contains a preponderance of recent immigrants. As Table 6:7 shows, the proportion for every major ethnic origin group living in metropolitan areas increased between 1941 and 1961. The continuing rural-urban movement of population has, no doubt, contributed to this increase as has the notable tendency for recent immigrants to settle in urban areas in disproportionate numbers. In 1961, 86.4 per cent of all post-World War II immigrants had settled in urban areas compared to 75.7 per cent of the earlier immigrants and 67.5 per cent of native born.[7]

Table 6:7

PERCENTAGE OF THE TOTAL POPULATION OF CANADA
LIVING IN CENSUS METROPOLITAN AREAS[a] BY ETHNIC
GROUP, 1961, 1951, AND 1941

Ethnic Group	1961	1951	1941
British Isles	46.2	43.7	41.0
French	39.3	35.8	34.1
Other European	49.9	39.4	32.2
German	39.4	27.5	21.9
Italian	75.2	63.1	61.0
Jewish	94.0	93.0	89.9
Netherlands	35.0	24.0	19.8
Polish	55.6	46.3	35.7
Russian	46.1	35.3	22.7
Scandinavian	36.8	29.2	21.1
Ukrainian	44.5	35.2	21.9
Other	56.5	43.8	33.6
Asiatic	68.6	59.9	57.8
Other and not stated[b]	33.1	30.8	11.2

SOURCE: Dominion Bureau of Statistics, *1961 Census of Canada*, Bulletin 7:1-6, Ottawa, The Queen's Printer, 1966, Table VIII.
[a] Areas as of 1961.
[b] Includes 220,121 Native Indian and Eskimos, 32,127 Negroes and 210,382 other and not stated origins in 1961.

Ethnic Group Differentials

In addition to differences in size, growth, and distribution, ethnic populations vary significantly with respect to their nativity and age-sex structure. These too can have significant social, political, and economic consequences, so that no examination of ethnicity and race in Canada would be complete without their inclusion.

Sex ratios by ethnic origin groups. The balance between males and females is influenced by the following: (1) the sex ratio at birth, (2) sex differentials in mortality which increasingly tend to favour females, (3) sex ratios of arriving and departing migrants, (4) relative proportions of native and foreign born, and (5) the age structure which in turn is determined by the group's fertility, mortality, and age and sex characteristics of its net migrants.

Table 6:8

SEX RATIO, PERCENTAGE AGE DISTRIBUTION, AND PER CENT FOREIGN BORN, SELECTED ETHNIC ORIGIN GROUPS, CANADA: 1961

Ethnic Origin Group	Sex Ratio	Percentage Age Distribtion					Per Cent Foreign Born
		Total	Under 15	15–44	45–64	65+	
British Isles	998	100.0	32.1	38.9	19.0	10.0	14.4
French	1,001	100.0	37.4	42.1	15.1	5.4	1.6
German	1,036	100.0	33.2	44.3	16.4	6.2	27.4
Hungarian	1,223	100.0	28.6	46.7	19.6	5.1	56.9
Italian	1,150	100.0	34.0	49.7	12.8	3.5	58.9
Jewish	1,029	100.0	28.8	38.1	25.1	8.0	37.8
Netherlands	1,065	100.0	38.3	42.6	14.5	4.7	36.2
Polish	1,121	100.0	32.2	41.0	21.4	5.4	39.9
Russian	1,064	100.0	29.5	39.9	21.4	9.2	27.1
Scandinavian	1,118	100.0	32.1	40.8	18.6	8.5	27.1
Ukrainian	1,087	100.0	31.7	43.3	18.9	6.2	23.3
Asiatic	1,339	100.0	30.3	43.4	15.9	10.4	46.0
Native Indian and Eskimo	1,035	100.0	46.7	38.2	10.8	4.3	0.7
Total Origins[a]	1,022	100.0	34.0	41.1	17.4	7.4	15.6

SOURCE: Dominion Bureau of Statistics, *1961 Census of Canada*, Bulletin 1:3-2, Ottawa, The Queen's Printer, 1963; Table 81 and Bulletin 7:1-6, 1966, Table XI and XVII. Per cent foreign born based on data presented in W. E. Kalbach, *The Impact of Immigration on Canada's Population*, Ottawa, The Queen's Printer, 1970, Table C1.
[a] Includes all other origins and not stated.

Sex ratios, as indicated in Table 6:8 for 1961, varied from a low of 998 males (per 1,000 females) for British Isles origins to a high of 1,631 for the Chinese. All ethnic groups listed, except the British, had an excess of males in 1961; but only the French, with a sex ratio of 1,001, in addition to the British, had what might be regarded as a balanced population insofar as the sex distribution is concerned. The French-origin population appears to have achieved this through continuing high fertility aided by immigration characterized by a slight excess of females. On the other hand, the British Isles origin group achieved their low sex ratios through the immigration of excess numbers of women and the assistance of excess mortality of males in the older ages. "Other Europeans" had an excess of 92 males for every 1,000 females, while Asiatics had an excess of 339 males per 1,000 females. This latter imbalance was due mainly to the large number of Chinese male survivors of coolie labour imported to assist in the building of Canada's transcontinental railroad. Among "Other Europeans", those groups with sex ratios greater than the average for the group as a whole were Austrians, Czechs and Slovaks, Hungarians, Italians, Poles, and Scandinavians. Here again, the effects of recent heavy male immigration resulting from political and economic conditions in Europe can be seen. This total was augmented by the survivors of the early twentieth century influx of predominantly male labour. The Jewish, with 1,029, had the lowest sex ratio within this category and the third lowest among all the ethnic groups shown.

Variations in age distributions. Like sex ratios, the age characteristics of Canada's ethnic populations varied significantly and for many of the same reasons. Those groups experiencing relatively high fertility and minimal immigration would tend to have both high proportions of their populations in the younger age groups and smoothly tapering age-sex pyramids, much like the age structure of a developing country with an agrarian economy. The most extreme example of this situation would be the Native Indian and Eskimo population, illustrated in Figure 6:6. This group had almost half, or 46.7 per cent, of its population under 15 years of age in 1961, and only 4.3 per cent 65 years of age and over. The distribution for French origins was quite similar although not nearly as extreme in either its excess population under 15 years of age or its under-representation in the older age groups.

The British origin population reflects another somewhat unique combination of low fertility, low mortality, and declining immigration. The obvious consequences are the below average proportions of young people and disproportionately greater numbers among the aged.

Those ethnic groups which have experienced heavy immigration for limited periods are characterized by yet another type of population profile. The Italian origin population in Figure 6:6, for example, shows the effects of heavy current immigration of young adults through both the concentration of its population in the 20–39 year age range and above average proportions of

Fig. 6:6

**AGE AND SEX COMPOSITION
SELECTED ETHNIC ORIGINS
CANADA: 1961**

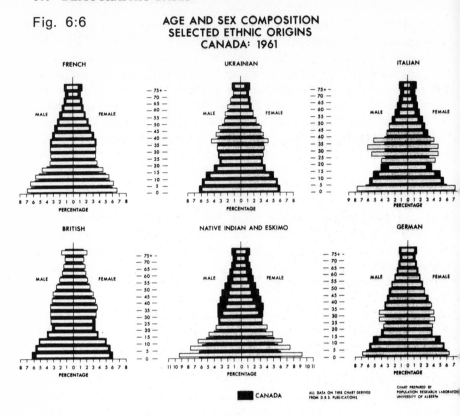

children 0–4 years of age. Closer examination will also reveal the higher sex ratios for all age groups 25 years and over typical of populations having participated in the earlier male-dominated international migrations. Ukrainians, on the other hand, exhibit the characteristics of a population that is aging and not being replaced by either a fresh inflow of new immigrants or high birth rates. The excess of older males, reflecting the survivors of heavy immigration during the early 1900s, is still visible, and above average proportions are found in the older age groups rather than the young. The remaining pyramid for German origins illustrates the effects of heavy post-war immigration on a population which has shown sufficient growth through the years to maintain itself as the third largest ethnic population. It also exhibits those characteristics typical of immigrant populations, i.e., over-representation in the young adult ages between 20 and 35 years, and excess of children under five years of age, but not to the same extent as the smaller and more recent immigrant populations, e.g., the Italians.

Native and foreign-born components. In general, the differences in native and foreign-born content of ethnic groups reflect the relative contribution of natural increase and net migration. Natural increase has been paramount for the growth of the French origin population and of increasing importance for British origins as immigration has declined. The native-born content of the French origin population, already very high, increased from 97.0 per cent in 1921 to 98.4 per cent in 1961, while the corresponding percentages for the British Isles were 74.1 and 85.6 per cent respectively.[8] With respect to the recent growth of other European origins, immigration has been a much more significant factor. However, during the era of the Great Depression, when immigration virtually ceased, the native-born component increased from 55.3 to 63.8 per cent; yet post-war immigration between 1951 and 1961, in reaching historic proportions, had the opposite effect of reducing the proportion native born from 66.3 per cent tn 1951 to 62.9 per cent in 1961.[9]

Dominance of Canadian population by the predominantly native-born British Isles and French origin groups limits the impact of the foreign immigrant on Canadian society. However, as may be seen in Table 6:8, the situation is quite different for specific origin groups where the foreign-born component comprised a significant proportion of their total number in 1961, e.g., Italians, Hungarians. It would be an elaboration of the obvious to suggest that the significance of ethnicity for the Canadian population varies directly with the size of its foreign-born component. A considerable amount of research has been done on the ethnic populations in Canada, exploring the significance of such factors as settlement and migration patterns, length of residence, mother tongue, religion, etc., for the persistence of ethnicity as a positive value within Canadian society.[10]

REFERENCES

Dominion Bureau of Statistics: *1961 Census of Canada. General Review: Origins of the Canadian Population,* Vol. 7:1–6. Ottawa, The Queen's Printer, 1966.
Hurd, W. B.: *Ethnic Origin and Nativity of the Canadian People.* 1941 Census Monograph. Ottawa, The Queen's Printer, 1965.
Kalbach, W. E.: *The Impact of Immigration on Canada's Population,* 1961 Census Monograph. Ottawa, The Queen's Printer, 1970.

FOOTNOTES

[1]The ethnic or cultural group question has been subjected to considerable criticism because of its lack of precision and because of the considerable difficulty encountered in the field in getting the people to understand its intent. Neither the question nor the instructions given to enumerators have been consistent from one census to the next so that in actual practice the enumerator has had considerable leeway in establishing the respondents' ethnic or cultural background. In 1961, each person was asked to indicate "the ethnic or cultural group that he or his ancestor (on the male side) belonged to on coming to this continent." If the respondent didn't understand the question, the enumerator was instructed to ask for the language spoken by him on

arrival, or by his ancestor on the male side when they first arrived in North America. If this failed to elicit an answer, the enumerator was then instructed to ask "Is your ethnic or cultural group on the male side English, French, Jewish, Negro, North American Indian, Norwegian, Scottish, Ukrainian, etc.?" Obviously, no amount of special instruction or care can overcome all the difficulties associated with attempts to determine ethnic or cultural background, and those who use these data are advised to do so with considerable caution.

²Dominion Bureau of Statistics, *1961 Census of Canada,* Bulletin 7:1–6, Ottawa, The Queen's Printer, 1966, pp. 3–4.

³*Ibid.,* Table II.

⁴*Ibid.,* pp. 6–9.

⁵Remember that the crucial factor in the determination of ethnic origin in Canada is the person's "ethnic or cultural group that he or his ancestors (on the male side) belonged to *on coming to this continent.*" (Italics added). See note no. 1.

⁶*Ibid.,* pp. 6–23.

⁷*Ibid.,* Table VII, pp. 6–24.

⁸*Ibid,* Table XVII.

⁹*Ibid.*

¹⁰For collections of articles dealing with ethnic populations in Canada, see B. R. Blishen, (et. al.) *Canadian Society: Sociological Perspectives,* Third Edition, Toronto, Macmillan of Canada, 1968; and R. Laskin, editor, *Social Problems: A Canadian Profile,* Toronto, McGraw-Hill Co. of Canada, Ltd., 1964. For comprehensive bibliographies, see Department of Citizenship and Immigration, *A Bibliography of Research, 1920–58,* and *1962–64,* Ottawa, The Queen's Printer, 1961 and 1964; and M. B. Stone and J. V. Kokich, *A Bibliography of Canadian Demography,* Dominion Bureau of Statistics, Census Division, (Technical Paper no. 5), Ottawa, 1966.

Religious Composition

The early scattered settlements in the New World took on the cultural complexion of the immigrants' national origins. As would be expected, French settlements would reflect the dominant influence of the Roman Catholic Church, while those communities established by immigrants from the British Isles were characteristically Protestant. In the latter case, the degree of religious homogeneity was probably much less than might appear on the surface in view of the many denominations to be found within the Protestant community. In any event, the religious balance achieved in any specific locality depended upon the relative size of migrant streams both into and out of these areas, and also upon the religious composition of the net migrants. It is to be expected that the continuing Roman Catholic-Protestant dualism in Canada's history should produce both the high degree of religious homogeneity within areas and the considerable diversity between areas which is so apparent today.

Information on religious composition of early settlements in Canada is sketchy, but it can be presumed that during the period of French domination Roman Catholics were predominant. This is borne out by the earliest detailed information, resulting from the census of Lower Canada in 1831, which indicated that three-fourths of the approximately 500,000 inhabitants were Roman Catholic. As may be seen in Table 7:1, of the six other specific denominations reported, the next largest numbers were affiliated with the Church of England and Church of Scotland. Other censuses clearly indicate that Roman Catholics did not enjoy this same degree of dominance in other areas of settlement. Further west, in the Territory of Assiniboia, for example, a census of 460 family heads in the two settlements of Red River and Gran-

Table 7:1

POPULATION OF LOWER CANADA BY RELIGIOUS DENOMINATIONS, 1831

Denomination	Number	Per Cent
Roman Catholic	412,717	74.6
Church of England	34,620	6.3
Church of Scotland	15,069	2.7
Presbyterian	7,810	1.4
Methodist	7,018	1.3
Baptist	2,461	0.4
Jewish	107	—
Other	5,577	1.0
Not given	67,755	12.3
Total	553,134	100.0

SOURCE: *Census of Canada*, 1870-71, Vol. 4, Ottawa, 1876, Table III, p. 109

town showed that only a slight majority, or 57 per cent, were Roman Catholics.[1]

While data are lacking for Upper Canada during the earlier period, the 1842 Census would suggest that most of the several hundred thousand people in this area were non-Catholic. Protestants were dominant in Nova Scotia as early as 1767 when the census of that year reported 84.6 per cent Protestants.[2] A later and more detailed census, in 1827, revealed that Presbyterians constituted the largest Protestant denomination with 30.4 per cent, followed by the Church of England with 23.2 per cent, and by Baptists with 16.0 per cent. Methodists comprised 7.6 per cent of the population while the Dissenters, with 3.6 per cent, outnumbered the 2.4 per cent who were Lutherans.[3]

The first comprehensive reports on the religious character of the population for both Upper and Lower Canada took place in the Censuses of 1842 and 1844 respectively. As these provide the earliest comparison between the major areas of French and British settlement, the distributions are presented in Table 7:2. The contrast is quite striking with Roman Catholics comprising 82.1 per cent of the population of Lower Canada compared to just 13.4 per cent for Upper Canada. Note that while most of the major Protestant denominations were represented in Lower Canada, their numbers were relatively small. For example, the second largest denomination in Lower Canada, the Church of England, accounted for only 6.2 per cent compared to 22.1

Table 7:2

POPULATION BY RELIGIOUS DENOMINATION FOR UPPER CANADA, 1842, AND LOWER CANADA, 1844

Denomination	Upper Canada, 1842		Lower Canada, 1844	
	Number	Per Cent	Number	Per Cent
Baptist	16,411	3.4	4,063	0.6
Roman Catholic	65,203	13.4	572,439	82.1
Church of England	107,791	22.1	43,527	6.2
Congregational	4,253	0.9	3,906	0.6
Jewish	1,105	0.2	154	0.0
Lutheran	4,524	0.9	101	0.0
Methodist:				
British Wesleyan	23,342	4.8	10,797	1.6
Canadian	32,315	6.6	2,993	0.4
Episcopal	20,125	4.1	719	0.1
Other	7,141	1.5	1,315	0.2
Moravian	1,778	0.4	—	—
Presbyterian:				
Church of Scotland	77,929	16.0	26,702	3.8
Other Presbyterian	18,220	3.7	5,279	0.8
Dutch Reform	946	0.2	—	—
Quaker	5,200	1.1	—	—
Other Denominations	19,422	4.0	6,291	0.9
No response	81,348	16.7	18,798	2.7
Total	487,053	100.0	697,084	100.0

SOURCE: *Census of Canada, 1870-71*, Vol. 4, Ottawa, 1876, pp. 135 and 147.

per cent in Upper Canada where they were the single largest denomination. The second largest group in Upper Canada was the Church of Scotland with 16.0 per cent. All Presbyterian churches combined amounted to 19.9 per cent compared to 17.0 per cent for all Methodist groups.

Many of the early churches established in Canada maintained ties with their parent organizations in Europe; but, as national consciousness began to emerge, more and more effort was directed towards the establishment of independence from extra-national controls. S. D. Clark has argued that the movement towards union and autonomy, beginning as early as 1824 for the Methodists and culminating in the United Church of Canada in 1925, was part of a general movement towards national autonomy that characterized all forms of association.[4] However, Clark hastens to point out that movement towards union and autonomy, while clearly evident among the larger denominations, left many divided churches and new sects in its wake.[5]

Analysis of religious organization in Canada is difficult, at best, when using census data since it is not practical to identify all of the different religious groups with which the population identifies. Perhaps an unfortunate consequence is the misleading impression of simplicity of structure presented by use of the major religious denominational categories which tends to obscure the hundreds of existing religious bodies. Not only is diversity hidden within the "other" category, but much is also hidden within the major categories themselves. As late as 1942, *The Vital Statistics Instruction Manual* for Canada (containing instructions for coding religious affiliations stated on marriage, death, and birth certificates) listed 45 different designations referring to distinctly different Lutheran groups. While there is undoubtedly considerable overlap in many of the terms used, there are differences reflected by such terms as American Lutheran, German Reform, Lutheran Evangelical, Swinglion, and Zion Lutheran.[6] The fact remains that the census classification for religious denominations used in the following discussion of trends, like so many other general classification systems, exhibits considerable heterogeneity within categories. While there is little doubt as to the general sociological validity of the classification used, the reader must not lose sight of the greater complexity concealed within the data as presented in this chapter.

Growth of Religious Denominations in Canada

The Census of 1871, four years after Confederation, shows that 42.9 per cent of the population was Roman Catholic. For Quebec, the percentage was 85.7 per cent, or just slightly higher than for Lower Canada in 1844. Catholics were also proportionately larger in Ontario with 17.1 per cent compared to 13.4 per cent in 1842. Methodists and Presbyterians were approximately equal in number for Canada as a whole; but in Ontario the Methodists were the somewhat larger group, their percentages being 28.8 and 22.2 per cent respectively.[7]

Between 1871 and 1901, the proportions Catholic and Anglican continued to decline. The former decreased slightly to 41.7 per cent while Anglicans experienced a greater relative decline to 12.8 per cent. On the other hand, numerical gains for Lutherans, Methodists, and other religious denominations were sufficient to increase their proportionate share of the total population.

Trends in size for the eight principal denominations in 1961 are presented in Figure 7:1 for the period 1901 to 1961. A comparison of the rates of growth (revealed by the slope of the curve) for Roman Catholics and Anglicans indicates that the number of Anglicans increased at a more rapid rate than Catholics before 1921, and at a slower rate between 1921 and 1961. Not directly apparent from Figure 7:1 is the fact that in 1921 the proportion of Anglicans in the population reached its maximum value of 16.1 per cent while Roman Catholics simultaneously reached their minimum relative level of 38.7 per cent. It is quite clear that after 1921 the Anglican rate of growth never again exceeded that of the Roman Catholic; and, while they continued to increase in numbers, the numerical increase was not sufficient to prevent a decline in their relative size. By 1961, Anglicans constituted only 13.2 per cent of the total while Roman Catholics reached 45.7 per cent.

Fig. 7:1

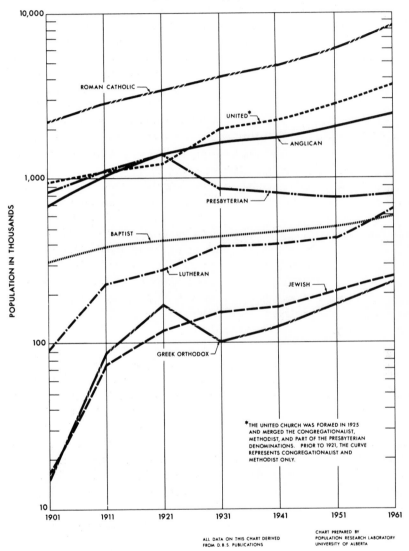

POPULATION TRENDS
SELECTED RELIGIOUS DENOMINATIONS
CANADA: 1901-1961

POPULATION IN THOUSANDS

ROMAN CATHOLIC

UNITED*

ANGLICAN

PRESBYTERIAN

BAPTIST

LUTHERAN

JEWISH

GREEK ORTHODOX

*THE UNITED CHURCH WAS FORMED IN 1925
AND MERGED THE CONGREGATIONALIST,
METHODIST, AND PART OF THE PRESBYTERIAN
DENOMINATIONS.   PRIOR TO 1921, THE CURVE
REPRESENTS CONGREGATIONALIST AND
METHODIST ONLY.

ALL DATA ON THIS CHART DERIVED
FROM D.B.S. PUBLICATIONS

CHART PREPARED BY
POPULATION RESEARCH LABORATORY
UNIVERSITY OF ALBERTA

Lutherans experienced their most rapid expansion during the first decade of the twentieth century and between 1951 and 1961 when their proportion increased from 3.2 to 3.8 per cent. Erratic growth curves for Presbyterians and the United Church of Canada between 1921 and 1931 reflect the upheaval and aftermath of the merger of Methodists, Congregationalists, and part of the Presbyterian denominations. Whereas the growth rate for the United Church has actually increased each decade since its inception, the number of Presbyterians declined until the 1951–61 decade when their numbers again showed an increase. As would be expected, the proportion of Presbyterians declined sharply from 16.1 to 8.4 per cent as a result of the formation of the United Church; and thereafter, their proportionate share continued to decline reaching 4.5 per cent in 1961. Methodists and Congregationalists ceased to exist in any significant numbers; and while the United Church increased from just over two million to three and two-thirds million in 1961, their proportion of the total population increased only perceptibly from 19.5 per cent in 1931 to 20.1 per cent in 1961.

That segment of the population claiming Judaic affiliation has shown continued growth from the earliest period for which information has been available, but they did not reach perceptible proportions until 1911 when they reached 1.0 per cent of the total. Between 1931 and 1951, the proportion Jewish reached 1.5 per cent; but, with a growth rate of only 24.2 per cent for the 1951–61 decade compared to 30.2 per cent for Canada, their proportionate share declined slightly to 1.4 per cent. Since the Jews are a highly urbanized and educated population, and as such have the low fertility associated with these characteristics, their continued growth has been maintained primarily through continuing immigration.

The Baptists, who were the sixth largest denomination in Canada in 1961, have shown steady numerical increases throughout this period reaching 593,553 members in 1961. However, since their rate of growth has been continually below that for all denominations combined, the proportion who were Baptists has steadily declined from 5.9 per cent in 1901, to 3.3 per cent in 1961. The drop in numbers for Greek Orthodox shown in Figure 7:1 has no sociological relevance as it is simply a consequence of removing approximately 187,000 Ukrainian (Greek) Catholics in 1931 from the previously combined category consisting of both Greek Orthodox and Greek Catholics.

Minor religious denominations. A number of smaller religious groups have been visible in Canadian census data for close to 100 years, but most made their statistical debut at the beginning of the twentieth century during the era of large scale European immigration. However, as early as the 1871 Census, 6,202 Adventists, 539 Mormons, 2,289 Unitarians, and 62,874 members of other miscellaneous denominations were enumerated. Two other groups increased to the point where separate recognition was given in the published census reports prior to 1901. In 1881, Churches of Christ Disciples accounted

Table 7:3

ADHERENTS OF SPECIFIED SMALLER RELIGIOUS DENOMINATIONS, CANADA, 1901–1961

Denomination	1901	1911	1921	1931	1941	1951	1961
Adventist	8,092	10,462	14,200	16,058	18,485	21,398	25,999
Buddhist	10,531	10,072	11,316	15,921	15,676	8,184	11,611
Christian and Missionary Alliance	—	128	283	3,560	4,214	6,396	18,006
Christian Science	2,644	5,099	13,856	18,499	20,261	20,795	19,466
Churches of Christ, Disciples	17,250	14,610	13,125	15,831	21,260	14,920	19,512
Doukhobor	8,858	10,616	12,674	14,978	16,878	13,175	13,234
Free Methodist Church of Canada	—	—	—	7,740	8,805	8,921	14,245
Jehovah's Witnesses	101	938	6,689	13,582	7,007	34,596	68,018
Mennonite[a]	31,949	44,972	58,874	88,837	111,554	125,938	152,452
Mormon	7,061	16,115	19,657	22,041	25,328	32,888	50,016
Pentecostal	—	515	7,012	26,349	57,742	95,131	143,877
Salvation Army	10,360	18,909	24,771	30,773	33,609	70,275	92,054
Ukrainian (Greek) Catholic	—[b]	—[b]	—[b]	186,879[c]	185,948[c]	191,051[c]	189,653[c]
Unitarian	2,032	3,275	4,943	4,453	5,584	3,517	15,062
Other	93,307	160,627	173,703	177,904	179,519	241,395	420,151

SOURCE: Dominion Bureau of Statistics, *1961 Census of Canada*, Bulletin 7:1-11, Ottawa, The Queen's Printer, 1965, Table III.

[a] Includes Hutterite.

[b] "Greek Catholic" and "Greek Orthodox" combined under "Greek Church".

[c] Includes "Other Greek Catholic".

for 20,253 persons; and in 1891, members of the Salvation Army were separated from the "other" category and 14,131 were listed in that year. As may be seen in Table 7:3, four new denominations were identified in the 1901 Census, including Buddhists, Christian Scientists, Doukhobors, Jehovah's Witnesses, and Mennonites. The latter group, which includes Hutterites, had been included with Baptists in 1871 and 1881 but were identified for the first time as a separate group in 1901. By 1911, the Christian Missionary Alliance with 128 members and Pentecostal with 515 achieved separate census recognition. Of the remaining denominations in Table 7:3, only the Free Methodists constituted a new census group, having come into existence as a result of the emergence of the United Church in 1925. Predecessors of the 186,879 Ukrainian Catholics in 1931 had been previously combined with the Greek Orthodox Church as noted above.

Regional distribution. If the various religious denominations were evenly distributed throughout the population, each province would have the same proportion of Anglicans, Catholics, and other denominations in its population as they are found in the total population. Thus, the larger provinces, by virtue of their larger size, would tend to have more of each denomination than the smaller ones. But the important question to answer here is: "To what extent do specific religious denominations tend to be over- or under-represented in each of the provinces?" Knowing that religion is an important dimension of ethnic identity, and having already shown the unique distributional patterns for specific ethnic and racial groups, it is not surprising to find in Figure 7:2 that certain religious denominations also show distributional patterns similar to those for ethnic populations.

The most obvious concentration of any religious group in 1961 is the Roman Catholics in Quebec. They account for 55.6 per cent of all Catholics in Canada and constitute 88.1 per cent of that province's population, compared to 45.7 per cent for the country as a whole. Another 22.4 per cent were living in Ontario in 1961, but this represented only 30 per cent of the province's population. The only other area which had an over-representation of Roman Catholics was New Brunswick where they comprised 52.0 per cent of the total. Members of Greek Orthodox and Ukrainian Catholic Churches were heavily concentrated in the Prairies where the former were to be found more in Saskatchewan and Alberta while the latter were located in disproportionately greater numbers in Manitoba and Saskatchewan.

Numbers of Anglicans, relative to their respective provincial populations, had their highest concentrations in the Northwest Territories, Yukon, Newfoundland, and British Columbia. While 46.4 per cent of their total was located in Ontario, Anglicans constituted just 17.9 per cent of that province's population compared to 13.2 per cent for Canada. For the United Church, their highest relative concentrations were to be found in the West, especially Saskatchewan, Alberta, and British Columbia. Presbyterians who did not

Fig. 7:2

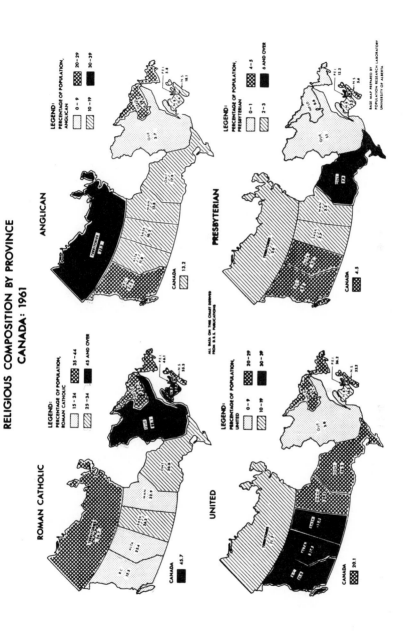

RELIGIOUS COMPOSITION BY PROVINCE
CANADA: 1961

join with the Methodists in forming the United Church, were most heavily concentrated in Prince Edward Island, and to a considerably lesser extent in Ontario.

Lutherans were found primarily west of Ontario and in the Yukon, while Baptists were more concentrated in the Atlantic Provinces of Prince Edward Island, Nova Scotia, and New Brunswick. For the other lesser Protestant denominations, considerable variation characterized their distributional patterns. The Salvation Army was most highly concentrated in Newfoundland where they comprised 7.9 per cent of the population compared to 0.5 per cent for Canada as a whole. Lesser concentrations were found in Nova Scotia; and, in Ontario, which claimed 34.6 per cent of all Salvation Army members, they constituted only 0.5 per cent of the province's population. Others, like the Churches of Christ Disciples were situated in both the Maritimes and western Prairie Provinces. Pentecostal had its heaviest concentration in Newfoundland, followed by New Brunswick, Northwest Territories, and British Columbia. Other smaller groups were located primarily in the West, e.g., Adventists, Christian Scientists, Doukhobors, Evangelical United Brethren, Jehovah's Witnesses, Mennonites, and Mormons.

The Jews had their highest relative concentrations in Manitoba, Quebec, and Ontario respectively. The Oriental religions, i.e., Confucian and Buddhists, were primarily in Alberta and British Columbia with lesser concentrations in Ontario, Manitoba, and the Yukon. Table 7:4 presents the percentage distribution of the population by religious denominations for provinces in 1961. The relative degree of concentration may be determined rather easily by comparing the proportion for a particular denomination in a province with its corresponding proportion for Canada as a whole.

Rural-urban distribution. Generally, regional settlement patterns appear to be closely associated with the degree of urbanization experienced by specific denominations with those settling primarily in the Prairies and Maritimes being less urbanized than the population as a whole. Of the larger denominations shown in Figure 7:3, the Jews were almost completely urbanized with 99.0 per cent living in urban areas in 1961. Presbyterians, Anglicans, Greek Orthodox, and Roman Catholics were all above the average for the country as a whole (69.6 per cent), although the latter group, with 70.4 per cent urban, was only slightly more urbanized. United Church, Lutheran, and Baptist all fell below the average with 66.6, 65.2, and 62.4 per cent respectively.

Of the 20 denominations shown in Table 7:5, only three more in addition to the four already mentioned above had proportions urban higher than that for Canada as a whole. It is interesting to note that only the Greek Orthodox had fewer than two-thirds of their members living in the three provinces of Quebec, Ontario, and British Columbia. The most urbanized, the Jews, had

Table 7:4

PERCENTAGE DISTRIBUTION OF THE POPULATION BY RELIGIOUS DENOMINATIONS FOR PROVINCES, 1961

Denomination	Canada	Nfld.	P.E.I.	N.S.	N.B.	Que.	Ont.	Man.	Sask.	Alta.	B.C.	Yukon	N.W.T.
Adventist	0.1	0.1	0.1	0.2	0.2	—	0.1	0.1	0.3	0.4	0.4	—	—
Anglican	13.2	28.5	5.8	18.1	11.4	3.7	17.9	13.8	10.2	11.8	22.5	30.9	38.5
Baptist	3.3	0.2	5.7	13.7	15.7	0.3	4.0	1.9	1.8	3.2	3.0	4.8	0.8
Christian Reformed	—	—	—	—	—	—	0.7	0.2	—	0.8	0.4	0.1	—
Christian Science	0.1	—	0.1	0.1	—	—	0.1	0.1	0.1	0.1	0.3	0.1	—
Churches of Christ, Disciples	0.1	—	1.1	0.2	0.2	—	—	—	—	0.2	—	—	—
Confucian and Buddhist	0.1	—	—	—	—	—	0.1	0.1	0.2	0.2	0.5	—	—
Doukhobor	0.1	—	—	—	—	—	—	—	0.4	0.1	0.6	0.1	—
Evangelical United Brethren	—	—	—	—	—	—	0.1	0.1	0.3	0.5	0.2	—	—
Greek Orthodox	1.3	0.2	—	0.1	0.2	0.6	1.3	3.0	3.5	3.6	1.0	—	0.8
Jehovah's Witnesses	0.4	0.1	0.2	0.4	0.2	0.1	0.4	0.5	0.8	0.6	0.9	0.8	0.1
Jewish	1.4	0.1	—	0.3	0.3	2.0	1.8	2.2	0.3	0.4	0.5	0.4	0.1
Lutheran	3.6	—	0.1	1.6	—	0.4	3.9	6.9	10.3	9.2	6.2	6.0	2.1
Mennonite	0.8	—	—	—	—	—	0.5	6.2	3.0	1.2	1.2	0.1	0.1
Mormon	0.3	—	—	—	—	—	0.2	0.1	0.2	1.9	0.4	0.2	0.1
Pentecostal	0.8	4.4	0.4	0.6	2.0	0.1	0.8	0.8	1.0	1.1	1.2	0.7	1.4
Presbyterian	4.5	0.6	12.2	5.6	2.3	1.1	7.9	3.2	2.7	4.2	5.5	5.6	1.4
Roman Catholic	45.8	35.7	46.1	35.3	52.0	88.1	30.0	22.9	26.2	22.4	17.5	27.2	42.9
Salvation Army	0.5	7.9	0.2	0.6	0.3	0.1	0.5	0.2	0.3	0.2	0.4	0.2	—
Ukrainian Catholic	1.0	—	—	0.1	—	—	0.8	6.3	3.8	2.6	0.4	0.3	0.3
United Church	20.1	21.4	26.2	22.2	14.3	3.0	26.3	29.3	32.0	31.4	31.0	17.2	8.2
Other	2.5	0.1	1.6	0.8	0.7	0.4	2.4	1.9	2.7	3.8	5.9	5.0	3.2
Total	100.0	100.0	100.0	100.0	100.0	100.0	100.0	100.0	100.0	100.0	100.0	100.0	100.0

SOURCE: Dominion Bureau of Statistics, *1961 Census of Canada*, Bulletin 7:1-11, Ottawa, The Queen's Printer, 1965, Table VI, and Table I.

Table 7:5

RANK ORDER OF POPULATION BY PER CENT URBAN FOR RELIGIOUS DENOMINATIONS SHOWING DISTRIBUTION BY URBAN SIZE GROUPS AND TYPES OF RURAL AREAS, CANADA, 1961

Denomination	Rank Order	Total	Urban					Rural Non-farm	Rural farm
			Total	100,000 and over	30,000 to 99,999	10,000 to 29,999	Under 10,000		
Jewish	1	100.0	99.0	94.5	2.6	0.9	1.0	0.7	0.3
Christian Science	2	100.0	82.6	64.3	8.0	4.4	5.9	11.9	5.5
Confucian and Buddhist	3	100.0	82.0	65.7	5.7	5.1	5.5	11.4	6.6
Presbyterian	4	100.0	75.5	48.0	9.5	7.0	11.0	14.7	9.8
Anglican	5	100.0	74.1	48.9	9.3	5.9	10.0	20.2	5.7
Greek Orthodox	6	100.0	72.7	57.6	6.9	2.6	5.6	10.3	17.0
Roman Catholic	7	100.0	70.4	43.0	10.2	5.6	11.6	18.6	11.0
Salvation Army	8	100.0	68.3	28.0	10.4	10.7	19.2	29.5	2.2
Other	9	100.0	68.2	47.0	6.2	5.4	9.6	19.2	12.6
Mormon	10	100.0	66.9	31.1	11.9	5.9	18.0	18.0	15.1
United Church	11	100.0	66.6	39.4	9.1	6.2	11.9	20.4	13.0
Lutheran	12	100.0	65.2	43.5	7.2	5.1	9.4	17.0	17.8
Baptist	13	100.0	62.4	33.5	10.2	6.8	11.9	26.7	10.9
Jehovah's Witnesses	14	100.0	60.0	34.2	8.7	6.1	10.5	25.3	14.7
Ukrainian (Greek) Catholic	15	100.0	59.9	41.8	8.3	3.0	6.8	13.2	26.9
Pentecostal	16	100.0	57.4	26.5	7.7	8.1	15.1	30.4	12.2
Churches of Christ, Disciples	17	100.0	52.8	27.1	8.2	6.4	11.1	29.2	18.0
Christian Reformed	18	100.0	52.0	28.4	8.0	7.2	8.4	20.5	27.5
Adventist	19	100.0	51.2	27.9	10.5	4.8	8.0	28.8	20.0
Evangelical United Brethren	20	100.0	51.0	27.7	1.5	8.5	13.3	20.9	28.1
Mennonite	21	100.0	34.5	16.3	5.1	1.6	11.5	19.3	46.2
Total		100.0	69.6	43.4	9.3	5.8	11.1	19.0	11.4

SOURCE: Dominion Bureau of Statistics, *1961 Census of Canada*, Bulletin 7:1-11, Ottawa, The Queen's Printer, 1965, Table 2.

Fig. 7:3

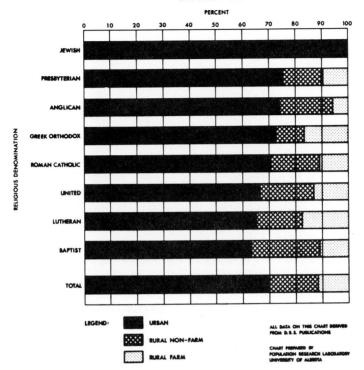

PLACE OF RESIDENCE
BY SELECTED RELIGIOUS DENOMINATIONS
CANADA: 1961

87.3 per cent residing in the three largest provinces compared to 71.9 per cent for all religious groups combined.

Data in Table 7:5 show that, with the exception of Roman Catholics, those denominations with above average proportions residing in urban areas tended to have disproportionately greater numbers living in the larger urban areas of 100,000 population and over. Roman Catholics exceeded the average for Canada because of slightly larger proportions residing in urban places 30,000–99,999 and under 10,000 population. By way of contrast, Christian Reformed, Evangelical United Brethren, Mennonites, and Ukrainian Catholics have more than double the national average living on rural farms. Adventists are most heavily concentrated in rural farm and somewhat less in non-farm rural areas. Pentecostals tend to be concentrated in rural non-farm areas and urban areas under 30,000 while the Salvation Army and Baptists tend to be concentrated in rural non-farm areas and urban places up to 100,000 in population.

It is interesting to speculate on rural-urban trends as they may affect religious composition of the population in the future. Analysis of changes between 1951 and 1961 indicate that urbanization has not proceeded any more uniformly for the various religious denominations than it has regionally. Since religious composition of regions can be affected by conversions and fertility differentials, as well as shifts in character of immigration streams and changes in internal migration, projections of future trends become very difficult. Between 1951 and 1961, Lutherans in rural areas decreased from 54.2 to 34.8 per cent, while their urban numbers increased by 112.0 per cent compared to 47.2 per cent for all denominations combined. The Mennonites increased from 19.6 to 34.5 per cent urban, and Greek Orthodox from 53.7 to 72.7 per cent over the same period. Roman Catholics and Pentecostal denominations also showed larger percentage increases than for the total combined population.[8] All of these groups experienced significant increases in their urban populations between 1951 and 1961. However, during the same period the proportion foreign born increased significantly only among Lutherans, Greek Orthodox, and Roman Catholics. For Mennonites and Pentecostals, the native-born component increased at a faster rate so that their proportion foreign born actually declined.[9] Thus, the increase among urban Lutherans, while reflecting many of the factors previously mentioned, in all probability was due more to heavy urban immigration during this particular decade than to rural-urban movement of the native born. For Mennonites, the reverse appears to be true; i.e., the relatively small increase in foreign born through immigration suggests that the primary source of urban growth was rural-urban movement.

Factors Affecting Changes in Religious Composition

Each religious denomination is made up of native- and foreign-born components that vary in age-sex structure. For the native born, probably the most important factor affecting their size is the natural increase of their members and their ability to retain their children within their denomination. For the foreign born, growth is assured only if the number of net migrants exceeds the numbers dying plus those dropping out of the church. No doubt conversions are important for both groups, but the absence of relevant and reliable data do not permit analysis of its significance. Data on inter-marriage, which have been included, show the extent to which marriage patterns tend to support the existing religious structure; but the extent of pre-marriage conversions reflected in these data is indeterminate.

Immigration. Data presented in Table 7:6 show number and per cent foreign born for the major religious denominations in 1951 and 1961. All groups, except Ukrainian Catholic, increased their numbers because immigration exceeded the combined effects of mortality and emigration. However, only in the case of five specific denominations was this gain in foreign born sufficient to exceed the growth rate among native born, and thus achieve

Table 7:6

NUMBER AND PER CENT FOREIGN BORN FOR MAJOR RELIGIOUS DENOMINATIONS, CANADA, 1951 AND 1961

Denomination	1951			1961		
	Total	Number Foreign Born	Per Cent Foreign Born	Total	Number Foreign Born	Per Cent Foreign Born
Anglican	2,060,720	487,400	23.6	2,409,068	510,980	21.2
Baptist	519,585	62,372	12.0	593,553	69,274	11.7
Greek Orthodox	172,271	70,209	40.7	239,766	111,629	46.5
Jewish	204,836	91,096	44.5	254,368	104,636	41.1
Lutheran	444,923	164,696	37.0	662,744	272,848	41.2
Mennonite	125,938	27,283	21.7	152,452	30,657	20.1
Pentecostal	95,131	12,424	13.0	143,877	17,380	12.1
Presbyterian	781,747	184,886	23.6	818,558	193,932	23.7
Roman Catholic[a]	6,069,496	434,289	7.1	8,342,826	886,111	10.6
Ukrainian Catholic[a]	191,051	74,386	38.9	189,653	63,951	33.7
United Church	2,867,271	332,962	11.6	3,664,008	381,436	10.4
All Others	476,460	117,908	24.7	767,374	201,429	26.2
Totals	14,009,429	2,059,911	14.7	18,238,247	2,844,263	15.6

SOURCE: W. E. Kalbach, *The Impact of Immigration on Canada's Population*, Ottawa, The Queen's Printer, 1970, Table 2:16.
[a] Includes Greek Catholic.

an increase in their proportion of the total. Percentage increases during the 1951–61 decade were highest for Roman Catholics, Greek Orthodox, and Lutherans. Foreign born belonging to all Catholic denominations combined have increased from 28.1 to 37.3 per cent, while Jewish and Protestant totals declined from 71.9 to 62.7 per cent.[10] Clearly, immigration since 1931, and especially during the 1951–61 decade, has contributed to an increasing proportion of population belonging to Catholic denominations.

Natural increase. There is little evidence to support any hypothesis as to the existence of significant religious differentials in age-sex specific mortality. However, unless the differences are considerable, the important factor is the age-sex structure. An older population will produce more deaths relative to births than a young population so that certain denominations, with many members beyond the childbearing ages, will tend to have lower rates of increase than other groups having relatively young populations. Thus, the age structure provides some evidence as to the balance between births and deaths and the population's potential for future growth. High fertility levels will produce high proportions of the population under 15 years of age and rela-

Fig. 7:4

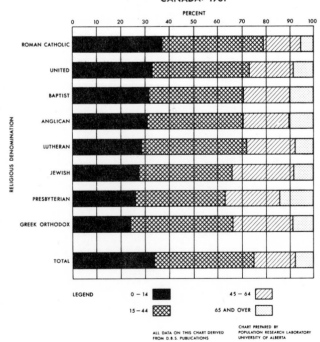

RELIGIOUS COMPOSITION
BY SELECTED AGE GROUPS
CANADA: 1961

tively small numbers 65 and over. Conversely, those denominations whose members are characterized by low fertility will have larger proportions in the older age groups. In the case of religious populations, there is an additional factor which must be taken into account when considering the importance of the differences in age structures visible in Figure 7:4. Significant changes in membership can occur as a result of reorganization, as in the case of the founding of the United Church. Those Presbyterians not joining the new church were undoubtedly many of the older members who tend to have difficulty adapting to change. Certainly the unusually large proportion of Presbyterians 65 years of age and over cannot be explained in terms of fertility alone, as their fertility was not the lowest for the various denominations considered in Table 7:7.

A more accurate picture of the relative fertility levels of the various denominations can be obtained by examining their age-sex structure in greater detail, which is possible with the population pyramids presented in Figure 7:5. By examining the relative sizes of the age groups under five years and the number of women in the childbearing ages, i.e., 15–44 years, an estimate of the effective fertility of the several denominations can be obtained. It is immediately apparent that both Mennonite and Roman Catholic populations are high fertility populations. It is equally apparent that the Jewish, Greek

Table 7:7

CHILDREN 0–4 PER 1,000 WOMEN, 15–44, BY RELIGIOUS DENOMINATIONS, FOR CANADA, 1951 AND 1961

Denomination	1951	1961
Mormon	638	713
Mennonite	581	712
Salvation Army	696	696
Roman Catholic	616	666
Pentecostal	583	652
United Church of Canada	529	574
Baptist	510	565
Churches of Christ, Disciples	509	564
Confucian and Buddhist	375	557
Lutheran	440	533
Anglican Church of Canada	525	533
Adventist	466	531
Ukrainian (Greek) Catholic	415	501
Presbyterian	441	487
Greek Orthodox	383	426
Jewish	444	421
Christian Science	341	365
Total	555	606

SOURCE: Dominion Bureau of Statistics, *1961 Census of Canada*, Bulletin 7:1-11, Ottawa, The Queen's Printer, 1965, Table IX.

Orthodox, and Presbyterians are low fertility groups. Furthermore, in the case of the Jews, the declining proportions under 15 years of age is suggestive of declining fertility. However, there are other factors which could produce a similar effect, such as young families with small children who cease to identify themselves as being affiliated with a particular denomination.

Inferences concerning relative fertility levels for the various denominations illustrated in Figure 7:5, are consistent with, and supported by, the child-woman ratios presented in Table 7:7. Interestingly, all groups but the Jews showed increasing levels of fertility between 1951 and 1961. Thus, the Jewish religious population structure may be expected to age relatively quickly if this trend should persist for any length of time. In general, those with the lowest child-woman ratios in 1961 tended to have the highest proportions of their population 45 years of age and over. Christian Scientists, for example, with the lowest ratio both in 1951 and 1961, had the highest proportion 45 years of age and over (46.1 per cent). The four next lowest groups, shown in Table 7:7, had proportions 45 years of age and over ranging from 36.9 to 31.2 per cent, including the Jews, who showed a decline in their fertility ratio.[11] By contrast, the five denominations with the highest fertility had considerably lower proportions 45 years and over.

It is not unexpected to find that Roman Catholics, like the French origin population of which they constitute the major share, have depended heavily on natural increase for continued growth. The small part played by immigration is reflected in the fact that only 10.6 per cent of Roman Catholics were foreign born in 1961. More surprising, perhaps, is the fact that Mormons, Mennonites, and the Salvation Army all had higher fertility as measured by the child-woman ratio. Barring the possibility of other significant attenuating factors, these particular denominations can be expected to increase their proportionate share at a faster rate than other denominations are able to through fertility. The expected overall effect on the balance between Catholic and other denominations will be rather insignificant as these high fertility groups are relatively small in numbers. Evidence of this may be found in the fact that the proportion of native-born Catholics has continued to increase since 1931. At that time, 47.5 per cent of the population was reported as Catholic compared to 50.1 per cent in 1961.[12] The trend for both foreign and native-born populations has been towards an increasing proportion of Catholics. The native born exceeded the 50 per cent mark in 1961, while the proportion Catholic among foreign born increased rapidly between 1951 and 1961. Canada should achieve its Catholic majority very soon.

Inter-marriage. In 1967, 65.0 per cent of the 331,758 persons marrying that year married someone of the same religious faith.[13] It is quite possible that in many of these marriages either the bride or groom may have been converted from their faith to that of their marriage partner's prior to the actual ceremony. To the extent that this happens, the degree of homogeneity

Fig. 7:5

AGE AND SEX COMPOSITION
SELECTED RELIGIOUS DENOMINATIONS
CANADA: 1961

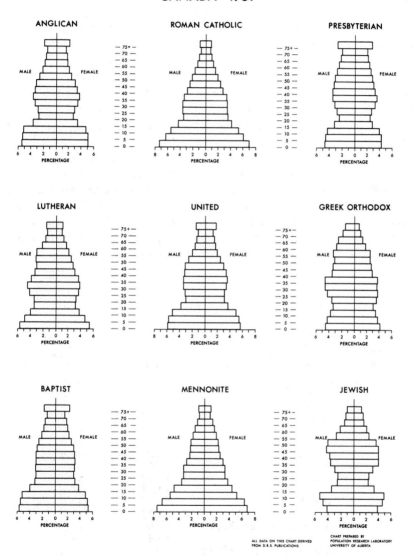

ALL DATA ON THIS CHART DERIVED
FROM D.B.S. PUBLICATIONS

CHART PREPARED BY
POPULATION RESEARCH LABORATORY
UNIVERSITY OF ALBERTA

might appear greater than is actually the case. However, regardless of the degree of conversion which might occur at this stage, additional evidence suggests that further conversion occurs subsequent to marriage. A comparison of religious characteristics of married persons reported in the 1941 Census with marriage statistics for the preceding decade showed a much closer agreement in the religious characteristics of husbands and wives than at the time of marriage.[14] The data do suggest that the propensity to marry within one's own religious group is relatively strong whether the reasons are social, cultural, or due to such contingencies as residential propinquity. Jews and Roman Catholics had the highest proportions of brides and grooms reporting the same religion, with 87.6 and 84.4 per cent respectively; and Mennonites, with 67.0 per cent, had the third largest proportion.[15]

A degree of consistency in religious intra-marriage over time is evident from an examination of data in Table 7:8 which give the proportion of brides having the same religious affiliation as the groom. Note that in these data, representing total marriages for the three-year period 1959–61, Jewish grooms also had the highest proportion of any denomination, 89.0 per cent, marrying brides of their own faith. Catholic grooms, with 88.2 per cent were second, followed by Mennonites with 75.9 per cent. Of all denominations listed, only the Christian Scientists had a higher proportion of grooms marrying brides of another denomination than of their own faith. In this case, 31.1

Table 7:8

AVERAGE PERCENTAGE OF BRIDES HAVING SAME RELIGIOUS
AFFILIATION AS GROOMS, CANADA, 1959–1961

Denomination of Groom	Number of Marriages	Per Cent of Brides
Jewish	1,533	89.0
Roman Catholic	60,564	88.2
Mennonite	1,149	75.9
Greek Orthodox	2,607	63.8
United Church	23,996	61.6
Adventist	171	59.6
Pentecostal	1,102	58.5
Mormon	342	53.5
Greek Catholic	1,549	50.8
Anglican	14,851	49.6
Salvation Army	578	47.8
Baptist	4,533	45.8
Evangelical United Brethren	207	44.9
Lutheran	5,590	44.5
Churches of Christ, Disciples	155	41.3
Presbyterian	4,843	36.7
Christian Science	74	28.4

SOURCE: Dominion Bureau of Statistics, *1961 Census of Canada*, Bulletin 7:1-11, Ottawa, The Queen's Printer, 1965, Table XII.

per cent of the grooms married brides who reported belonging to the United Church compared to 28.4 per cent who married other Christian Scientists.[16]

The significance for the total population's religious character of approximately one-third of its marriages being inter-denominational is impossible to ascertain on the basis of vital statistics alone. Census data, while restricted to cross-sectional pictures of religious composition at various points in time, do show the net effect of religious inter-marriage on the religious character of the total population in combination with the effects of net migration and natural increase. However, the extent of conversions or the processes by which they occur within families and how children acquire their religious identity can only be revealed through original field research.

REFERENCES

Clark, S. D.: *The Developing Canadian Community*. Toronto, University of Toronto Press, 1962.
Dominion Bureau of Statistics: *1961 Census of Canada, General Review: Religious Denominations in Canada*, Bulletin 7:1–11. Ottawa, The Queen's Printer, 1965.

FOOTNOTES

[1]*Census of Canada, 1870–71*, Vol. 4, Ottawa, 1876, "Census of Assiniboia, 1831, Table III", p. 105.

[2]*Ibid.*, Table II.

[3]*Ibid.*, p. 94.

[4]S. D. Clark, *The Developing Canadian Community*, Toronto, University of Toronto Press, 1962, pp. 115–117.

[5]Clark presents a very interesting analysis of the efforts to achieve unity among the major denominations and the emergence of religious sects as a concomitant of success in achieving union, autonomy, and social status. See his discussion in *The Developing Canadian Community, op. cit.*, pp. 117–130.

[6]By way of further illustration, the general Presbyterian category had 23 identifiable groups including Calvinists, Burning Bush, MacDonaldites, etc. The general residual category "Other" included 124 different entries among which were such groups as the Amana Society, Anglo-Israelites, Druids, Evening Lights, Johannites, Rosecrucians, Round Church and Theosophists.

[7]Dominion Bureau of Statistics, *1961 Census of Canada*, Bulletin 7:1–11, Ottawa, The Queen's Printer, 1965, Table I.

[8]*Ibid.*, Table V.

[9]W. E. Kalbach, *Impact of Immigration on Canada's Population*, Ottawa, The Queen's Printer, 1970, Table 2.16.

[10]*Ibid.*, Table 2.17, p. 69.

[11]Dominion Bureau of Statistics, *1961 Census of Canada*, Bulletin 7:1–11, Ottawa, The Queen's Printer, 1965, Table VIII, pp. 11–13.

[12]W. E. Kalbach, *op. cit.*

[13]Dominion Bureau of Statistics, *Vital Statistics, 1967*, Ottawa, The Queen's Printer, 1969, Table M7.

[14]Census Division, Dominion Bureau of Statistics, "Some Characteristics of Husbands and Wives Indicated in the Census and Vital Statistics", Reference Paper No. 10, 1950, Ottawa.
[15]Dominion Bureau of Statistics, *Vital Statistics, 1967, op. cit.*
[16]Dominion Bureau of Statistics, *1961 Census of Canada, op. cit.,* Table XII.

Educational Attainment

At the turn of the nineteenth century, most people still retained the belief that education was the primary concern of church and home. Without taxation to support schools and the means to train teachers, there was obviously no need for compulsory attendance laws. What few elementary or common schools there were in Upper Canada had been established with local support only, and the use of tutors was limited to those who could afford them. During the early settlement of Canada, the Roman Catholic Church as well as others played important roles in the education of the young. In Lower Canada, i.e., Quebec, the Roman Catholic Church continued to be a dominant factor in education; but elsewhere the power of the Church waned as education became increasingly secularized.[1]

The first act to provide free education was passed in Prince Edward Island in 1852, with others following in Nova Scotia and New Brunswick in 1864 and 1871 respectively.[2] The British North American Act of 1867 insured that education would remain the responsibility of the provinces with the exception of those Canadians living outside the ten provinces and Indians and Eskimos, regardless of their place of residence.[3] Following Confederation, the provinces formed departments of education, compulsory attendance laws were established, and tax measures were introduced to provide the necessary revenues to build, maintain, and staff the facilities required to meet the educational needs of the provinces.

Canada's churches, in addition to their contribution to primary and secondary education, were also responsible for the establishment of the nation's first universities and academies of higher learning. The Anglican King's College of Nova Scotia, founded in 1802, was the first university. This was followed by the Baptist academies of Pictou and Horton, Dalhousie University in 1818, McGill University in 1821, Anglican King's College at York (Toronto) in 1827, the Anglican King's College of New Brunswick in 1829, and the Roman Catholic College of Laval in 1852.[4]

From these early and modest beginnings, the federal and provincial educational systems of Canada had expanded to 21,547 public and separate elementary and secondary schools, and 370 institutions of higher education by 1964. In addition, there were 1,135 private and 416 special schools for students at elementary and secondary levels and 122 teacher's colleges.[5] Following Confederation, illiteracy was gradually reduced to the point where it was no longer considered necessary to collect information on this problem. In the Census of 1941, attention was directed to the task of evaluating the level of educational attainment; and, for this reason, the analyses in this chapter deal primarily with (1) school attendance and (2) educational attainment.

Historical Trends in School Attendance

The population attending schools in Canada has increased by 370 per cent, from 892,831 in 1901 to 4,198,165 in 1961.[6] This increase was considerably greater than either the 240 per cent increase in total population or the 207 per cent increase in population 5–19 years of age during the same period. Rates of growth, calculated on the basis of data in Table 8:1, show that the decade growth rates for the population attending school have fluctuated considerably more than similar rates calculated for the population 5–19 years of age. This would suggest that social and economic factors are significant for changes in school attendance beyond variations in decade rates of growth exhibited by the specific population at risk, i.e., those of school age.

With the exception of the depression decade, 1931–41, the proportion of population 5–19 years of age attending school increased throughout the 60-year period with the largest increase occurring during the decade of heavy immigration and high fertility just prior to the census of 1961. The number attending school increased from 2,386,780 to 4,198,165—the largest absolute gain ever experienced in any decade. Note in Figure 8:1 that the age group with the most spectacular improvement since 1921 was the 15–19 year-olds. While all age groups under 20 years of age showed significant increases during the 1950s, the 15–19 year-old males experienced the largest relative gains. In fact, 1951 marked the first time since 1921 that the percentage of males in this age group exceeded that for females, and the gap increased markedly during the subsequent decade. Significant changes also occurred in the attendance trends for the 20–24 year age group. Rates for both males and females have increased through time; but, following World War II, the attendance for males increased at a more rapid rate than for females.

Table 8:1

THE SCHOOL AGE POPULATION, 5–19 YEARS, AND PROPORTION ATTENDING SCHOOL, CANADA,[a] 1901–1961

Year	Total Population	Population 5-19		Population Attending School		Ratio of Attendance and Population Growth Rates by Decade
		Number	Per Cent	Number	Per Cent of Pop. 5-19 Yrs.	
1901	5,371,315	1,745,521	32.5	892,831[b]	51.1	—
1911	7,206,643	2,161,217	30.0	1,144,184	52.9	1.18
1921	8,787,949	2,761,092	31.4	1,694,430	61.4	1.73
1931	10,376,786	3,242,213	31.2	2,128,907	65.7	1.47
1941	11,506,655	3,261,997	28.3	2,131,567	65.3	0.20
1951	14,009,429	3,580,083	25.6	2,386,780[c]	66.7	1.23
1961	18,238,247	5,357,331	29.4	4,198,165	78.4	1.53

SOURCE: Dominion Bureau of Statistics, *1961 Census of Canada*, Bulletin 7:1-10, Table I, and Bulletin 7:1-4, Table 2, Ottawa, The Queen's Printer, 1965.
[a] Includes Newfoundland in 1951 and 1961. Excludes Yukon and Northwest Territories for all years.
[b] School attendance figures for all ages for 1901 only.
[c] Attendance at Kindergarten was not counted as school attendance in the 1951 Census.

Fig. 8:1

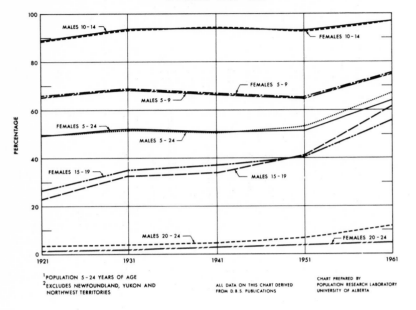

SCHOOL ATTENDANCE TRENDS[1]
BY SELECTED AGE GROUPS AND SEX
CANADA: 1921 – 1961[2]

[1]POPULATION 5 - 24 YEARS OF AGE
[2]EXCLUDES NEWFOUNDLAND, YUKON AND NORTHWEST TERRITORIES

ALL DATA ON THIS CHART DERIVED FROM D.B.S. PUBLICATIONS

CHART PREPARED BY POPULATION RESEARCH LABORATORY UNIVERSITY OF ALBERTA

Fig. 8:2

ENROLMENT TRENDS
CANADA: 1951 – 1961

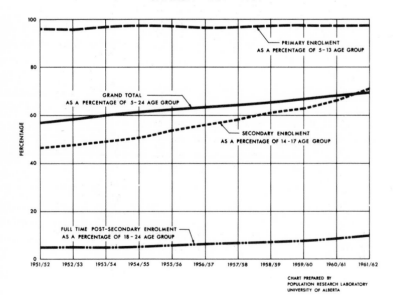

CHART PREPARED BY
POPULATION RESEARCH LABORATORY
UNIVERSITY OF ALBERTA

Figure 8:2 gives a more detailed picture of annual enrolment trends in Canada between 1951 and 1961, showing that the proportion of the school age population 5–24 years of age increased steadily during this decade. The most significant increases in enrolments occurred at the secondary level, particularly following the 1954–55 year, and the post-secondary level, where full-time enrolment as a percentage of the 18–24 year-old group increased from 4.9 to 9.5 per cent.[7]

Just as important were the relative rates of change of the total population 5–19 years of age and the numbers actually attending school. Comparing increases by decades for these two groups, the 1911–21 period shows that the rate of increase in attendance exceeded the growth rate for this age group by 73 per cent, compared to 53 per cent for the more recent 1951–61 decade. This would suggest that periods of high immigration and economic growth are also periods of greater educational participation (at least as measured by school attendance in relation to the total eligible population). Conversely, periods of economic depression tend to reduce immigration, fertility, as well as the level of school attendance. Note that while the population 5–19 years of age increased by 0.6 per cent between 1931 and 1941, the population attending school increased by only 0.1 per cent; hence, the proportion of this age group actually attending school declined from 65.7 to 65.3 per cent.

Educational Attainment of the Population in 1961

Assessing a population's educational quality in terms of the highest grade or year of schooling attained by its members represented a departure from earlier census procedures. While this change was consistent with recommendations made by the Statistical Office of the United Nations and will facilitate comparative analyses at the international level, it presents certain difficulties for any historical analysis of educational trends in Canada. However, it is important to know both how the school population is distributed throughout the educational system for those currently attending school as well as the educational attainment of the population 15 years of age and over not attending school. The loss in comparability with earlier data is more than compensated for by the gain in information.

Of the 6,551,726 who were 5–24 years of age in 1961, 65.6 per cent (4,299,131) were attending school. As may be seen in Table 8:2, slightly more than three-fourths of those in school were in elementary grades or kindergarten. Of the remaining million, 912,054 were enrolled in secondary schools and only 89,253 in university. According to the Economic Council of Canada, the proportion of those of secondary school and post-secondary school age who were in school increased very rapidly during the post-World War II period. However, while the proportions are still significantly lower than those found in the United States, they have been rising considerably

Table 8:2

NUMBER AND PERCENTAGE OF POPULATION 5–24 YEARS OF AGE
BY HIGHEST LEVEL OF SCHOOLING, CANADA, 1961

Highest Level of Schooling	Population 5-24 Years of Age Attending School	
	Number	Per Cent
Kindergarten or elementary	3,297,824	76.7
Secondary	912,054	21.2
University	89,253	2.1
Total	4,299,131	100.0

SOURCE: Dominion Bureau of Statistics, *1961 Census of Canada*, Bulletin 7:1-10, Ottawa, The Queen's Printer, 1965, Table XII.

faster since the mid-1950s,[8] reflecting improvements in both quantity and quality of institutions of higher learning.

Rates of increase for enrolments in secondary schools were 56 and 53 per cent for the 1951–56 to 1960–61 and 1960–61 to 1965–66 periods respectively, while the rate of increase for full-time university enrolments accelerated from 56 to 81 per cent. In contrast, the rate of increase for primary grades actually declined from 23 per cent to 15 per cent during this same period.[9] These trends are a direct reflection of the post-war baby boom and its abatement during the mid-1950s. The more rapid increases in secondary and university enrolments indicate that the proportions in the population having attained secondary and post-secondary levels of education may be expected to increase beyond those shown for 1961 in Table 8:3.[10]

Table 8:3

NUMBER AND PER CENT OF POPULATION 15 YEARS OF AGE
AND OVER NOT ATTENDING SCHOOL BY HIGHEST
LEVEL OF SCHOOLING, CANADA, 1961

Highest Level of Schooling Attained	Population 15 Years and Over	
	Number	Per Cent
No Schooling	176,524	1.6
Elementary	4,989,822	45.2
Secondary	5,209,423	47.1
Some university	343,933	3.1
University degree	326,903	3.0
Total	11,046,605	100.0

SOURCE: Dominion Bureau of Statistics, *1961 Census of Canada*, Bulletin 7:1-10, Ottawa, The Queen's Printer, 1965, Table XIII.

Regional Variations in Educational Characteristics

School attendance by province. The pattern of change in proportion of the population 5–24 years of age attending school since 1931 in Canada was relatively uniform throughout Canada as may be seen in Table 8:4. With only one exception, every province experienced a decline in proportion attending school during the depression decade, 1931–41. Only in Quebec did the increase in those attending schools match the increase in total numbers in this age range; but their proportion of the population 5–24 years attending school during this period was the lowest for any province. Two provinces, Manitoba and Saskatchewan, actually experienced declines in the size of their school-age population as well as in the numbers attending school. The Yukon and Northwest Territories combined actually showed an increase in the proportion attending school; but their level of attendance, which varied from 10.6 to 13.1 per cent, was extremely low and involved less than 1,000 students in 1941.

All of the provinces and territories experienced consistent increases in proportions attending school from 1941 to 1961. This was particularly interesting in the case of Manitoba and Saskatchewan as both experienced numerical declines in their population in this age group as well as in numbers attending school between 1941 and 1951. The most spectacular period of growth in school attendance, which occurred during the 1951–61 decade, was centred in Ontario which moved to first place in 1961 with 68.9 per cent in attendance. In 1951, it had ranked only ninth with 53.3 per cent. British

Table 8:4

PER CENT OF POPULATION 5–24 YEARS OF AGE ATTENDING SCHOOL
FOR CANADA AND PROVINCES, 1931–1961

Province	1931	1941	1951	1961
Newfoundland	—	—	54.9	65.2
Prince Edward Island	52.1	52.0	56.8	65.4
Nova Scotia	54.6	51.8	58.2	67.5
New Brunswick	51.1	49.2	54.7	65.0
Quebec	47.5	47.5	47.8	61.3
Ontario	54.4	52.3	53.3	68.9
Manitoba	52.6	50.5	53.7	66.6
Saskatchewan	53.4	52.6	56.1	66.6
Alberta	53.9	53.0	54.5	65.6
British Columbia	53.6	51.7	55.0	67.9
Yukon and N.W.T.	10.6	13.1	22.3	49.2
Canada	51.8	50.5	52.2	65.6

SOURCE: Dominion Bureau of Statistics, *1961 Census of Canada*, Bulletin 7:1-10, Ottawa, The Queen's Printer, 1965, Table I.

Columbia moved from fourth place in 1951 to second place in 1961; Manitoba moved from eighth to a tie for fourth place; and Alberta moved from seventh to sixth. All other areas either retained their rank order position relative to the other provinces or dropped in rank from what they had been ten years earlier. While the Yukon and Northwest Territories have consistently had the lowest proportion attending school in this age group, their relative increase from 1951 to 1961 was the greatest for any area in Canada. In the latter instance, any increase in economic activity, e.g., oil exploration and construction, and an influx of workers and their families will have a significant impact on the relatively small populations in these areas.

There does not seem to have been any consistent regional pattern throughout this 30-year period other than the persistent tendency of Quebec and the northern areas to have the minimal proportions attending school. By 1961, however, a very clear distinction had emerged between East and West, with the former tending to have proportions below the national average and the latter exceeding the average for Canada as a whole. This major regional difference, visible only in 1961 with attendance figures for the population 5–24 years of age, is more evident throughout the 30-year period if attendance figures for the 15–19 year olds are used instead. Data for this group are perhaps more indicative of the schools' holding power since they relate for the most part to those ages beyond the compulsory school ages. On this basis, Ontario and the other Western Provinces have had proportions attending school which have consistently exceeded the national average each decade since 1931. British Columbia, which has had the highest proportion during this period, increased from 42.9 per cent in 1931 to 68.0 per cent in 1961. Quebec, with the lowest proportions of any province, increased from 23.6 per cent to 50.1 per cent during the same period.[11] Overall, whether the analysis includes or excludes the North, the extent of variation between areas has diminished during this 30-year period.

Provincial variations in educational attainment. It has been previously noted that somewhat less than half, or 46.8 per cent, of the population 15 years of age and over in 1961 had not gone beyond an elementary level of education. The highest proportion was found in the Northwest Territories where 63.5 per cent had not attained any secondary schooling, followed by Newfoundland, New Brunswick, and Quebec with 58.2, 56.6, and 55.2 per cent respectively. With the exception of Saskatchewan, all provinces west of Quebec had proportions less than the average for Canada as a whole.

Considering the other end of the educational attainment scale, i.e., those with some university or university degree, the same general East-West differential can be discerned.[12] British Columbia, Alberta, and the combined Northern Territories had the highest proportions with 8.4, 7.2, and 6.6 per cent respectively; and Newfoundland, Prince Edward Island, and New Brunswick with 3.2, 4.4, and 4.6 per cent respectively, had the lowest. In-

Fig. 8:3

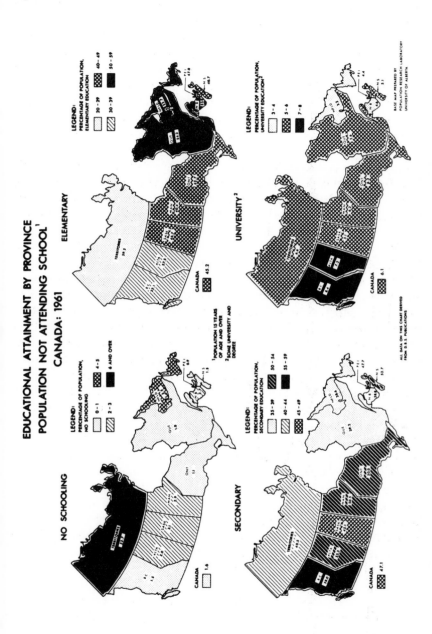

EDUCATIONAL ATTAINMENT BY PROVINCE
POPULATION NOT ATTENDING SCHOOL[1]
CANADA: 1961

terestingly, the Northwest Territories, with 5.7 per cent, still had a higher proportion than any of the Eastern Provinces; but then, this is undoubtedly due to the presence of the more highly trained professionals in both government and businesses related to the administration of the native populations of the North and to the development of its oil and mineral resources.

Figure 8:3 also shows educational attainment by province for those with elementary and secondary education. Again, those provinces with the higher proportions attaining only elementary levels were in Eastern Canada, while those with the highest proportions attaining secondary levels were located west of Quebec. Saskatchewan is the only exception to these general regional patterns.

Rural-urban contrasts. The use of attendance data as a measure of the educational quality of populations produces some difficulties when making rural-urban comparisons for a population which has experienced a large rural-urban movement. The actual difference in proportions attending school between 5 and 25 years of age in 1961 was very slight, being 65.7 per cent for urban areas and 65.4 per cent for rural. However, if all those born in rural areas remained there, instead of migrating to the urban areas, the difference would be considerably greater. The reason is quite obvious. As rural youth stop attending school and move to the city to seek employment, they become a part of the urban population. This transfer tends to reduce the number of youths 5–24 years of age still residing in rural areas, and those attending schools in rural areas become a larger proportion of the total rural population in this age group. For urban areas, the effect is just the opposite; i.e., in-migrant rural youths seeking jobs increase the total number in the 5–24 year age group without increasing the number attending schools, thereby reducing the proportion of the total attending school. For females 15–19 years of age, this migration effect is so great that the proportion of females attending schools in urban areas is less than that for those living in rural areas. For all other age and sex groups within the 5–24 year age group, the proportions in urban areas tend to exceed those for rural areas.[13]

Data for highest level of schooling attained for those 15 years of age and over not attending school are presented by type of locality in Table 8:5 below. Again, it is evident that those living in urban areas tend to exceed those in rural farm and non-farm areas in their proportion with secondary or higher educational attainment. The relatively high proportion of rural non-farm population with no schooling reflects the tendency for Eskimos and native-born Indians to reside in rural non-farm communities rather than on farms. The migration effect is also present here in that educational attainment of the population is presented by current place of residence rather than by place of birth.

Figure 8:4 shows the percentage distributions for provincial populations

Fig. 8:4   SELECTED LEVELS OF EDUCATIONAL ATTAINMENT[1]
BY PLACE OF RESIDENCE
CANADA AND PROVINCES: 1961

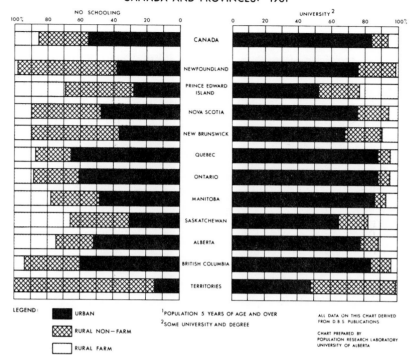

LEGEND:
■ URBAN
▨ RURAL NON—FARM
□ RURAL FARM

[1]POPULATION 5 YEARS OF AGE AND OVER
[2]SOME UNIVERSITY AND DEGREE

ALL DATA ON THIS CHART DERIVED
FROM D.B.S. PUBLICATIONS

CHART PREPARED BY
POPULATION RESEARCH LABORATORY
UNIVERSITY OF ALBERTA

Table 8:5

PERCENTAGE DISTRIBUTION OF THE POPULATION 15 YEARS AND OVER NOT ATTENDING SCHOOL, BY HIGHEST LEVEL OF SCHOOLING ATTAINED FOR CANADA BY TYPE OF LOCALITY, 1961

Type of Locality	Population 15 Years and Over (in 000's)	No School	Elementary	Secondary	Some University or Degree
Rural	3,125	2.9	57.7	36.4	3.0
Farm	1,162	1.7	62.8	33.5	2.0
Non-farm	1,963	3.6	54.7	38.2	3.5
Urban	7,921	1.1	40.2	51.4	7.3
Canada	11,047	1.6	45.2	47.1	6.1

SOURCE: Dominion Bureau of Statistics, *1961 Census of Canada*, Bulletin 7:1-10, Ottawa, The Queen's Printer, 1965, Table XIV, p. 10-24.

reporting no schooling, and for those who attained some university or degree by residence. The amount of inter-provincial variation is very striking in both cases. As would be expected, the largest proportions of those with university training lived in urban areas where employment opportunities would be greatest. However, the range varied among the provinces from a maximum of 85.5 per cent for Ontario, to a low of 52.3 per cent for Prince Edward Island. However, this low was exceeded by the northern areas where the percentage was slightly less than half, and 51.1 per cent were living in rural non-farm areas. The only other areas where the proportions with university training living in rural non-farm areas failed to exceed those on rural farms were the three Prairie Provinces where large scale and generally profitable farming exists.

More than half of all the 661,676 persons with no schooling in 1961 lived in urban areas. Provinces with the highest urban concentrations were Quebec with 65.7 per cent, Ontario with 60.6 per cent, and British Columbia with 59.9 per cent. By way of contrast, Prince Edward Island, Saskatchewan, and the Northern Territories had the lowest urban concentrations. In the latter area, only 14.7 per cent were urban in contrast to the 85.3 per cent residing in rural non-farm areas.

Educational Differentials

Educational attainment by age and sex. For those 15 years of age and over not attending school in 1961, very distinct differences in school attainment existed by age and sex. The proportions with only an elementary education, or less, consistently increased with age. Of those who had attended school, 30 per cent of the 20–24 year olds had not progressed beyond elementary school, compared to 64 per cent of those 65 years and over. As would be expected, larger proportions of the younger age groups had some secondary education, with the proportions declining for the successively older age groups. Perhaps reflecting in part the increasing opportunity in recent years for higher education, those 25–34 years of age had the highest proportion with some university or degree. However, it is interesting to note that members of this particular group were becoming of university age between 1944 and 1954, a period of rapid economic expansion and growth for Canada. Those of the next younger age group, born during the early war years and reaching university age during a less favourable period of economic activity between 1955 and 1960, had a somewhat smaller proportion with university training. Economic conditions existing at the time of the student's graduation from secondary school would appear to have a significant impact on his family's ability to provide financial support for the pursuit of post-secondary education.

As may be seen in Table 8:6 and Figure 8:5, sex differences were fairly

Table 8:6

PERCENTAGE DISTRIBUTION BY HIGHEST LEVEL OF SCHOOLING OF THE POPULATION 15 YEARS OF AGE AND OVER NOT ATTENDING SCHOOL, BY AGE GROUP AND SEX, CANADA, 1961

Age and Sex	Population 15 Yrs. + Not Attending School	Highest Level of Schooling				
		No Schooling	Elementary	Secondary	Some University	University Degree
Males	5,498,252	1.7	48.3	42.5	3.3	4.2
15–19	282,694	1.3	46.8	51.2	0.7	—
20–24	520,532	0.7	34.6	59.3	3.9	1.5
25–34	1,234,408	0.8	39.0	50.6	4.1	5.5
35–44	1,182,029	0.9	43.4	46.0	3.9	5.8
45–54	953,720	1.3	51.3	39.6	3.2	4.6
55–64	652,582	2.5	62.3	28.7	2.8	3.7
65 and over	672,287	5.4	66.8	22.9	2.2	2.7
Females	5,548,353	1.5	42.2	51.7	2.9	1.7
15–19	311,582	0.9	34.4	63.7	1.0	—
20–24	568,962	0.6	26.5	67.8	3.7	1.4
25–34	1,212,873	0.7	33.5	60.0	3.5	2.3
35–44	1,191,608	0.7	39.4	54.8	3.1	2.0
45–54	915,572	1.3	46.0	47.6	3.0	2.1
55–64	632,576	2.7	55.4	37.9	2.5	1.5
65 and over	715,180	4.3	60.7	32.1	2.0	0.9

SOURCE: Dominion Bureau of Statistics, *1961 Census of Canada*, Bulletin 7:1-10. Ottawa, The Queen's Printer, 1965, Table XVII. p. 10-28.

consistent throughout the age range for each of the levels of educational attainment shown. Females had higher proportions than males with some secondary education throughout the entire age range. For the two extremes of the educational continuum, the reverse was true; i.e., larger proportions of males had not progressed beyond elementary schooling, while at the same time relatively more males than females had attained some university or a university degree. In the latter case, the maximum difference in proportions for males and females occurred in the 35–44 year age group who were born between 1917 and 1927, and who most likely started university during the late depression or early war years. For those not progressing beyond elementary levels, the difference in educational attainment between males and females was least for those in this same age group.

Fig. 8:5

**EDUCATIONAL ATTAINMENT BY AGE,[1]
SEX AND NATIVITY
CANADA: 1961**

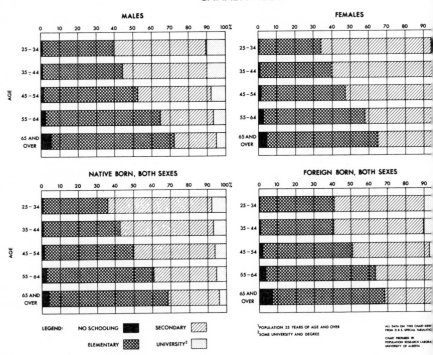

Educational attainment by nativity and period of immigration for the foreign born. Comparing all immigrants 15 years of age and over with native born of the same age group reveals that the immigrant population tends to have higher proportions with some university or degree as well as higher proportions who have not progressed beyond the elementary grades.[14] Data presented in Table 8:7, limited to the population 25 years of age and over, show that this educational superiority of the foreign born is due to the high proportion of post-World War II immigrants with some university or degree, as pre-war immigrants have a somewhat lower proportion than do the native born. Actually, the poorer showing by pre-war immigrants is due entirely to those who arrived in Canada before 1931 and were 45 years of age and older in 1961. All of the remaining groups of pre-war immigrants had higher proportions with some university than either native-born or post-war immigrants. However, since the numbers of immigrants arriving during the 1931–45 period, as well as those under 45 years who arrived prior to 1931, were relatively few, they had no significant effect on the average for all pre-war immigrants combined.[15]

Table 8:7

HIGHEST LEVEL OF EDUCATIONAL ATTAINMENT FOR POPULATION 25 YEARS OF AGE AND OVER BY NATIVITY AND PERIOD OF IMMIGRATION FOR FOREIGN BORN, CANADA, 1961

Nativity and Period of Immigration for Foreign Born	Number	Educational Attainment		
		None or Elemen.	1-5+ yrs. Secondary	Some Univ. or Degree
Native born	7,105,373	47.2	46.2	6.6
Foreign born				
Pre-war imm.	1,325,488	59.4	35.7	4.9
Post-war imm.	998,674	45.3	44.4	10.3
Total Pop. 25+	9,429,535	48.8	44.5	6.7

SOURCE: W. E. Kalbach, *The Impact of Immigration on Canada's Population*, Ottawa, The Queen's Printer, 1970, Table 4:13.

Data showing educational attainment by age for native- and foreign-born populations (in Figure 8:5) reveal the larger proportions of foreign born with no schooling for each age group in contrast to the native born, even though the proportions for both groups increase with age. At the other extreme is the noticeably greater proportion of foreign born, in contrast to the native born, with some university or degree in each of the age groups under 55 years of age. The other interesting difference between these two populations is the consistently higher proportions of native born with some high school for all age groups under 65 years of age.

It is quite evident that the older foreign born, like the older native born, are part of a passing pre-urban era. The younger generations of both groups have achieved levels of educational attainment much more appropriate for an urban-industrial society. While the larger proportions of native born with secondary schooling in the younger age groups, in contrast to the foreign born, may partially reflect the better educational opportunities for the native born in Canada, the high proportions of foreign born with university training reflect the increasingly selective nature of immigration.

Ethnic origins and educational attainment. Ethnic differentials in educational attainment for the population 25 years of age and over are summarized in Table 8:8 and Figure 8:6. Using the proportion attaining some university or degree as an index of relative achievement reveals considerable variation between the various ethnic origin groups. Notable is the very high proportion for those of Jewish origin with 15.3 per cent, followed by Hungarians with 9.9 per cent, Asiatics with 9.2 per cent, Russians with 8.4 per cent, and the British with 8.3 per cent. Equally striking, but in a negative sense, are the low proportions for native-born Indians and Eskimos with 0.4 per cent and Italians with just 2.2 per cent. The remaining groups, shown specifically in Table 8:8 and Figure 8:6, are all below the average for Canada as a whole.

Having already shown in previous sections how educational attainment is related to place of residence, age, sex, nativity, and period of immigration for the foreign born, the interpretation of ethnic differentials becomes quite difficult if these other factors cannot be controlled in the analysis. However, the ethnic differentials, while not revealing any intrinsic capability for intellectual achievement, do show the net effects of the unique historical and demographic experiences of each ethnic group insofar as they are relevant

Table 8:8

PERCENTAGE DISTRIBUTIONS FOR ETHNIC POPULATIONS 25 YEARS OF AGE AND OVER BY HIGHEST LEVEL OF EDUCATIONAL ATTAINMENT, CANADA, 1961

Ethnic Origin	Population 25 yrs. +	Educational Attainment		
		None or Elemen.	1-5+ yrs. Secondary	Some Univ. or Degree
British	4,377,840	37.3	54.4	8.3
French	2,558,144	61.7	33.8	4.5
German	547,141	51.2	43.3	5.5
Netherlands	202,417	49.7	44.1	6.2
Scandinavian	208,418	43.6	49.9	6.5
Hungarian	73,614	52.2	37.9	9.9
Polish	182,807	59.9	34.1	6.0
Russian	69,431	56.5	35.0	8.4
Ukrainian	260,097	61.9	33.7	4.4
Italian	234,470	76.6	21.2	2.2
Jewish	102,180	36.3	48.4	15.3
Asiatic	68,848	54.9	35.9	9.2
Native Indian and Eskimo	78,260	91.4	8.2	0.4
Total[a]	9,429,535	48.8	44.5	6.7

SOURCE: Dominion Bureau of Statistics, *1961 Census of Canada,* unpublished tabulations.
  [a] Includes other origins and not stated.

Fig. 8:6

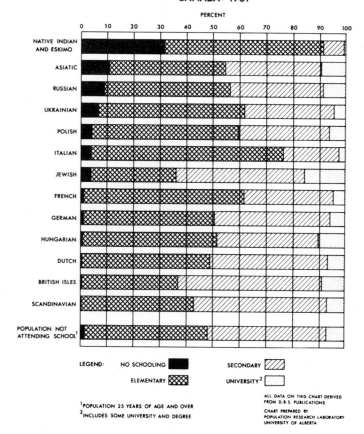

**EDUCATIONAL ATTAINMENT
SELECTED ETHNIC ORIGINS¹
CANADA: 1961**

LEGEND: NO SCHOOLING ▮   SECONDARY ▨

ELEMENTARY ▧   UNIVERSITY² ▢

ALL DATA ON THIS CHART DERIVED
FROM D.B.S. PUBLICATIONS

CHART PREPARED BY
POPULATION RESEARCH LABORATORY
UNIVERSITY OF ALBERTA

¹POPULATION 25 YEARS OF AGE AND OVER
²INCLUDES SOME UNIVERSITY AND DEGREE

to their educational resources at the time of the 1961 Census. In Table 8:9, distributions for those with some university or degree are shown for the native- and foreign-born components of each ethnic population. Most striking perhaps is the fact that the post-war immigrants of Jewish and Italian origins are the only ones with lower proportions with some university or degree than their native born. Post-war immigrants of German, Netherlands, Polish, and Ukrainian origins all have proportions below that for all post-war immigrants combined, while the remaining groups exceeded the average. For pre-war immigrants, only two exceptions may be noted as only those of French and Netherlands origin had higher proportions than their native-born counterparts. The relative significance of the educational character of the population by nativity and period of immigration for the foreign born can be obtained by comparing the distributions of Table 8:9 with the comparable distribution in Table 8:8. In the case of the two founding groups, the educational character of their native-born components, which comprise the largest part of their total number, determines their overall educational character. For those groups consisting primarily of recent arrivals, the character of their post-war immigrants have over-riding significance as in the case of the Italian ethnic population. It may seem odd that so many of one particular ethnic group should have so little education during a period where the demand has been so great for highly trained and educated immigrants. Of course, labourers have been needed for primary-type industries as well as for construction work, and the southern rural areas of Italy have had an abundance of able-bodied men willing to emigrate from their homeland. In addition, the system of sponsored immigration has allowed many skilled immigrants to bring relatives to Canada without any special consideration of their educational or occupational qualifications. Changes in the immigration laws made in 1962 and the introduction of the point system in 1967 have tended to increase the proportions of professional and technical workers among arriving immigrants, and such changes will undoubtedly contribute indirectly to the upgrading of the educational levels of their dependents as well.

Status of family heads and retention of children in school. Socio-economic status has been well established as an explanatory factor in accounting for variations in both educational aspirations and achievements among school

Table 8:9

PERCENTAGE OF THE POPULATION 25 YEARS OF AGE AND OVER
WITH SOME UNIVERSITY OR DEGREE FOR SELECTED ETHNIC
ORIGINS BY NATIVITY AND PERIODS OF IMMIGRATION
FOR FOREIGN BORN, CANADA, 1961

Ethnic Origin	Native Born	Foreign Born	
		Pre-war Imm.	Post-war Imm.
British	8.4	6.0	13.9
French	4.3	6.0	18.8
German	4.9	4.4	7.8
Netherlands	5.3	6.3	7.4
Scandinavian	7.1	3.9	13.0
Hungarian	4.9	2.6	17.4
Polish	5.9	2.6	10.0
Russian	8.3	4.8	20.8
Ukrainian	5.0	1.4	9.5
Italian	5.0	1.7	1.3
Jewish	22.4	7.0	15.1
Asiatic	11.1	2.2	14.3
Total	6.6	4.9	10.3

SOURCE: W. E. Kalbach, *The Impact of Immigration on Canada's Population*, Ottawa, The Queen's Printer, 1970, Table 4:15.

age populations. The 1961 Census data provide additional support for this general relationship for the Canadian population if per cent of children in families (ages 19–24, still attending school) be accepted as a rough measure of educational attainment. This is acceptable, of course, to the extent that children of this age group would normally be attending post-secondary educational institutions.

The following tables relate three separate characteristics indicative of the socio-economic status of family heads to the proportions of children 19–24 years of age still attending school. For both education and wage earnings of family heads, as shown in Tables 8:10 and 8:11, there are very consistent and positive relationships with retention of older children in school.

Table 8:10

EDUCATION OF FAMILY HEAD AND PROPORTION OF CHILDREN 19–24 YEARS OF AGE IN FAMILIES STILL ATTENDING SCHOOL, CANADA, 1961

Education of Family Head	Percent of Children 19-24 Still Attending School
None	6.9
Elementary: under 5 years	8.5
Elementary: 5 years +	14.6
Secondary: 1–2 years	21.5
Secondary: 3 years	28.9
Secondary: 4–5 years	34.6
Some university	45.5
University degree	63.7
Total	20.0

SOURCE: Dominion Bureau of Statistics, *1961 Census of Canada*, Bulletin 7:1-10, Ottawa, The Queen's Printer, 1965, Table XI.

Table 8:11

EARNINGS OF WAGE-EARNING HEADS OF FAMILIES SHOWING PROPORTION OF CHILDREN 19–24 YEARS OF AGE STILL ATTENDING SCHOOL, CANADA, 1961

Wage Earnings of Family Head	Per Cent of Children 19-24 Still Attending School
Under $3,000	12.0
$3,000–$4,999	18.4
$5,000–$6,999	29.4
$7,000 and over	50.0
Total	21.3

SOURCE: Dominion Bureau of Statistics, *1961 Census of Canada*, Bulletin 7:1-10, Ottawa, The Queen's Printer, 1965, Table X.

Occupational data presented in Table 8:12 for heads of families also reflect the importance of status to the extent these selected occupations have been logically ordered on a status continuum. Lacking an occupational prestige scale based on the 1961 Census, perhaps it is sufficient to point out the major differences between the white-collar and blue-collar types of occupations so obvious in these data. Physicians and surgeon heads of families had 73.6 per cent of their children, ages 19–24 years, still in school compared to only one-third for those who were commercial travelers, and slightly less than one-tenth for those who were non-farm labourers or fishermen. The most obvious fact of life reflected in these data is that heads of families with low-paying occupations find it more difficult to keep their children in school beyond secondary school. While there may be cultural factors operating to keep children of blue-collar families from continuing their education into post-secondary levels, the data presented here suggest that a healthy economy with minimal unemployment and a rising standard of living is absolutely necessary for increasing the educational resources of Canada's population. In the absence of such favourable conditions, upgrading the population in terms of its educational attainment will clearly require federal or provincial assistance in the form of tuition grants or scholarships to students with the potential for post-secondary training and who wish to continue their education.

Table 8:12

SELECTED OCCUPATIONS OF HEADS OF FAMILIES SHOWING PROPORTION OF CHILDREN 19–24 YEARS OF AGE STILL ATTENDING SCHOOL, CANADA, 1961

Occupation of Family Head	Percentage of Children 19-24 Still Attending School
Manager	37.8
Professional	57.0
School teacher	57.9
Physicians and surgeons	73.6
Accountants and auditors	46.0
Clerical	23.9
Commercial travellers	33.4
Policemen and detectives	21.3
Taxi drivers and chauffeurs	12.5
Farmers and stock raisers	15.2
Fishermen	9.5
Carpenters	15.5
Mechanics and repairmen	16.5
Construction foremen	17.5
Non-farm labourers	9.8
All occupations	21.9

SOURCE: Dominion Bureau of Statistics, *1961 Census of Canada*, Bulletin 7:1-10, Ottawa, The Queen's Printer, 1965, Table X.

REFERENCES

Dominion Bureau of Statistics: *1961 Census of Canada. General Review: Educational Levels and School Attendance,* Bulletin 7:1–10, Ottawa, The Queen's Printer, 1965.

Wilkinson, B. W.: *Studies in the Economics of Education.* Occasional Paper No. 4. Economics and Research Branch, Department of Labour, Ottawa, The Queen's Printer, 1966.

Zsigmond, Z. and Wolfgang M. Illing: *Enrolment in Schools and Universities, 1951–52 to 1975–76.* Staff Study No. 20, Economic Council of Canada. Ottawa, The Queen's Printer, 1967.

FOOTNOTES

[1]J. A. Lower, *Canada, An Outline History,* Toronto, The Ryerson Press, 1966, pp. 86–87.

[2]Dominion Bureau of Statistics, *Canada, One Hundred, 1867–1967,* Ottawa, The Queen's Printer, 1967, p. 361.

[3]A brief, but more detailed, discussion of the organization and administration of education in Canada, including the full text of Section 93 of the British North American Act of 1867 dealing with the powers of the provinces to enact laws concerning education may be found in *Canada, One Hundred, 1867–1967,* pp. 361–363.

[4]J. A. Lower, *op. cit.,* p. 87.

[5]Dominion Bureau of Statistics, *Canada Year Book, 1967,* Ottawa, The Queen's Printer, 1967, pp. 352–353.

[6]In 1961, a person was considered as attending school if his main daytime activity at any time between September, 1960, and the census date of June 1, 1961, was attending an elementary or secondary school, university, or an institution providing an equivalent type of general education.

[7]W. M. Illing and Z. E. Zsigmond, *Enrolment in Schools and Universities, 1951–52 to 1975–76,* Staff Study No. 20, Economic Council of Canada, Ottawa, The Queen's Printer, 1967, Appendix Table B-2.

[8]Economic Council of Canada, *Fourth Annual Review,* Ottawa, The Queen's Printer, 1967, pp. 64–71.

[9]*Ibid.,* Table 3–10, p. 66.

[10]For an excellent study of the educational requirements of Canada's labour force and problems arising from migration, see Bruce W. Wilkinson, *Studies in Economics of Education,* Occasional Paper No. 4, Department of Labour, Economics and Research Branch, Ottawa, The Queen's Printer, 1965.

[11]Dominion Bureau of Statistics, *1961 Census of Canada,* Bulletin 7:1–10, Ottawa, The Queen's Printer, 1965, Table 1, pp. 35–37.

[12]*Ibid.,* Table XIII, p. 23.

[13]*Ibid.,* Table V, p. 10.

[14]*Ibid.,* Table XIX, p. 32.

[15]*Ibid.*

Labour Force Participation

Changes in census definitions and procedures over the years make it virtually impossible to accurately reconstruct the historical records of Canada's labour force growth. The expansion of the labour force has always been closely linked to population growth even though actual participation by various age and sex groups has varied according to the customs and conditions of the times. However, as Canada has moved from an agricultural to an industrial society, the extent of participation in the labour force, as well as the nature of that participation, has undergone radical change.

When Canada was predominantly rural, any attempt to distinguish between the participants in the labour force and the general population would have had limited utility. All able-bodied members of farm families, including young children, worked so that, theoretically speaking, the labour force participation rates were very high. With urbanization and industrialization, the picture has changed dramatically; and it is with these changes, during the years following Confederation, that this chapter is particularly concerned.

The Potential Labour Force

During the century following Confederation, Canada's population increased almost sixfold with maximum increases coinciding with the heavy immigrations of the 1901–11 and 1951–61 decades. Of course, the more relevant segment of the total population, insofar as potential labour force is concerned, is that portion between 15 and 65 years of age. However, the rate of growth for this particular age group has not always coincided with that for the total population, as may be seen in Table 9:1.

Table 9:1

DECADE RATES OF GROWTH FOR TOTAL POPULATION, POPULATION
15–64 YEARS OF AGE, AND THE LABOUR FORCE POPULATION,
14 YEARS OF AGE AND OVER, CANADA: 1881–1961

Decade	Percentage Increase		
	Total Population	Population[a] 15-64 Years of Age	Labour Force Population[a] 14 Years and Over
1881–1891	11.8	15.5	17.5[b]
1891–1901	11.1	13.9	9.6[b]
1901–1911	34.2	38.2	48.5
1911–1921	21.9	18.9	18.0
1921–1931	18.1	22.0	22.4
1931–1941	10.9	15.7	15.1
1941–1951	18.6	12.4	12.9
1951–1961	30.3	22.9	26.1

SOURCE: Based on data from Dominion Bureau of Statistics, *1961 Census of Canada*,
Bulletin 7:1-4, Ottawa, The Queen's Printer, 1964; and F. T. Denton and S. Ostry,
Historical Estimates of the Canadian Labour Force, Ottawa, The Queen's Printer,
1967, Tables 3-7, 10 and 11.
[a] Excluding Newfoundland.
[b] Population 10 years of age and over.

Generally speaking, population growth for the major working ages has
exceeded that of the total population, i.e., the population 15–64 years of age
compared to all age groups combined. Only during the 1911–21 and post-
World War II decades did this group fail to match the total decade growth
rates. While the combined dependent populations grew at a much more rapid
rate, the rate of growth was not consistent for the younger and older portions
of these dependent populations. During 1911–21 and 1951–61, the highest
rates of growth were experienced by the population under 15 years of age,
whereas during the immediate post-war decade, it was the population 65
years of age and older that had the highest growth rate.

Growth of the Labour Force

Definition of labour force status. Not everyone within the generally accepted
range of working ages, i.e., 15–64 years, works or seeks employment. Many,
particularly in the younger ages, continue their formal education. Others
often stop working either for reasons of poor health or retirement. Many
simply do not seek employment because they lack the necessary skills or
because they believe jobs are not available for persons with their particular
qualifications. Traditionally, most women have worked as homemakers and
generally have not sought employment outside the home, unless forced to do
so through economic necessity or because they needed a greater challenge
than can be found in homemaking activities alone. However, even here,

significant changes are occurring. What is important to keep in mind is that the labour force is not a fixed pool of individuals capable of performing specific tasks, but a flexible resource whose growth tends to parallel that of the total population while responding to changes in technology and in levels of economic activity and opportunity. This sensitivity of the labour force to change produces a variability that makes the precise determination of the actual size of the labour force and unemployment levels difficult to achieve.

Other methodological difficulties have been introduced by frequent changes in definitions of the "economically active" person. Prior to 1951, specifically the period 1911–41, the gainfully occupied concept stressing the person's *usual* activity was used. The labour force approach, stressing employment characteristics at a *given point in time*, was first used in the 1951 Census. In 1961, the labour force was defined to include "all persons 15 years of age and over who were reported as having a job of any kind, either part-time or full-time (even if they were not at work) or were reported as looking for work during the week prior to enumeration."[1]

Labour force trends, 1901 to 1961. Trends in labour force size and participation rates from 1901 to 1961 are depicted in Figure 9:1.[2] The 1901 labour force of 1,885,000 increased by 4,736,000 (or 251.2 per cent) in 60 years to 6,621,000 in 1961. This contrasted with an increase of 231.0 per cent for the total population during the same period of time. Growth was not consistent throughout this period; and, as would be expected, the largest increases occurred during the decades of heavy immigration, i.e., 1901–11, and 1951–61. As both Figure 9:1 and Table 9:2 indicate, labour force participation rates for both sexes combined were also highest in 1911, but subsequently declined until 1951. In 1961, the census revealed the first increase in the overall participation rate since 1911.

Data for the total labour force during this period tend to obscure very significant changes which took place in the female population. For example, in 1901 women constituted only 14.8 per cent of the total labour force, while in 1961 their proportion had increased to 35.9 per cent. The percentage of women in the labour force increased significantly each decade, with the largest increase of 49.8 per cent occurring during the 1901–11 period, closely followed by the 49.4 per cent increase during the 1951–61 decade. Thus, the upturn in the total participation rate between 1951 and 1961, shown in Figure 9:1, is the sole result of the significant increase in participation by women. The rate for males continued its long term decline from its peak in 1911.

Fluctuations in the labour force. The preceding analysis does not reveal the highly variable nature of the labour force. The total number belonging to the labour force at one time or another during the year preceding the census was larger than the current labour force count for 1961 given in Table 9:2. For males, the total number who had been in the labour market during the

Fig. 9:1

LABOUR FORCE[1] TRENDS
CANADA: 1901–1961

NUMBER

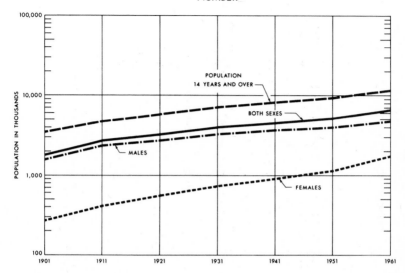

PERCENT

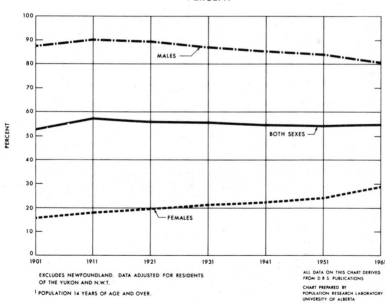

EXCLUDES NEWFOUNDLAND. DATA ADJUSTED FOR RESIDENTS
OF THE YUKON AND N.W.T.

[1] POPULATION 14 YEARS OF AGE AND OVER.

ALL DATA ON THIS CHART DERIVED
FROM D B S. PUBLICATIONS

CHART PREPARED BY
POPULATION RESEARCH LABORATORY
UNIVERSITY OF ALBERTA

Table 9:2

POPULATION 14 YEARS OF AGE AND OVER IN THE LABOUR FORCE, PERCENTAGE DISTRIBUTION OF THE LABOUR FORCE BY SEX, AND LABOUR FORCE PARTICIPATION RATES BY SEX, CANADA: 1901–1961

Census Year	Total	Labour Force			Labour Force Participation Rates[a]		
	Number (in 1,000s)	Per Cent	Males	Females	Total	Males	Females
1901	1,885	100.0	85.2	14.8	53.0	87.8	16.1
1911	2,799	100.0	82.4	17.6	57.4	90.6	18.6
1921	3,303	100.0	79.5	20.5	56.2	89.8	19.9
1931	4,042	100.0	77.2	22.8	55.9	87.2	21.8
1941	4,652	100.0	74.7	25.3	55.2	85.6	22.9
1951	5,250	100.0	71.3	28.7	54.5	84.4	24.4
1961	6,621	100.0	64.1	35.9	55.3	81.1	29.3

SOURCE: F. T. Denton and S. Ostry, *Historical Estimates of the Canadian Labour Force*, Ottawa, The Queen's Printer, 1967, Tables 3-7, and 10.
[a] Per cent of the population 14 years of age and over in the labour force. Male and female participation rates based on male and female populations 14 years of age and over respectively.

year was almost 220,000, or 4.7 per cent larger than those reported in the labour force at the time of the census. In addition, there were approximately 243,000 more women who had had jobs during the year but who were not in the labour force during the week prior to the census. Because of the much smaller size of the female labour force, the relative number of females with a labour force attachment at some time during the year was considerably higher than it was for males. A comparison of these data by sex suggests that the female labour force tends to be more mobile than the male labour force, i.e., there is greater movement by females into and out of the labour force.[3] More detailed analyses by Ostry show that this mobility varies significantly by age and marital status. The least mobile women were found to be those who were single and over 20 years of age, while the most mobile were married and between 15 and 35 years of age.[4]

While some of this mobility must reflect short term variations in economic and social conditions, it also includes a periodic or "seasonal" component of labour force demand. A more precise determination of the relative sizes of these two components would be difficult with available data. Nevertheless, examination of seasonal fluctuations alone should substantiate the variable nature of the labour force in Canadian society.

Analysis of employment by month reveals low levels of employment during winter months and high levels during the summer. However, this common seasonal pattern is not reflected consistently in all age-sex specific rates. To be more specific, monthly participation rates based on 1963–65 averages show maximum seasonal variations for young males under 25 years of age, young females under 20 years, and for both males and females 65 years and over.[5] Thus, students entering the labour force during summer vacations, and older workers close to retirement exhibit the greatest variations in seasonal employment. For males between 25 and 65 years of age, the seasonal variation is only 2 per cent or less; and for women, variation is lowest for those 45–64 years of age. Interestingly, female participation rates tend to be lowest during the vacation months of July and August which correspond to the peak rates for those 14–19 years of age. This is not, however, the case for males where minimum participation rates tend to occur in the fall and winter for every age group. Summer employment for those under 25, and 65 and over, appears to be an additional increment of workers added to a very stable labour force comprised of those between 25 and 65 years of age.

Regional Variations

Distribution of the labour force and change by provinces. Between 1911 and 1961, the Canadian labour force, 15 years of age and over, increased from 2,698,000 to 6,458,000,[6] or by 139.3 per cent. As would be expected, labour force growth during the same period was not uniform throughout Canada, as may be seen in both Figure 9:2 and in Table 9:3 below. Generally, labour force growth has reflected total population growth so that those areas in Canada experiencing minimal population change were also the areas experiencing little change in the size of their labour force. For example, Prince Edward Island showed the smallest increases in population as well as in its labour force, while Alberta experienced the greatest relative growth for both. Quebec was the only province whose labour force experienced a greater relative growth than its total population.

For the entire 50-year period, the regional distribution of the labour force has changed relatively little. By way of illustration, Ontario and Quebec combined accounted for 62.7 per cent of the population 15 years of age and older in 1911 and 63.4 per cent in 1961. During the same period, their combined proportion of the labour force increased from 60.2 to 64.5 per cent. However, these summary data obscure several significant changes. Data for intervening decades show that Quebec and Ontario's proportion of the population 15 years of age and over had actually been declining, reaching a minimum of 61.0 per cent in 1921 and again in 1931. Their combined share of the labour force population also declined between 1911 and 1921, reaching a minimum of 59.9 per cent in 1921 before the upswing commenced in 1931. Apparently, one of the consequences of the heavy immigration destined for the Prairie Provinces during the early 1900s was a more uniform distribution of population throughout Canada by reducing the relative concentrations in Ontario and Quebec. Not until the depression decade did this trend towards equalization falter. With the advent of World War II and the post-war period

Table 9:3

GROWTH OF THE LABOUR FORCE BY PROVINCE, 1911 TO 1961

Province	Labour Force 15 Yrs. and Over		Per Cent Increase 1911 to 1961	
	1911	1961	Labour Force	Tot. Pop. 15 Yrs. and Over
Prince Edward Island	31,766	34,148	7.5	11.6
Nova Scotia	171,861	236,819	37.8	49.7
New Brunswick	118,906	178,355	50.0	69.9
Quebec	644,966	1,768,119	174.1	162.2
Ontario	980,911	2,393,015	144.0	146.7
Manitoba	176,666	342,642	93.9	99.8
Saskatchewan	207,532	325,589	56.9	87.9
Alberta	160,811	489,511	204.4	344.0
British Columbia	205,062	577,648	181.7	315.1
Total	2,698,481	6,345,846	135.2	144.0

SOURCE: Dominion Bureau of Statistics, *1961 Census of Canada*, Bulletin 3:1-1, Ottawa, The Queen's Printer, 1964, Table 1.

Fig. 9:2

LABOUR FORCE TRENDS BY SEX
CANADA[1] AND PROVINCES: 1911 – 1961[2]

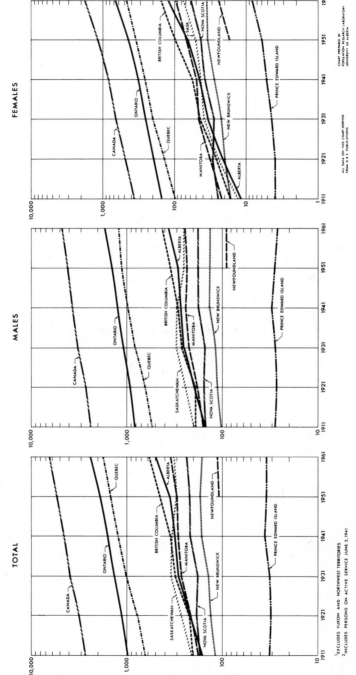

[1] EXCLUDES YUKON AND NORTHWEST TERRITORIES
[2] INCLUDES PERSONS ON ACTIVE SERVICE JUNE 2, 1941

of rapid industrialization, economic forces were again developing to increase the concentration of population in a relatively small number of areas.

Other analyses of the distribution of the labour force relative to the total population have shown similar results for the same period of time. Ostry has shown a significant decline in the degree of concentration of the labour force during the 1911–21 decade; but not until 1951 do Ostry's indexes of concentration reveal a reversal of the long term decline.[7]

Variations in participation rates. Participation rates show a fairly consistent decline during the 50 years between 1911 and 1961. As data in Table 9:4 indicate, all provinces except two had lower participation rates in 1961 than they did in 1911. The trend for Prince Edward Island turned downward only after 1941, but the participation rates for Ontario have consistently increased since 1921.

Prior to 1941, the highest participation rates were to be found in the Western Provinces. In 1941, and the following decades, the picture altered considerably. Of the Western Provinces, only Alberta has persistently shown rates equal to or above the national average; and it had the highest rates both in 1941 and 1961. Ontario had the second highest rates in these two years, and the highest of any province in 1951. Only one other province exceeded the national average in 1961, and that was the Western Province of Manitoba.

To a certain extent, higher participation rates for the West have been a function of their somewhat unique age and sex distributions. When these differences were taken into account (e.g., in 1911), the geographical varia-

Table 9:4

LABOUR FORCE PARTICIPATION RATES, POPULATION 15 YEARS OF AGE AND OLDER, BY PROVINCE, 1911–1961

Province	Per Cent of Population 15 Years of Age and Over in the Labour Force					
	1911	1921	1931	1941[a]	1951	1961
Newfoundland	—	—	—	—	48.4	42.2
Prince Edward Island	50.3	51.5	53.3	53.5	51.9	51.0
Nova Scotia	52.7	53.2	52.2	52.4	50.9	49.3
New Brunswick	52.3	53.0	52.7	52.4	50.9	48.1
Quebec	52.3	52.8	54.8	54.2	54.6	52.1
Ontario	54.9	54.3	54.3	54.8	56.1	56.6
Manitoba	58.4	55.7	56.0	53.8	53.8	55.1
Saskatchewan	63.9	57.9	56.8	54.1	52.3	53.4
Alberta	63.5	57.5	58.0	55.0	54.2	56.8
British Columbia	68.1	58.4	58.5	53.4	51.6	51.6
Canada	56.0	54.6	55.2	54.2	54.2	53.7

SOURCE: Dominion Bureau of Statistics, *1961 Census of Canada*, Bulletin 3:1-1, Ottawa, The Queen's Printer, 1967, Table 1.
a 1941 participation rates include persons on active service on June 2, 1941.

tions in "standardized" participation rates were almost eliminated, although the effects of standardization were considerably lessened in subsequent years.[8] Furthermore, there appears to be no discernable trend towards convergence of provincial participation rates for males. The evidence, in fact, reveals an increase in inter-provincial variation between 1951 and 1961.[9] For females, the situation is somewhat different. Their increasing participation in the labour force appears to have contributed to greater uniformity throughout Canada.[10]

Labour Force Differentials

Age and sex differences in participation rates. The difference between male and female participation in the labour force is more than just a difference in degree, as revealed in Table 9:2. Each sex group, in addition, has its own distinctive age distribution. The most obvious difference visible in Figure 9:3 is that the age group of maximum participation is younger for females than for males. In addition, female rates drop off very sharply while those for males continue at a fairly high level until the 45–54 year age group, after which the decline becomes increasingly greater.

Changes in male participation rates during the 1941–61 period are somewhat difficult to ascertain in Figure 9:3 because the 1941 data, in this particular series, exclude those who were on active service in the armed forces at the time of the census. This, of course, would tend to depress the level of participation for the younger age groups below that which might otherwise be expected. For this reason, the general overall decline in male participation rates for the entire period between 1941 and 1961 is clearly evident only for those age groups 55 years and over. However, the decline between 1951 and 1961 was consistent throughout the entire age range. By way of contrast, the increasing participation by females over the same period was shared, with several minor exceptions, by all age groups. While the maximum rates for females each year occurred in the 20–24 year age group, the greatest absolute and relative increases occurred for the older ages between 35 and 65 years.

Estimates of male labour force participation rates, incorporating those on active service in 1941, produced a clearer and more complete picture of trends for males. For each of the three age groups between 20 and 65 years, participation rates remained high and relatively stable, varying less than two percentage points over the entire 20 years. The significant declines occurred for those under 20 years of age and for those 65 and over, with rates decreasing 26 and 36 per cent respectively.[11]

Rural-urban residence. Historical data, previously presented in Table 9:4, have already suggested that levels of labour force participation were associated with region of residence, especially prior to 1941 when participation rates in Canada's West consistently exceeded the national norms. These data

Fig. 9:3

LABOUR FORCE PARTICIPATION RATES[1]
BY AGE AND SEX
CANADA: 1941, 1951, AND 1961

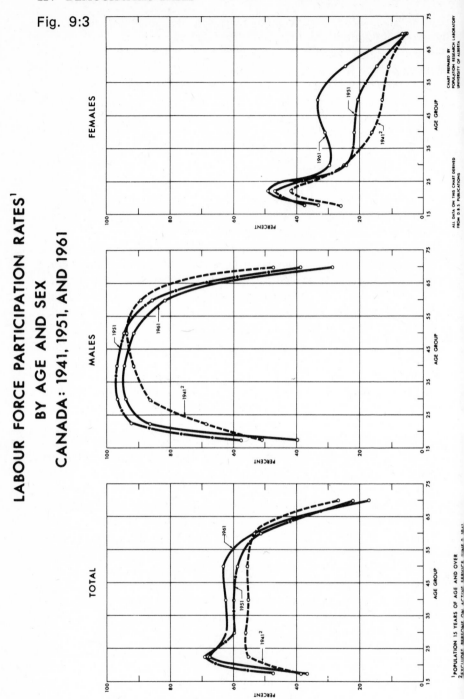

[1] POPULATION 15 YEARS OF AGE AND OVER

also revealed a shift to higher participation rates in rapidly urbanizing areas, such as Ontario, during the post-war period. Analysis by area of residence in 1961 further confirms the existence of higher rates in Canada's urban areas.[12] Specifically, labour force rates were 55.7 for urban areas and 49.9 per cent for rural areas. However, if the farm and non-farm components of rural areas are considered separately, it becomes evident that the lower rural rates are due entirely to the low participation rates for rural non-farm populations. Again, an analysis of the combined male and female populations has limited value because of the highly significant differences in their labour force behaviour. This is clearly evident in Figure 9:4. For all ages combined, males living in rural farm areas had the highest participation rate of 82.7 per cent. Next highest was the rate for urban males with 79.5 per cent, followed by rural non-farm with 70.0 per cent in the labour force. By way of contrast, urban females had the highest labour force participation, followed by those in farm and non-farm areas, with 33.0, 22.0, and 19.9 per cent respectively for all ages combined.[13]

As Figure 9:4 illustrates, residence differentials were not consistent throughout the age range. Rural farm males had the highest participation rates only for those 15–19 years of age, those in the 35–44 years and

Fig. 9:4   **LABOUR FORCE PARTICIPATION RATES**
BY AGE, SEX AND RESIDENCE
CANADA: 1961

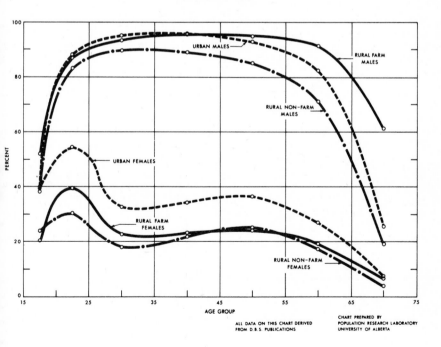

ALL DATA ON THIS CHART DERIVED
FROM D.B.S. PUBLICATIONS

CHART PREPARED BY
POPULATION RESEARCH LABORATORY
UNIVERSITY OF ALBERTA

older age groups. Only in the 20–24 and 25–34 year age groups did urban males exceed those living in rural farm areas. While the rates were almost identical for the 35–44 year olds, the rates for urban males declined quite rapidly with increasing age. Males in rural non-farm populations had consistently lower rates than did those living in the other areas. Of course, the significance of the higher rates for rural farm males is attenuated by the fact that this population constitutes only 13.1 per cent of all males in these five labour force age groups.

The participation pattern by age for the three residence areas is fundamentally different for women. Rates for urban females are consistently higher throughout the entire age range. Unlike the rates for males, which tend to diverge with increasing age, female participation rates by residence show a tendency towards convergence. Rates for rural farm and non-farm women, 35–44 years of age and older, are very similar.

Participation by marital status and sex. The labour force participation rates for married males in Table 9:5 are consistent with the fact that the age groups with high participation rates are the same ones in which large proportions are married. The higher median age for divorced males as contrasted with married males is also consistent with their somewhat lower participation rates. Very low rates for widowed males reflect their heavy concentration in the oldest age groups, while the below average rates for single males reflect their concentration at the younger end of the age continuum.

Table 9:5

PERCENTAGE OF THE POPULATION, 15 YEARS OF AGE AND OVER, IN THE LABOUR FORCE, BY MARITAL STATUS AND SEX, CANADA, 1951–1961

Sex and Marital Status	1951	1961
Males		
Single	76.0	62.4
Married	90.0	86.8
Widowed	44.2	34.6
Divorced	85.1	78.3
Total	83.8	77.7
Females		
Single	58.1	54.2
Married	11.2	22.0
Widowed	17.2	20.3
Divorced	70.3	73.2
Total	24.0	29.5

SOURCE: Dominion Bureau of Statistics, *1961 Census of Canada*, Bulletin 7:1-12, Ottawa, The Queen's Printer, 1967, Table 8.

More than half of the single females were employed in 1961, even though they still do not participate in the labour force to the same extent as the single male. In the case of married women, their reliance upon their husbands for economic support is clearly reflected in the low labour force rates for both married and widowed females. The somewhat lower rates for widows in 1961, as compared to married women, reflect the generally lower levels of participation associated with older ages as well as the significant increase in participation by married women between 1951 and 1961. Those who legally dissolve their marriage usually must support themselves, a fact clearly reflected in the extremely high level of participation for divorced women.

Data in Table 9:5 also reveal that neither the decade decline in rates for males nor the increase for females was uniformly consistent throughout the range of marital statuses. The decline for married males from 90.0 per cent in 1951 to 86.8 per cent in 1961 was minimal in comparison to the relatively large declines experienced by widowed males, or declines experienced by either the single or divorced. For females, those who were single actually experienced a decline, contrary to the increases for all other groups. Like the single males, the decline for this group undoubtedly reflected an increase in the numbers continuing in school. The proportion of working married females almost doubled from 11.2 to 22.0 per cent, whereas the rate for widowed women increased by only 18 per cent.

Because of the increasing importance of labour force participation by women and the recent emergence of the unique two-phase working life cycle, it is important to examine the relationship between marital status and age of females in more detail. Figure 9:5 shows the proportion by age of women who make up the three classes of marital status in the labour force. In view of the high rate for divorced females revealed in Table 9:5, it is unfortunate that they have been combined with the group having the lowest rate. However, it should be remembered that this combined group of widowed and divorced is relatively insignificant in terms of its numerical size. Since the married population was approximately three times as large as the group of single females, it tends to set the general form of the distribution and consequently deserves the closest scrutiny. The only major exception occurs for the 20–24 year olds where the high participation rate of 81.6 per cent for single females combines with an almost equivalent number of married women to produce a significant effect on the curve representing all groups combined.

Neither the high participation rates for the single nor the combined rates for the divorced and widowed is perhaps as unusual as the relatively stable rates for married females between 15 and 55 years of age. However, within this age range the lowest participation rates of 21.4 per cent for females 25–34 years of age reflected the presence of young children at home. Thus, the presence of young school age children exerts a depressing effect on the labour force participation of mothers, although the effect is not as great as might be

Fig. 9:5   MARITAL STATUS AND AGE DIFFERENTIALS
              FEMALE LABOUR FORCE
              CANADA: 1961

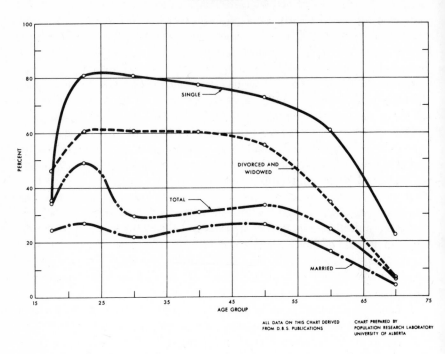

ALL DATA ON THIS CHART DERIVED   CHART PREPARED BY
FROM D.B.S. PUBLICATIONS   POPULATION RESEARCH LABORATORY
                                         UNIVERSITY OF ALBERTA

expected. Perhaps the most interesting feature of the distribution for married women is the high participation level for those 45–54 years of age. Their participation rate of 26.4 per cent was almost as high as the 27.4 per cent observed for the 20–24 year age group. Furthermore, the rate of 16.1 per cent for women 55–64 years of age was greater than that for all married women in 1951, as previously shown in Table 9:5. Thus, the emergence of the two-phase pattern for women in 1961, observed in Figure 9:3, appears to have been due to the re-entry of middle-aged women into the labour force as their children become less dependent upon their presence in the home.

Consistent with this is the fact that the effect of children in the home appears to be greatest for those under 35 years of age. Those 25–34 years of age with no young children at home have a participation rate of approximately 60 per cent, which was somewhat more than three times as great as those married women with one or more children, 15 years of age and under, at home.[14] Further analyses have shown that those women with children under six years of age had relatively low participation rates compared to those with no children under six. The difference was greatest for the youngest age group of women, but diminished with increasing age of married females.[15]

Thus, the increase in labour force participation for married women from the age group 25–34 years to the 45–54 year olds, evident in Figure 9:5, appears to be the result of increasing proportions of women whose children have reached the 6–15 age group or beyond.

Education and labour force participation. Generally speaking, the greater the amount of schooling the greater the probabilities of participating in the current labour force. As data in Table 9:6 indicate, significant increases in participation rates occur with each additional level of educational attainment. For males, only 58.0 per cent of those with less than five years elementary education were in the labour force compared to 87.4 per cent of those with some university or university degree. The greatest relative, as well as absolute, difference occurs for those with more than five years of elementary schooling in comparison with those with less than five years. According to Figure 9:6, this appears to hold throughout the age range, with the possible exception being the youngest and the oldest age groups. The only major inconsistency in this positive relationship between participation and educational attainment is found in those younger age groups of males with some university experience whose educational activities appear to have precluded greater participation in the labour force.

While women tend to have considerably lower participation rates than men, differences in educational attainment have a much greater effect on their labour force behaviour than in the case of males. For all ages combined, only 14.3 per cent of the women with less than five years elementary schooling were in the labour force compared to 47.5 per cent of those who had attended university. Figure 9:6 shows that the significance of education for

Table 9:6

LABOUR FORCE PARTICIPATION OF THE POPULATION 15 YEARS OF AGE AND OVER, BY EDUCATIONAL ATTAINMENT AND SEX, CANADA,[a] 1961

Educational Attainment	Males	Females
Less than five years elementary schooling[b]	58.0	14.3
More than five years elementary schooling	78.4	23.1
Secondary schooling	80.6	34.4
University	87.4	47.5
Total	78.1	29.7

SOURCE: Dominion Bureau of Statistics, *1961 Census of Canada,* Bulletin 7:1-12, Ottawa, The Queen's Printer, 1967, Table XXI.
[a] Includes Yukon and Northwest Territories.
[b] Includes persons with no schooling or kindergarten only.

Fig. 9:6

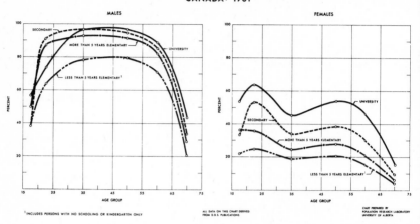

EDUCATIONAL DIFFERENTIALS BY AGE
MALE AND FEMALE LABOUR FORCE
CANADA: 1961

labour force participation of women, like that for men, varies with age. For example, the increase in participation rates for females 20–24 years of age is greatest between those with more than five years of elementary schooling and those with secondary education. On the other hand, the greatest increase for older women occurred between those with university and those with only secondary education.

The positive relationship between participation and education for the total female population also holds for married women, regardless of the presence or age of children in the home.[16] It would appear that the more educated the woman, the greater the employment opportunities, and the greater the pull or attractiveness of the labour market. However, to what extent is actual employment a response to economic need? It would be reasonable to expect that participation rates would be highest where husband's income is lowest, since the economic motivation would be very strong. That this is, in fact, the case is evident from the data presented in the first row of Table 9:7. It is also interesting to note that the positive relationship between participation and education of married women holds for each of the income groups under $10,000 regardless of family type, i.e., the age and number of children at home. Only in the highest income category, and specifically in the case of younger families, does this positive relationship disappear. The evidence strongly supports an economic explanation for working wives, since they are more likely to choose housekeeping and child care as their husband's earnings reach a level high enough to provide for their family needs without the additional increment of income provided by the working wife.

It is quite apparent that the male still carries the major burden as economic

Table 9:7

LABOUR FORCE PARTICIPATION RATES OF MARRIED WOMEN,[a] BY FAMILY TYPE (number and age group of children) AND SCHOOLING, BY INCOME OF HUSBAND: CANADA, 1961

Family type by number and age group of children and schooling of wife	Income of Husband					Total
	Under $3,000	$3,000-4,999	$5,000-6,999	$7,000-9,999	$10,000-and over	
Total	26.0	24.9	20.2	14.2	9.4	22.4
One or more children under 6						
Elementary or less	12.0	9.7	6.2	5.2	6.2	9.7
High School	19.0	15.3	10.0	5.2	4.5	12.8
University	36.2	24.5	15.7	8.8	6.6	15.3
Some children, none under 6						
Elementary or less	23.5	21.8	17.1	12.4	10.6	20.8
High School	38.6	36.4	28.7	18.1	9.7	29.8
University	56.1	53.7	44.2	29.0	11.4	33.3
No children						
Elementary or less	28.1	27.0	21.2	14.2	15.6	26.1
High School	46.9	49.9	42.4	27.9	14.1	44.0
University	60.2	63.0	57.3	40.6	20.5	51.4

SOURCE: Sylvia Ostry, *The Female Worker in Canada*, Ottawa, The Queen's Printer, 1968, Table 12.
[a] In husband-wife families, living in urban and rural non-farm areas, husband in labour force.

provider in Canadian society. There are few viable alternatives for able-bodied males within the major working ages. The changes which are occurring are directly affecting the age of entry into, and departure from, the labour force through voluntary or forced retirement. The most significant changes in the labour force have been related to the participation of women. Since World War II, they have enjoyed increasing freedom to choose the attractive alternative to marriage, i.e., a career with economic independence. Even for married women, their family role no longer needs to be restricted to the care of their children. However, since women are not under the same compulsion as men to enter the labour force, the factors influencing their decision are both numerous and complex. For this and other reasons, the extent of their participation in the labour force is quite variable. The data have shown the importance of age, residence, marital status, the extent and timing of fertility behaviour, and education of wives, as well as the income and occupational characteristics of their husbands. The importance of education, revealed in the 1961 data, suggests that participation rates for women will continue to increase as their educational levels continue to improve. Similarly, because of the importance of children in the home, any change which encourages the provision of adequate child care for working mothers will contribute to further increases in the participation of women in Canada's labour force.

Native- and foreign-born populations in the labour force. Comparison of participation rates for native- and foreign-born populations in 1961, presented in Table 9:8, shows that native-born males slightly exceed the foreign born while participation rates for females are about equal. Previous analyses of the age-sex structure of the foreign born (in Chapter 5) would suggest that this was due primarily to the fact that the median age for the male foreign-born population was somewhat higher than that for the native born, and that the difference would be greater for males than females.

It is also important to recognize that the total foreign-born population is comprised of two significantly different groups, i.e., pre-World War II and post-World War II immigrants, with respect to their age and sex characteristics. Analyzing these two component groups separately reveals the significantly higher levels of participation characteristic of recent immigrants, both male and female, to Canada. For post-war immigrant males, 88.9 per cent were in the experienced labour force in 1961 compared to 78.1 and 65.0 per cent for native born and pre-World War II immigrants respectively. The same contrast also appears for females with participation rates of 39.2, 29.5 and 20.3 per cent for post-war, native-born, and pre-war immigrants respectively.

Because of the distinctive age distributions for these three populations, it might be thought that the higher participation rates for post-war immigrants

Table 9:8

LABOUR FORCE PARTICIPATION RATES[a] OF THE POPULATION
15 YEARS OF AGE AND OVER BY SEX, NATIVITY, AND PERIOD
OF IMMIGRATION FOR FOREIGN BORN, CANADA, 1961

Nativity	Males	Females
Native born	78.1	29.5
Foreign born	76.5	29.4
Pre-war immigrants	65.0	20.3
Post-war immigrants	88.9	39.2
Total	77.8	29.5

SOURCE: Dominion Bureau of Statistics, unpublished special tabulations (A19) for W. E.
Kalbach, *The Impact of Immigration on Canada's Population*, Ottawa, The Queen's
Printer, 1970.
[a] Current experienced labour force includes those with jobs during week prior to
census plus those looking for work who have worked before.

are due entirely to their younger average age. However, post-war immigrants,
both males and females, actually had higher participation rates for all age
groups (as illustrated in Figure 9:7 for females only). For pre-war immigrants, the situation was somewhat different. While participation rates for
both males and females between 20 and 55 years of age also tended to be
higher than their native-born counterparts, it was the heavy concentration of

Fig. 9:7   FEMALE LABOUR FORCE
            NATIVITY DIFFERENTIALS BY AGE
                    CANADA: 1961

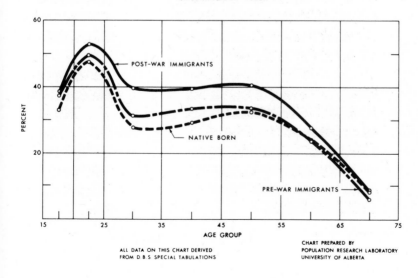

ALL DATA ON THIS CHART DERIVED
FROM D.B.S SPECIAL TABULATIONS

CHART PREPARED BY
POPULATION RESEARCH LABORATORY
UNIVERSITY OF ALBERTA

pre-war immigrants in the 65 years of age and over category that produced the low participation rates for all ages combined.

Labour force by ethnic origins. The centrality of value systems for explanations of behavioural differences is generally recognized; and differences in value systems between various ethnic, religious, and nationality groups have been amply demonstrated. For this reason, variations in labour force participation rates between Canada's numerous ethnic origin groups is to be expected. In Figure 9:8, participation rates for both males and females are shown for selected ethnic origins. The range for males in 1961 was from 85.0 per cent for those of Italian origin to 49.4 per cent for Native Indian and Eskimos. For the opposite sex, Hungarian females had the highest participation rate, 38.1 per cent, while Native Indian and Eskimos, with 11.3 per cent, had the lowest.

There is little correspondence between the rank order of participation rates for males and females by ethnic origin. Since all able-bodied males are expected to work, the significant factor affecting their participation would be ethnic differences in age structure. Those groups with large proportions in either the older ages or the youngest age groups would tend to have lower

Fig. 9:8   **ETHNIC ORIGIN DIFFERENTIALS**
MALE AND FEMALE LABOUR FORCE[1]
CANADA: 1961

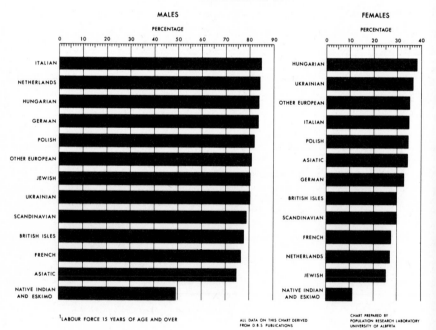

[1] LABOUR FORCE 15 YEARS OF AGE AND OVER   ALL DATA ON THIS CHART DERIVED FROM D B S PUBLICATIONS   CHART PREPARED BY POPULATION RESEARCH LABORATORY UNIVERSITY OF ALBERTA

participation rates than those groups with fewer young and old workers. The influence of age differences is reflected in the rank order of male participation rates by ethnic origins presented in Figure 9:8. Standardizing the rates to control for the effects of differences in their age distributions resulted in a reduction of almost 50 per cent in the average deviation in ethnic participation rates.[17]

The fact that female participation rates exhibited greater relative variability by ethnic origin than males suggests that cultural differences are more important in determining female labour force behaviour than they are for males. For females 15 years of age and over, standardization failed to significantly reduce the amount of inter-ethnic variation, indicating that factors other than age differences were primarily responsible for the observed variations. Low participation rates for Jewish females, for example, may in part be the result of their higher socio-economic status as reflected by their husbands' above-average income. In a more extreme case, minimal participation by Native Indian and Eskimo females would appear to reflect a combination of low educational achievement, high fertility, a general lack of employment opportunities in the areas in which they live, and the widespread existence of prejudice in the dominant white population.

REFERENCES

Denton, F. T., Y. Kasahara, and S. Ostry: *Population and Labour Force Projections to 1970,* Economic Council of Canada, Staff Study No. 1, Ottawa, The Queen's Printer, 1965.

Denton, F. T., and S. Ostry: *Historical Estimates of the Canadian Labour Force,* 1961 Census Monograph, Ottawa, The Queen's Printer, 1967.

Department of Labour: *Women at Work in Canada.* Ottawa, The Queen's Printer, 1965.

Dominion Bureau of Statistics: *1961 Census of Canada. General Review: The Canadian Labour Force,* Bulletin 7:1–12. Ottawa, The Queen's Printer, 1967.

Economic Council of Canada: *Fourth Annual Review.* Ottawa, The Queen's Printer, 1967.

Hall, O. and B. McFarlane: *Transition from School to Work.* Report No. 10, Department of Labour, Ottawa, The Queen's Printer, 1965.

Ostry, S.: *The Female Worker in Canada.* 1961 Census Monograph, Ottawa, The Queen's Printer, 1968.

Ostry, S.: *Geographic Composition of the Canadian Labour Force.* 1961 Census Monograph, Ottawa, The Queen's Printer, 1968.

Ostry, S.: *Provincial Differences in Labour Force Participation.* 1961 Census Monograph, Ottawa, The Queen's Printer, 1968.

Ostry, S.: *Unemployment in Canada.* 1961 Census Monograph, Ottawa, The Queen's Printer, 1968.

Poduluk, J. R.: *Incomes of Canadians.* 1961 Census Monograph, Ottawa, The Queen's Printer, 1968.

FOOTNOTES

[1]Dominion Bureau of Statistics, *1961 Census of Canada*, Bulletin 3:1–1, "Introduction", Ottawa, The Queen's Printer, 1964. The labour force definition in 1951 was quite similar to the definition in 1961. However, they are not directly comparable since in 1951 the population 14 years of age was included while in 1961 the labour force population was limited to those 15 years of age and older.

[2]Data presented in Figure 9.1 are labour force estimates prepared by F. T. Denton, and S. Ostry, *Historical Estimates of the Canadian Labour Force*, Ottawa ,The Queen's Printer, 1967, Tables 3–7 and 10. Their definition varies somewhat from the 1961 Census definition in that it includes the population 14 years of age. Also, these estimates include residents of the Yukon and Northwest Territories, Indians living on reserves, and members of the Armed Forces. Inmates of institutions are excluded.

[3]Dominion Bureau of Statistics, special tabulations of the 1961 Census data for the census monograph on post-war immigration. See Appendix H, tabulation A27, in W. E. Kalbach, *The Impact of Immigration on Canada's Population*, Ottawa, The Queen's Printer, 1970.

[4]S. Ostry, *The Female Worker in Canada*, Ottawa, The Queen's Printer, 1968, Table 4.

[5]Dominion Bureau of Statistics, *Canadian Statistical Review*, July, 1966, Vol. 41, No. 7, p. xiii.

[6]Including Newfoundland in 1961.

[7]S. Ostry, *Geographic Composition of the Labour Force*, Ottawa, The Queen's Printer, 1968, pp. 3–7.

[8]S. Ostry, *Provincial Differences in Labour Force Participation*, Ottawa, The Queen's Printer, 1968, pp. 17–19.

[9]*Ibid.*

[10]*Ibid.*, pp. 19–22.

[11]F. T. Denton and S. Ostry, *op. cit.*, Tables 5–7. This series of estimates excludes Newfoundland but includes the Yukon and Northwest Territories and adjustments for Indians living on reservations.

Male Labour Force Participation Rates, Canada: 1941–1961

Age Group	1941	1951	1961
14–19	54.6	53.7	40.6
20–24	92.6	94.2	94.4
25–34	98.7	98.2	98.4
35–64	96.1	95.0	95.3
65+	47.9	39.5	30.6

[12]Dominion Bureau of Statistics, *1961 Census of Canada*, Bulletin 7:1–12, Ottawa, The Queen's Printer, 1967, Table IV.

[13]*Ibid.*

[14]S. Ostry, *The Female Worker in Canada*, Ottawa, The Queen's Printer, 1968, p. 18.

[15]*Ibid.*

[16]*Ibid.*, Table II, p. 31.

[17]In the absence of age-sex-ethnic specific participation rates, ethnic participation rates were standardized by the indirect method using age-sex specific rates and the age-sex distribution for Canada, 1961.

Occupational
Characteristics

The kind of work people must perform in order to feed, clothe, and shelter themselves reveals more about the nature of their society than any other single characteristic. A society's level of social and economic development is not only reflected in the proportion of its population that must work, but also by the relative distribution of its labour force among the various work activities. Since the kind of work an individual performs reflects something of his social background and education, as well as his potential earning power, it can also reveal something about the nature of his housing, the size of his family, and whether or not his political attitudes will tend to be conservative or radical. Since occupation is linked to education and income, it has a crucial influence on a person's life style; and the combined factors have a significant effect on the probability of his survival, as well as the likelihood of dying from specific causes. In short, the nature of one's society and the state of its development set the limits of available work opportunities. Within these limits, the kind of occupational commitment made by the individual carries with it specific economic, political, psychological, and social consequences. The significance of early work experience and career commitment is generally not appreciated by young people entering the labour force for the first time.

Examination of the industrial composition of a country's labour force provides a quick way of obtaining a basic perspective as to its nature and organization. If all economic activity is somewhat arbitrarily subsumed under the general industrial categories shown in Table 10:1, the following picture of the Canadian economy in 1961 emerges: For every 100 persons in the current labour force, only 10 were needed for the basic production of food;

Table 10:1

EXPERIENCED LABOUR FORCE, 15 YEARS OF AGE AND OVER BY INDUSTRY DIVISION, CANADA, 1961

Industry	Per Cent
Agriculture	9.9
Forestry	1.7
Fishing and trapping	0.6
Mines, quarries, oil wells	1.9
Manufacturing	21.7
Construction	6.7
Transportation, communication, and other utilities	9.3
Wholesale and retail trade	15.3
Finance, insurance, and real estate	3.5
Community, business, and personal service	19.5
Public administration and defence	7.5
Industry unspecified	2.4
Total: Per Cent	100.0
Number	6,471,850

SOURCE: Dominion Bureau of Statistics, *1961 Census of Canada*, Bulletin 3:2-1, Ottawa, The Queen's Printer, 1963, Table 1A.

22 were engaged in the manufacturing of goods; 15 were needed to handle wholesale and retail trade activities; and 9 were occupied in providing transportation, communication, and other utilities. In addition to these basic activities, almost 20 out of every 100 persons were engaged in performing community, business, and personal services—including educational, health and welfare, religious, recreational, and other services; and 8 persons were required for public administration and defence.

By way of comparison, it is interesting to note that in 1960 the United States required only 6.6 per cent of its labour force for food production, employed a slightly larger proportion of its population, or 27.1 per cent, in the manufacture of goods, and utilized only 5.0 per cent for public administration.[1] While these data are not strictly comparable, because of definitional differences, they suggest that further industrialization and urbanization in Canada should bring additional reductions in its agricultural labour force. Canada's position, relative to that of the United States, is reflected in the fact that the proportion of its labour force required for food production in 1961 was less than that for the United States in 1950, when 12.2 per cent of the latter's labour force were engaged in agriculture.[2]

The Changing Occupation Structure

The decline of agriculture. Changes in Canada's labour force since Confederation have been highly significant. The Census of 1871, for example, indicates that 55 per cent of those who provided information on their occupation were classified as agricultural. The remainder were distributed as follows:[3] commercial, 8.7 per cent; industrial, 24.6 per cent; domestic, 6.9 per cent; and professional, 4.5 per cent. The subsequent reduction in the proportion of the labour force engaged in agricultural pursuits, from 55.3 to 9.9 per cent during a period of 90 years, has been of utmost importance in terms of the general life style and standard of living for the Canadian population.

The description and classification of specific occupations in both the early and recent censuses of Canada illustrate two very important aspects of the nature of the labour force and changes which have taken place over this period of time. First, the emergence of new industries requires new occupational skills; and second, as established industries grow and change, additional workers are needed as well as alterations in existing job skills.

Reflective of these changes is the fact that while the Census of 1871 listed 131 separate occupations, the 1961 Census provided tabulations for over 300 occupations, including numerous general categories which obscured even greater occupational specialization. As would be expected, many occupations appear in both censuses. More indicative of the basic changes which have occurred is the virtual disappearance of what used to be common occupations (e.g., saddlers, sail makers, and carriage makers), and the appearance of new specializations, such as bus drivers, aircraft pilots, computer programmers, and radio and television announcers. Shifts in the relative numbers of persons engaged in certain occupations have more than mere historical interest. For example, interesting evidence as to one consequence of secularization of society, albeit a minor one, can be observed in the change which has occurred in the relative number of bartenders and religious workers since 1871. Bartenders increased from 2.1 per 10,000 population (in Canada's four original provinces) to 5.2 per 10,000 in 1961, a relative increase of 147.6 per cent. On the other hand, the proportion of religious workers decreased by 14.7 per cent, from 21.7 to 18.5 per 10,000. Some may still find hope for the future in the fact that religious workers still outnumber, by four times, those who minister to man's frustrations and pleasure in the country's pubs and cocktail lounges. While hardly the most significant of the changes which have occurred, this does illustrate the manner in which occupational change can reflect changes in a society's value system. Changing values are also apparent in the number of teachers and professors which had increased from 39 to 104 per 10,000 total population during this same period. As impressive as this growth is, the figures still do not reveal the total growth of the labour force connected with the provision of basic educational services which include an increasing number of secretaries, clerks, technicians, and maintenance staff. Closer examination of the occupational struc-

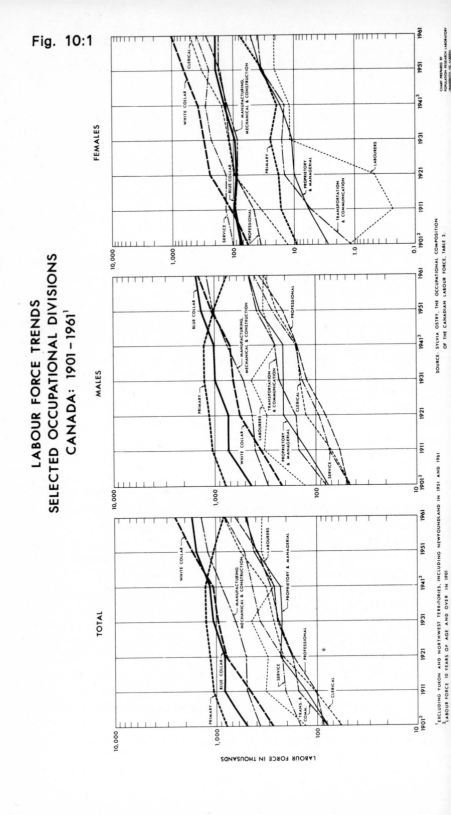

Fig. 10:1

LABOUR FORCE TRENDS
SELECTED OCCUPATIONAL DIVISIONS
CANADA: 1901–1961[1]

TOTAL

MALES

FEMALES

LABOUR FORCE IN THOUSANDS

[1] EXCLUDING YUKON AND NORTHWEST TERRITORIES, INCLUDING NEWFOUNDLAND IN 1951 AND 1961
[2] LABOUR FORCE 10 YEARS OF AGE AND OVER IN 1901

SOURCE: SYLVIA OSTRY, THE OCCUPATIONAL COMPOSITION
OF THE CANADIAN LABOUR FORCE, TABLE 3.

CHART PREPARED BY
POPULATION RESEARCH LABORATORY
UNIVERSITY OF ALBERTA

ture of Canada's labour force in 1961 is the primary concern of the following sections of this chapter.

Ascendency of the white-collar worker. The decline in the importance of primary occupations between 1901 and 1961 coincided with the rise of blue-collar occupations associated with manufacturing, mechanical, and construction activities. As may be seen in Figure 10:1, the size of the labour force associated with primary occupations reached its peak in 1941 when 1,275,-367, or 30.5 per cent, were reported as having occupations associated with agriculture, fishing, hunting and trapping, logging, and mining and quarrying. During the post-World War II period of rapid industrialization, this component of the labour force declined rapidly, dropping to 830,180, or just 12.8 per cent of the labour force. On the other hand, the number of workers in manufacturing, mechanical, and construction jobs continued their rapid rate of growth, reaching 1,372,819 in 1961, and comprising 21.3 per cent of the labour force. The other significant trend during this 60-year period was the emergence of white-collar workers as the dominant occupational category.

In 1901, white-collar occupations constituted only 15.3 per cent of the labour force; but after 60 years of rapid growth they increased their proportionate share to 37.9 per cent. However, growth was not uniform throughout this period. After a period of extremely rapid expansion from 1901 to 1921, the rate of growth subsided somewhat, only to revive during the post-World War II era. While the size of the white-collar class came close to that of blue-collar workers in 1921, it was not until the 1941–51 decade that the white-collar group emerged as the largest. Further examination of Figure 10:1 will reveal that, of the white-collar occupations shown, the growth rate for clerical workers exceeded that for the white-collar group as a whole during the 1941–51 decade, while professional occupations expanded most rapidly during the 1951–61 decade. Both transportation and communications, and proprietary and managerial occupations made notable gains during the immediate post-war decade before declining somewhat during the 1951–61 decade. On the other hand, the growth rate for service and recreation occupations increased significantly during this latter decade, reflecting the increase in leisure time and related activities.

Changes in male and female labour forces were generally similar to those for the total labour force with several notable exceptions. Most important is the observation that the emergence of the white-collar group into a position of dominance between 1951 and 1961 was due primarily to the increase in female workers. At the same time, the number of white-collar male workers was rapidly approaching the size of the blue-collar labour force during the post-war period.

Rapid gains were made by women in clerical, professional, and proprietary and managerial occupations. Of particular interest is the fact that the number of female clerical workers first surpassed the number of males in 1941, and in each subsequent decade have increased their margin of numerical superiority. Women professionals actually outnumbered men by a considerable margin in 1921, but this was the only exception to the general numerical dominance by males which has prevailed through time. However, in spite of their larger numbers in 1961, the only white-collar occupations in which men claimed a greater proportionate share of their labour force than women were proprietary and managerial, and financial positions. For professional and clerical occupations, the proportions of women were 15.5 and 28.6 per cent respectively, compared to 7.7 and 6.7 per cent for men.

A second exception to the general trends for the combined labour force is to be found in the comparison of males and females in primary occupations. The decline since 1941 has been due entirely to the decline experienced by the male labour force, since the number and proportion of females has increased significantly during this same period. Practically all of this increase was due to the growth of agricultural workers from 18,800 to 75,900, representing an increase from 2.3 to 4.3 per cent of the female labour force.

The other notable change in the female labour force was the emergence of the clerical workers in 1951 to replace those in service occupations as the largest single group in the female labour force. In addition, the women in professional occupations increased enough between 1951 and 1961 to put them ahead of the combined blue-collar group consisting of manufacturing, mechanical, and construction workers, and labourers.

Regional Variations

The effects of the decline in primary occupations, and the increase in those associated with industrialization and urbanization, would be felt in varying degrees throughout the country, as the type of economic activity has varied significantly by region. Predominantly rural areas, for example, would feel the greatest impact from the reduction of the labour force engaged in primary occupations, whereas the urban centres themselves were expanding as a result of the growth of business and industry in these areas.

It is evident in Table 10:2 that all regions experienced large declines in their proportions of the male labour force in primary occupations between 1951 and 1961. The Atlantic and Prairie Provinces experienced declines of −41.2 and −21.3 per cent respectively; but, nevertheless, the Prairies, with 31.3 per cent, still had the largest proportion engaged in primary occupations in 1961, most of which was accounted for by agricultural activities.

White-collar occupations for males increased by 36.6 per cent throughout Canada during the 1951–61 decade, growing from 25.3 to 30.3 per cent of

Table 10:2

PERCENTAGE DISTRIBUTION OF THE MALE LABOUR FORCE,[a] 15 YEARS OF AGE AND OVER, BY BROAD OCCUPATIONAL GROUPINGS AS OF 1961, FOR CANADA AND REGIONS, 1951 AND 1961, AND PERCENTAGE CHANGE, 1951 TO 1961

Occupational Grouping	Atlantic Provinces			Quebec			Ontario		
	1951	1961	Per Cent Increase	1951	1961	Per Cent Increase	1951	1961	Per Cent Increase
White-collar workers	18.7	23.9	26.5	25.8	30.9	37.0	28.4	33.0	37.4
Blue-collar workers	30.9	33.4	6.9	38.0	37.7	13.4	40.3	37.6	10.2
Transport and communication occupations	8.3	8.5	2.4	7.5	8.2	24.6	7.1	7.2	19.4
Service and recreation occupations	7.2	11.9	63.4	5.8	7.5	49.0	7.0	8.6	45.2
Primary occupations	33.5	19.9	−41.2	21.0	12.8	−30.4	16.1	11.1	−18.7
All occupations[b]	100.0	100.0	−1.0	100.0	100.0	14.4	100.0	100.0	18.2

Occupational Grouping	Prairie Provinces			British Columbia			Canada		
	1951	1961	Per Cent Increase	1951	1956	Per Cent Increase	1951	1961	Per Cent Increase
White-collar workers	21.7	26.6	35.8	27.0	31.6	42.3	25.3	30.3	36.6
Blue-collar workers	22.2	25.8	28.6	37.9	37.3	19.8	35.1	35.0	13.9
Transport and communication occupations	6.0	6.5	19.5	8.4	8.1	17.8	7.2	7.5	18.7
Service and recreation occupations	5.4	7.5	52.5	8.7	9.7	36.6	6.5	8.5	48.4
Primary occupations	44.0	31.3	−21.3	16.5	10.4	−23.5	24.6	16.0	−25.8
All occupations[b]	100.0	100.0	10.7	100.0	100.0	21.9	100.0	100.0	14.1

SOURCE: Dominion Bureau of Statistics, 1961 Census of Canada, Bulletin 7:1-12, Ottawa, The Queen's Printer, 1967, Table VIII.
[a] Excludes those seeking work who have never been employed.
[b] Includes occupations not stated.

the total labour force. On the other hand, the growth rate for blue-collar occupations was not quite sufficient to maintain its proportionate share of the male labour force. In the latter case, a growth rate of only 13.9 per cent, compared to 14.1 per cent for all occupations combined, just barely managed to maintain its proportionate share of blue-collar occupations at approximately 35 per cent. The two provinces with the highest proportions of white-collar workers in 1951, Ontario and British Columbia, experienced the greatest decade growth with increases of 37.4 and 42.3 per cent respectively. The blue-collar segment of the labour force remained the same, or declined relative to the other components, in those areas having the highest proportions of white collar occupations, e.g., Quebec, Ontario, and British Columbia. Only in the Atlantic and Prairie Provinces was the numerical increase sufficient to increase their proportionate share of the labour force.

Although comprising a relatively small proportion of the total, e.g., 6.5 per cent in 1951, male workers in service occupations showed the largest relative gain of any major occupational group, increasing by 48.4 per cent to 8.5 per cent in 1961. Relative increases were greatest in the Atlantic and Prairie Provinces, which experienced growth rates of 63.4 and 52.5 per cent respectively. Only in British Columbia did the growth rate of this segment fall below that of any other group, and in this case it was exceeded by the white-collar workers. Again, it must be kept in mind that the greatest share of the absolute growth in service and recreation occupations, over half, occurred in Ontario and Quebec, regions with large urban concentrations.

Regional comparisons are generally sufficient to clarify the salient aspects of changes in occupational patterns. However, to avoid leaving a false impression of regional homogeneity, the percentage composition of provincial labour forces for both sexes combined, for selected occupations, is shown in Figure 10:2. These data delineate more accurately the regional concentrations of key segments of the labour force. Note for example, the relatively uneven concentrations of farmers and farm workers in the Prairie Provinces. Saskatchewan, with 36.7 per cent, had by far the greatest proportionate share of its labour force in agriculture in 1961. Variations in proportions of farmers and farm workers are even greater in the Atlantic Provinces, ranging from 26.9 per cent for Prince Edward Island to only 1.5 per cent for Newfoundland where the primary emphasis is on fishing and logging rather than on agriculture. Those provinces with high proportions of farmers and farm workers tend to have the lowest proportions of craftsmen and production workers, and vice versa. The strongholds for blue-collar craftsmen and production process workers are clearly Quebec, Ontario, and British Columbia, with 27.5, 25.9, and 24.1 per cent respectively. The same three provinces also have the highest proportions of professional, technical, and managerial workers in their respective labour forces.

Fig. 10:2

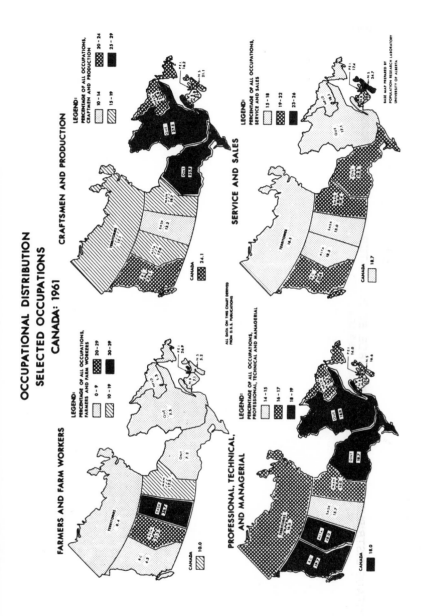

Table 10:3

PERCENTAGE DISTRIBUTION OF THE LABOUR FORCE, BY OCCUPATION AND SEX, FOR RURAL AND URBAN AREAS, CANADA, 1961

Occupational Division	URBAN		Total		RURAL Non-Farm		Farm	
	Male	Female	Male	Female	Male	Female	Male	Female
Managerial, professional, and technical	21.6	18.2	8.7	21.1	13.7	25.0	2.1	14.8
Clerical and sales	15.9	41.2	4.4	19.3	6.5	25.2	1.6	10.2
Service and recreation	9.7	22.2	5.5	23.5	9.0	29.7	1.0	13.9
Transport and communication	8.2	2.1	6.0	2.2	8.6	2.8	2.6	1.1
Craftsmen and production process	32.2	12.6	20.4	7.3	29.8	8.6	8.0	5.3
Farmers and workers	1.4	0.2	38.1	22.3	7.9	3.1	77.9	52.5
Loggers, trappers, etc.	0.7	—	6.6	—	10.0	—	2.3	—
Miners, quarrymen, etc.	1.3	—	1.6	—	2.4	—	0.4	—
Labourers	6.2	1.2	6.4	1.2	8.7	1.4	3.3	0.4
Total occupations[a]	100.0	100.0	100.0	100.0	100.0	100.0	100.0	100.0

SOURCE: Dominion Bureau of Statistics, *1961 Census of Canada*, Bulletin 7:1-12, Ottawa, The Queen's Printer, 1967, Tables VI and VII.
[a] Includes occupation not stated.

Alberta's position is somewhat unique by virtue of its dual economic nature. A high proportion of farmers and farm workers is found in conjunction with a low proportion of craftsmen and production workers. However, the considerable investment in oil and gas exploration and production activity, beginning with the big discovery of the Leduc field in 1946, has contributed to a fairly high proportion of professional, technical, and managerial occupations. Nova Scotia and New Brunswick are also somewhat atypical in that these provinces have low proportions of their labour force in agricultural, manufacturing, and professional, technical and managerial positions. Lacking strength in these areas, they would, by default, tend to have above average proportions in sales and service occupations.

Urban-rural variations in occupational characteristics. Data in Table 10:3 show more clearly the distinctive variations in occupational character of the labour force population by area of residence. As would be expected, proportionately more urban type occupations are found in the labour force as one moves from rural farm to rural non-farm, and urban. Males in white-collar occupations comprise 37.5 per cent of urban labour compared to 20.2 per cent and 3.7 per cent for rural non-farm and rural farm labour force respectively.

Craftsmen and production process workers, who constitute only 8.0 per cent of the male labour force living in rural farm areas, account for 29.8 per cent in rural non-farm and 32.2 per cent in urban areas. Similarly, by far the largest proportion of clerical and sales workers is found in urban areas followed by rural non-farm and rural farm areas. The same general pattern holds for service and recreational occupations; but, for transportation and communications, logging and fishing, mining and general labourers, the largest proportions are found in the rural non-farm population which includes many of those living in the suburban fringe areas adjacent to Canada's urban centres. Relatively few farmers or farm workers are found among urban or rural non-farm populations. As would be expected, they comprise over three-fourths, or 77.9 per cent, of the rural farm labour force.

For working females in rural farm populations, slightly more than half were reported as farmers or farm workers (mainly unpaid family workers); 13.9 per cent were in service and recreation occupations; and 14.8 per cent were in the professional, technical, and managerial category, most of whom were teachers.[4] The contrast with urban females is considerable. Approximately 41 per cent were in clerical and sales occupations, followed by 22.2 per cent in service and recreation, with an additional 18.2 per cent in professional, technical, and managerial positions. The rural non-farm female labour force had the largest proportion in service and recreation, 29.7 per cent, and had higher proportions of its labour force in transportation and communication, managerial, professional and technical, and sales than either the urban or rural farm groups.[5] These data clearly emphasize the fact that

Fig. 10:3

SELECTED OCCUPATIONS
BY PLACE OF RESIDENCE
CANADA: 1961

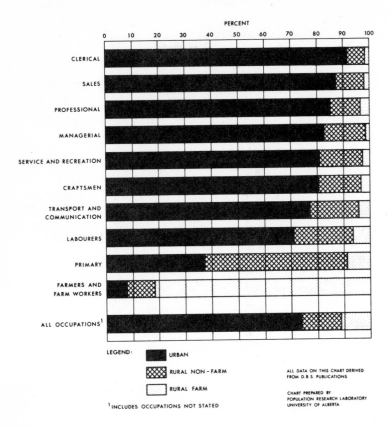

LEGEND:

■ URBAN

▨ RURAL NON - FARM

☐ RURAL FARM

[1] INCLUDES OCCUPATIONS NOT STATED

ALL DATA ON THIS CHART DERIVED
FROM D.B.S. PUBLICATIONS

CHART PREPARED BY
POPULATION RESEARCH LABORATORY
UNIVERSITY OF ALBERTA

the area of residence, i.e., urban or rural within region or province, determines both the type and number of availability of jobs. The relationship between occupations and the rural-urban character of the labour force is
summarized in Figure 10:3 which presents the rural-urban distribution for
selected occupations for the total experienced labour force in 1961. In
assessing the significance of the distribution for each occupational group,
keep in mind that in 1961 approximately 74 per cent of the total experienced
labour force who had jobs (or were looking for jobs) lived in urban areas,
15 per cent lived in rural non-farm areas, and 11 per cent in rural farm areas.
As would be expected from the previous discussion, the most significant
deviations are to be found for clerical occupations which are highly concentrated in urban areas, farmers and farm workers primarily in rural farm
areas, and primary occupations with disproportionate numbers in rural non-
farm areas.

Occupational Differentials

Variations in occupations by sex. Occupational variations by sex for Canada in 1961 are summarized in Table 10:4. The major distinctions between the two groups are readily apparent. For males, approximately two-thirds of the labour force are accounted for by white- and blue-collar occupations, with primary occupations accounting for an additional 16 per cent. Female white-collar, and service and recreational occupations account for 78.3 per cent of their total labour force, with 55.9 per cent in white-collar occupations alone. In three of the major occupational groupings, i.e., white collar, service and recreation, and primary, as well as the residual category, the decade rate of increase exceeded that for males. Of particular interest is the large increase for females in primary occupations (mainly agriculture) compared to a decline of 25.8 per cent for males. Males still tended to numerically exceed females by a considerable margin in all major groups except service and recreation where the number of females about equalled the number of males in 1961.

Figure 10:4 provides a more detailed picture of the relative sizes of nine selected occupational categories for both males and females. Of the female labour force, 28.8 per cent reported clerical occupations. Those in service occupations, 22.4 per cent, exceeded the number of female professional

Table 10:4

PERCENTAGE DISTRIBUTION OF THE LABOUR FORCE, 15 YEARS OF AGE AND OVER, BY BROAD OCCUPATIONAL GROUPINGS AND SEX, FOR CANADA,[a] 1961, AND PERCENTAGE CHANGE, 1951 TO 1961

Occupational Grouping 1961	Males (N = 4,694,294)		Females (N = 1,763,862)	
	Per Cent	Per Cent Change: 1951-61	Per Cent	Per Cent Change: 1951-61
White collar	30.3	36.6	55.9	56.9
Blue collar	35.0	13.9	12.8	7.5
Transportation and communication	7.5	18.7	2.2	15.0
Service and recreation	8.5	48.4	22.4	60.9
Primary	16.0	−25.8	4.3	135.3
Occupation not stated	2.6	140.9	2.4	228.2
Total occupations	100.0	14.1	100.0	51.8

SOURCE: Dominion Bureau of Statistics, *1961 Census of Canada*, Bulletin 7:1-12, Ottawa, The Queen's Printer, 1967, Table VIII.
[a] Excludes Yukon and Northwest Territories.

Fig. 10:4   OCCUPATIONAL DISTRIBUTION BY SEX
CANADA: 1961

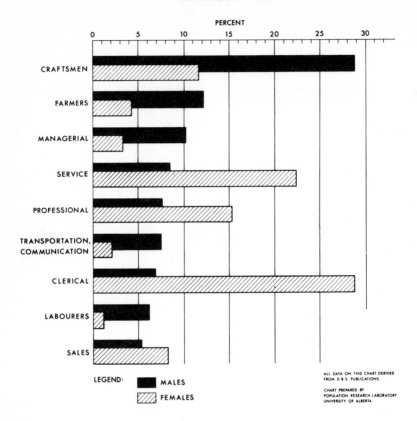

workers who accounted for an additional 15.4 per cent. Of the remaining occupations shown, sales jobs accounted for only 8.3 per cent, and managerial positions another 3.3 per cent. Within the service and recreational group, somewhat more than three-fourths of the women were "housekeepers, waitresses, cooks, and related workers"; and, among professionals, somewhat less than half were teachers and slightly more than one-third were health professionals.

Again, a more detailed examination of sex differentials for two of the larger occupational categories of the female labour force is possible in Figure 10:5. With almost 90 per cent of all professional females either teachers or health professionals, relatively few are found in other categories. Males are not as highly concentrated in any one specific professional occupa-

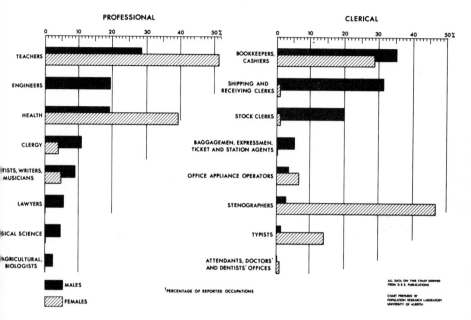

Fig. 10:5

PROFESSIONAL AND CLERICAL OCCUPATIONS¹
DETAILED DISTRIBUTIONS BY SEX
CANADA: 1961

tion; yet teachers, engineers, and health workers account for two-thirds of all those for whom occupation was known.

Of the clerical positions identified in Figure 10:5, women were highly concentrated in stenographic, bookkeeping, and cashiering positions. Males had a somewhat higher proportion in the latter-type positions, and significantly greater proportions working as stock, shipping, and receiving clerks. Baggagemen, expressmen, ticket and station agents were also predominantly males. For the service and recreation occupations (not shown in Figure 10:5), which had approximately equal numbers of males and females, the major difference was to be found in the concentration of males in the protective services in contrast to the concentration of females in housekeeping and waitressing. Males also had about twice the number and proportion employed as athletes and entertainers as compared to females, and again somewhat more in the residual category. The 1961 Census did report 43 specific occupations where females constituted more than half of the labour force. Those exhibiting the greatest dependence upon females for workers, i.e., those with 90 per cent or more women, are shown in Table 10:5.

Age variations in occupations by sex. Previous analysis of participation rates by age and sex would suggest that the female labour force would tend to be younger than the male labour force, and that age variations by occupations would tend to be greater for women. This is essentially substantiated

Table 10:5

OCCUPATIONS WITH MORE THAN 90 PER CENT FEMALES, CANADA, 1961

Occupation	Number of Females	Per Cent of Total
Nurses in training	22,667	98.6
Baby sitters	12,214	97.4
Stenographers	160,843	97.2
Dietitians	1,849	96.6
Attendants, doctor and dentist	3,761	96.5
Graduate nurses	59,345	96.2
Lodging and boarding housekeepers	24,650	95.8
Dressmakers and seamstresses	15,516	95.8
Typists and clerk typists	48,799	95.2
Telephone operators	33,706	95.2
Sewer and sewing machine operators	50,593	90.5

SOURCE: Dominion Bureau of Statistics, *1961 Census of Canada*, Bulletin 7:1-12, Ottawa, The Queen's Printer, 1967, Table X.

by data presented in Table 10:6 which show the average age for women to be 36 years compared to 39 years for men for all occupations combined. Also, the range of average ages for the major occupational divisions is from 33 to 46 years for females compared to 36 to 44 years for males.

In general, it would appear that those occupations with lower average ages tend to be those which require the least experience or formal education.

Table 10:6

AVERAGE AGE OF THE LABOUR FORCE, 15 YEARS OF AGE AND OVER, BY OCCUPATIONAL DIVISION, CANADA, 1961

Occupation Division	Males	Females
Managerial	44	46
Professional and technical	38	35
Clerical	36	33
Sales	36	37
Service and recreation	39	38
Transportation and communication	37	33
Farmers and farm workers	43	41
Loggers, fishermen, etc.	36	—
Miners, quarrymen, etc.	37	—
Craftsmen and production	39	35
Labourers	36	33
Occupation not stated	38	35
All occupations	39	36

SOURCE: Dominion Bureau of Statistics, *1961 Census of Canada*, Bulletin 7:1-12, Ottawa, The Queen's Printer, 1967, Table 5.

Conversely, those in managerial positions requiring maximum experience, or education and experience, have the highest average age. On the other hand, the rather high average age for farmers is the consequence of the aging of the rural population and loss of youth to other and more urban occupations. Percentage distributions presented in Figure 10:6 reveal additional interesting details of the age characteristics of selected occupations. For example, of the four occupational groups of males with the youngest average age, the labourers have the highest proportion, or 29.9 per cent, below the age of 25 years. Clerical workers are a close second with 27.8 per cent, but their peak is more concentrated between the ages of 20 and 25 years. The largest proportions for sales workers fall in the younger ages with the peak occurring in the 25–34 year age range. The shift in modal age groups between labourers and craftsmen clearly reflect a component of mobility as the unskilled gain experience with increasing years of labour force experience.

Age distributions for females by occupations, for the most part, show the typical distribution of female participation rates, i.e., an early peak between 15 and 25 years followed by a secondary peak of participation between 35 and 45 years before diminishing rapidly with increasing age. Where experience is a crucial factor, as in managerial positions, the proportion builds up gradually to its peak in the 45–54 year age group before diminishing. The age distribution for female farmers and farm workers is similar, but the peak occurs earlier (between 35 and 45 years) and reflects to a considerable degree the aging of the farm population as well as the exodus from rural-farm areas by younger people.

It is also interesting that clerical, and transportation and communications occupations show minimal evidence of the increase in participation rates for middle age groups, a characteristic of most occupations. By contrast, the significant increase in proportions of female sales worker in the age groups 40–44 and 45–49 years suggests that this is one type of employment which permits relatively easy entry either for older women beginning to work for the first time or re-entering the labour force after their children have outgrown their early dependency.

One additional comparison, using part of the same data in Figure 10:6, may be useful in highlighting differences in occupational structure for different age groups. The major distinctions between the two age groups shown in Figure 10:7 are (1) the disproportionate number of farmers and farm workers among those 55 years of age and over and (2) the generally larger proportions of older workers in managerial and in service and recreation occupations, especially females.

A number of factors would appear to have explanatory value for these differences. Perhaps most fundamental is the tendency for the older worker to drop out of the labour force with increasing age, a tendency not uniformly consistent within each of these major occupational categories. For those jobs

Fig. 10:6   # AGE DISTRIBUTION BY SEX
SELECTED OCCUPATIONS
CANADA: 1961

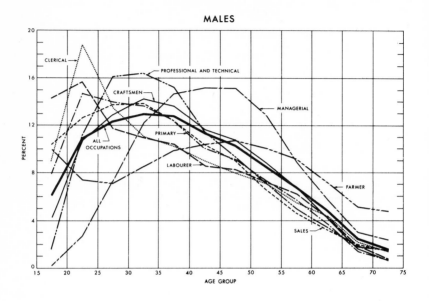

MALES

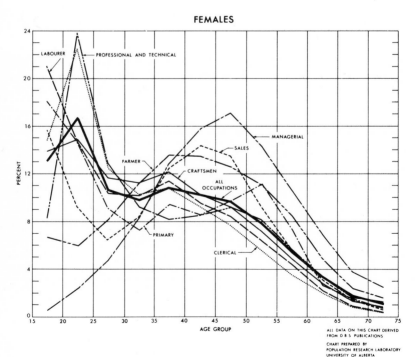

FEMALES

ALL DATA ON THIS CHART DERIVED
FROM D B S PUBLICATIONS

CHART PREPARED BY
POPULATION RESEARCH LABORATORY
UNIVERSITY OF ALBERTA

Fig. 10:7   OCCUPATIONAL DISTRIBUTIONS
SELECTED AGE GROUPS AND SEX
CANADA: 1961

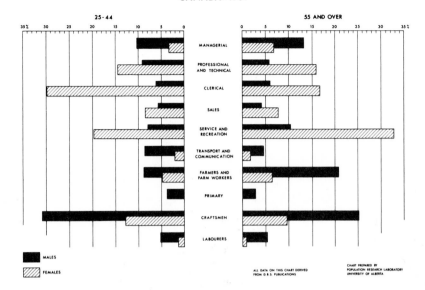

placing a premium on experience, or where one type of position recruits from upwardly mobile workers, e.g., professional or managerial positions, the decline in numbers with increasing age is apt to occur more slowly than for all occupations combined. The same is true for the agricultural worker but for a somewhat different reason. The easiest alternative for the aging farmer whose sons have moved to the city is to continue to work the farm until retirement, or as long as his health permits. This "excess" of older farmers and farm workers will then gradually decline through the normal effects of aging and mortality and in the absence of replacement by younger men. In other job areas, the older worker is phased out somewhat earlier as a result of increasing competition from the younger worker and must revert either to part-time work or seek more suitable employment, e.g., in service and recreational occupations, or as unskilled labourers where the working hours, wages, and other conditions may not be as attractive to the younger worker. The expansion of service and recreational occupations appears to have provided just such an opportunity for suitable employment of relatively unskilled but older women who might otherwise experience considerable difficulty in competing with younger women for many clerical and sales jobs.

Native and foreign born in the labour force. Historically, the foreign-born immigrant was relatively uneducated and unskilled. For these reasons, foreign-born workers were found in disproportionately greater numbers in the unskilled occupations. In 1911, 33.2 per cent of the males 10 years of

Fig. 10:8

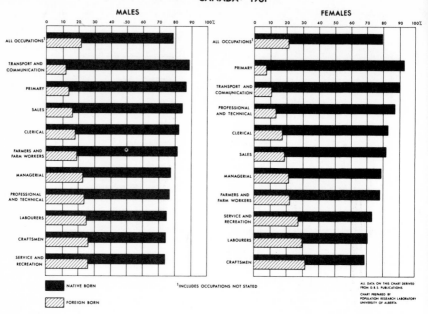

OCCUPATIONAL DISTRIBUTION BY NATIVITY
CANADA: 1961

age and older and engaged in gainful occupations were foreign born. Although the foreign born were somewhat under-represented among agricultural workers in general, they were disproportionately over-represented among agricultural labourers, ranging from a minimum of 40.8 per cent of the general farm labourers to 81.4 per cent of all labourers working on ditching and irrigation works. For the major occupational categories, they were most over-represented in mining occupations (52.3 per cent), domestic and personal services (48.6 per cent), and in transportation occupations, (54.4 per cent).[6]

Figure 10:8 shows that in 1961, the greatest concentration of foreign-born males to be found in any of the major occupational groups was in the service and recreation category (26.0 per cent), followed by craftsmen (25.8 per cent) and labourers (25.0 per cent). The increasing selectivity of recent immigration is reflected in the above average concentration of foreign-born males in professional and managerial occupations (23.6 and 23.1 per cent respectively, compared to 21.7 per cent for all occupations combined). For females, the foreign born comprised greater than average proportions of craftsmen (31.5 per cent), labourers (29.7 per cent), service and recreation (27.0 per cent), and a slightly larger than average proportion of managerial jobs (21.5 per cent). Both males and females are significantly under-represented in transportation and communications, and primary occupations with the exception of mining and related occupations for males.[7]

Occupations by ethnic origin groups. Differences in occupational distributions for major ethnic-origin groups reflect many factors in addition to cultural differences in values and attitudes towards work. Differences in age and sex composition, marital status, proportion foreign born, recency of immigration, and level of educational attainment also have significance to

Table 10:7

PERCENTAGE DISTRIBUTION OF THE LABOUR FORCE, 15 YEARS OF AGE AND OVER, BY OCCUPATION DIVISION AND SEX, FOR BRITISH ISLES, FRENCH, AND TOTAL ORIGINS, CANADA,[a] 1961

Occupational Division and Sex	Total Origins	British Isles	French
Males:			
Managerial	10.2	12.1	7.6
Professional and technical	7.6	9.3	5.9
Clerical	6.9	8.2	6.7
Sales	5.6	6.6	5.2
Service and recreation	8.5	9.2	7.7
Protective service	4.0	5.5	3.4
Transport and communication	7.5	8.0	8.9
Operators, road transport	5.3	5.1	7.0
Farmers and farm workers	12.2	10.7	10.8
Loggers, fishermen, trappers, etc.	2.4	1.9	3.8
Miners, quarrymen, etc.	1.4	1.2	1.5
Craftsmen, production process	28.8	25.5	31.4
Labourers	6.2	4.6	7.5
Occupation not stated	2.6	2.6	3.0
Total	100.0	100.0	100.0
Females:			
Managerial	3.3	3.4	3.1
Professional and technical	15.4	17.5	17.0
Teachers	7.1	7.6	9.5
Health professionals	5.4	6.7	4.5
Clerical	28.8	35.4	21.9
Sales	8.3	9.7	7.0
Service and recreation	22.4	18.8	24.4
Housekeepers, waitresses, etc.	17.3	14.6	19.3
Transport and communication	2.1	2.6	2.0
Farmers and farm workers	4.3	2.6	3.8
Craftsmen, production process	11.6	6.8	16.3
Labourers[b]	1.2	0.8	1.4
Occupation not stated	2.4	2.3	3.1
Total	100.0	100.0	100.0

SOURCE: Dominion Bureau of Statistics, *1961 Census of Canada,* Bulletin 7:1-12, Ottawa, The Queen's Printer, 1967, Table 13.
[a] Includes Yukon and Northwest Territories.
[b] Includes primary workers other than "farmers and farm workers".

Table 10:8

PERCENTAGE DISTRIBUTION OF THE LABOUR FORCE, 15 YEARS OF AGE AND OVER, BY OCCUPATIONAL DIVISION FOR SELECTED ETHNIC ORIGIN GROUPS, CANADA,[a] 1961

Occupation Division	British Isles 2,886,476	French 1,778,494	German 410,410	Hungarian 57,416	Italian 183,787	Jewish 65,191
Professional, technical and managerial	21.4	15.3	14.3	14.2	8.4	46.1
Sales and clerical	23.4	16.5	15.9	12.2	10.4	29.0
Craftsmen, production process	20.2	27.4	26.8	30.0	43.5	14.4
Transport and communication	6.4	7.1	5.0	3.3	3.7	2.3
Primary (including farmers)	10.6	12.8	19.2	17.7	4.0	0.4
Service and recreation	11.9	12.1	12.2	14.5	12.2	3.8
Labourers	3.6	5.8	4.4	6.4	15.4	1.0
Total[b]	100.0	100.0	100.0	100.0	100.0	100.0

Occupation Division	Nether- lands 149,350	Polish 130,970	Scandi- navian 145,318	Ukrain- ian 191,680	Other European 298,577	Asiatic 42,294	Native Indian 33,123
Professional, etc.	14.9	14.9	16.2	12.4	15.7	28.2	2.8
Sales and clerical	14.8	14.7	15.9	15.7	14.6	16.8	3.5
Craftsmen, etc.	24.9	29.6	22.2	24.0	28.0	15.8	16.5
Transport and communication	5.5	3.9	5.5	5.0	3.5	2.7	3.2
Primary	20.9	15.4	22.3	22.9	15.3	6.9	41.8
Service and recreation	11.9	12.6	11.3	12.6	15.5	24.4	16.8
Labourers	5.0	6.0	4.0	5.3	5.5	3.5	12.4
Total[b]	100.0	100.0	100.0	100.0	100.0	100.0	100.0

SOURCE: Dominion Bureau of Statistics, *1961 Census of Canada*, Bulletin 7:1-12, Ottawa, The Queen's Printer, 1967, Table 13.
aIncludes Yukon and Northwest Territories.
bIncludes occupation not stated.

the extent that they are related to ethnic differences. Therefore, any meaningful discussion of occupational differences by ethnic origins must take these other factors into consideration.

Because of the bicultural nature of Canadian society, considerable interest has been focused on British-French differences and their implications for the relative status positions of these two "founding" groups. Data in Table 10:7 clearly show the greater proportions of male white-collar workers among the labour force of British origins, and under-representation of those of French origins. This same relationship appears in each of the major components within the combined occupational categories shown. The British origin group also has an above average proportion of service and recreation workers, while the French are again under-represented in terms of the average of all ethnic groups combined. On the other hand, French origin males have a greater proportion in transportation and communication, primary occupations (except farmers and farm workers), and among blue-collar workers.

For women, the pattern is quite similar, but with three exceptions. Those of French origin also have (1) an above average proportion of professional and technical workers (primarily teachers), (2) higher proportions in service and recreation occupations, and (3) higher proportions of transportation and communication workers than women of British origin. Percentage distributions for both sexes combined, for the selected origin groups presented in Table 10:8, still show the relative advantage of those of British origin in the professional, technical, managerial, clerical, and sales occupational groups compared to those in the labour force of French ethnic origin.

With the exception of the British, Jewish, Asiatic, and Native Indian labour forces for both sexes combined, all major ethnic origins had their largest proportion engaged in craftsmen and production process activities. Among the exceptions, the Jewish labour force had, by far, the highest percentage (75.1 per cent) in managerial, professional, technical, sales, and clerical occupations of any origin group. Asiatics, with 28.2 per cent, were higher than those of British origin in the professional and managerial category, but relatively fewer in sales and clerical. The second largest proportion for Asiatics was 24.4 per cent in service occupations. The remaining groups, e.g., the Native Indians, had 41.8 per cent of their labour force in primary occupations, with an additional 16.8 per cent in service occupations, and another 12.4 per cent working as labourers.

Primary occupations were second in relative size for German, Hungarian, Netherlands, Polish, and Ukrainian origin groups. For Scandinavians, those in primary occupations had a slight numerical edge over craftsmen and production process workers because of a large proportion of farmers and farm workers among their pre-war immigrants.[8] For Italians, the second largest group, comprising 15.4 per cent, consisted of labourers. This was a reflection of the heavy post-war immigration of Italians, and the fact that of those in the experienced labour force in 1961, half were craftsmen and production process workers, and an additional 20.0 per cent were working as labourers.[9]

Variations in income and education by occupation. Two characteristics generally accepted as indicative of an occupation's status position are (1) the amount of skill or training required and (2) its earning power. It is true that the prestige accorded certain occupations in a given population does not always correspond to its socio-economic status ranking based on indicators of skill and earnings. This is certainly the case for some religious professionals and teachers. However, the relationship is sufficiently close to warrant their use in assessing the relative importance of the various occupations within Canada's labour force.

The major occupational divisions are ranked in Table 10:9 by average income reported for the non-farm male population, 25–64 years of age, in the current labour force in 1961. Those in professional and technical occupations and in managerial positions ranked first and second in terms of average total income. However, it should be pointed out that, because of the range of positions within these two general categories, it is to be expected

Table 10:9

AVERAGE TOTAL INCOME FOR MAJOR OCCUPATIONAL GROUPINGS FOR THE NON-FARM MALE POPULATION, 25–64 YEARS OF AGE, IN THE CURRENT LABOUR FORCE, CANADA, 1961[a]

Occupational Group	25–64 Years	35–44 Years	45–54 Years
Professional and technical	7,224	7,980	8,251
Managerial	7,088	7,203	7,562
Sales	4,924	5,272	5,114
Miners, quarrymen, etc.	4,344	4,474	4,357
Clerical	4,030	4,187	4,109
Craftsmen, production process and related workers	3,974	4,128	3,989
Transportation and communication workers	3,966	4,148	4,043
Service and recreation	3,678	4,128	3,620
Labourers, n.e.s.	2,668	2,781	2,652
Loggers, etc.	2,505	2,687	2,482
Farm workers and other agricultural occupations	2,054	2,258	2,061
Fishermen, trappers, and hunters	2,021	2,197	2,025
Occupations not stated	3,858	3,989	4,100
All occupations	4,602	4,905	4,868

SOURCE: Dominion Bureau of Statistics, *1961 Census of Canada*, Bulletin 4:1-2, Ottawa, The Queen's Printer, 1965, Table B6.
[a] Year ended May 31st.

that average incomes for some managerial positions would exceed those for some classes of professional and technical jobs. For example, average total incomes ranged from $5,739 for managers in retail businesses to $9,079 for those in finance, insurance, and real estate. On the other hand, the range for professional and technical workers ran from a low of $3,279 for religious professionals to $15,627 for physicians and surgeons.[10]

Years of formal schooling attained by individuals in specific jobs is generally accepted as an indicator of the degree of skill required, although this is not necessarily a valid assumption for all occupations. However, a ranking of occupations by income will generally correlate very highly with a ranking by years of formal education. This is illustrated in the partial listing of specific occupations by size of their average reported total earnings presented in Table 10:10. The data reveal a tendency for income to vary directly with the proportion having above average schooling.[11] The combined effect of

Table 10:10

SELECTED OCCUPATIONS OF NON-FARM MALE LABOUR FORCE RANKED BY AVERAGE INCOME FROM EMPLOYMENT, SHOWING PER CENT WITH ABOVE AVERAGE SCHOOLING, AND BLISHEN'S SOCIO-ECONOMIC INDEX, CANADA, 1961

Occupation	Average Earnings in Dollars	Per Cent With Above Average Schooling	Blishen's Socio-Economic Index
Physicians and surgeons	15,822	99.3	75.57
Judges and magistrates	13,009	90.5	72.24
Lawyers and notaries	12,459	98.8	75.41
Optometrists	10,064	93.4	73.77
Architects	9,389	95.6	74.52
Mechanical engineers	7,823	89.1	72.78
Accountants and auditors	7,324	83.5	68.80
Toolmakers and diemakers	4,882	32.8	44.82
Social welfare workers	4,543	70.2	55.62
Bookbinders	4,393	18.8	38.54
Bookkeepers and cashiers	3,775	61.6	49.55
Bricklayers, stone masons, tile setters	3,516	7.3	29.93
Barbers, hairdressers	3,489	11.0	30.94
Bartenders	3,007	14.6	33.29
Waiters	2,311	15.8	30.47
Fishermen	2,197	3.6	27.17
Trappers and hunters	1,228	0.8	25.36

SOURCE: Dominion Bureau of Statistics, *1961 Census of Canada*, Bulletin 4:1-2, Table B4; Bulletin 3:1-9, Table 17; and Bernard Blishen, "A Socio-Economic Index for Occupations in Canada", *Canadian Review of Sociology and Anthropology*, Vol. IV, No. 1, Feb., 1967, Table 1, pp. 44-50.
  a Percentage in occupation having attained four or five years of secondary schooling or having some university training or university degree.

income and education for measures of socio-economic status is also shown in Table 10:10, which presents socio-economic indices assigned to specific occupations using Blishen's revised scale and is based on 1961 Census data.[12] This particular selection of occupations, while being far from complete, is sufficient to demonstrate several aspects of the relationship between occupation, education, and income. Note that there is a tendency for the socio-economic index to vary directly with income. However, there are several discrepancies worthy of note. These data show very clearly the overlap of blue-collar workers with certain white-collar occupations, e.g., the higher income of tool and diemakers compared to social welfare workers. In terms of the educational attainment of the latter, they would be expected to show considerably higher incomes than they, in fact, reported in 1961. A similar situation appears to exist for bookkeepers and cashiers. On the other hand, in terms of their educational attainment, bricklayers reported higher earnings than would have been expected. Some of these inconsistencies might tend to disappear if other factors such as age and maturity were controlled. Nevertheless, many of the discrepancies do reflect both gains made by blue-collar workers through unionization, and status inconsistencies experienced by low paid, but highly educated, white-collar workers. The strong labour movement will continue to improve the income position of blue-collar workers at the expense of many semi-professional, white-collar workers.

REFERENCES

Department of Labour: *Occupational Trends in Canada 1931–1961*. Report No. 11, Ottawa, The Queen's Printer, 1965.

Ostry, S.: *The Occupational Composition of the Canadian Labour Force.* 1961 Census Monograph, Ottawa, The Queen's Printer, 1967.

Parai, L.: *Immigration and Emigration of Professional and Skilled Manpower During the Post-War Period.* Economic Council of Canada, Ottawa, The Queen's Printer, 1965.

Podoluk, J. R.: *Incomes of Canadians.* 1961 Census Monograph, Ottawa, The Queen's Printer, 1968.

FOOTNOTES

[1]*U.S. Census of Population, 1960, General Social and Economic Characteristics,* U.S. Summary, Table 92. For a more detailed discussion of the industrial composition of the U.S. labour force see D. J. Bogue, *Principles of Demography,* New York, John Wiley and Sons Inc., 1969, pp. 259–264.

[2]*Ibid.*

[3]*1918 Census of Canada,* Vol. 2, Table XIII.

[4]Dominion Bureau of Statistics, *1961 Census of Canada,* Bulletin 7:1–12, Ottawa, The Queen's Printer, 1967, p. 14.

[5]Females in sales occupations were 8.6, 9.7 and 2.9 per cent, respectively, of urban, rural non-farm, and rural labour force populations.

[6]*1911 Census of Canada,* Vol. VI, Table IV.

[7]Dominion Bureau of Statistics, special unpublished tabulations (A21) for W. E. Kalbach *The Impact of Immigration on Canada's Population,* 1961 Census Monograph, Ottawa, The Queen's Printer, 1970.

[8]*Ibid.,* Table 4.27, pp. 234–237.

[9]*Ibid.*

[10]Dominion Bureau of Statistics, *1961 Census of Canada,* Bulletin 4:1–2, Ottawa, The Queen's Printer, 1965, Table B6.

[11]These data are similar to those presented by Jenny R. Podoluk in *Incomes of Canadians,* Ottawa, The Queen's Printer, 1968, Table 4:12. Podoluk indicates that the median years of schooling for the male labour force was one year of secondary schooling and defines "above average" as those having attained four or five years of secondary schooling, or having some university training or degree. Data in Table 10:10 are for males only so as to be comparable with data used by Blishen in his 1961 socio-economic index. See note 12.

[12]B. Blishen, "A Socio-Economic Index for Occupations in Canada", *The Canadian Review of Sociology and Anthropology,* Vol. 4, No. 1, February, 1967, pp. 41–53.

Marital Status

Three "vital" events are of crucial importance to human societies. Births and deaths, already discussed in Chapter 3, initiate and terminate the life cycles of their individual members, while marriage and its family of related statuses, i.e., single (never married), widowed, and divorced (all in conjunction with one's age and sex characteristics), delineate the bounds of appropriate behaviour. Besides being of central importance to the individual, the marital status of persons in a population has crucial significance for the survival of society through the determination of the size and character of its reproductively active population. While prevailing marriage customs directly affect fertility behaviour, i.e., the number and timing of births, the two are interrelated in such a way that variations in fertility can, in turn, have an indirect influence on the marital status of a population by altering its age structure. On the other hand, changes in mortality also exert an influence on the relative size of the various age and sex groups, especially affecting the sex ratios and consequently the marital status of the older population. This chapter presents data on trends in marital status from 1901 to 1961 as well as analyses of marital status composition and differentials.

Marriage and Divorce Trends

Marriages: 1921–61. The potential number of marriages is basically a function of the supply of marriageable individuals. However, if this were the sole determinant of the decision to marry, the number and rate of marriages would vary directly with changes in the size of the eligible population. Obviously, many other factors exert an influence on the decision to marry,

264

among which are (1) the sex ratios within the relevant age groups, (2) pressures to extend or shorten the period of formal education, and especially, (3) variations in level of economic activity.

Since 1921, the annual number of marriages has gradually increased from 71,254 in 1921 to a peak of 133,186 in 1957, just a few years prior to the 1961 Census.[1] Interestingly, the marriage rate (number of marriages per 1,000 population) for 1957 was only 8.0 compared to 7.9 in 1921. However, between these two points in time, the rate at which people married varied considerably. The effects of changing levels of economic activity, as well as World War II, are plainly visible in Figure 11:1, and they appear to account for the major fluctuations during this period. Marriage rates reached a peak of 7.7 in 1929, before dropping sharply with the onset of the economic recession to 5.9 in 1932. Thereafter the rates recovered slowly, then, during the early war years from 1940 to 1942, increased rapidly to peaks of 10.8, 10.6, and 10.9 as employment levels rose with Canada's involvement in the war. The effects of World War II, especially the movement into the armed forces and overseas, are clearly visible in the declining marriage rate which reached its minimum in 1944. Returning service men, following the end of hostilities in 1945, triggered another year of peak marriage rates in 1946 as couples made up for war time delays and prolonged absences. Following this post-war peak came a decline in marriage rates which did not abate until 1963 when it reached a low of 6.9 per 1,000. While social and economic

Fig. 11:1   MARRIAGE AND DIVORCE TRENDS
                        CANADA: 1921-1961

ALL DATA ON THIS CHART DERIVED
FROM D.B.S. PUBLICATIONS

CHART PREPARED BY
POPULATION RESEARCH LABORATORY
UNIVERSITY OF ALBERTA

factors cannot be totally excluded, a more significant factor in this decline was the influx of smaller cohorts of the depression-era babies into the marriageable age groups. Marriage rates for those marrying for the first time between 15 and 25 years of age actually increased between 1941 and 1961, as did the proportion married of the total population 15 years of age and over; but these increases were not sufficient to overcome the effects of smaller age and sex cohorts.[2]

Examination of marriage rates by province reveals the same general pattern as for Canada as a whole. The major inter-provincial differences appear to be in the levels of marriage rates during this period. Rates for Quebec, the Atlantic Provinces, and Saskatchewan have been persistently lower than Canada between 1921 and 1961, while rates for Alberta, Ontario, Manitoba, and British Columbia tended to be higher.[3] The latter provinces, with the possible exception of Manitoba, have been the rapid growth areas. Generally speaking, marriage rates tend to be higher in those areas where economic conditions are favourable or promising, while they tend to be below average in areas experiencing slower economic growth. The factors affecting inter-provincial differences in the decision to marry are very similar but less dramatic than those which operated to lower the marriage rates throughout Canada between 1931 and 1935.

Divorces: 1921–61. Canada may have the distinction of having the lowest divorce rates of any westernized country, but then Canada has never been known for its liberal divorce laws. Perhaps Quebec has had the greater reputation in this regard, but the residents of Newfoundland (and until recently those of Prince Edward Island) also could not obtain a divorce except by a Private Act of the Parliament of Canada.[4] One consequence of relatively tough divorce laws has been the absence of reliable data on family dissolution in Canada. The number of "official" divorces quite likely provides an unrealistic estimate of the number of disrupted families where husband and wife have separated, or where either husband or wife has simply deserted. Unless man and wife have received a formal divorce, they are listed as married in the Canadian Census, regardless of their living arrangement. Divorce statistics provide, at best, only a rough indication of family disorganization; and even the census statistics are suspected of underestimating the actual number of divorced persons living in Canada.[5]

The number of divorces, as well as divorce rates, increased during the years following 1921, reaching record highs during the immediate post-World War II years, 1946 and 1947, when divorce rates reached 62.6 and 65.5 per 100,000 population.[6] After the disruptive effects of the war had taken their toll, divorce rates gradually declined, albeit somewhat erratically, until 1961 when they reached 36 divorces, compared to 700 marriages per 100,000 population.

Table 11:1

MARRIAGE AND DIVORCE RATES FOR SELECTED YEARS, IN CANADA, 1941 TO 1961

Year	Marriage Rate per 1,000 population	DIVORCE RATES		
		Number per 100,000 population	Number per 100,000 pop. 15 years and over	Number per 100,000 married pop. 15 years and over
1941	10.6	21.4[a]	32.0	56.2
1946	10.9	63.1[a]	79.3	131.9
1951	9.2	37.6	57.0	88.8
1956	8.3	37.3	59.0	89.5
1961	7.0	36.0	57.3[b]	85.9[b]

SOURCE: Dominion Bureau of Statistics, *Vital Statistics, 1967*, Ottawa, The Queen's Printer, 1969, Tables M1 and M9; and *1961 Census*, Bulletin 7:1-5, Ottawa, The Queen's Printer, 1964, Table X.

[a] Newfoundland not included prior to 1951.
[b] Yukon and Northwest Territories included in 1961 only.

More precise measurements of divorce, in which divorces are related to more relevant portions of the total population, are shown in Table 11:1 along with crude marriage and divorce rates. They also reflect the sharp rise during the immediate post-war period and decline to a plateau during the 1951–61 decade at a somewhat higher level than that which occurred in 1941. The marriage rate, in the same period, continued to decline.

Trends in Marital Status of the Population

The married population increases through the addition of newly-weds and arrival of married immigrants, and decreases through divorce, emigration, mortality, and changes in status of the surviving members of marriages broken by death. The net effect of these continuing events has been the steady increase in married population from 1,833,043 in 1901, to 8,024,304 in 1961, as shown in Figure 11:2. This represents a rate of growth significantly higher than that for the population 15 years of age and over for the same period, a growth rate which produced an increase from 52.0 per cent to 66.6 per cent in the proportion of married population. Only in 1931 did the proportion married fail to show an increase over the preceding decade. This short term reversal, reflected in an increase in the proportion single, was most likely caused by numerous postponements of marriage in response to the depressed economic situation. The increase in the widowed population has been fairly constant, thus its proportion has remained unchanged.

Another socially significant trend during this period was the continued and rapid increase in divorced population. Although still relatively insignificant numerically, the divorced population has shown important and consistent

Fig. 11:2   **MARITAL STATUS TRENDS[1]**
                       CANADA: 1901 - 1961[2]

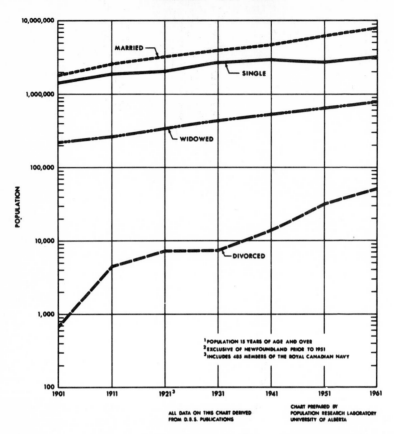

increases in its proportionate share of the population, particularly since 1931. While this undoubtedly reflects a change in the social acceptability of divorce, it is also a logical consequence of the rapidly increasing proportion of the population getting married. As more of the population marries, so will an increasing number of "marginal marital risks", and an increasing number of marriage failures can be expected.

Regional Variations in Marital Status

Provincial differences. There were marked variations in marital composition by province in 1961. From the data presented in Table 11:2, it can be stated that the Western Provinces had lower than average proportions of single population and an above average proportion of married. This is entirely consistent with the earlier analysis of regional differences in marriage rates

Table 11:2

PERCENTAGE DISTRIBUTION BY MARITAL STATUS, POPULATION
15 YEARS OF AGE AND OVER, CANADA AND PROVINCES, 1961

Province	Total	Single	Married	Widowed	Divorced
Newfoundland	100.0	30.2	63.7	6.1	—
Prince Edward Island	100.0	30.4	61.9	7.5	0.1
Nova Scotia	100.0	28.3	64.1	7.3	0.4
New Brunswick	100.0	28.8	64.2	6.6	0.3
Quebec	100.0	32.0	62.2	5.6	0.2
Ontario	100.0	23.0	69.9	6.9	0.5
Manitoba	100.0	25.6	67.2	6.8	0.5
Saskatchewan	100.0	26.1	67.1	6.5	0.3
Alberta	100.0	24.5	69.1	5.7	0.7
British Columbia	100.0	22.4	69.2	7.4	1.0
Yukon	100.0	30.3	64.8	3.4	1.5
Northwest Territories	100.0	34.3	60.3	4.7	0.7
Canada	100.0	26.5	66.6	6.5	0.4

SOURCE: Dominion Bureau of Statistics, *1961 Census of Canada*, Bulletin 7:1-5, Ottawa, The Queen's Printer, 1964, Table 1.

where it was shown that Ontario and the Western Provinces, excepting Saskatchewan, have had higher than average marriage rates for the period 1921 to 1961. The situation in the Yukon and Northwest Territories was more similar to that of the Eastern Provinces in that they also had above average proportions of single and were below average with respect to their married populations. In fact, the Northwest Territories, with 34.3 per cent, had the highest percentage single, and, with 60.3 per cent, the lowest proportion married of any era in Canada. Both of the Northern Territories also had relatively large numbers of divorced, but the Yukon with 1.5 per cent exceeded all other areas. Since it has already been shown that there are significant inter-provincial variations in age structure, it is possible that Table 11:2 might reflect these, rather than differences in propensity to marry or divorce. However, standardizing these rates on the age structure for Canada as a whole in 1961 does not basically alter the more general east-west pattern already noted. After standardization, Prince Edward Island shows the highest proportion of single persons rather than Quebec, and Alberta replaces British Columbia as the province with the lowest. Alberta also replaced Ontario as the area with the highest proportion married, while Quebec replaced Prince Edward Island as having the lowest. Eliminating the effects of differences in age structure on the proportions widowed and divorced further reveals that the proportion of widows was highest in Newfoundland, rather than Prince Edward Island, while British Columbia and Alberta retained their distinction of having the highest proportion divorced. Percentage distributions by marital status for the provinces, standardized on the age composition of Canada for 1961, are presented in Table 11:3.

Table 11:3

PERCENTAGE DISTRIBUTION BY MARITAL STATUS, POPULATION 15 YEARS OF AGE AND OVER, FOR THE PROVINCES STANDARDIZED ON THE AGE COMPOSITION OF CANADA, 1961

Province	Total	Single	Married	Widowed	Divorced
Newfoundland	100.0	25.6	67.5	6.9	—
Prince Edward Island	100.0	29.8	64.2	5.9	0.1
Nova Scotia	100.0	27.0	65.9	6.7	0.4
New Brunswick	100.0	26.8	66.6	6.3	0.3
Quebec	100.0	29.7	63.4	6.7	0.2
Ontario	100.0	24.6	68.3	6.6	0.5
Manitoba	100.0	26.3	67.2	6.1	0.4
Saskatchewan	100.0	26.5	67.5	5.7	0.3
Alberta	100.0	24.5	68.8	6.0	0.7
British Columbia	100.0	24.6	68.3	6.1	1.0
Canada	100.0	26.5	66.6	6.5	0.4

SOURCE: Dominion Bureau of Statistics, *1961 Census of Canada*, Bulletin 7:1-5, Ottawa, The Queen's Printer, 1964, Table II.

Rural-urban differences in marital status. In Table 11:4, the proportion of the population 15 years of age and over and single varies from a maximum of 32.3 per cent in rural farm areas to a minimum of 25.6 per cent in urban areas. Since the rural non-farm populations are generally in closer proximity to urban centres, their marital composition tends to be more like that of urban localities than rural farm. Similarly, the proportions married in urban and rural non-farm areas are more alike than when compared to the rural non-farm population. The relative number of widowed and divorced also increased from minimal levels in rural farm areas to maximum proportions in urban areas. Here again, differences in the age-sex structure of rural and urban populations would contribute to the observed variations in addition to behavioural differences associated with rural-urban residence.

Table 11:4

PERCENTAGE DISTRIBUTION BY MARITAL STATUS, POPULATION 15 YEARS OF AGE AND OVER, FOR RURAL AND URBAN AREAS, CANADA, 1961

Marital Status	Total	Urban	Rural Non-farm	Rural Farm
Single	26.5	25.6	26.5	32.3
Married	66.6	67.1	66.7	63.4
Widowed	6.5	6.8	6.5	4.2
Divorced	0.4	0.5	0.3	0.1
Total: Per Cent	100.0	100.0	100.0	100.0
Number	21,046,325	8,614,648	2,132,893	1,298,784

SOURCE: Dominion Bureau of Statistics, *1961 Census of Canada*, Bulletin 7:1-5, Ottawa, The Queen's Printer, 1964, Table 2.

Marital Status Differentials

The changing age at marriage. One of the crucial variables affecting both the marital status composition of a population and the changes in level of fertility, is age at marriage. All other things being equal, where early marriage is the norm, larger proportions of the population will be married and the potential fertility levels will tend to be higher because of the longer exposure to the risk of pregnancy. Clearly, the picture is far more complex than this because during the 45-year period covered by Table 11:5, fertility made a dramatic post-war revival following minimal depression levels, while the average age at marriage declined by 2.9 years for bridegrooms and 1.1 years

Table 11:5

AVERAGE AGE AT MARRIAGE FOR BRIDES AND BRIDEGROOMS, CANADA, 1921 TO 1966

Year	Brides	Bridegrooms
1921	25.5	29.9
1926	25.1	29.3
1931	24.9	29.2
1936	25.0	29.1
1941	25.1	28.9
1946	25.3	28.6
1951	25.3	28.3
1956	25.0	27.9
1961	24.7	27.7
1966	24.4	27.0

SOURCE: Dominion Bureau of Statistics, *Nuptiality, 1950-1964*, Cat. No. 84-523, Ottawa, The Queen's Printer, May, 1967, Tables 4 and 5.

for brides. Data presented in Table 11:5 for both sexes show this long term decline.

Since these data are for all marriages, the trends for those marrying for the first time are somewhat obscured. Older persons marrying for a second time, i.e., those who have been widowed or divorced, even though comprising less than 10 per cent of all marriages, can produce a considerable effect on the average age at marriage. This may be confirmed by comparing data in Table 11:6 with those for corresponding years in Table 11:5. Such a comparison reveals that the decline in age at marriage between 1941 and 1966 was actually greater for those women marrying for the first time than for all brides combined. For males the drop in age was somewhat greater than for females, but the decline for those never previously married was somewhat less than for all bridegrooms. Age at marriage for previously divorced brides and bridegrooms increased only slightly between 1950 and 1964, while that for widows and widowers entering their next marriage increased by 3.9 and 3.2 years respectively, i.e., from 46.4 to 50.3 years for females, and from 53.2 to 56.4 years for males.[7]

These data reflect two highly significant trends: (1) the increasing social acceptability of younger marriages (a trend only temporarily interrupted by a major economic depression, and World War II) and (2) the increasing longevity of married persons, hence an older age at marriage for those persons choosing to remarry after the death of their spouse.

Provincial variations in age at marriage. The overall decline in age at marriage between 1921 and 1961 is also evident at provincial levels, as may be seen in Figure 11:3. The decline has been much greater and more consistent for males than for females, and the general pattern for each sex is evident in all provinces except Quebec. For females, the most pronounced declines occurred between 1921 and 1931, with the age at marriage subsequently increasing to peak values between 1941 and 1951 before again re-

Table 11:6

AVERAGE AGE AT MARRIAGE OF PERSONS NEVER PREVIOUSLY
MARRIED, FOR BRIDES, AND BRIDEGROOMS, CANADA,
1941 TO 1966

Year	Brides	Bridegrooms
1941	24.4	27.6
1946	24.1	27.1
1951	23.8	26.6
1956	23.4	26.1
1961	22.9	25.8
1966	22.6	25.2

SOURCE: Dominion Bureau of Statistics, *Vital Statistics, 1967*, Ottawa, The Queen's Printer, 1969, Table M3.

suming a downward trend. Apparently the Great Depression and World War II had a more direct effect on the age at which women married than it did for men, whose age decline appears to have been relatively unaffected.

For individual provinces, there are interesting exceptions to the general trends. Quebec's patterns of change were unique in that they were similar for both males and females, and they increased from 1926 to peaks in 1941 before entering a period of gradual decline. For British Columbia, age at marriage, for both males and females, has been consistently higher than any other province, while Newfoundland had the lowest age during the period for which data were available. Prince Edward Island is unique in terms of its changing age level relative to the other provinces at the beginning and end of the period. During the early 1920s, its age at marriage was the second highest, and unusually high *vis-à-vis* the other Maritime Provinces; but, during the late 1950s, it was next to the lowest and consistent with the pattern for the Atlantic Provinces in general. Northern areas, especially the Yukon, exhibited a remarkable rise in age at marriage between 1951 and

Fig. 11:3   AVERAGE AGE AT MARRIAGE BY SEX
CANADA AND PROVINCES: 1921 – 1961

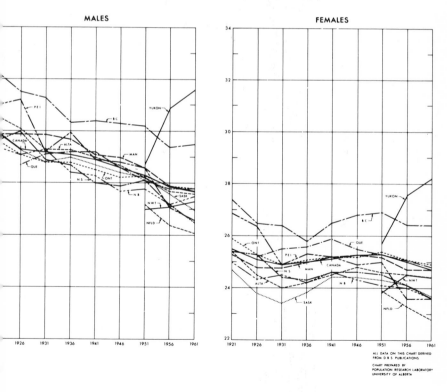

ALL DATA ON THIS CHART DERIVED
FROM D B S PUBLICATIONS

CHART PREPARED BY
POPULATION RESEARCH LABORATORY
UNIVERSITY OF ALBERTA

1961. The reasons for this are not immediately apparent, but adequate explanations are difficult to find when limited to the analysis of infrequent events in small populations which have an inherent statistical instability.

Variations in marital status by age and sex. Two immediately apparent consequences of the tendency for women to marry earlier than men, and the declining age at marriage for both sexes are (1) higher proportions of females married in the younger age groups than males, and (2) an increasing proportion of the population, 15 years of age and over, married. The latter trend has already been dealt with in an earlier section of this chapter, while the first consequence may be clarified by referring to Figure 11:4. Note that the proportion of females married significantly exceeds that for males up to the middle-age group of 40–44 year olds, at which point the situation is reversed and the proportion of married males becomes greater and the difference increases dramatically with increasing age. Since the proportions of males who are single consistently exceeds that for females throughout the age distribution, the explanation for variations in the relative position of the proportions married must lie with the other marital statuses. For the relatively small number under 55 years of age who were divorced, women outnumbered men relatively and absolutely, while for all age groups above 60 years

Fig. 11:4   MARITAL STATUS BY AGE AND SEX
                        CANADA: 1961

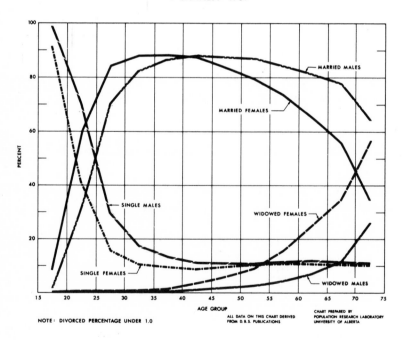

NOTE: DIVORCED PERCENTAGE UNDER 1.0

Fig. 11:5 MARITAL STATUS BY AGE AND SEX
AREA OF RESIDENCE
CANADA: 1961

RURAL-FARM

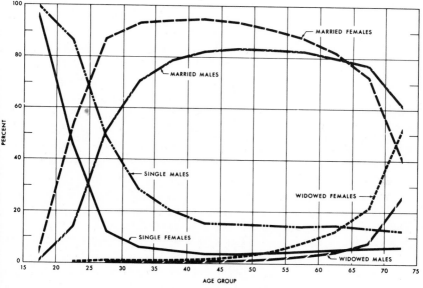

URBAN

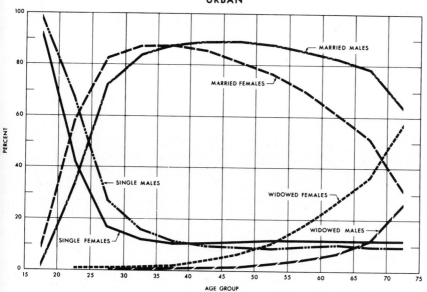

NOTE: DIVORCED PERCENTAGE UNDER 1.0

ALL DATA ON THIS CHART DERIVED
FROM D.B.S. PUBLICATIONS

CHART PREPARED BY
POPULATION RESEARCH LABORATORY
UNIVERSITY OF ALBERTA

the men outnumbered the women. This would suggest that even though men tend to marry later than women, men under 50 years of age are more likely to remarry than women. The fact that there are proportionately and numerically more widows than widowers in all age groups indicates that women not only tend to marry older men (with lower life expectancies), but are also less likely to remarry after the death of their spouse.

The proportion single in the population drops rapidly during the prime marrying ages and then stabilizes between 10 and 11 per cent for all age groups 45 years and over, with single females being both proportionately and numerically smaller in size. The proportion married, as would be expected, increases rapidly, reaching peak proportions in the 35–39 and 40–44 year age groups. For males the maximum proportion is found for the 40–44 year age group, while for women it is the 35–39 year age group, reflecting again the tendency for females to marry older males. For ages beyond 45 years, the relative numbers married decline as divorce and mortality take their toll. Maximum proportions of divorced women are found between 45 and 55 years, whereas for males it is the 50–54 year age group. In each case, the maximum number of divorced persons were in the 45–49 year age group.

Marital status and area of residence. Distributions for marital status, by age and sex, are shown for rural farm and urban areas in Figure 11:5. The same general distribution by age for the single population holds for both areas, but the levels vary somewhat by sex. For example, the relative number of males in rural farm areas is greater than females in the older age groups. Apparently those women who do not marry and settle in rural farm areas migrate to rural non-farm or urban centres. Thus, the proportion married for women in rural farm areas is consistently higher for all age groups 25–29 years of age and over. An examination of data for the widowed will also show a tendency for greater proportions of widows to stay on the farm than widowers. This, of course, could reflect the higher remarriage rates for widowers.

The percentage of divorced males is greater than divorced females in rural farm populations, but in both cases their numbers are significantly higher in urban areas. This is true for all age groups, and undoubtedly reflects both the greater social acceptability of this status in urban areas as well as greater social and economic opportunities for divorced persons. Urban areas appear to be more attractive than rural farm areas for both widows and widowers. In addition, the proportions widowed are consistently higher for females than for males in both areas and for all age groups.

Marital status and nativity. The foreign born of both sexes, 15 years of age and over, have had higher proportions married than native born, and relatively greater numbers of widowed and divorced since 1931. As may be seen in Table 11:7, almost three-fourths of the foreign-born males were

Table 11:7

PERCENTAGE MARRIED, WIDOWED AND DIVORCED, FOR NATIVE- AND FOREIGN-BORN POPULATIONS, 15 YEARS OF AGE AND OVER, BY SEX, CANADA, 1921 TO 1961

Year	Per Cent Married			Per Cent Widowed and Divorced		
	Total	Native Born	Foreign Born	Total	Native Born	Foreign Born
Males						
1921	56.5	53.8	62.0	4.4	4.7	3.8
1931	54.7	49.7	65.0	4.4	4.2	4.6
1941	55.2	49.8	71.2	5.0	4.4	6.9
1951	63.8	60.8	75.4	4.1	3.4	6.6
1961	66.4	64.1	74.7	3.7	3.1	5.7
Females						
1921	59.1	54.8	70.1	9.0	9.0	9.0
1931	57.3	51.4	72.8	8.6	8.3	9.6
1941	56.9	52.5	72.4	10.1	8.8	14.6
1951	64.5	64.4	64.7	9.8	8.5	14.7
1961	66.8	65.6	71.5	10.2	8.4	16.9

SOURCE: W. E. Kalbach, *The Impact of Immigration on Canada's Population,* Ottawa, The Queen's Printer, 1970, Tables 2:13 and 2:14.

married, compared to somewhat less than two-thirds of the native born. For females, the situation was very similar, but the differences have been somewhat less since 1941. For widowed and divorced, the differences by nativity have increased primarily because of consistent increases in proportions widowed and divorced among foreign born, as well as a significant decline for native-born males. Changes in the proportion married among the foreign born have been such that since 1951 relatively more males are married than females.

Both the increasing proportions of widowed and divorced and married among males reflect in part the higher average age of the foreign born, and in part the fact that the proportions of married males tend to exceed those for married females for all age groups beyond 40 years of age. Another factor contributing to the higher proportion married among the foreign born is the large proportion of adult immigrants who are already married when they arrive in Canada. Between 1933 and 1961, with the exception of the war years 1943–46, more than half of all immigrants 15 years of age and over were already married when they arrived in Canada.[8]

Inter-marriage of Ethnic and Cultural Groups

In the absence of total ethnic, religious, and cultural segregation, thousands of people with varying cultural backgrounds and differing social, psychological, and economic characteristics meet and interact during the course of their daily activities in any modern society. Industrialization has not only worked to increase this mixing in Canada by encouraging urbanward migration, but also by creating such a demand for skilled workers that the country's manpower needs can only be met through immigration of workers from foreign countries. Migrants bring their cultural heritage with them, and it is only natural that they should attempt to preserve their customary way of life in their new homes. However, there are many forces impinging on the immigrant that tend to produce attitudinal and behavioural changes, not the least of which are the consequences of the inter-marriage of persons from diverse ethnic and cultural groups. Analyses of the religious affiliation of brides and grooms who were married during 1959–61, previously discussed in Chapter 7, revealed significant variations in the degree of mixing observed for many of the denominations in Canada. Other studies of Canadian data, notably by Burton Hurd, have also reported significant variations in the propensity to marry within ethnic origin groups.[9] Similar data on ethnic origins of spouses, in husband-wife families, from the 1961 Census are examined in this section. The analysis is carried one additional step by examining inter-marriage patterns for native-born males in order to factor out the extraneous and confounding effect introduced by the presence of foreign-born immigrants who were married before arriving in Canada.

Comparison of ethnic origins of husbands and wives living together at the time of the 1961 Census reveals a strong tendency for persons to marry within their own ethnic origin groups, with just over three-fourths of all husbands living with wives of the same origin. There is, however, considerable variation between ethnic groups, as one can readily determine by examination of the data in Table 11:8. At one extreme are the Native Indian and Eskimo husbands, with almost 92 per cent living with wives of the same ethnic origin, followed closely by Jewish and French husbands with 91.1 and 88.3 per cent respectively. Proportions were also high for British Isles and Asiatic origin males with close to 80 per cent reporting wives of the same origin. Scandinavian males were least endogamous in their mate selection with less than one-third living with women of Scandinavian origin at the time of the census.

These data provide only a rough indication of propensity to marry within one's ethnic or racial group as they do not distinguish between the native and foreign born within the group. It has already been pointed out that this is important because a high proportion of the latter were married before they arrived in Canada. The problem is of less consequence for those groups with high proportions of native born, e.g., the French and Native Indian and

Eskimo populations. On the other hand, it is quite serious for groups like the Italians, comprised of a relatively large proportion of foreign born. Thus, a more precise measure of the propensity to inter-marry, one that would have greater relevance for the assessment of the significance of ethnicity in the assimilation process, would be the proportion of native-born husbands with wives of the same origin. These data for 1961, have also been included in Table 11:8. The interesting features of these data, which are revealed in

Table 11:8

PERCENTAGE OF FAMILY HEADS WITH WIVES OF SAME ETHNIC ORIGIN FOR TOTAL AND NATIVE-BORN HEADS, CANADA, 1961

Ethnic Origin of Family Head	All Family Heads	Native born Heads
British Isles	81.2	79.9
French	88.3	88.6
German	52.0	37.9
Italian	76.6	27.2
Netherlands	54.9	29.5
Jewish	91.1	87.5
Polish	49.0	25.5
Russian	47.7	44.7
Scandinavian	31.2	18.0
Ukrainian	61.8	50.5
Asiatic	79.9	67.7
Native Indian and Eskimo	91.8	92.0

SOURCE: Dominion Bureau of Statistics, unpublished special tabulations. See W. E. Kalbach, *The Impact of Immigration on Canada's Population*, Ottawa, The Queen's Printer, 1970, Appendix H.

comparisons with those for total husband-wife families are the following: (1) the persistence of high proportions of endogamous marriages for French, Jewish, and British Isles origins, even after controlling for the presence of foreign-born males; (2) the radical drop in the levels of such marriages for other origins; and (3) changes in the relative positions of ethnic groups, with respect to their tendency towards endogamous marriage.

Native-born males of Scandinavian origin still had the lowest proportion of endogamous marriages, but the relative position of Italian family heads changed remarkably. Note that the propensity for intra-marriage among native-born Italian males is now less than that for those of German, Netherlands, Ukrainian, and Russian origins. Such factors as relative size, sex ratio, age distribution, and geographical concentration of ethnic populations are important determinants of inter-marriage patterns. Native Indians and Eskimos, for example, living in the more isolated and remote parts of the country are limited in their contacts with other origin groups, not to mention the additional difficulties created by the prevalence of prejudice, and social and economic discrimination. For somewhat similar reasons, the high concentration of French in Quebec precludes any significant degree of inter-marriage, apart from other cultural and religious considerations. While the Jewish population represented only one per cent of the total population in 1961, their high degree of ecological concentration in urban centres combined with their strong ethnic and religious identity has produced a high proportion of endogamous marriages. Also of considerable significance in each of these cases are the socio-economic status differences which tend to structure interaction between various ethnic groups, as well as within.

Analyses which have taken into consideration the distributional factor show very clearly the significance of early settlement patterns on the propensity of certain ethnic origins to marry outside their own group. A number of ethnic groups show higher proportions of endogamous marriages in their areas of original settlement, and lower proportions in areas of secondary settlement. In a general sense, this is illustrated by the intra-ethnic marriage rates for native-born Italians, Asiatics, and Jews living in metropolitan areas when compared to non-metropolitan urban and rural areas. The proportions of native-born Italians with Italian wives were 30.1, 24.5, and 12.6 per cent for these areas respectively. The importance of residence for native-born Jews is perhaps even more clearly demonstrated as their proportion of endogamous marriages decreases from a high of 88.9 per cent in metropolitan areas, to 72.7 and 31.4 per cent for non-metropolitan urban and rural areas respectively. Because of their initial tendency to settle in rural areas, those of Netherlands origin show the reverse effect, with the highest proportion of intra-ethnic marriages occurring in non-metropolitan rural areas, e.g., 42.4 per cent compared to 23.5 per cent for non-metropolitan urban and 17.2 per cent for metropolitan areas.[10] Thus, it would appear that for those who stay in their, or their family's, original area of settlement, the chances of marrying someone of similar ethnic origin are much greater than if they moved elsewhere. This is not only because of the greater supply of eligible persons, but also because of prevailing social expectations. Those who leave not only escape these group constraints, but increase their opportunities for meeting individuals of other ethnic, religious, and cultural backgrounds.

REFERENCES

Dominion Bureau of Statistics: *1961 Census of Canada. General Review: Marital Status of the Population.* Bulletin 7:1–5, Ottawa, The Queen's Printer, 1964.

Dominion Bureau of Statistics: *Nuptiality, 1950–1964.* Catalog No. 84-523, Ottawa, The Queen's Printer, 1967.

FOOTNOTES

[1] Dominion Bureau of Statistics, *Vital Statistics, 1954,* Ottawa, The Queen's Printer, 1956, Table 39, and *Vital Statistics, 1967,* Ottawa, The Queen's Printer, 1969, Table M1.

[2] Dominion Bureau of Statistics, *1961 Census of Canada,* Bulletin 7:1–5, Ottawa, The Queen's Printer, 1964, Tables VII and VI.

[3] Dominion Bureau of Statistics, *Vital Statistics, op. cit.*

[4] J. D. Payne, *The Law & Practice Relating to Divorce and Other Matrimonial Causes in Canada,* Second Edition, Toronto, the Carswell Co., Ltd., 1964, pp. 22–23.

[5] Dominion Bureau of Statistics, *1961 Census of Canada, op. cit.,* p. 22.

[6] Dominion Bureau of Statistics, *op. cit.,* Tables 46 and M9.

[7] Dominion Bureau of Statistics, *Nuptiality, 1950–1964,* Cat. No. 84-523, May, 1967, Tables 10 and 11.

[8] W. E. Kalbach, *The Impact of Immigration on Canada's Population,* Ottawa, The Queen's Printer, 1970, Chart 2.20.

[9] As an example of an earlier study of this kind, see Burton W. Hurd, *Ethnic Origin and Nativity of the Canadian People,* Dominion Bureau of Statistics, 1941 Census, pp. 96–113.

[10] W. E. Kalbach, *op. cit.,* pp. 333–335.

Characteristics of Families

Sociologically speaking, two or more persons living within the same household, related by blood, marriage, or adoption, would be said to constitute a family. The most basic grouping would be the *nuclear family*, where membership is limited to spouses and their children, while the *extended family* would include related individuals in addition to those comprising the nuclear family. Definitional problems arise from the fact that the groupings of persons which actually occur for purposes of sharing shelter are not always limited to these pure family types, but often include other families, or portions of families, in addition to unrelated individuals.

Thus, it is important to keep in mind the basic distinction which is currently made between "households" (i.e., all persons occupying a single dwelling) and "families" (i.e., parents with children). Clearly, households may consist of several families or even unrelated individuals. In early censuses, no distinction was made between these terms; but, with increased knowledge of the nature and types of living groups in modern society, more precise definitions are needed for identification and enumeration of dwelling units, households, and families in the national censuses. Current definitions in use since 1941, are as follows:[1] a *dwelling unit* is "a structurally separate set of living quarters, with a private entrance either from outside the building, or from a common hall, lobby, vestibule, or stairway inside (which must not be through anyone else's living quarters)"; a *household* "consists of a person or persons occupying one dwelling"; and, a *family*[2] "consists of a husband and wife (with or without children who have never been married),[3] or a parent with one or more children never married, living together in the same dwelling. Adopted children and stepchildren have the same status as own children;

and in fact, a family, for census purposes, may comprise a man or woman living with a guardianship child or ward under 21 years of age."

Number of Families

As of June 1, 1966, there were 17,681,728 persons living in families, while 2,187,784 persons, or 11.0 per cent of those for whom family status could be determined, were living alone or in non-family groups.[4] This represented an increase of 77.9 per cent in the number of persons living in families since 1941, compared to an increase of 74.2 per cent for the total population. While the number of families increased by 79.2 per cent, the average number of persons per family, 3.9, was still the same in 1966 as it had been in 1941. However, this comparison hides the fact that there was a significant shift in relative growth rates during this period resulting in a drop in family size between 1941 and 1951, followed by an equally quick recovery during the 1951–61 decade. High rates of natural increase accompanied by a level of immigration comparable to the 1920s and a declining rate of family formation combined to produce a much greater increase in the number of persons living in families than the number of families.

Structure of Families

Characteristics of family heads. Almost all, or 94.3 per cent, of family heads were married in 1966, representing a slight increase over 1951 when 93.0 per cent were listed as married. Since the proportions of heads who were either divorced or never married also increased during this period, family heads who were widowed had to decline relative to the other statuses. Widowed persons constituted just 5.0 per cent of family heads in 1966 compared to 6.6 per cent in 1951. Trends in marital status of family heads for the 1951–66 period are summarized in Table 12:1.

Culturally, traditionally, and statistically, males continue to dominate the family in Canada. If the husband is present in the family, he is generally the family head. Of all families with male heads, 98.1 per cent were married with wife present in the home, and only 0.7 per cent were families with only the husband present. Families where the male head was widowed represented only 1.1 per cent of the total, while those who were divorced accounted for only 0.1 per cent. The number of families with female heads has continued to increase, reaching more than 300,000 by 1966; but, as a proportion of all families, they have remained at 6.6 per cent of the total since 1956.

Because of the large numbers of males relative to females in Table 12:1, sociologically significant variations in the characteristics of female heads of families are obscured. The situation is clarified by Figure 12:1. Note that of the 272,215 female heads of families, the greatest proportions were heads

Table 12:1

PERCENTAGE DISTRIBUTIONS BY MARITAL STATUS FOR FAMILY HEADS, CANADA, 1951 TO 1966

Marital Status of Head	1951	1956	1961	1966
Married	93.0	93.7	94.2	94.3
Widowed	6.6	5.8	5.2	5.0
Divorced	0.3	0.3	0.4	0.5
Never married	0.1	0.1	0.2	0.2
Total	100.0	100.0	100.0	100.0

SOURCE: Dominion Bureau of Statistics, *1966 Census of Canada*, Vol. II (2-12), Ottawa, The Queen's Printer, 1969, Table 78. *1961 Census of Canada*, Bulletin 2:1-7, Ottawa, The Queen's Printer, 1963, Table 72.

because of their husband's death. Another 29.8 per cent were heads because their husbands were not present in the home, and 7.2 per cent achieved their status by divorcing their husbands or because they had assumed the responsibility of family heads even though they had never married. The proportion of widowed heads of families increases with age, as would be expected, until they comprised 92.9 per cent of all female heads 65 years of age and over. Conversely, the proportion of females who were heads because of absent husbands declined rapidly with increasing age. Through remarriage, or marriage, the proportion of divorced or never married females declines rapidly with increasing age.

Age of husbands and wives. An average age at marriage of approximately 28 years for bridegrooms and 25 years for brides, circa 1961, combined with the normal effects of aging, mortality, and net migration to produce an age distribution where slightly more than one-half of all family heads were under 45 years of age, and approximately 70 per cent were between the ages of 25 and 55. At the extremes of the distribution, only 4.5 per cent were under the age of 25 years, and 12.4 per cent, 65 years of age and over.[5]

Sociologically more interesting to the student of the family is the discrepancy between the ages of husbands and wives resulting from the preference of males for younger women, a tendency which increases directly with the male's age. Note in Table 12:2 that the proportion of male heads of families with wives in the same age group was highest for those under twenty years of age; and that the proportion steadily declines, reaching a minimum of 27.7 per cent for the 65–69 year age group, before increasing sharply to 50.0 per cent for those 70 years and over. For the oldest age group, the trend reversal probably reflects a combination of fewer opportunities to interact with younger women and the increasing availability of widows. While the cultural

Fig. 12:1

FAMILY STATUS
FEMALE HOUSEHOLD HEADS BY AGE
CANADA: 1961

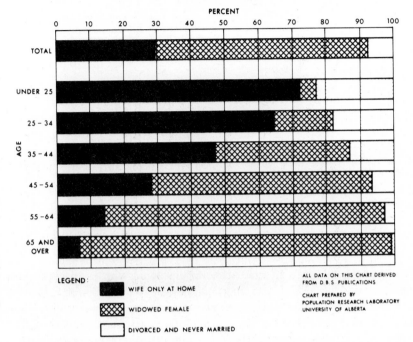

preference for younger women exists at all ages, remarriage at older ages tends to increase the age differentials.

Preference for wives older than their husbands was minimal and remained fairly constant throughout the age range. The major exception, in the case of those under 20 years of age, illustrates an interesting dilemma faced by the younger male who intends to marry. Normally, he would be expected to marry a younger female, but marrying anyone much younger than himself at this age would actually tend to be less socially acceptable. For this reason, he must look to females in his own age group; but these, according to custom, are marrying older men. As the data indicate, if the young male were to marry at all, it is much more probable that he would marry someone older than himself.

A similar situation can be produced for females as a consequence of rapid increases in the size of successive birth cohorts, such as occurred during the years following 1945. Again, the general pattern is for women to marry older men, i.e., those belonging to earlier birth cohorts. However, during the immediate post-war years, females outnumbered by far the number of males in each of the preceding cohorts so that there was essentially a shortage of

Table 12:2

PER CENT OF WIVES IN A YOUNGER, THE SAME, OR OLDER AGE GROUP THAN THE HUSBAND BY AGE OF HUSBAND, CANADA, 1961

Age of Husband	Total Husband-Wife Families	Age of Wife		
		In a Younger Age Group	In the Same Age Group	In an Older Age Group
Under 20 years	6,654	—	76.9	23.1
20–24	167,920	21.6	68.7	9.6
25–29	412,400	43.0	48.5	8.5
30–34	508,471	48.2	43.2	8.6
35–39	521,716	49.7	41.6	8.7
40–44	467,425	56.1	36.1	7.9
45–49	430,762	58.5	34.3	7.3
50–54	361,507	61.7	31.8	6.5
55–59	285,747	63.5	30.1	6.4
60–64	219,362	64.4	28.8	6.8
65–69	170,685	65.2	27.7	7.1
70 and over	247,377	50.0	50.0	—

SOURCE: Dominion Bureau of Statistics, *1961 Census of Canada*, Bulletin 7:2-1, Ottawa, The Queen's Printer, 1967, Table XXV.

eligible males. Women in these cohorts are faced with a dilemma quite similar to that faced by young males. If they try to maintain the traditional marriage pattern, their chances of marrying decrease significantly. Thus, they must be willing either to marry men of their own age or younger, remain single, or be content with having affairs with older married men.

Educational attainment of family heads and wives. In terms of the highest grade achieved, family heads were almost identical to the total male population 15 years of age and over, as almost half of each group had attained less than a secondary education. At the higher levels, e.g., some university or degree, family heads, with 8.1 per cent, had a very slight edge over all males 15 years of age and over who had only 7.5 per cent attaining this level.

Earlier chapters have dealt with the significance of ethnic origin and religion in mate selection as reflected in the characteristics of husbands and wives. Data on educational attainment presented in Table 12:3 suggest another important consideration influencing choice of mate in Canadian society. Note that in general, as the schooling of the husband increases, so does that of his wife, hence husbands and wives tend to have attained approximately the same educational levels. In addition, the wives of husbands who had not completed secondary school generally had achieved higher educational levels. However, if husbands went beyond secondary schooling, they tended to have more schooling than their wives.

The significance of these differences and similarities in educational attainment of husbands and wives is not limited to the nature of their marital

Table 12:3

PERCENTAGE DISTRIBUTION OF WIFE'S EDUCATIONAL ATTAINMENT BY ATTAINMENT OF HUSBAND, CANADA, 1961

Schooling[a] of Husband	Total	Schooling[a] of Wife							
		No Schooling	Elementary		Secondary			University	
			Less than Five	Five or more Years	One and Two Years	Three Years	Fourth and Fifth	Some University	University Degree
No Schooling	47,449	37.8	27.6	27.8	4.5	1.0	1.1	0.2	—[b]
Elementary:									
Less than fifth	307,475	3.9	36.8	44.9	9.5	2.2	2.4	0.2	0.1
Fifth year plus	1,482,498	0.7	5.6	57.6	20.6	6.7	7.8	0.9	0.2
Secondary:									
First and second	789,686	0.2	1.8	26.4	39.1	13.5	16.8	1.8	0.4
Third year	307,037	0.1	1.0	17.5	28.5	26.1	23.4	2.6	0.8
Fourth and fifth	540,747	0.1	0.8	13.9	20.9	14.8	44.1	3.9	1.6
Some University	136,058	0.1	0.6	10.1	16.8	13.6	40.0	14.6	4.2
University degree	189,076	—[b]	0.2	4.1	8.6	9.8	43.9	14.5	19.1
Canada	3,800,026	1.1	6.1	35.9	23.3	10.8	18.5	2.8	1.6

SOURCE: Dominion Bureau of Statistics, *1961 Census of Canada*, Bulletin 7:2-1, Ottawa, The Queen's Printer, 1967, Table XXVI.
[a] Highest grade of schooling attended.
[b] Less than 0.05 per cent.

interactional patterns and personal life styles, but has considerable import for the socialization and education of their children. Census data for 1961 clearly show that the higher the educational attainment of the family head, the greater the proportion of children in the family between 15 and 19 years of age who are still attending school.[6] To illustrate, 51.8 per cent of the children 15–18 years of age in families where the family head had less than five years of elementary education were still in school, compared to 93.8 per cent where the family head had a university degree. For these same two categories of families, the proportions of children 19–24 years of age still in school were 8.5 per cent and 63.7 per cent respectively. It is quite obvious that education is not only crucial in determining the general patterns of mate selection, but also of importance in setting the educational norms or goals for children in the family. Further research will hopefully reveal the significance of educational attainment for supporting, or weakening, the constraints imposed by ethnic and religious considerations in the courtship and marriage process.

Type of family living arrangements. Almost all families maintain their own households. In 1961, the proportion was 94.3 per cent, and this increased to 96.0 per cent by 1966. However, whether or not a family maintains its own household is a function of the marital status and sex of the head, as may be seen in Table 12:4. When both husband and wife are present, the proportion tends to be almost 100 per cent, e.g., 96.9 per cent

Table 12:4

NUMBER AND PERCENTAGE DISTRIBUTION OF FAMILIES CLASSIFIED ACCORDING TO MARITAL STATUS AND SEX OF HEAD, BY TYPE OF LIVING ARRANGEMENT, CANADA, 1966

Marital Status and Sex of Head	Total Families	Main-taining own household	Not Maintaining Own Household		
			Total	Related	Lodging
Total family heads	4,526,266	96.0	4.0	3.0	0.8
Husband and Wife at Home	4,154,381	96.9	3.1	2.3	0.7
One Parent Only:					
Husband only	24,511	78.8	21.2	17.3	3.6
Wife only	87,540	75.3	24.7	18.2	4.4
Widowed male	40,143	92.2	7.8	6.8	0.8
Widowed female	186,807	93.4	6.6	5.5	0.7
Divorced male	3,494	78.1	21.9	17.6	4.1
Divorced female	18,621	80.2	29.8	15.1	3.0
Single male	3,354	54.7	45.3	38.1	6.3
Single female	7,415	70.2	29.8	7.5	14.8

SOURCE: Dominion Bureau of Statistics, *1966 Census of Canada,* Vol. II (2-12), Ottawa, The Queen's Printer, 1969, Table 79.

in 1966. Death of one spouse does not reduce the proportion very much as 93.4 per cent of widows still maintained their own households and only a slightly smaller proportion of widowers. Homes broken by divorce have relatively fewer independent households. For divorced female heads, the percentage was 80.2, compared to 78.1 per cent for males who also exhibit a slightly greater tendency to live with related or lodging families.

Divorced females who are heads of families appear to be more independent than wives who are family heads in the absence of their husbands, insofar as maintaining a separate household is evidence of a greater degree of independence than living with a related or lodging family. Single males and females show the least independence in this respect. Over one-third of the single male family heads were living with related families, and 7.5 per cent of single female heads, compared to just 3.0 per cent for all family heads. On the other hand, single female heads had the largest proportion living with lodging families, 14.8 per cent, compared to only 0.8 per cent for all family heads. The pattern of living arrangements in 1966 appeared to be fairly consistent with the pattern displayed in the 1961 Census data, except where the number of cases are relatively small, e.g., single male and female heads maintaining their own households.

Two other important factors are associated with sharing households with others: (1) age of head of family and (2) earnings of heads of wage-earner families. Sharing of households was highest, 17.8 per cent, for those under 25 years of age and declined with increasing age,[7] most likely as a consequence of increasing psychological and economic independence. Further, if the family head was under 25 years of age, and earning less than $2,000 as a wage earner, the proportion sharing households with others was over one-third or 33.5 per cent. Again, the proportion declined with increasing earnings; but it was always greater for the younger heads of households at every income level.[8]

Working wives. Income is a primary determinant of family life style. While the exact amount that constitutes the poverty line is debatable, there would be little question that the 329,949 wage-earning families in 1961 making under $2,000 were living under less than desirable conditions, and sharing fewer of the amenities of life that most people take for granted in a society where average income for family heads was $4,133. More careful consideration suggests that this picture is misleading in its simplicity. Income is not static, but varies with the age of family head, reaching a peak in the latter part of the middle age range and subsequently declining with increasing age. It also must be remembered that the income required to fulfill family and personal needs varies considerably so that adequacy of income is relative not only to the stage in the family life cycle, but also to one's life style expectations.

Regardless of the specific reasons, need for income in addition to that

Table 12:5

PERCENTAGE DISTRIBUTIONS BY LABOUR FORCE STATUS OF FAMILY MEMBERS, FOR HUSBAND–WIFE FAMILIES, RURAL AND URBAN AREAS, CANADA, 1961

Family Members in Labour Force		Canada	Urban	Rural Non-farm	Rural Farm
Total husband–wife families	N	3,800,026	2,728,557	672,087	399,382
	%	100.0	100.0	100.0	100.0
Members in the labour force:					
Husband but not wife[a]		68.3	67.8	66.7	74.7
Both husband and wife[a]		19.5	21.3	13.0	18.5
Other than husband		3.2	3.0	3.9	2.3
None		9.0	7.9	16.4	4.5

SOURCE: Dominion Bureau of Statistics, *1961 Census of Canada*, Bulletin 7:2-1, Ottawa, The Queen's Printer, 1967, Table XXI.
[a] With or without children in labour force.

ordinarily provided by the family head appears to have increased substantially, if the increase in labour force participation rates by married women since World War II is any indication. This is not to deny the importance of noneconomic motivation for women seeking a more meaningful role in modern society, but these more subtle motives would be more difficult to substantiate on the basis of census data alone. Table 12:5 shows that for slightly more than two-thirds of all husband-wife families, only the husband was in the labour force. Both husbands and wives worked in almost one-fifth of the families, while members other than the husband worked in 3.2 per cent of the cases. No one worked in 9.0 per cent of the cases.

Rural-urban variations in joint husband-wife participation undoubtedly reveal the greater employment opportunities in urban localities, as well as on the farm; but the differences also suggest the consequences of greater involvement in childrearing characteristic of families living in rural non-farm areas, and the limitations which are placed on the activities of mothers with young children.

The largest proportion of working wives for husband-wife families, tends to be found among wives under 25 years of age. The relative number drops sharply during the childbearing years before achieving a second peak between the ages of 45 and 55 years when many are again free of childrearing responsibilities. While there may be many reasons why wives need or want to work, the economic dimension is revealed sharply in Table 12:6. Average earnings of husbands whose wives work are consistently lower at every age level than those whose wives are not in the labour force. The discrepancy is lowest for those under 25 years of age; but average earnings are also low for

Table 12:6

LABOUR FORCE STATUS[a] OF HUSBAND AND WIFE BY AGE,
AND AVERAGE EARNINGS OF HUSBAND BY LABOUR FORCE
STATUS AND AGE OF WIFE, CANADA, 1961

Age Group	Head in Labour Force	Wife in Labour Force[b]	Average Earnings of Husband (in dollars)	
			Wife Not in Labour Force	Wife in Labour Force
Under 25 years	95.7	25.9	3,376	3,367
25–34	96.8	20.3	4,307	3,889
35–44	96.4	23.9	4,694	4,101
45–54	94.5	24.7	4,557	3,991
55–64	85.9	14.6	4,087	3,446
65+	34.2	3.2	3,211	2,581
Total	87.8	20.8	4,303	3,867

SOURCE: Dominion Bureau of Statistics, *1961 Census of Canada*, Bulletin 7:2-1, Ottawa, The Queen's Printer, 1967, Tables XXII, XXIV.
[a] Per cent in labour force.
[b] Labour force status by age of wife.

the youngest ages, and wives are free to work or continue to work until their first child arrives. The discrepancy between earnings of husbands whose wives do not work and those who do increases as the husband ages, a fact suggesting that the need for additional income increases throughout the life cycle of these particular families.

This is also shown, but in a slightly different manner, by the data in Table 12:7 which breaks down the sources of total family income by age of head in those families where there are other contributors to family income.[9] Wives under 25 years of age made the maximum contribution, but the proportion rises again in the later age groups. Note that the family is most dependent upon the income of the family head between 35 and 55 years of age when his contribution represented approximately 86 per cent of the total family income. The interesting aspect of Table 12:7 is the rapid increase in the contribution made by unmarried children. Their contribution reaches its peak when the family head is 55–64 years of age, decreasing only slightly with increasing age of the head. In the past, unmarried children have been the most important source for supplementary income; but, as Podoluk points out in her extensive analysis of the incomes of Canadians, wives have now taken over this role. This is not necessarily so much through personal choice, but because the extended period of schooling for children, combined with the tendency towards earlier marriage, puts more pressure on the wife to enter the labour force to help meet the family's financial needs.[10] Podoluk's

Table 12:7

PERCENTAGE OF FAMILY INCOME CONTRIBUTED BY HEAD, WIFE, AND UNMARRIED CHILDREN, BY AGE OF HEAD OF FAMILY, CANADA, 1961[a]

Age of Head	Head	Wives	Unmarried Children
Under 25	77.9	19.3	—
25–34	86.0	10.9	0.1
35–44	86.2	8.8	2.5
45–54	75.7	9.0	12.0
55–64	71.8	8.7	15.2
65–69	68.5	10.6	15.1
70 and over	60.3	17.9	14.7
Totals[b]	79.6	10.1	7.0

SOURCE: J. R. Podoluk, *Income of Canadians*, Ottawa, The Queen's Printer, 1968, Table 6:11.
[a] Year ended, May 31st.
[b] Totals do not add to 100 per cent as income from other relatives in family not shown.

analysis is highly suggestive as to the effects of changing economic and social conditions on the role and status structure of the family, as well as the importance of the family life cycle.

Variations in Family Size

In 1941, the number of persons per family in Canada averaged 3.9. During the immediate post-war period, the number of families increased much more rapidly than the population in families, with the consequence that average family size declined to 3.7 by 1951. During the 1951–61 decade the situation reversed, with the family population increasing by 31.8 per cent compared to a 26.3 per cent increase in the number of families. Family size increased to 3.9 and remained at this level between 1961 and 1966. Table 12:8 summarizes these changes in family size for Canada between 1941 and 1966, as well as for the provinces and territories.

Perhaps the most striking feature of these data is the clear demarcation in family size between Eastern and Western Canada. All the Eastern Provinces, as well as the North, exceeded the average for Canada as a whole, whereas Ontario, the Prairie Provinces, and British Columbia fell below the national norm. All provinces, with the possible exception of Newfoundland, experienced declines between 1941 and 1951; and all but Quebec experienced increases in family size following 1951. Where increases did occur, most

Table 12:8

AVERAGE NUMBER OF PERSONS PER FAMILY, CANADA AND
PROVINCES, 1941 TO 1966

Province	1941	1951	1956	1961	1966
Newfoundland	4.4[a]	4.4	4.6	4.7	4.6
Prince Edward Island	4.2	4.0	4.1	4.2	4.2
Nova Scotia	4.0	3.9	3.9	4.0	4.0
New Brunswick	4.3	4.1	4.2	4.3	4.3
Quebec	4.5	4.2	4.2	4.2	4.2
Ontario	3.6	3.4	3.5	3.6	3.7
Manitoba	3.8	3.6	3.6	3.7	3.8
Saskatchewan	4.1	3.7	3.8	3.8	3.9
Alberta	3.9	3.7	3.7	3.8	3.9
British Columbia	3.4	3.3	3.4	3.6	3.6
Yukon and N.W.T.	—	3.9	4.1	4.3	4.5
Canada	3.9	3.7	3.8	3.9	3.9

SOURCE: Dominion Bureau of Statistics, *1961 Census of Canada*, Bulletin 7:2-1, Ottawa,
The Queen's Printer, 1967, Table 1; and *1966 Census of Canada*, Vol. II (2-9),
Ottawa, The Queen's Printer, 1968, Table 52.
[a] Based on the 1945 Census of Newfoundland.

returned to their 1941 levels with several notable exceptions. Family size in
British Columbia had exceeded the 1941 level by 1961, whereas in Ontario
the higher level was not reached until 1966. Saskatchewan experienced the
greatest drop between 1941 and 1951, declining from 4.1 to 3.7, and by
1966 its average family size had only returned to 3.9 persons per family.
The greatest absolute change was recorded for families in the Yukon and
Northwest Territories, where their average size increased from 3.9 to 4.5 in
15 years.

Number of Children. The trend in number of children per family since
1941 followed very closely that of family size, varying from 1.9 in 1941 to
1.7 in 1951, and recovering again to 1.9 in 1961 where it remained through
1966.[11] Eastern Canada again exceeded the average for the country as a
whole, with Newfoundland having the highest average of 2.6 in 1966. For
the rest of Canada, both Ontario and British Columbia, with averages of 1.7,
had the lowest number of children per family.

As would be expected, considerable variation was also observed for rural
and urban areas. Average number of children varied from 2.4 for rural farm
to 2.2 for rural non-farm, and 1.7 for urban areas compared to 1.9 for

Canada as a whole. Figure 12:2 illustrates the relative distribution of family size as measured by number of children under 25 years of age living at home. The proportion of families with either none, one, or from two to three children at home, or the cumulative percentage for all three groups, is maximum (at 86.8 per cent) for urban families and minimum for rural farm families (at 77.2 per cent). For families with four or more children, the proportions increase as one moves from urban (13.4 per cent) to rural non-farm (22.8 per cent), and to rural farm areas of residence (26.2 per cent). Rural farm areas in Quebec, with 3.5 children per family, had the highest average while the highest rates for rural non-farm and urban areas were found in Newfoundland.

Fig. 12:2

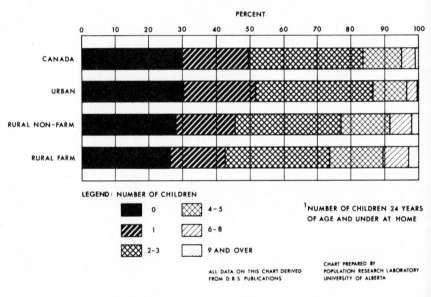

FAMILY SIZE[1]
BY PLACE OF RESIDENCE
CANADA: 1961

Obviously, changes in the average number of children reflect more than changes in reproductive behaviour since fertility rates increased between 1941 and 1951 while average number of children per family decreased. Variations in age of marriage, rate of family formation, variations in family life cycle, and the increasing divorce rate all affect this particular indicator of family size. A large increase in new families, with their characteristically small number of children, as occurred after World War II, would tend to reduce the average number of children for all families. In addition, the number of children living at home decreases with increasing age of family head,

Table 12:9

PERCENTAGE DISTRIBUTION OF FAMILIES BY NUMBER OF CHILDREN
PER FAMILY, CANADA, 1941 TO 1966

Number of Children per Family	1941[a]	1951	1961	1966
None	31.2	32.3	29.3	28.9
One	23.6	23.5	20.2	19.5
Two	17.5	19.8	20.6	20.5
Three	10.6	10.9	13.4	13.9
Four	6.4	5.8	7.5	8.0
Five	3.9	3.2	3.9	4.2
Six–Eight	5.3	3.7	4.1	4.1
Nine or more	1.5	0.9	0.9	0.9

SOURCE: Dominion Bureau of Statistics, *1961 Census of Canada*, Bulletin 7:2-1, Ottawa,
The Queen's Printer, 1967, Table VII; and *1966 Census of Canada*, Vol. II (2-10),
Ottawa, The Queen's Printer, 1968, Table 58.
[a] Not including Newfoundland, the Yukon and Northwest Territories.

so that the proportion of families with older family heads is a factor which
must be taken into account.

More informative as to the specific nature of the changes in the Canadian
family which occurred between 1941 and 1966 are the data on the distribution of families by number of children, presented in Table 12:9. In 1966, the
proportions of very large families, i.e., six or more children, and families
with no children (or just one child), were lower than 1941 levels. Families
with four and five children increased consistently after 1951, and were at
higher levels in 1966, when they accounted for 12.1 per cent of all the
families, than they were in 1951 when they accounted for 10.3 per cent.
Families with two to three children also showed relatively greater growth,
increasing from 28.1 per cent to 34.5 per cent in 1966. Thus, it would seem
that while the families at the extremes of the distribution, i.e., families with
none, one, or more than six, were declining relative to the others, those with
two, three, four, and five children were still increasing. Since 1951, the
largest proportionate increases have occurred in families with three and four
children. The range of the distribution appears to have narrowed as well as
becoming more uniform. This trend is consistent with the decline in the
average number of children in husband-wife families between 1951 and
1961 with heads 55 years of age and over, evident in Table 12:10. At the
same time the average for heads of families 34–44 has increased from 2.5
to 3.0, and for heads 45–54 years of age from 2.3 to 2.4. There is additional

Table 12:10

AVERAGE NUMBER OF CHILDREN UNDER 25 YEARS OF AGE AT HOME
FOR HUSBAND-WIFE FAMILIES BY AGE OF HEAD, CANADA, 1951–1966

Age of Head	1951	1956	1961	1966
All ages	1.7	1.8	1.9	1.9
Under 35 years	1.5	1.7	1.8	1.8
35–44	2.5	2.7	2.8	3.0
45–54	2.3	2.2	2.3	2.4
55–64	1.1	1.1	1.0	1.0
65 and over	0.3	0.3	0.2	0.2

SOURCE: Dominion Bureau of Statistics, *1966 Census of Canada*, Vol. II (2-12), Table 79;
1961 Census of Canada, Bulletin 2:1-7, Table 73; *1951 Census of Canada*, Vol.
III, Table 136; and *1956 Census of Canada*, Vol. 1-19, Table 56, Ottawa, The
Queen's Printer.

evidence from the more recent censuses that the average number of children
for heads under 25 years of age declined from 0.9 to 0.8 while the average
remained constant for those between 25 and 35 years of age.

Fertility of women ever-married. Figure 12:3 illustrates, in a somewhat
different manner, the increase in fertility which has contributed to the in-

Fig. 12:3   CUMULATIVE FERTILITY[1] BY AGE AND RESIDENCE
CANADA: 1961

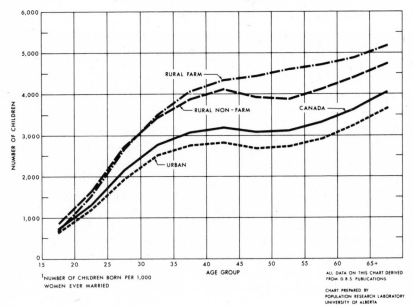

[1] NUMBER OF CHILDREN BORN PER 1,000
WOMEN EVER MARRIED

ALL DATA ON THIS CHART DERIVED
FROM D.B.S. PUBLICATIONS

CHART PREPARED BY
POPULATION RESEARCH LABORATORY
UNIVERSITY OF ALBERTA

creasing number of children in families. The cumulative fertility curve for the total population of women ever-married shows that women aged 35–39 had achieved approximately the same level of fertility by 1961 as had women 45–49 years of age who had essentially completed their childbearing years. This might be interpreted to mean that these younger women had either completed their childbearing earlier than had been expected or that their completed fertility will be greater if they continue to produce children, even at a drastically reduced rate, for another five years. The increase in fertility for younger women, i.e., those 35–39 and 40–44 years of age, relative to the older age groups who had already completed their childbearing, is more apparent for women living in rural non-farm and urban areas. For rural non-farm women, those 45–49 years of age had produced 3,952 children per 1,000 ever-married women, compared to the older cohort, 50–54 years, which had produced only 3,919. For those 40–44 years of age the difference was significantly greater in that they had already produced 206 more children per 1,000 women than had the 50–54 year age group. Similarly for urban women, those 35–39 as well as 40–44 years of age have already exceeded the completed fertility of those cohorts of women who were 45–49 and 50–54 years of age in 1961. Whether or not this will also be true of the younger cohorts in urban areas will depend on their fertiltiy behaviour subsequent to 1961. But the evidence is clear that completed fertility reached a low point for the 45–49 year age cohort of urban women and the 50–54 year age cohort of rural non-farm women, and that completed fertility for the next two or three younger five-year cohorts will be higher. It is still too early to tell which of the younger cohorts will reverse this trend of increasing completed fertility, but the 1971 Census should provide a few clues.

Family Size Differentials

Variations in family size by nativity. Analyses of the 1961 Census data have established the lower fertility of foreign-born women relative to native born.[12] In view of this, families with foreign-born heads, and presumably in most cases married to foreign-born wives, would be expected to have smaller families than native-born heads. Data on size of families, both in terms of average number of persons per family as well as average number of children, do in fact provide evidence of smaller family size for foreign-born heads. In addition, the family size increases with increasing length of residence in Canada for post World War II immigrants, as may be seen in Figure 12:4.

Family size for the most recent arrivals in 1961 was 3.2; but, for those who had arrived after World War II, i.e., 1946–50, the average size was 3.7. Native-born heads with an average of 4.0 persons per family had the largest families, while pre-war immigrant heads had the smallest with 3.0 persons. The same relationship to nativity held for number of children under 25 years

Fig. 12:4

FAMILY SIZE BY NATIVITY
CANADA: 1961

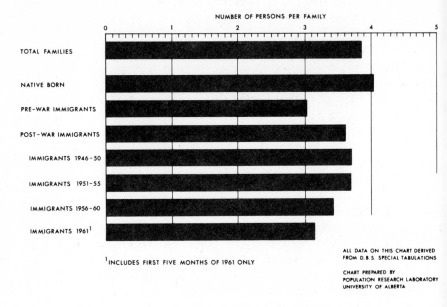

NUMBER OF PERSONS PER FAMILY

TOTAL FAMILIES

NATIVE BORN

PRE-WAR IMMIGRANTS

POST-WAR IMMIGRANTS

IMMIGRANTS 1946-50

IMMIGRANTS 1951-55

IMMIGRANTS 1956-60

IMMIGRANTS 1961[1]

[1]INCLUDES FIRST FIVE MONTHS OF 1961 ONLY

ALL DATA ON THIS CHART DERIVED
FROM D.B.S. SPECIAL TABULATIONS

CHART PREPARED BY
POPULATION RESEARCH LABORATORY
UNIVERSITY OF ALBERTA

of age living at home. Pre-war immigrants again had the smallest average, i.e., 1.0 compared to 1.6 for all post-war immigrants and 2.0 for native born.[13]

It is quite likely that the anomalous situation for pre-war immigrant heads of families was due to their higher average age. While they actually might have had smaller families *per se*, it is quite possible that more of their children had already left home and established their own families. In any event, all families with foreign-born heads did have smaller families on the average than native-born heads at the time of the 1961 Census.

Variations by ethnic origins. The association between ethnic, religious, educational, and locational characteristics is again evident in Figure 12:5 showing variations in average family size by ethnic origin. Native Indian and Eskimo families were significantly larger with an average of 5.1 persons per family, followed by French origins with 4.4, and Netherlands with 4.1 persons per family. Interestingly, each of these groups ranks high among all ethnic origins, but for somewhat different reasons. For example, Native Indians and Eskimos have the high fertility characteristic of poorly educated, low-income minority groups living on marginal lands. The French origins reflect the persistence of religious and rural influences, while the families of Netherlands origin are characteristic of rural farm populations.

At the other extreme are the Jewish and Hungarian families with averages

Fig. 12:5

**FAMILY SIZE
SELECTED ETHNIC ORIGINS[1]
CANADA: 1961**

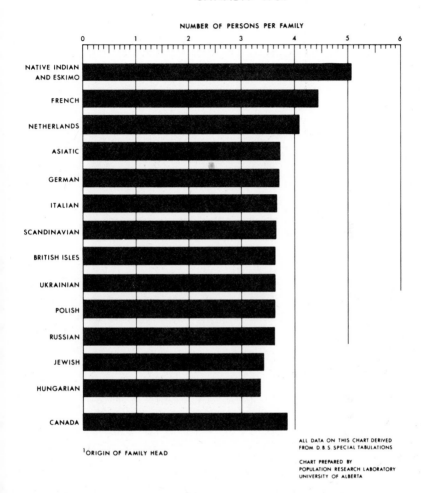

NUMBER OF PERSONS PER FAMILY

NATIVE INDIAN AND ESKIMO
FRENCH
NETHERLANDS
ASIATIC
GERMAN
ITALIAN
SCANDINAVIAN
BRITISH ISLES
UKRAINIAN
POLISH
RUSSIAN
JEWISH
HUNGARIAN
CANADA

[1]ORIGIN OF FAMILY HEAD

ALL DATA ON THIS CHART DERIVED
FROM D.B.S. SPECIAL TABULATIONS

CHART PREPARED BY
POPULATION RESEARCH LABORATORY
UNIVERSITY OF ALBERTA

of 3.4 and 3.3 persons per family respectively. The Jewish population is highly educated, concentrated in the professions, has high income levels, and is urban oriented, all of which are factors associated with small families. To the extent that the population of Hungarian origin reflects the heavy immigration associated with the Hungarian revolt of the late 1950s, they too would possess characteristics consistent with small families, i.e., highly educated, professional, and urban. It is also quite possible that those who fled their homeland did not leave with intact families, a factor that would contribute to their smaller family size in Canada.

Family Life Style and Life Cycle[14]

Differences in structural characteristics of the family, such as age, sex, income, and education of family head, type of living arrangement, and variations in family size, are all indicative of differing life styles to be found in an urban society as well as of changes that occur within families with the passage of time. Every family, beginning at marriage, proceeds through a typical sequence of events as its individual members age, begin childbearing, watch their children leave home, and finally are broken through the death of one and then both of the original pair. The various stages often overlap, sometimes they may occur in a different sequence, while some are omitted entirely because of the absence of childbearing or premature death in the family. Social, political, and economic change will affect the timing and duration of the various stages, and the ease with which families negotiate each stage is highly dependent upon the family head's work experiences and the family's financial resources.

The relative level and variation in income throughout the family's life history sets the basic limits of its material and non-material wealth. However, the parent's educational attainment, cultural background, and aspirations for social mobility direct both the nature of its expression in patterns of family consumption and activity and the transmission of values and attitudes to their children. Many changes which are occurring in society will continue to have considerable impact on the family. Paramount among recent events has been the declining age at first marriage and the earlier onset and termination of childbearing, mentioned in earlier chapters. This, coupled with increasing longevity and increasing economic opportunities for women has already radically altered the present-day family. On the one hand, extension of the period of formal education has kept the children dependent for a longer period of time, while the declining age at marriage has hastened their departure. One important consequence, mentioned before in this chapter, has been the emergence of the wife as the major source of supplementary family income. Earlier termination of childbearing has encouraged the return of women to the labour force to help bolster the declining earnings of the family head, characteristic of the latter part of his working life. Increasing longevity and sex differentials in mortality increase the time that parents will spend together in the "empty nest" and the period that women will live alone as widows.

The need for better housing and recreational facilities and for activities designed for older and economically inactive population is obvious. Development of retirement communities is one type of response; but beyond this lie the needs of an increasing number of widows, and to a lesser extent widowers, who must find a meaningful life for themselves, either alone or in second marriages. While fewer women are being left with the responsibility of caring for small children because of the death of their husbands, the proportion who must re-enter the labour force to support their families because of divorce or separation is increasing. The implications of these changes for changing life styles are hard to foresee. The remarkable increase in labour force participation among married women and the concomitant changes in family statuses and role behaviour are but several of many consequences. The growth of adult education and community recreation programs, the increase in retirement communities, and housing for the aged are but a few of the many changes that can be traced to basic demographic events. On the other hand, only time will tell what some of the specific consequences will be for the family and the individual. There is no question that statuses and roles in the family will continue to change in response to the larger external forces of societal change.

REFERENCES

Charles, Enid: *The Changing Size of the Canadian Family*. 1941 Census Monograph, Ottawa, King's Printer, 1948.

Dominion Bureau of Statistics: *1961 Census of Canada. General Review: Canadian Families*. Bulletin 7:2-1. Ottawa, The Queen's Printer, 1967.

Elkin, F.: *The Family in Canada*. Canadian Conference on the Family, Ottawa, 1964.

Henripin, J.: *Tendances et facteurs de la fécondité au Canada*. Monographie sur le recensement de 1961, Ottawa, Imprimeur de la Reine, 1968.

FOOTNOTES

[1] Dominion Bureau of Statistics, *1961 Census of Canada*, "Introduction", Bulletin 2:1-1 and 2:1-5, Ottawa, The Queen's Printer, 1962 and 1963.

[2] The definition of "family" used in the 1961 Census was first adopted in 1941. The major change at that time was the exclusion of related individuals beyond the immediate parent-child relationship, and one person households.

[3] "For census purposes 'children in families' are defined as unmarried sons and daughters 24 years of age and under living at home. Thus, those older than 24 years of age who have never married and are living at home with a parent or parents are considered as 'members' of a family, but not as 'children' ". For further elaboration of the definition and a discussion of changes from earlier censuses, see the *1961 Census of Canada*, Bulletin 7:2-1, Ottawa, The Queen's Printer, 1967, p. 3.

[4] Non-family groups are related or unrelated persons living together but not meeting the census criteria for "families". Examples of unrelated persons would be lodgers, employees, or partners of head, persons living in hotels, and inmates of institutions.

[5] Dominion Bureau of Statistics, *1961 Census of Canada*, Bulletin 7:2-1, Ottawa, The Queen's Printer, 1967, Table 6.

[6] *Ibid.*, Table xxviii.

[7] *Ibid.*, Table x.

[8] *Ibid.*, Table xi.

[9] Podoluk's analyses of family income includes all sources of income including social security, pensions, veterans' allowances, pensions to the blind and disabled, etc. Thus, the nature of the wife's income contribution may change considerably from the time she is first married to her later years.

[10]J. R. Podoluk, *Incomes of Canadians,* Ottawa, The Queen's Printer, 1968. See especially her Chapter 6, "Structure of Family Income", pp. 123–150.

[11]Dominion Bureau of Statistics, *op. cit.,* Table iv.

[12]See W. E. Kalbach, *The Impact of Immigration on Canada's Population,* Ottawa, The Queen's Printer, 1970, pp. 102–115. Also, for a more comprehensive analysis of Canadian fertility, see J. S. Henripin, *Tendances et facteurs de la fécundité au Canada,* Monographie du recensement de 1961, Bureau fédéral de la Statistique, Division du Recensement, Ottawa, 1968.

[13]Special tabulations provided by the Dominion Bureau of Statistics for the 1961 monograph series.

[14]For a comprehensive treatment of the methodological problems associated with estimating the onset and duration of the various stages of the family life cycle see P. C. Glick and R. Parke Jr., "New Approaches in Studying the Life Cycle of the Family," *Demography,* Vol. 2, 1965, pp. 187–202.

Housing the Canadian Population

Every individual in society is faced at some time in his life with the prospect of selecting a form of housing to accommodate his personal living arrangement—whether in terms of living alone, or with a friend, or spouse and children. Shifts in living arrangements of the population, often necessitated by scarcity of housing as well as changes in housing technology, have produced new emphases in the quantity and form of shelter in today's society.

In recent times, the modal living arrangement has been the typical nuclear family, with the husband, wife, and children occupying a single residential housing unit. As the number of families increase, more and more pressure is brought to bear on the housing industry to provide more shelter of various types to house these new families. There are a variety of ways that such housing needs may be met; for example, accommodation through newly constructed homes, rental units, renting or buying older homes, house trailers, or sharing single housing units with other families.

Even though the family is the basic social unit, it is not necessarily the best indicator to utilize in estimating the present housing stock. This is primarily due to the process called "doubling"—where two or more families may, through choice, economic necessity, or because of a tight housing market, live in the same housing unit. For this reason, the household is the concept most often utilized for providing a reliable measure of the housing in an area. Basically, the household is an economic unit rather than a social unit in that it can refer to a single person or a group of persons occupying either one dwelling unit or structurally separate set of living quarters. Using the household concept, two families "doubling" in one housing unit would be

303

labelled a two-family household and would be indicated as only one household in the census tabulations. Furthermore, households are categorized as either family households or non-family households. Unrelated individuals sharing common living arrangements and individuals living by themselves are not considered family households. This more refined classification scheme blends the social character of the family with the economic aspect of the household.

Family and Non-Family Household Patterns

The family household pattern has continued to be the predominant form of living arrangement in 1961. However, between 1951 and 1966 their rate of increase has slowed; yet the rate for non-family households has increased significantly. Between 1951 and 1966, non-family households increased from 385,010 to 804,064, or 109.0 per cent as compared to a 44.7 per cent increase in family households. Contributing to this increase in non-family households has been the trend toward more people electing to live by themselves in addition to an increase in the number of divorced, widowed, and separated members of society. These factors have influenced the increase in the number of younger and older non-family household heads. Table 13:1

Table 13:1

PERCENTAGE CHANGE IN FAMILY AND NON-FAMILY HOUSEHOLDS BY AGE OF HOUSEHOLD HEAD, 1951–1966

Age of Household Head	Percentage Change			
	1951–1956	1956–1961	1961–1966	1951–1966
Family Households				
Total	14.5	14.0	10.8	44.7
Under 35 years	21.6	14.9	10.2	53.9
35–44 Years	16.0	13.8	9.8	44.8
45–64 Years	9.8	15.4	13.5	43.9
65 and over	12.2	9.0	6.8	30.5
Non-Family Households				
Total	19.3	31.9	32.8	109.0
Under 35 Years	29.4	46.1	65.4	212.8
35–44 Years	16.3	24.4	31.4	90.0
45–64 Years	12.9	28.8	12.9	64.1
65 and over	23.4	31.7	29.4	110.3

SOURCE: Dominion Bureau of Statistics, *1951 Census of Canada*, Vol. III, Table 100; *1961 Census of Canada*, Vol. 7:2-3, 1967, Table 2; and *1966 Census of Canada*, Vol. II (2-6), 1969, Table 41A.

indicates that between 1951 and 1966, the non-family households with heads under the age of 35 years increased 212.8 per cent, and the households with older heads increased 110.3 per cent.

A limited housing market is available to these two non-family household age groups. The younger household heads are not likely to be in a position to buy their own homes, and, therefore, for economic reasons are attracted to the rental housing market. In addition, they are apt to have locational preferences, and given the choice are likely to locate close to the central area in the urban complex where they can be close to their place of work, school, and "where the action is." In this case, the housing market for these non-families is further restricted to either boarding houses or rental apartments. Older household heads are somewhat disadvantaged. With increasing age, level of income decreases and lowers their economic viability for participating in the housing market. A considerable proportion of the older population already own their homes; however, increasing numbers are vacating their larger dwellings in favour of more convenient rental apartments and condominium living.

Figure 13:1 illustrates the differential increases between the family and non-family households in Canada by age of the household head. It is interest-

Fig. 13:1   FAMILY AND NON-FAMILY HOUSEHOLD TRENDS
BY AGE OF HOUSEHOLD HEAD
CANADA: 1951 - 1966

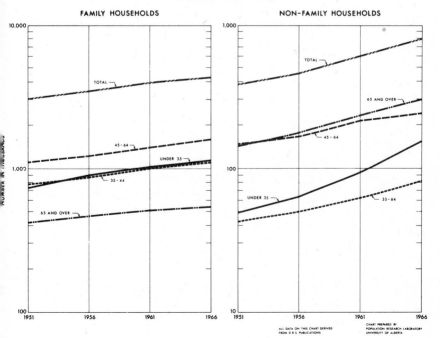

ing to note that the two potential rental housing consumer groups—the household heads under the age of 35 and the 65 and over age group—are expanding at an increasing rate. The growth rate for all family households appears to be levelling, whereas non-family households are continuing to increase markedly.

The Family Life Cycle and Housing Expenditure

To further understand the housing needs of the family household in relation to the market, it is useful to utilize the family life cycle framework. The family tends to adjust to the existing housing supply. At the same time, however, the needs of the family are continually changing as they move from one stage in the life cycle to another. Each life cycle stage in the maturation of the family dictates different housing requisites that the family attempts to satisfy. The young, newly married couple—the stage of family formation—may have minimal housing needs, particularly in terms of space. As the young couple progresses into the stage of childbearing, the housing needs modify accordingly. They are now concerned with an extra bedroom for the infant, more storage space, and perhaps a change in location from the inner area of the city to one of the peripheral areas, commonly referred to as "suburbia," with its attendant age-selective services. Usually, during this stage, the family is characterized by mobility as its freedom of movement is enhanced by its small size. As the level of income improves, the family becomes better equipped to "up-grade" their housing situation by moving to better quality and more expensive dwellings. Coupled with this "up-grading" is an improvement in the locational setting as well—another factor influencing the total cost. Eventually, improvement in income will allow the family to become potential home owners, and subsequently will open a wider housing market for them. Conversely, the process of "down-grading" occurs when the family's housing needs change but their income level remains relatively static, thus making them potential clients for the less expensive, older residential unit. Several housing moves may be made during this stage in the life cycle, all of which are dependent upon changes that take place in the size of family, in the ages of the children, and changes in employment.

Following the stage of childbearing and childraising, a third stage in the family life cycle begins which has an additional set of implications for housing expenditure. As the children mature and leave home, the parents may no longer wish to pay the maintenance costs of their large house and may elect to move back to one of the inner areas of the city where they will become likely candidates for apartment-house living once more. In addition, the differential mortality rate increases the chance of females to out-live their spouses, resulting in an excess of widows with their own unique housing needs.

The family households associated with early and middle stages of the family life cycle, the formative and childraising stages, influence the single, family-type dwelling construction throughout the nation. The non-family households may be involved in any stage of the life cycle. Single individuals living alone and those living with unrelated individuals do not fit in this framework; however, the majority will eventually progress to the family formation stage of the life cycle.

Determinants of Housing

Demographic factors. The most important single influence on the size of the housing stock is the population growth. Concomitant with this phenonmenon are the changes which take place in family formation—as the population increases, increasing numbers of new families are formed. For example, following the post-war baby boom of the late 1940s and early 1950s there was an increase in the number of marriages and, consequently, new families. With this increase in family formation came a change in the number and type of households in that there has been an increase in the number of single-family households and non-family households. The increase in households, either family or non-family, is contingent upon the balance between marriages, divorces, separations, and deaths.

Of equal importance to the shaping of the housing market are the demographic characteristics which reflect the nature of the household and associated housing needs. Foremost among these are the age of the household head, household income, household size, and the number and age of the children— all of which permit associating the household with its appropriate stage in the life cycle framework. Age of household head and level of income determine the type and cost of housing. Household size and the age and number of children serve to delimit the level and type of space requirements in housing, as well as the locational preferences. These demographic characteristics combine to shape the housing requisites of the household—the number of bedrooms needed, whether it be rental or a home purchase, located in the central city or in the suburbs close to a school. The net result of these requisites in turn influence the housing choice of the household.

The migratory character of the population serves to shift the housing demand spatially within the country. Urbanization with concomitant depopulation of rural farm areas has placed severe strains on the urban housing market. Exhaustion of resources, shifting market and transportation networks, and modern agricultural technology have influenced the migration patterns in the rural areas.

Population settlement patterns within urban areas also influence the housing market. For some population sub-groups there has been the tendency to centralize and for others to decentralize in terms of residence in the North

American city. The young, single adults and the newly married tend to locate near the central portions of the city while the typical family households tend to locate in peripheral areas. Both of these trends have consequences for the housing industry by indicating where new housing should be located and what type to construct.

Non-demographic determinants. Housing ages in much the same manner as the human population. It is characterized by longevity and loses useful members of its population through deterioration, demolition, fire, and locational blight. In most instances, an attempt is made to replace or maintain the housing stock exposed to these mortality conditions. For example, in the process of urban renewal the resident population may be forced to relocate in other areas of the city. Because of this shift in land use, older housing units must be replaced with similar low-cost dwellings. In several North American cities this replacement in housing stock has taken the form of subsidized low-income housing. In other cities, rejuvenation of the core areas has taken the form of refurbishment of the existing housing stock; or the mortality of housing has simply exceeded replacement resulting in a net loss.

Coupled with these trends is the city's effort to rejuvenate or "up-grade" the transitional areas in the older part of the urban complex. Housing in these areas has deteriorated over time; and, as they become financially able, the resident population tend to relocate in areas with less locational blight. These deteriorating residential areas, an unattractive mosaic in the city, face several alternatives. The city may elect to improve the existing housing stock for new residents, or curb locational blight by imposing stringent regulations on invading commercial and industrial use and encourage private rehabilitation of the residential structures. A recent trend in the larger metropolitan areas is towards rezoning for multiple apartment structures in the transitional areas. While this may up-grade the area, this type of housing generally does not serve the housing needs of the former residents of the area; hence it creates another demand on the total housing market.

In sum, the up-grading process may be initiated either by the municipality or the household itself, or both. The city may up-grade through rejuvenating the residential area and the household may up-grade by moving to a better area. In many cases, while one blighted residential area of the city will contribute to the decentralization of segments of the population, another area, through land-use changes or up-grading, will attract residents. As the population redistributes within the city, the housing demand and market realign.

The cost of renting or owning a dwelling unit may act as a deterrent in the sense that families may opt for doubling with another family. This is particularly true for younger families who will often live with relatives. In recent years, increasing income levels have enabled many families to "undouble," resulting in an increased demand for housing. The cost of housing is the net sum of land, labour, and material expenses. The initial investment, particularly in terms of home ownership, acts as a very real deterrent for the low-income household. In addition to the initial cost of housing would be such items as operating and maintenance expenses, cost of borrowing, rental deposits, insurance payments, and tax assessments.

Housing Trends in Canada

The number of occupied dwellings in the nation has increased four-fold since 1901, from 1,018,015 to 4,544,493 in 1961, reflecting an increase of almost 350 per cent. The trends portrayed in Figure 13:2 reflect significant increases in occupied dwellings consistent with the general rise in both population growth and economy since the turn of the century. A significant slow-down in the increase of dwelling units occurred during the 1931–41 decade. This slackening is accounted for by the tendency for families to double up during periods of economic recession. In addition, the war period in the latter stage of this decade, and the subsequent mobilization, dissolved many households. A consequence of undoubling, following the war years, was the marked increase in occupied dwelling units for all regions in Canada.

The changes indicated in Table 13:2 for the Prairie Provinces and British Columbia parallel the marked increase in population experienced in the west as a result of large scale immigration. The table also evinces housing fluctuations following internal migratory shifts in the population as well as regional variations in economy. With the exception of the Atlantic Provinces,[1] all other

Table 13:2

PERCENTAGE CHANGE IN OCCUPIED DWELLING UNITS,
CANADA[a] AND REGIONS, 1901–1961

Region	Percentage Change					
	1901–1911	1911–1921	1921–1931	1931–1941	1941–1951	1951–1961
Atlantic	6.7	10.9	7.1	15.5	50.9	17.8
Quebec	16.7	17.1	34.7	21.3	32.5	38.8
Ontario	18.8	20.5	24.2	15.7	29.2	39.2
Prairies	254.5	43.1	23.4	10.8	18.7	23.9
B.C.	102.2	59.4	49.7	25.3	52.1	36.4
Canada	38.4	25.2	26.2	16.6	31.7	33.8

SOURCE: Dominion Bureau of Statistics, *1961 Census of Canada, Housing, Introductory Report to Volume II* (Part 2), Bulletin 2:2-13, Ottawa, The Queen's Printer, 1970, Table 1.
[a] Excluding the Yukon and N.W.T.

Fig. 13:2

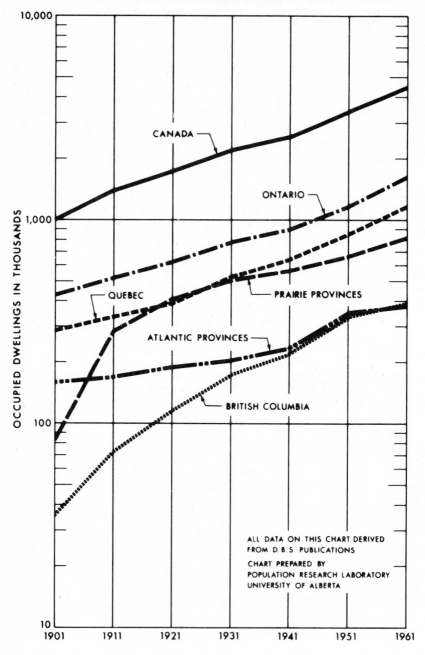

HOUSING TRENDS
CANADA AND REGIONS: 1901-1961

ALL DATA ON THIS CHART DERIVED
FROM D.B.S. PUBLICATIONS

CHART PREPARED BY
POPULATION RESEARCH LABORATORY
UNIVERSITY OF ALBERTA

Table 13:3

HOUSING TRENDS BY TYPE OF DWELLING UNIT, CANADA, 1921–1966

Year	Total	Single Detached	Single Attached	Apartment	Mobile[a]
1921	100.0	84.9	12.6	2.0	—
1931	100.0	76.4	7.8	15.5	—
1941	100.0	70.6	7.7	20.8	—
1951	100.0	66.7	7.0	26.0	0.3
1961	100.0	65.4	8.9	25.3	0.4
1966	100.0	62.4	7.8	29.3	0.5

SOURCE: Dominion Bureau of Statistics, *1921 Census of Canada*, Vol. III, Table 9, p. 26; *1931 Census of Canada*, Vol. I, Table 109, p. 1399; *1941 Census of Canada*, Vol. V., Table 4, p. 6; *1951 Census of Canada*, Vol. III, Table 8-1; *1961 Census of Canada*, Bulletin 2:2-1, 1963, Table 5; *1966 Census of Canada*, Vol. II (2-2), 1968, Table 3.
[a] Mobile units were not categorized separately in the 1921, 1931, and 1941 censuses.

regions experienced lower increases in occupied dwellings consistent with the economic depression years and pre-war years reflecting doubling up by families and decreased housing activity. The post-war years demonstrated the reverse. With economic prosperity, renewed security, and the returning military personnel, available housing accommodations were quickly occupied and new construction activity surged upward.

Type of housing in Canada. To further understand the complexity of the housing market in present-day Canada, it is advantageous to examine the trends in various housing characteristics. Foremost among these is the type of housing. The population of a country is housed in many kinds of structures, ranging from the mobile trailer home to the luxury high-rise apartment complex. As indicated in Table 13:3, rather interesting shifts in the type of construction have been taking place in Canada. In 1921, the most common type of dwelling unit available was the single-detached unit, with 85 per cent so classified. On the other hand, apartments, which are primarily an urban structure, only accounted for two per cent of the total housing stock. By 1966, apartment units accounted for almost one-third (29.3 per cent) of the housing in Canada, whereas construction of single-detached dwelling units declined to 62.4 per cent. It is apparent that the single-detached dwelling is still the most common type of construction; however, the trends indicate a decline in its importance on the housing scene.

Most of the apartment construction has been located in urban areas, and more specifically, in the central cities of the nation. Two rather distinct trends in the urban scene have fostered demands on the housing industry. First, the rural-to-urban movement, which Canada has experienced in increasing intensity since the turn of the century, created a demand for more urban-type dwellings. The apartment and the single-attached dwelling, commonly known as the "duplex" has been the housing industry's answer. Second, the suburb-

Table 13:4

PERCENTAGE DISTRIBUTION OF RURAL AND URBAN DWELLINGS BY TYPE, CANADA, 1921–1966

Locality	Total		Single Detached		Single Attached		Apartment, Flat, Etc.		All Other	
	Number	Per Cent	Number	Per Cent	Number	Per Cent	Number	Per Cent	Number	Per Cent
1921[a]	1,764,129	100.0	1,497,305	100.0	222,172	100.0	35,095	100.0	9,557	100.0
Rural	920,541	52.2	898,643	60.0	15,480	7.0	3,490	7.1	3,928	41.1
Urban	843,588	47.8	598,662	40.0	206,692	93.0	32,605	92.9	5,629	58.9
1931[a]	2,205,228	100.0	1,683,023	100.0	171,925	100.0	342,659	100.0	7,621	100.0
Rural	1,005,523	45.6	975,873	58.0	17,845	10.4	9,285	2.7	2,520	33.1
Urban	1,199,705	54.4	707,150	42.0	154,080	89.6	333,374	97.3	5,101	66.9
1941	2,573,155	100.0	1,817,646	100.0	196,874	100.0	534,912	100.0	23,723	100.0
Rural	1,158,585	45.0	1,082,079	59.5	31,242	15.9	34,356	6.4	10,908	46.0
Farm	703,782	27.3	684,984	37.7	9,775	5.0	4,825	0.9	4,198	17.7
Non-farm	454,803	17.7	397,095	21.8	21,467	10.9	29,531	5.5	6,710	28.3
Urban	1,414,570	55.0	735,567	40.5	165,632	84.1	500,556	93.6	12,815	54.0
1951	3,409,295	100.0	2,275,615	100.0	237,655	100.0	885,565	100.0	10,460	100.0
Rural	1,254,260	36.8	1,131,610	49.7	58,875	21.8	58,520	6.6	5,255	50.2
Farm	629,785	18.5	592,940	26.0	24,725	10.4	10,605	1.2	1,515	14.5
Non-farm	624,475	18.3	538,670	23.7	34,150	14.4	47,915	5.4	3,740	35.7
Urban	2,155,035	63.2	1,144,005	50.3	178,780	75.2	827,045	93.4	5,205	49.8
1961[b]	4,544,493	100.0	2,978,501	100.0	404,933	100.0	1,151,098	100.0	19,961	100.0
Rural	1,274,025	28.0	1,146,033	38.5	73,234	18.1	42,444	3.7	12,314	61.7
Farm	449,553	9.9	427,559	14.4	15,580	3.8	5,626	0.5	788	3.9
Non-farm	824,472	18.1	718,474	24.1	57,654	14.3	36,818	3.2	11,526	57.8
Urban	3,280,468	72.0	1,832,468	61.5	331,699	81.9	1,108,654	96.3	7,647	38.3
1966[b]	5,180,473	100.0	3,234,123	100.0	401,754	100.0	1,516,419	100.0	28,177	100.0
Rural	1,239,014	23.9	1,128,454	34.9	52,839	13.1	41,662	2.7	16,059	57.0
Farm	427,238	8.2	413,124	12.8	9,007	2.2	3,346	0.2	1,761	6.2
Non-farm	811,776	15.7	715,330	22.1	43,832	10.9	38,316	2.5	14,298	50.8
Urban	3,941,459	76.1	2,105,669	65.1	348,915	86.9	1,474,757	97.3	12,118	43.0

SOURCE: Dominion Bureau of Statistics, *1921 Census of Canada*, Vol. III, Table 10; *1931 Census of Canada*, Vol. I, Table 109; *1941 Census of Canada*, Vol. V, Table 4; *1951 Census of Canada*, Vol. III, Table 8-1; *1961 Census of Canada*, Bulletin 2:2-1, 1963, Table 5; *1966 Census of Canada*, Vol. II (2-2), 1968, Table 5-1.
[a] Rural Farm and Rural Non-Farm Categories were not used in the 1921 and 1931 Censuses of Canada.
[b] Includes Yukon and N.W.T.

anization movement, i.e., the shifting of population to peripheral locations in the urban complex, has created additional demands for the single-detached dwelling unit.

With the subsequent decline in farm population, there has been less demand for housing in rural Canada. The dominant form of housing in the rural areas has been the single-detached dwelling as indicated in Table 13:4. Consistently since 1921, this type of housing has constituted over 90 per cent of the total rural housing stock. When comparing the distribution of the housing between the rural and urban areas of the country, a rather interesting shift is distinguishable. Sixty per cent of the single-detached dwellings were located in the rural areas in 1921 compared to 34.9 per cent in 1966. Partly due to the suburbanization process, single-detached dwellings increased from 40 per cent to 65.1 per cent in the urban areas. Again, the trend toward apartment construction is evident in urban areas with an increase from 3.9 per cent to 37.4 per cent over the same period of time.

Many demographic trends have accounted for this shift in priorities since the turn of the century. Obviously, the apartment with its bachelor suite is not conducive to childrearing, hence it is not suitable accommodation for the family in its formative years. The apartment structure, however, does meet certain special types of demand for housing. It is suitable for the single person, the young married without children, the divorced, the widowed or separated person, and the older, retired couple. The size of these populations has been influenced by several demographic changes that have occurred in our society. The decreasing age at marriage has increased the number of young married couples, and the postponement of childbearing serves to increase the length of time that an apartment will serve their needs. In addition, increasing numbers of females are entering the labour market, a factor which further influences the delay in childbearing and for some the postponement of marriage. The improvement in mortality conditions has added years to the longevity of the population, simply meaning that married couples will continue to enjoy many years together after their children have matured and left home to form their own families. As a consequence, the proportion of aged populations increases and the demand for smaller accommodations in the form of light-housekeeping apartment units appears. More and more college-age populations are attending institutions of higher learning than ever before and, again, creating a need for housing of the apartment variety close to university locations. These essentially demographic trends have served to bring about change in life style and, necessarily, living arrangements.

Rental versus Home Ownership

It is important to reiterate that rental housing is comprised mainly of apartment units, over 90 per cent of which are located in urban areas. Consequently, any demographic, social, or economic factors that may influence the values, preferences, life styles, and living arrangements of the urban population will also have implications for the housing industry.

Rental housing fulfills the demands of several family and non-family groups. Most notably among these are the single persons, newly married and childless couples, and the older couples whose children have left home. Several factors make rental housing the ideal form of accommodation and in some cases the only alternative available to these segments of the population. In the earlier stages of the family life cycle, single persons or young married couples may not have achieved the level of income that would allow them access to the home ownership market or have need for larger accommodations. The older couple, beyond the childrearing stage, will again be in a situation where smaller, less demanding accommodations would best serve their needs.

There are several trends in Canadian society that tend to favour the rental market by influencing the aforementioned segments of the population in terms of age distribution. The 20 to 29 year age group—a principal source of renters—is expected to increase by approximately 2.1 million by 1980.[2] Comparatively, the projected growth for the 30 to 49 year age group is 1.2 million.[3] It is significant that this is the age group predominantly in the childbearing and childraising years of the life cycle. This group has been the strongest contender in the home buying market because of increased housing needs. Consequently, family households with heads in the 30 to 49 year range receive the greatest attention of the housing industry. One other important group, the population over 65 years of age, is expected to increase by 1980 to 2,109,400.[4] In light of current trends, it can be assumed that an increasing share of this age group will be potential consumers in the rental housing market.

The increasing number of married females participating in the labour force has an additional consequence for the rental housing market. Almost half of the women who worked in 1961 were married, in contrast to only ten per cent in 1931.[5] These working wives are predominantly younger women who most likely have continued to work after marriage and will continue to do so until they start their own families. They are at an early stage in their life cycle, still shifting their priorities as to careers, and generally not willing or able to take on the financial burden of purchasing a home or give up the mobility which goes with apartment living. This particular group, then, would be a major candidate for the rental market.

Modern housing technology coupled with the housing industry's concern for the desires of the client has brought about a rather significant change in the rental unit of today. Aiding the rental unit in its competition with home ownership has been the inclusion of extra living features and conveniences.

The rental unit, with the attendant features of location, maintenance, services, labour-saving devices and appliances, and with many other amenities of the single-detached home, is satisfying the needs of the potential home owner. Families with changing housing requisites in the childbearing and rearing stages of the life cycle are increasingly being accommodated by the new apartment rental unit. The employed wife and husband with their outer-directed activities and the need for an accommodation requiring little attention are attracted to these self-contained and maintained rental units. The differences between the single-detached unit and the rental apartment unit are narrowing; and, as this continues, the apartment type of accommodation will increase their share of the market.

The rural to urban population movement, in contrast to earlier years, has been increasingly diverted from the central city to the suburbs of metropolitan areas. Suburban areas are now receiving the major share of this influx due to the saturation of the central cities in recent decades. Corollary to this shift in population is the more recent phenomenon of population exchange between urban areas, or inter-city movement. Both trends bear import for the rental scene. In addition, the trend toward new family formation, and particularly toward new, younger, family household heads with relatively low incomes will provide additional consumers for this alternative to home ownership. As indicated in Figure 13:3, the proportion of household heads owning rather than renting was significantly lower in the younger age groups.

Home ownership. Most new home owners are rental graduates, as the rental unit merely serves as a preparatory stage until consumers can realize their goals as home owners. Young married couples and immigrants utilize the rental market until they can afford to finance the purchase of a home. The proportion of renters declines to 33 per cent in 1961 for the 35 to 44 year age group and stabilizes at this point for the older age groups. It appears that between 30 and 35 years of age, the head of the household makes the decision for home ownership. For the age group 35–44 years, home ownership exceeds 60 per cent, and for the remaining age groups stays at this level.

In comparison, the home ownership levels are significantly higher in the non-urban areas for household heads of all ages. For rural farm, the proportion who are home owners levels at the 55 to 64 year age group with 96.8 per cent, whereas the home ownership curve for the urban dweller begins to level at the much younger ages of 35 to 44 years. The urban home-ownership proportion does not reach its peak of 69.6 per cent until the household head is 65 years of age and over. It is interesting to note that this peak is about equal to that of the youngest rural-farm household head age groups. Factors influencing the differences between home-ownership levels for the urban and rural areas would be (1) fewer rental housing units available in rural areas, (2) lower number of population in the age groups for rural areas, and (3) relatively less expensive housing in rural areas.

Fig. 13:3

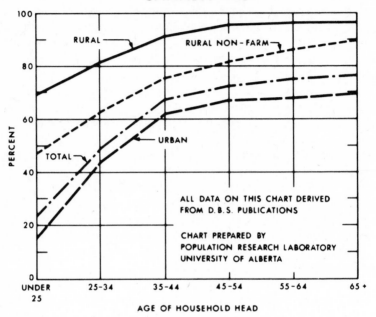

HOME OWNERSHIP
BY RESIDENCE AND AGE OF HEAD
CANADA: 1961

ALL DATA ON THIS CHART DERIVED
FROM D.B.S. PUBLICATIONS

CHART PREPARED BY
POPULATION RESEARCH LABORATORY
UNIVERSITY OF ALBERTA

AGE OF HOUSEHOLD HEAD

Table 13:5

PERCENTAGE DISTRIBUTION OF OCCUPIED DWELLINGS BY TENURE, CANADA, 1931–1966

Year	Total Dwellings[a]	Owner-Occupied		Tenant-Occupied	
		Number	Per Cent	Number	Per Cent
1931	2,252,729	1,362,896	60.5	889,833	39.5
1941	2,573,155	1,457,526	56.6	1,115,629	43.4
1951	3,409,295	2,236,955	65.6	1,172,340	34.4
1961	4,546,573	3,001,295	66.0	1,545,278	34.0
1966	5,171,542	3,265,476	63.1	1,906,066	36.9

SOURCE: Dominion Bureau of Statistics, *1931 Census of Canada*, Vol. I, Table 110; *1941 Census of Canada*, Vol. V, Table 4; *1961 Census of Canada*, Bulletin 7:2-4, 1966, Table viii.
[a] Excludes Yukon and N.W.T.

As can be seen in Table 13:5, home ownership remains a dominant force on the Canadian housing scene. Only in the 1941 Census did the home ownership rate fall below 60 per cent. This was probably a reflection of the war years and aftermath of the depression when the economic situation was not favourable for home ownership and doubling developed as a more viable solution to housing needs. There is evidence of a new trend in tenure emerging between 1961 and 1966 where rentership has increased to 36.9 per cent. If, in fact, this trend continues to develop, it will signify a major change in the value orientations of the population toward home ownership.

In the past, studies have consistently indicated favourable attitudes of the population toward home ownership.[6] Home ownership in itself provides a large measure of prestige and social status to the consumer, i.e., demonstration of personal success. In addition to the socio-psychological factors, home ownership decisions are based on family size, space needs, employment changes, income levels, and locational preferences.

Length of Occupancy

As expected, the mobility of the population influences the length of time that a household occupies a dwelling unit. Portrayed in Table 13:6 the greatest percentage of owned dwelling units—41.6 per cent—had been occupied for more than ten years. Conversely, only 11.5 per cent of the rental units had been occupied this length of time. It is also evident that renter-occupied dwellings experience shorter-term occupancy than owner-occupied dwellings, with the major share, 77.9 per cent, of the rental units being occupied less than five years. This figure is influenced by the relatively higher mobility of the renter population, particularly its younger components. For example,

Table 13:6

PERCENTAGE DISTRIBUTION OF OCCUPIED DWELLINGS, CLASSIFIED ACCORDING TO TENURE, BY LENGTH OF OCCUPANCY, CANADA, 1961

Tenure	Total Dwellings	Less Than One Year	1–5 Years	6–10 Years	More Than 10 Years
Total	4,554,493	15.3	36.7	16.6	31.4
Owner-Occupied	3,005,587	7.1	31.5	19.8	41.6
Renter-Occupied	1,548,906	31.3	46.6	10.5	11.5

SOURCE: Dominion Bureau of Statistics, *1961 Census of Canada*, Bulletin 7:2-4, Ottawa, The Queen's Printer, 1966, Table XIV.

at the time of the census enumeration, the respondent may have recently changed residence from one rental unit to another, and therefore still be classified as a "less than one year" occupant.

Generally, mobility decreases as the age of the population increases. When young married heads of households mature, start to raise children, and improve their income level, they begin to establish themselves in the homeowner market. Prior to this stabilizing, the apartment rental unit is very compatible with a highly mobile population as it requires no long-term commitment.

Figure 13:4 shows that as the age of the household head increases, length of occupancy increases. Assuming that the major share of younger household heads are living in rental accommodations because of their financial inability to participate in the home-ownership market, they would not become home owners until at a later stage in their life cycle. This is consistent with the patterns revealed in the chart where the younger household heads reflect shorter occupancy behaviour, either due to rentership or to becoming recent

Fig. 13:4

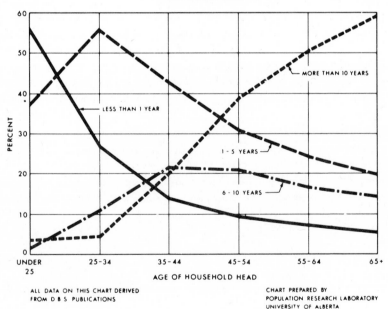

LENGTH OF OCCUPANCY
BY AGE OF HOUSEHOLD HEAD
CANADA: 1961

ALL DATA ON THIS CHART DERIVED
FROM D B S PUBLICATIONS

CHART PREPARED BY
POPULATION RESEARCH LABORATORY
UNIVERSITY OF ALBERTA

home owners. Conversely, the older household heads demonstrate longer periods of occupancy reflecting more stable living arrangements. A possible explanation for the peak in the one to five year occupancy curve for the 25 to 34 year age group may be found in the tendency for people to enter the home-ownership market at this stage in their life cycle. When this age group matures and their life styles stabilize, the proportions occupying dwelling units in the 35 to 44 year age range would be relatively high.

The relationship between age of household head and length of occupancy is consistent with the present understanding of consumer behaviour. Donald McAllister, in a study of rental housing, points out that there is evidence of change in attitude toward home ownership during the early stages of the life cycle.[7] A marked shift in saving patterns occurs as the household head approaches 30 years of age, primarily reflecting the active planning and saving for home purchase. Hence, as the age of household head increases, so does his ability to participate in home ownership; and conversely, rentership will continue to decline as age increases.

Quality of Housing

The quality of housing, as indicated in preference surveys,[8] is one of the least dominant factors in the shaping of housing preferences and choice. The consumer may sacrifice housing quality in order to fulfill other housing requisites such as space, location, design, availability of play space for children, and the like. This balancing of criteria is more noticeable for larger families where they are subjected to greater expenditures for other necessities, and hence must compromise on quality.

The adequacy of the housing stock in Canada can be measured by using four basic indicators: the age of the structure, the condition, the type of facilities servicing the structure, and the number of persons per room. New construction accounts for a relatively small proportion of the housing stock at any given point in time; for example, only 3.7 per cent of the housing was constructed between 1960 and 1961.[9]

New housing. Construction of new housing units is primarily in response to the increase in family formation, household formation patterns,[10] and the replacement of losses in the existing housing stock. This new housing is largely limited to the single-detached dwellings designed for families in the childbearing and raising stage of the life cycle who are in the middle-income bracket and who have popular tastes. These consumers, although exerting a minor influence on total supply, will dictate what will be available to most later home purchasers. In other words, these "new" houses will eventually filter down to other consumers—consumers not having purchasing power in the new home market and to whom quality is of less importance.

It is noteworthy that housing, in contrast to an automobile product, is characterized by extreme longevity and slow design change. With these factors in mind and the long-term investment involved, the filtering down process is much slower than with a shorter-term product. Lower-income families, by circumstance, have to wait until lower-priced, older homes become available to them.

Table 13:7

PERCENTAGE OF OCCUPIED DWELLING UNITS BY PERIOD OF CONSTRUCTION FOR RURAL FARM, RURAL NON-FARM, AND URBAN LOCALITIES, CANADA, 1961

Locality	Total Dwellings	Before 1920	1920–1945	1946–1961[a]
Canada	4,554,493	30.6	25.2	44.2
Rural	1,274,025	37.9	25.1	36.9
Farm	449,553	52.1	26.4	21.5
Non-farm	824,472	30.3	24.4	45.3
Urban	3,280,468	27.7	25.3	47.0

SOURCE: Dominion Bureau of Statistics, *1961 Census of Canada*, Volume 2:2-1, Ottawa, The Queen's Printer, 1963, Table 15.
[a] Includes first five months of 1961 only.

The age structure of housing. The housing stock can be treated in terms of its age structure, in a manner somewhat analogous to the demographer's analysis of a population age structure. New units enter the housing age structure at its base as in the normal age-sex pyramid. Similarly, as the housing stock ages, there is housing mortality in that there are losses due to fire, demolition, and land use changes. The shape of the housing age structure would be influenced by the past population growth, the national economy, and any changes occurring in household and family formation patterns.

In 1961, approximately 97 per cent of the existing housing stock were used dwellings. Less than half—44.2 per cent—of all dwelling units were constructed since World War II as portrayed in Table 13:7. Indicative of the population shift from rural to urban areas is the fact that only 21.5 per cent, about one-fifth, of the rural farm housing had been constructed since 1945 as compared to 47.0 per cent for urban areas. Both rural and urban areas reflected lower construction activity during the 1920 to 1945 period due to the combined effects of the Great Depression and the war years. In the postwar period, the urban and rural non-farm areas demonstrated an upsurge in the proportion of new dwelling units in response to migration patterns, improving economy, undoubling of families, and the rising marriage rates following the war.

Provincial variations in the age structure of dwellings are portrayed in Table 13:8, where, as expected, the Western Provinces having experienced the major share of growth since the turn of the century have lower proportions of older dwellings than their eastern counterparts. Newfoundland, with 48.7 per cent of its housing constructed during the post-war period, is the major exception. Accounting for this increased building activity is the combined effects of a significantly high rate of natural increase, substantial

Table 13:8

PERCENTAGE OF OCCUPIED DWELLING UNITS BY PERIOD OF CONSTRUCTION, CANADA AND PROVINCES, 1961

Province	Total Dwellings	Before 1920	1920–1945	1946–1961[a]
Canada	4,554,493	30.6	25.2	44.2
Newfoundland	87,940	24.1	27.2	48.7
Prince Edward Island	23,942	57.9	20.7	21.4
Nova Scotia	175,340	47.6	21.7	30.7
New Brunswick	132,714	43.6	22.9	33.5
Quebec	1,191,368	30.0	25.3	44.6
Ontario	1,640,750	34.9	22.1	43.0
Manitoba	239,754	31.5	27.7	40.9
Saskatchewan	245,424	28.2	32.2	39.6
Alberta	349,809	18.6	26.3	55.1
British Columbia	459,532	16.3	32.2	51.5
The Territories	7,920	4.6	18.2	77.2

SOURCE: Dominion Bureau of Statistics, *1961 Census of Canada*, Volume 2.2-1, Ottawa, The Queen's Printer, 1963, Table 15.
[a] Includes first five months of 1961 only.

growth rate, and governmental efforts to shift settlement patterns from small, relatively isolated fishing villages to larger, economically integrated communities.

The major proportion of the housing stock in the remaining three Atlantic Provinces was constructed prior to 1920. Housing activity increased for the remaining provinces in the post-war period when the proportion of housing units built was closer to the Canadian average of 40.5 per cent. Alberta, British Columbia, and the Territories had over 50 per cent of their housing constructed since 1945. Development of resources and the consequent increase in net migration contributed to increased construction during this period. Parallel developments in housing took place in the metropolitan areas of Canada as well. As expected, the 1961 Census revealed that the older eastern metropolitan areas contained high proportions of dwelling units built prior to 1920.[11]

Condition of Canadian housing. The condition of housing appeared to improve in Canada between 1951 and 1961 as demonstrated by the decline in the number and proportion of dwelling units in need of major repair—a drop from 457,570 units (13.5 per cent) in 1951 to 255,414 units (5.6 per cent) in 1961.[12] Several factors may have accounted for this improvement, such as the general increase in economic activity, the "catching up" on a backlog of home refurbishing postponed during the war years, and the addition of a larger proportion of new dwelling units to the total housing inventory.

Table 13:9

PERCENTAGE DISTRIBUTION OF OCCUPIED DWELLINGS BY
CONDITION FOR RURAL FARM, RURAL NON-FARM AND
URBAN LOCALITIES, CANADA, 1961

Locality	Total Dwellings	Good Condition	In Need of Minor Repair	In Need of Major Repair
Canada	4,544,493	74.1	20.3	5.6
Rural	1,274,025	63.0	27.6	9.4
Farm	449,553	60.1	30.5	9.4
Non-farm	824,472	64.6	26.0	9.4
Urban	3,280,468	78.4	17.5	4.1

SOURCE: Dominion Bureau of Statistics, *1961 Census of Canada*, Bulletin 2:2-1, Ottawa, The Queen's Printer, 1963, Table 15.

Urban and rural differences in the condition of housing are portrayed in Table 13:9. Over three-fourths of all dwellings in urban areas were reported as being in good condition, regardless of urban size. Urban areas with 100,000 population or more had the highest proportion, 80.9 per cent, of dwellings in good condition. The major differences appear between urban and rural housing, with the rural farm and non-farm areas having the lower proportions of good housing and the highest proportions in need of major repair. As noted earlier, the rural areas had the higher percentages of older dwellings; and, as housing ages, more effort is required in maintenance and repair. In addition, housing technology has improved considerably since 1920 when the major share of rural farm construction, 52.1 per cent, took place.

Housing equipment and conveniences. Age in itself is not an undesirable feature in housing; however, lack of adequate facilities is commonly associated with older dwellings. Important to the livability of the dwelling, as well as to the health of its occupants, is the mechanical equipment that it contains. The majority of housing consumers would consider running water, basic plumbing facilities, and adequate heating equipment as essential requirements in the selection of a home. As demonstrated in Table 13:10, not all Canadians enjoy these basic features in their accommodations; however, the urban dweller fairs much better than his rural counterpart in this regard. Four out of ten dwellings in rural farm areas are without running water, and about six out of ten units are without the exclusive use of a bath or shower and flush toilet. The rural non-farm dweller shows relatively little improvement in housing equipment over the rural farm dweller. Partial explanation for these conditions in the rural area of Canada is the lack of services, the age of structure, lower income levels, and the simple fact of opting for other kinds of expenditures. After considering the lower proportions of rural farm dwellings with "essential" facilities, it is interesting to note the higher proportions of households having refrigerators, television sets, and automobiles. This is indicative of the increasing importance of these conveniences, particularly in the relatively isolated rural setting. The need for food preservation and storage, communication and entertainment, and the necessity of automobiles for travelling longer distances than the urban dweller have firmly established these conveniences in the priority listing of necessities.

Overcrowdedness in housing. An important indicator of the general quality of the housing inventory is provided by the number of persons per room. The

Table 13:10

PERCENTAGE OF OCCUPIED DWELLING UNITS WITH SPECIFIED FACILITIES AND LIVING CONVENIENCES FOR RURAL FARM, RURAL NON-FARM, AND URBAN LOCALITIES, CANADA, 1961

Locality	Total Dwellings[a]	Running Water	Bath or Shower	Flush Toilet	Furnace Heating
Canada	100.0	89.1	77.1	79.0	67.5
Rural Farm	100.0	60.6	40.4	43.9	44.2
Rural Non-farm	100.0	68.1	49.7	54.3	42.5
Urban	100.0	98.3	89.0	90.1	76.9

Locality	Total Dwellings[a]	Refrigerator	Home Freezer	Television	Automobile
Canada	100.0	91.0	14.9	82.5	68.4
Rural Farm	100.0	80.0	40.7	67.3	77.5
Rural Non-farm	100.0	77.9	17.4	67.4	65.7
Urban	100.0	95.8	10.7	88.4	67.8

SOURCE: Dominion Bureau of Statistics, *1961 Census of Canada*, Bulletin 2:2-7, Ottawa, The Queen's Printer, 1963, Table 80.
[a] Includes mobile dwelling units.

Census of Canada defines a crowded household as a dwelling with more than one person per room. This is not an entirely adequate measure as it does not account for variations in the age and sex of household members, size of the rooms, or local customs.[13]

Overcrowding, as measured by this index, is closely related to income of the family. As an example, the heavy doubling up of families in single households during the depression period of the 1930s and the subsequent undoubling in the post-war period was found to parallel fluctuations in family income.[14] Conversely, an increase in "doubling up" may occur if there is a

Table 13:11

PERCENTAGE OF OCCUPIED DWELLING UNITS WITH MORE THAN
ONE PERSON PER ROOM BY PROVINCE, CANADA, 1961

Locality	Total Occupied Dwellings	Dwellings with More Than One Person per Room	
		Number	Per Cent
Canada[a]	4,546,573	747,350	16.4
Newfoundland	87,940	26,254	29.8
Prince Edward Island	23,942	4,080	17.0
Nova Scotia	175,340	31,832	18.2
New Brunswick	132,714	27,836	21.0
Quebec	1,191,368	259,985	21.8
Ontario	1,640,750	194,343	11.8
Manitoba	239,754	40,261	16.8
Saskatchewan	245,424	45,967	18.7
Alberta	349,809	61,308	17.5
British Columbia	459,532	55,484	12.1

SOURCE: Dominion Bureau of Statistics, *1961 Census of Canada*, Bulletin 2:2-12, Ottawa, The Queen's Printer, 1964, Table 107.
[a] Not including Yukon and N.W.T.

housing shortage as well, hence such a shortage may lead to overcrowding. In sum, families may double up in a single household voluntarily, while others may double up because of a deficiency in housing supply.

From Table 13:11 it may be seen that 16.4 per cent of all dwellings in Canada are categorized as overcrowded—a drop from the 18.8 per cent reported in 1951.[15] Crowded households are more prevalent among renter-occupied housing, primarily single-detached dwellings. Newfoundland, with 29.8 per cent of its housing stock classified as crowded, also reported that

31.3 per cent of its tenant-occupied single family dwellings fell into this category. This is a consequence of the higher birth rates, lower income levels, and the resettlement movement in this province. The result of these factors is both a deficiency in housing supply for specific segments of the population and also the economic necessity of accommodating to less space. Ontario and British Columbia reported the lowest index of crowdedness. In these two provinces, the economic viability of the population to participate in the housing market is greater and higher proportions of families maintain their own households. It is expected that crowdedness in Canada will decline in the future in that the number of families sharing accommodations is likely to decrease. Governmental concern and action in the area of low income housing, subsidized housing, and the general improvement in income levels will all be instrumental toward the achievement of further declines.

In retrospect, it is important to emphasize that concern with housing quality often detracts from the population aspect which is the more important element to consider in understanding differences in the adequacy of the housing stock. Variations in the housing inventory are associated with different segments of the population. It is known that the older segment of the population is more likely than the younger population to have deficient housing, and that the lower-income populations will also be limited to a very restricted housing choice.

The Aged, Low-Income, and Immigrant Households

Aged population. The comparison of aged households with all of the households in Canada reveals that this population sub-group is more likely to own rather than rent, live in a single-family dwelling, be associated with longer periods of occupancy, and consequently reside in older dwellings. Table 13:12 indicates that the quality of their housing is poorer than the average Canadian with 6.6 per cent of their dwellings in need of major repair. In addition, their older homes are less likely to have adequate facilities.

The elderly tend to develop strong social and psychological bonds with their neighbourhood; and, even if economically able, they are unlikely to move to areas with improved housing. These factors, along with their economic disadvantage, serve to explain the general immobility of the older population. It is probable that their residential area has deteriorated as well, further compounding their housing and community problems.

For older owners and renters alike, a greater share of a decreasing income is expended on housing. Moreover, additional expenditures are required in the area of health care as the incidence and prevalence of chronic disease increases with age. In brief, the older population are in an economically disadvantageous position to either maintain their present homes or afford better quality housing.

Table 13:12

SELECTED HOUSEHOLD AND DWELLING CHARACTERISTICS FOR SPECIFIED POPULATION SUB-GROUPS, CANADA, 1961

Household and Dwelling Characteristics	Total Households		Low Income[a] Households		Household Heads 65 Years of Age and Over	
	Number	Per Cent	Number	Per Cent	Number	Per Cent
Total Households	4,554,493	100.0	358,067[b]	100.0	746,792	100.0
Type of Housing						
Single-Detached	2,978,501	65.4	219,255	61.2	518,554	69.4
Single Attached	404,933	8.9	33,725	9.4	62,944	8.4
Apartments, Flats	1,151,098	25.3	103,348	28.9	164,455	22.0
Tenure						
Owned	3,005,587	66.0	202,617	56.6	574,780	77.0
Rented	1,548,906	34.0	155,450	43.4	172,012	23.0
Length of Occupancy						
10 Years or More	1,429,152	31.4	101,892	28.4	445,472	59.6
Housing Condition						
Needs Major Repair	255,414	5.6	41,548	11.6	49,092	6.6
Housing Facilities						
Running Water	4,058,313	89.1	286,596	80.0	630,577	84.4
Bath or Shower	3,512,110	77.1	205,155	57.3	526,564	70.5
Flush Toilet	3,599,468	79.0	231,606	64.7	549,304	73.6
Period of Construction						
Before 1920	1,391,719	30.6	136,376	38.1	341,535	45.8
1920–1945	1,148,389	25.2	95,806	26.8	221,359	29.6
1945–1961[c]	2,014,385	44.2	125,885	35.1	183,898	24.6

SOURCE: Dominion Bureau of Statistics, *1961 Census of Canada*, Bulletins 2:2-8, 1963, Tables 84 and 86 and 2:2-11, 1964, Tables 101 and 103.
[a] Wage-earner household heads earning less than $2,000.
[b] Includes mobile unit household heads, and household heads not reporting wages earned.
[c] Includes first five months of 1961 only.

Low-income households. While interpreting the figures for the low-income households in Table 13:12, the reader must keep in mind that the categories in this table are not mutually exclusive. For example, an aged couple with a reduced income could also be classified as a low-income household.

The low-income households reflect a high ownership rate, with 56.6 per cent owning their own homes, and report a lower proportion of dwellings occupied ten years or more. In this instance, it is possible that elderly populations with low incomes and high ownership rates may account for this pattern. The Economic Council of Canada reports that about 20 per cent of family heads classified in the low-income group were over 65 years of age.[16]

The inadequacy of housing for those with low incomes is greater in terms of housing condition and lack of basic facilities. A large proportion of older people, as well as low-income families with insufficient means of livelihood, are frequently located in the blighted central areas of the city.[17] Housing in these areas is usually older, not well maintained, and deficient in basic facilities. Residential structures are exposed to deterioration deriving from sheer usage and through the passage of time. As alluded to above, technological obsolescence and changes in land use have their impact on the quality of central area housing.

Immigrant households. One of the more salient features of Canada's population, historically, has been its composition by nativity. According to the 1961 Census, one-quarter of all households had immigrant heads of which 61.9 per cent had immigrated to this country prior to 1946. Of the 433,122 immigrants arriving in Canada during the post-war period, 297,337, or 26.1 per cent, came during the 1946 to 1955 period and 135,785 immigrants (12.0 per cent) arrived in the most recent period for which data are available, 1956 to 1961.[18]

In contrast to the pre-1946 immigrants, post-war arrivals tended to settle in those large urban areas noted for manufacturing industries. Within these urban complexes, the primary receiving area has been the central core, usually characterized by less than adequate, older housing. As the immigrants arrive they are faced with the prospect of a housing choice from an existing stock with some degree of deterioration. Except for the very few, rental units will be the only alternative; and, if attracted to the older, inner areas of the cities, these units will be of older stock.

Table 13:13 allows one to examine the housing character of households with immigrant heads by period of immigration. Similar characteristics for the non-immigrant or native-born population are provided for comparative purposes. In the gross comparison of housing characteristics for non-immigrant and immigrant households, very slight differences are revealed between the two population groups. Significant differences in housing begin to emerge when the immigrant population is subdivided by period of immigration. Emphasis on type of dwelling shifts from apartments for the recent

Table 13:13

SELECTED HOUSING CHARACTERISTICS FOR NON-IMMIGRANT HOUSEHOLDS AND IMMIGRANT HOUSEHOLDS BY PERIOD OF IMMIGRATION, CANADA, 1961

Housing Characteristics	Non-Immigrant Household Heads		Immigrant Household Heads		Period of Immigration					
					Before 1946		1946–1955		1956–1961	
	Number	Per Cent	Number	Per Cent	Number	Per Cent	Number	Per Cent	Number	Per Cent
Total Households[a]	3,417,316	100.0	1,137,177	100.0	704,055	100.0	297,337	100.0	135,785	100.0
Type of Dwelling										
Single-Detached	2,231,099	65.3	747,402	65.7	515,282	73.2	177,242	59.6	54,878	40.4
Single Attached	300,254	8.8	104,679	9.2	52,057	7.4	36,740	12.4	15,882	11.7
Apartment	868,998	25.4	282,100	24.8	135,146	19.2	82,415	27.7	64,539	47.5
Tenure										
Ownership	2,216,279	64.9	789,308	69.4	547,449	77.8	197,682	66.5	44,177	32.5
Rentership	1,201,037	35.1	347,869	30.6	156,606	22.2	99,655	33.5	91,608	67.5
Period of Construction										
Before 1920	1,064,966	31.2	326,753	28.7	211,470	30.0	77,627	26.1	37,656	27.7
1920–1945	823,008	24.1	325,381	28.6	229,167	32.5	66,002	22.2	30,212	22.2
1946–1961[b]	1,529,342	44.8	485,043	42.7	263,418	37.4	153,708	51.7	67,917	50.1
Length of Occupancy										
Less than 1 Year	527,850	15.4	170,284	15.0	57,942	8.2	56,209	18.9	56,133	41.3
1–5 Years	1,237,350	36.2	432,630	38.0	190,570	27.1	169,386	57.0	72,674	53.5
6–10 Years	565,358	16.5	191,869	16.9	131,499	18.7	57,453	19.3	2,383	1.8
More than 10 Years	1,086,758	31.8	342,394	30.1	324,044	46.0	14,289	4.8	—[c]	—[c]

SOURCE: Dominion Bureau of Statistics, *1961 Census of Canada*, Bulletin 2:2-10, Ottawa, The Queen's Printer, 1964, Tables 95 and 97.
[a] Includes mobile dwelling units.
[b] Includes first five months of 1961 only.
[c] Not applicable.

arrivals to single-detached dwellings for the earlier immigrants. Seven out of ten foreign-born households are housed in single-detached family dwellings which is higher than for non-immigrant households. It does not take very long for this change in accommodation to occur, as evinced in the data for the 1946 to 1955 period where 59.6 per cent of the immigrant housing were of this type. Similarly, tenure shifts from rentership for the recent arrivals (67.5 per cent) to ownership for the earlier immigrants (66.5 and 77.8 per cent). The changes in type of housing and tenure are likely to be associated with the improvement in the immigrant's economic position and his adjustment to the community.

Both the pre-war and post-war immigrants tend to live in housing constructed since 1946. Over half of the post-war immigrants reside in newer housing as compared to 37.4 per cent for the pre-war group. The pre-war immigrants are characterized by having more stable living arrangements in that almost 65 per cent of these households have occupied their dwellings for six or more years, considerably higher than the other immigrant groups and the non-immigrant group as well.

The combined effect of the historical process of urban growth and the aging of the dwelling units itself influences the character of the housing stock available to these special population segments. It must be remembered that physical condition, age, and kinds of facilities are only part of the measure of housing quality. An equally important factor is location. Although the housing unit may be physically adequate, it may be locationally unfit for the housing market and will rarely survive adverse environmental conditions.[19]

Summary
To indicate the current emphasis in the housing market, data on building permits[20] are presented in Figure 13:5. The most salient trend is the attention directed toward the construction of apartment units, the predominantly urban form of housing. While the single-family typé dwelling unit has increased in construction from 90,200 units in 1950 to 194,990 units in 1969, it has decreased proportionately from 76.2 per cent to 33.7 per cent of the annual housing construction. Apartment units are gaining in their proportionate share of building activity in recent years, and by 1969 they accounted for approximately 60 per cent of the annual construction.

Several factors will lend support to a continuation of this shift in building priority for the next several years. As the urban complex reclaims its inner areas through rezoning to higher density standards, the "high-rise" apartment structure will become a common sight on the urban scene. Increases in rental unit households (such as the single person, households of two or more unrelated persons, the young married couples, and the widowed, divorced, and separated populations) will gain more attention from the housing in-

Fig. 13:5

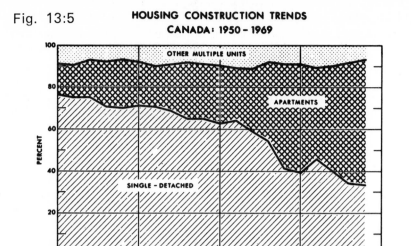

HOUSING CONSTRUCTION TRENDS
CANADA: 1950 – 1969

SOURCES:
W. M. ILLING, HOUSING DEMAND TO 1970, OTTAWA, ECONOMIC COUNCIL
OF CANADA, 1964, TABLE A-11, AND BUILDING PERMITS, ANNUAL SUMMARY,
OTTAWA: D.B.S., 1969, TABLE 1.

CHART PREPARED BY
POPULATION RESEARCH LABORATORY
UNIVERSITY OF ALBERTA

dustry. Housing and locational preferences will align with the maturation of the household as it is affected by its particular stage in the life cycle. The housing industry is in a position to offer to the wide range of households a variety of designs and types of accommodations. Foremost among these is the condominium designed to attract the urban dweller desirous of home ownership. The town house and garden apartment attracts the consumer who wants many of the amenities of home ownership in a rental accommodation. The less advantaged households will be courted with subsidized low-income housing, senior citizen apartment developments, and moderate-income row housing.

In conclusion, the average housing consumer may be exposed to the entire range of housing types throughout his life span. Of importance in the understanding of Canadian housing and its financing is that the typical single-detached dwelling unit is the "ideal" mode of shelter for a limited number of years in the family life cycle. In the 50 or more adult years of life, a mere 20 are years in which the family is composed of husband-wife and young children.[21] Any number of life cycle contingencies—all reducible to changes in status, fertility, mortality, and migration—will ultimately influence housing choice and demand.

REFERENCES

Dominion Bureau of Statistics: *1961 Census of Canada. General Review: Household Size and Composition*. Bulletin 7:2–3, Ottawa, The Queen's Printer, 1967.

Dominion Bureau of Statistics: *1961 Census of Canada. General Review: Housing in Canada*. Bulletin 7:2–4, Ottawa, The Queen's Printer, 1966.

Government of Canada: *Report of the Task Force on Housing and Urban Development*. Ottawa, The Queen's Printer, 1969.

Illing, Wolfgang M.: *Housing Development to 1970*. Economic Council of Canada, Staff Study No. 4, Ottawa, The Queen's Printer, 1965.

Lithwick, N. H. and G. Paquet: *Urban Studies: Canadian Perspective*. Toronto, Methuen, 1968.

FOOTNOTES

[1] Newfoundland was included in the data tabulation commencing with 1951 and accounted for the significant increase registered in the 1941–51 decade for the Atlantic Provinces.

[2] 1980 population projection of 4,450,600 for the 20 to 29 age group taken from Economic Council of Canada, Staff Study No. 19, *Population, Family, Household, and Labour Force Growth to 1980* by Wolfgang M. Illing, Ottawa, Queen's Printer and Controller of Stationery, 1967, pp. 40–41. It is interesting to note that the projected figure of 2,671,500 for the 20 to 29 year age group fell short of the actual census figure of 2,703,092 in 1966.

[3] *Ibid*. 1980 population projection for the 30 to 49 year age group is 5,946,000.

[4] *Ibid*. 1980 population projection for the 65 and over age group is 2,109,400.

[5] Department of Labour of Canada, *Women at Work in Canada*, Ottawa, Queen's Printer and Controller of Stationery, 1965, p. 21.

[6] Martin Meyerson, Barbara Terrett, and W. L. C. Wheaton, *Housing, People, and Cities*, Toronto, McGraw-Hill Book Company, Ltd., 1962, pp. 84–85; and Nelson N. Foote, *et al., Housing Choice and Housing Constraints*, Toronto, McGraw-Hill Book Company, Ltd., 1960.

[7] Donald McAllister, "The Demand for Rental Housing: An Investigation of Some Demographic and Economic Determinants," *The Annals of Regional Science*, Vol. 1, No. 2, (December, 1967), pp. 127–142.

[8] Meyerson, Terrett, and Wheaton, *op. cit.*, pp. 82–96.

[9] Dominion Bureau of Statistics, *1961 Census of Canada*, Vol. 2:2–1, Table 15.

[10] The undoubling phenomenon has increased in recent years, see, Wolfgang M. Illing, *Housing Demand to 1970*, Economic Council of Canada, Staff Study Number 4, Ottawa, Queen's Printer and Controller of Stationery, 1965.

[11] Dominion Bureau of Statistics, *1961 Census of Canada*, Vol. 7:2–4.

[12] *Ibid.*, p. 24.

[13] *Ibid.*, p. 22.

[14] Glen H. Beyer, *Housing and Society*, New York, The Macmillan Company, 1965, p. 120.

[15] Dominion Bureau of Statistics, *op. cit.*, Vol. 7:2–4, p. 22.

[16] Economic Council of Canada, *Fifth Annual Review: The Challenge of Growth and Change*, Ottawa, Queen's Printer and Controller of Stationery, 1968, p. 13.

[17] *Ibid.*

[18] Dominion Bureau of Statistics, *op. cit.*, Vol. 7:2–4, Table xxxii, p. 43.

[19] Meyerson, Terrett, and Wheaton, *op. cit.*, p. 39.

[20] It is necessary to point out a caution in the interpretation of building permit data. Permit data from 1963 to 1969 represent building permits issued and these figures may be distorted in two ways. First, there is a lag between a housing start and a housing completion and, secondly, a certain number of housing starts are never completed. Nevertheless, the data may serve as a general indicator of trends.

[21] Meyerson, Terrett, and Wheaton, *op. cit.*, p. 94.

A World Perspective, Recent Trends and the Future

In the midst of global concern over the population explosion of the mid-twentieth century, Canada stands as a demographic anomaly. Twenty-one and a half million people, occupying 3,500,000 square miles of territory and enjoying one of the highest standards of living in the world, hardly constitute a problem in the usual sense of the word. However, Canada, like the United States and other Western European countries, is an anomaly to the extent that the standard of living enjoyed in this country and in these other areas, which together account for only a small fraction of the total world population, appears to be an impossible goal for all mankind. Even if it were somehow conceivable within the limits of man's resourcefulness to extract, process, and consume the vast amounts of materials and energy that would be required, there are increasingly serious doubts as to man's ability to find substitute resources to replace those that are consumed, or to dispose of the waste products that are generated before they render man's habitat unlivable. The space age, if it accomplishes nothing else, will have served mankind well if it convinces man that his blue planet is a fragile and tenuous oasis in space that can not continue to be abused as it has been in the past.

Paradoxically, man's past successes in the struggle for survival stand to be his greatest obstacle for continuing survival. He has developed institutional systems that have encouraged and supported high fertility levels to compensate for milleniums of high mortality; and in recent times, he has achieved such notable technological achievements that most people firmly believe that man can now perpetually provide for his insatiable material needs. The notion that man is not only capable of, but is actively engaged in, destroying the very environment on which his existence depends seems totally inconceivable to most people—if they even bother to think about it.

World Population Growth

The struggle for survival has been underway for thousands of years, but not until about 300 years ago did the cumulative effect of man's efforts begin to appear in the form of accelerated population growth. It has been estimated that at about the time of Christ, the world's population was about half the number of people living in the United States in 1970; and that during the next 1,500 years, it increased to somewhere in the neighbourhood of 545 million. During the 200 years following 1650, estimates indicate that a doubling of the population occurred, a phenomenon which repeated itself again, but this time requiring only half the time as before. This second doubling produced a population of approximately 2,500,000,000 by 1950. At current rates of growth, the world's population is expected to reach somewhere between 6 and 7 billion by the year 2000. The present population, estimated at 3.6 billion, is expected to double again within 35 years.

A general description of total world growth, while emphasizing its recent acceleration, hides two important aspects of the population explosion: first, that the first stage was triggered off by a relatively small part of the world's population, i.e., the Europeans; and second, since as early as the 1920s the acceleration in growth has been spreading to the much larger non-European populations. The evidence for this is found in the declining proportion of the world's population living in the more developed regions. In 1921, the United Nations estimated this portion to be about 36.2 per cent. By 1960, this proportion had dropped to 32.6 per cent, and projections of future growth to the year 2000 indicate that the populations living in the developed areas will have declined to 23.5 per cent.[1]

The population explosion, triggered by the complex interaction of forces giving rise to, and resulting from, the commercial, agricultural, and industrial revolutions, has clearly spread to the larger underdeveloped areas of the world containing the bulk of the human population. The twentieth century has witnessed the beginning of the second and more critical phase of the world's population problem. Developments in medical and health sciences during the past 300 years in Western industrialized societies have become the triggering device for a potentially greater explosion. Rates of increase for Asia, Africa, and particularly for Central and South America since 1920 have accelerated mainly as a consequence of the diffusion of this information through aid programs and subsequent reductions of mortality in these areas. The major difference between the first and second phase is that mortality reductions can now be accomplished practically overnight. Little time is left

Fig. 14:1

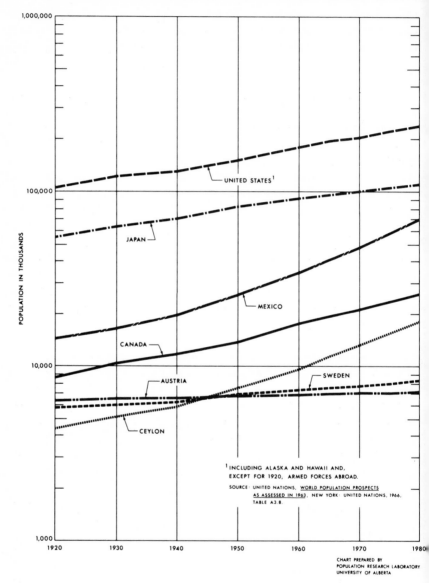

POPULATION TRENDS AND FORECASTS
CANADA AND SELECTED COUNTRIES: 1920 TO 1980

POPULATION IN THOUSANDS

UNITED STATES[1]

JAPAN

MEXICO

CANADA

AUSTRIA

SWEDEN

CEYLON

[1] INCLUDING ALASKA AND HAWAII AND, EXCEPT FOR 1920, ARMED FORCES ABROAD.

SOURCE: UNITED NATIONS, WORLD POPULATION PROSPECTS AS ASSESSED IN 1963, NEW YORK: UNITED NATIONS, 1966, TABLE A3.8.

1,000,000

100,000

10,000

1,000

1920   1930   1940   1950   1960   1970   1980

CHART PREPARED BY
POPULATION RESEARCH LABORATORY
UNIVERSITY OF ALBERTA

for changing people's attitudes and values related to their high levels of reproductive behaviour. Notwithstanding Japan's recent and spectacular success in reducing its birth rate, current family planning programs give little reason to hope for significant fertility declines in most problem areas in the immediate future.[2] Humanitarian hopes for further reductions in mortality, coupled with a continuation of high fertility which has been traditionally characteristic of these areas, gives promise of an even more spectacular growth in the era just ahead.

Canada in the World Perspective

In 1970, Canada's population was estimated at 21.4 million, with birth and death rates of 17.7 and 7.4 per cent respectively, providing an annual rate of increase of approximately 1.7 per cent. At this rate, Canada's population will double in just 41 years. While this is somewhat less than the growth rate for the world as a whole, it is still higher than the current rate of 1.0 per cent for the United States, and considerably higher than any European country, with the minor exceptions of Iceland and Albania. In only one other area occupied by European people was the growth rate higher, and this was in Australia where the rate was estimated at 1.9 per cent.

Canada, although highly urbanized and industrialized, with the third highest per capita gross national product among western countries, had some of the characteristics of less developed countries. For example, its gross reproduction rate of 1.9 in 1959 came very close to passing the limit of 2.0 used by the United Nations in classifying countries as underdeveloped areas. This is reflected in the fact that one-third of its population was under 15 years of age in 1970, a proportion considerably higher than normally found in Western Europe; whereas its infant mortality rate, at 22.0 per 1,000 births, was considerably higher than the pace-setting Scandinavian countries.

Canada's growth experience between 1920 and 1960, and projections to 1980 are shown in Figure 14:1 in conjunction with similar trends for selected countries. Decade growth rates for Canada have been consistently higher than those for the United States and most other European countries. Somewhat surprising, perhaps, is the fact that they have also been consistently higher than the growth rates for Japan. Evidence of the nature of the current phase of the population explosion can be found in a comparison of Canada's growth before and after 1930 with such underdeveloped countries as Mexico and Ceylon. Between 1920 and 1930, Canada's decade increase of 18.8 per cent exceeded that of both Ceylon and Mexico with 17.1 and 14.4 per cent respectively. Since 1930, however, growth rates for the latter two countries have tended to exceed Canada's by significant margins.

Recent Demographic Trends

Urbanization. Canada's growth has continued since 1961, in 1966 reaching 20,014,880, and an estimated 21,190,000 on June 1. Estimates of the rate of increase in recent years have been declining, and this is substantiated by rates which have declined from 20.3 in 1954 to 10.2 for the year ending May 31, 1970. Movement into urban areas has continued with the proportion urban reaching 73.6 per cent in 1966, compared to 69.6 in 1961. Most of this growth occurred in urban populations of 500,000 and over which increased their proportion of the total population from one-quarter to just under 30 per cent. All told, in 1966 just under one-half, or 47.3 per cent, of Canada's population lived in cities of 100,000 or more. Canada's population will continue to grow and become more concentrated in its biggest urban centres; but, as has been pointed out, when a population approaches the higher levels of urbanization, its rate of urbanization will begin to slow down as more and more of the growth occurs in the rural fringe areas.[3]

Fertility. The most significant phenomenon of the 1960s was the continuing decline in both numbers of births and the birth rate. The number of births declined consistently from its peak of 479,300 in 1959 to its low point of 364,300 in 1968, before increasing slightly in 1969 and again in 1970. The birth rate also declined from 1954 to 1968, dropping from 28.5 to 17.6. By 1970, it was still approximately the same at 17.5. An important consequence of this decline has been the shrinking proportion of population under 15 years of age. In 1961, this young age group constituted 34.0 per cent of the total. By 1966, it had declined slightly to 33.0, and in the span of the next three years had declined to 31.0 per cent.[4] Concomitant with this decline in the relative size of the younger age group was the perceptible increase in proportion of the population 65 years of age and over. Their proportion rose from 7.7 per cent in 1961 to 7.8 in 1969.

Number of marriages, families, and family size. The number of marriages has been increasing steadily since 1961, and the marriage rate just since 1964 when it was 7.2 climbed to 8.7 in 1970. Estimates indicate that in 1968 64.8 per cent of all males were married compared to 64.2 per cent of the females. The proportions divorced or widowed, for men and women combined, were 3.2 and 10.6 per cent respectively, down somewhat from the proportions in 1961 when 3.7 per cent were divorced and 10.2 per cent widowed. Proportions married in 1961, for men and women, were 66.4 and 66.8 per cent respectively, for their populations 15 years of age and over.[5]

On June 1, 1968, there were an estimated 4,969,000 families in Canada.[6] This represented an increase of 13.4 per cent over the number of families in 1961. However, the net family formation during this period was somewhat lower than the previous decade; and the number of persons per family remained constant at 3.9 during this period, as did the number of children per family at 1.9.[7]

It would appear that Canada is at an important demographic cross-roads. The marriage rate regained some of its lost ground as the post-war babies began to arrive at the marriageable ages, even while birth rates were still declining. It is still too early to say for certain just what the younger cohorts now entering marriage intend to do regarding the size and spacing of their families. Any decision that would postpone starting their families, or would induce them to space their children over a longer period of time than was characteristic of those women entering childbearing during the post-war period, would appear as apparent reductions in fertility even though family size might actually remain the same.

The most important question to be investigated at present is the determination of the significance of oral contraceptives for future childbearing patterns. Whether these new and more efficient methods will attract new contraceptive users or be adopted only by present users of the more traditional methods remains to be seen. In either case, its impact will have considerable social significance. A pioneering study carried out in Toronto, circa 1968, has shown that the "pill" has become the most widely used of all methods, and supports the position that the largest proportion of users of oral contraception have switched from other traditional and efficient methods.[8] This would suggest that the overall effectiveness would contribute less to a drastic decline in fertility than it would to increasing control over the timing of the first child and spacing of subsequent arrivals, i.e., more effective planning by those who are already convinced of the need for family planning. Thus, it will become imperative in the future to detect changes in attitudes concerning desired family size, if future trends in fertility are to be anticipated with any degree of accuracy.

Immigration during the 1960s. In 1961, immigration and unemployment rates hit their lowest and highest levels respectively for the entire post-war period. Subsequently, unemployment dropped sharply from 7.1 to 3.6 per cent of the labour force in 1966; and immigration not only recovered, but reached its second highest post-war peak when 222,876 immigrants arrived in Canada in 1967. Subsequently, immigration again declined and unemployment increased.[9] Thus, immigration appears to continue to react sensitively to changes in the economy and the demands of Canada's labour force. New changes in immigration regulations made in 1962, placing emphasis on education and occupational skills rather than ethnic origins of immigrants, appear to have been partially successful in achieving their stated objectives. The proportion of arriving immigrants who were professional, technical, and managerial workers increased during the latter part of the 1960s. In addition, those of the traditionally preferred origins, British Isles and other Northern and Western Europeans, have declined relatively to other origin groups as the volume of immigration increased subsequent to 1961. Analyses of immigration data for the late 1950s and 1960s also show that the number of immigrants arriving from the United States has increased steadily throughout the decade, apparently more as a consequence of events in the United States than in response to changing economic conditions in Canada. Although relatively small in numbers, the entire complexion of immigration from the United States—including as it does the managers and officials for United States subsidiaries, and professors and teachers, in addition to young draft-age men seeking relief from the anxieties of national military conscription—is causing growing concern among the more nationalistic elements of Canada's population.

It would seem that, with political stability and a high level of economic activity in Europe coupled with a rapidly expanding domestic labour market in Canada, immigration in the immediate future will not hit the same levels as during the decade of the 1950s. However, there are still shortages of specific skills that will no doubt serve as the catalyst for a continuing and sizeable immigration.

Labour force. Between 1961 and 1969, the labour force increased from 6,500,000 to over 8,000,000. All of this growth was accounted for by the non-agricultural sector, as the agricultural component decreased by 148,000 during this period. As the population 14 years of age and over increased at a slightly lower rate than the labour force, the net effect was an increase in labour force participation. Since 1953, the average annual growth rate for the labour force has been 2.5 per cent; but, from about 1961, the rate rose from below 2.0 per cent to over 3.0 per cent within a four-year period.[10] Growth rates at the mid-1960s were among the highest ever recorded for Canada and exceed by far the current rates for almost all other major industrialized countries. Only Germany, in recent years, experienced a higher increase in employment. Unlike Canada, this appears to have been due to a large influx of workers rather than to natural increase.[11] While the aging of post-war births accounts for most of this unprecedented growth, immigration and the increasing participation of women in the labour force have also made significant contributions.

Worth noting is the fact that the largest increases in employment occurred among part-time workers. Their average rate of growth was 9.5 per cent per year, while full-time employment increased by only 2.0 per cent per annum. This was true of both male and female workers, but it was much more characteristic of women. In 1969, for example, almost one out of every four employed women worked part time compared to somewhat more than five per cent of the men. In 1953, only one in ten women, and less than two per cent of the men worked part time.[12] The significance of this particular trend in part-time employment is somewhat difficult to assess. A large number of these are apparently unpaid family workers working on family farms or in family businesses. Others are students, retired persons, and the physically handicapped. Almost three-fourths of the total are employed in the trade and service industries. In any event, the role of the part-time worker, whether he be an unattached individual living by himself or a family member, must be examined carefully in the years ahead.

A more interesting aspect of Canada's rapidly increasing labour force is its contribution to the growth of real national income. Of the various contributing factors, it has been estimated that two-thirds of the increase between 1950 and 1962 was due to massive increases in labour and capital, while only one-third could be attributed to gains in productive efficiency.[13] Another positive effect of a labour force growing more rapidly than the total population is the concomitant decline in dependency ratios. As the size of the economically productive population increases relative to those under 15 years of age and 65 years and over, the cost of public services (e.g., education, health and medical care, and old age pensions) are spread over larger numbers, thus reducing the individual taxpayer's relative share of the total costs.

Standard of living. Much of what has been said about the population in general has had considerable relevance for the Canadian way of life, but little has been said directly about the problem of poverty or about those individuals who have not been able to share in Canada's generally high standard of living. Statistically, poverty is difficult to define as one's minimal needs vary with age, place of residence, state of health, marital status, size of family (if married), and with one's philosophy of life. In other words, not everyone at the lowest end of the income distribution is disadvantaged to the same extent. Furthermore, the assessment of either the economic or social significance of low incomes is difficult in the face of constantly changing incomes and price levels. Analyses have shown that between 1931 and 1951, the bottom 20 per cent of all families actually received a sizeable increase in their share of the total income; but that since 1951 their share has remained relatively the same, even while their incomes have continued to increase rather rapidly.[14]

Average income for non-farm families and unattached individuals increased about ten per cent every two years between 1951 and 1957. After a rather sharp drop, average income again increased but at an accelerated rate, from 6.5 per cent between 1959 and 1961, to 16.4 per cent for the 1963–65 period when average income for all non-farm families and unattached individuals rose from $5,195 to $6,049.[15] Perhaps more important was the fact that the percentage with incomes under $2,000 decreased from 20.3 per cent in 1961 to 15.1 per cent in 1965. Looking at the situation somewhat differently, one-quarter of all families and unattached individuals received incomes of less than $2,391 in 1961. By 1965, the upper limit for the first quartile had increased to $3,095.[16]

If "low-income" families and individuals are defined as those using 70 per cent or more of their incomes for food, clothing, and shelter, then 27 per cent of the total non-farm population in Canada in 1961 would have been classified as existing at the poverty level. If a cutting point of 60 per cent had been used instead, the proportion would have increased to 41 per cent.[17] While any single cutting point for all individuals and families is quite unrealistic, the fact remains that a sizeable portion of the population is living on the economic fringes of society.

While income is one of the major indices of living standards, there are other indicators which reflect serious deficiencies in the provision of food, clothing, and shelter for certain segments of the population. For example, mortality, and particularly infant mortality, is especially sensitive to the quality of life experienced by any group. The average age at death in Canada in 1965 was 61.7 for males and 65.4 for females, and slightly over 62 years for both sexes combined. However, in the Northwest Territories, with its predominantly native population, the average ages were less than half of that for Canada as a whole, being just 30.1 and 27.1 years for males and females respectively. More specifically, the averages for Eskimos and Indians in this part of Canada were only 20 and 36 years for their total populations respectively.[18] Similarly, infant mortality figures for Eskimos and Indians in the Northwest Territories, reveal the same marginal and sub-standard living conditions. Rates for these two groups were 108.8 and 46.2 respectively compared to 23.1 for Canada as a whole in 1966. Herein lies a national tragedy of growing proportions.

More generally, the various indicators of poverty conditions will show that the likelihood of living under marginal conditions is increased if any number of the following exist: an individual lives in rural areas; he has had little formal education; he was not a member of the labour force during the preceding year; he lived in a family where the head was 65 years of age or older, where no member of the family had worked during the year, or where the family head was a female. As revealing as these statistics might be, they are misleading if they suggest that poverty is only to be found in rural areas or among individuals having the kinds of particular characteristics mentioned above. Analyses of the 1961 Census data will show that almost two-thirds of the low-income non-farm families lived in urban areas, with more than half of these in the metropolitan centres. In addition, over 80 per cent lived outside the Atlantic Provinces, 87 per cent of the families had male heads, over three-fourths of the family heads were under 65 years of age, and 68 per cent had heads who were members of the labour force at some time during the year.[19] Thus, while it is patently obvious that conditions are tragic in the

North and elsewhere in Canada for relatively small but very important minority groups, this should not detract from the fact that the largest share of Canadians living under sub-standard conditions are very much like other Canadians, and are to be found in its urban centres where the amenities of life are supposedly available to all.

Demographic Projections

As revealing as the national censuses are of the social and economic condition of the country at a particular point in time, it is still incumbent upon the demographer to utilize these data in an effort to forecast future trends so that long range planning can have a rational basis. Thus, periodically there have been studies whose objectives are to provide demogrophic projections to serve as a basis for estimates of Canada's future economic growth. Those prepared for the Economic Council of Canada by Illing and Zsigmond in 1967 and 1970 are the most recent, and their major findings will be briefly summarized here to indicate the anticipated direction of Canada's future growth.[20]

Illing's population estimates for 1966, based on medium fertility and immigration assumptions, fell somewhat short of the 1966 Census results. Nevertheless, this particular set is used rather than the United Nation's projections as it provides the basis for projections of the number of families, labour force size, and school enrolments summarized in the following sections. To the extent that the population forecasts fall short of actual developments, the forecasts for special components of the total population may also be expected to exhibit the same deficiencies. However, their usefulness is not impaired if it is kept in mind that the various assumptions used in these projections provide a range of estimates varying from 23.8 to 26.7 million, rather than just the one estimate of 25.1 million for 1980 based on the "medium" assumptions. Actually, the upper limit of these projections just encompasses the United Nations "medium" variant estimate of 26.3 million for 1980.[21]

Projections to 1980, for anticipated increases in the number of families, enrolment in secondary and post-secondary schools, and the size of the labour force are presented in Figure 14:2.

Family formation. Illing sees the net effect of the baby boom and post-war immigration to be a continuing steep rise in the number of marriages and for net family formation. Projections for the latter indicate a rising trend from 100,500 in 1966 to approximately 150,000 by 1980. The number of families is expected to increase from 4,574,600 to 6,341,700 during the projection period. Thus, the annual percentage change in family formation, which had declined to 1.5 per cent for the 1960–65 period, has been projected to regain its 1950–55 level of 2.5 per cent by the 1975–80 forecast period.[22]

Fig. 14:2

TRENDS AND FORECASTS
POPULATION AND SELECTED COMPONENTS
CANADA[1]:   1950 TO 1980

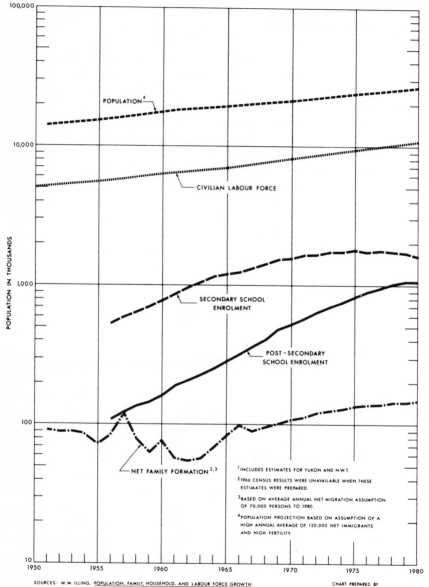

POPULATION[4]

CIVILIAN LABOUR FORCE

SECONDARY SCHOOL
ENROLMENT

POST-SECONDARY
SCHOOL ENROLMENT

NET FAMILY FORMATION[2,3]

[1] INCLUDES ESTIMATES FOR YUKON AND N.W.T.

[2] 1966 CENSUS RESULTS WERE UNAVAILABLE WHEN THESE
ESTIMATES WERE PREPARED.

[3] BASED ON AVERAGE ANNUAL NET MIGRATION ASSUMPTION
OF 70,000 PERSONS TO 1980.

[4] POPULATION PROJECTION BASED ON ASSUMPTION OF A
HIGH ANNUAL AVERAGE OF 120,000 NET IMMIGRANTS
AND HIGH FERTILITY.

POPULATION IN THOUSANDS

SOURCES: W.M. ILLING, POPULATION, FAMILY, HOUSEHOLD, AND LABOUR FORCE GROWTH,
OTTAWA: ECONOMIC COUNCIL OF CANADA, 1967, TABLES 2-9; 3-2; 3-3; 4-8; AND
Z.E. ZSIGMOND AND C.J.WENAAS, ENROLMENT IN EDUCATIONAL INSTITUTIONS BY
PROVINCE, 1951-52 TO 1980-81, OTTAWA: ECONOMIC COUNCIL OF CANADA, 1970,
TABLES A-1; A-2.

CHART PREPARED BY
POPULATION RESEARCH LABORATORY
UNIVERSITY OF ALBERTA

School enrolments. With most elementary school age children in attendance, the crucial years become the secondary and post-secondary years of education. Enrolment data for these years give the best indication of the schools' retention or holding power, as well as an indication of the degree of educational up-grading occurring within the population. The first of the post-war babies born in late 1945 and 1946 began entering secondary schools by the end of the 1950s, and the effects of this rapid increase in births continued to be felt for almost a decade. Overlaid with the effects of increasing size of successive birth cohorts is the increasing holding power of the schools beyond the compulsory school years. In 1951, less than half of the 14–17 year olds were attending secondary school, but by 1960, the proportion had increased to approximately two-thirds, and by 1980 the proportions have been projected to 92.4 per cent, a level comparable to that achieved in the United States during the mid-1960s. The total effect of these two trends by 1980 will have been to quadruple the enrolment level of 1951–52. A full-time secondary enrolment of 1,667,400 has been projected for the 1980–81 school year compared to 394,500 for 1951–52.[23]

Current and anticipated trends for post-secondary education are even more spectacular. Whereas the proportion of the 14–17 year old age group will have approximately doubled between 1951 and 1980, the proportion of 18–24 year olds engaged in post-secondary schooling almost doubled during the first decade, reaching 11.3 per cent in 1961–62. By 1980, the proportion will have tripled that of the 1961–62 level if the projections are reasonably correct. The proportions of 18–24 year olds attending post-secondary schools has been projected to increase from 14.2 per cent (in 1965–66) to 33.2 per cent by 1980. Translated into enrolments, this means that the number attending post-secondary schools in 1980–81 will reach 1,130,000, compared to 193,600 in 1961–62. Of these, 750,000 are expected to be attending universities or teacher colleges.[24]

Labour force growth. As is often the case, recent trends have exceeded expectations, requiring revision of earlier projections for the labour force. A slower decline in participation rates for young males and more rapid increases than expected for women, 20–24 years of age, resulted in an underestimate of the 1970 labour force. The latest revision, taking into account this new evidence, projects a 50 per cent increase in the size of the labour force between 1965 and 1980. By the projection date, a labour force of over 10,-500,000 is expected.[25]

In 1962 Canada had lower labour force participation rates than such countries as Britain, France, Germany, Sweden, and the United States. This discrepancy was particularly significant for females whose rate of 33.3 was considerably lower than the 43.5 per cent for the United States, and 49.0 for Britain.[26] This is partially the reason why women are expected to account for 1,500,000 of the 3,500,000 increase, as their participation rate is expected to reach 46.5 per cent by 1980.

In contrast to the picture of increasing participation for women, are the prospects for men. Rates for the major working age groups are expected to remain high and relatively constant. However, participation by those under 20 and 65 years and over is expected to continue to decline. Projected enrolment trends for post-secondary education suggest that the labour force participation rates for males 20–24 years of age will also decline as relatively more choose to continue their education.[27] Participation rates for all ages combined are expected to decline until 1975, at which time the trend will reverse with a slight increase expected to carry through until 1980.[28] This slight reversal in trend will reflect the changing age distribution of males rather than any underlying shift in work patterns for males in Canadian society.

The 1971 Census of Canada

Forecasting future events on the basis of historical trends is at best a risky undertaking. However, lacking the clairvoyance of the crystalball gazer, one must look to the past for clues as to the most probable future. In the last analysis, our knowledge of the present, as well as projections into the future based on past trends, must be constantly updated on the basis of new information. Thus we see the importance of the government's periodic censuses and special monthly surveys as sources of current information about changes occurring within the Canadian population.

The last complete enumeration, the quinquennial census of 1966, provided only a limited amount of information on the basic characteristics of the population. The 1971 decennial census, on the other hand, will provide the most complete updating of Canada's population inventory since 1961. New techniques of data collection are being introduced to improve both the efficiency and accuracy of this national inventory of human resources. As is always the case, the value of this undertaking will be totally dependent upon all Canadians recognizing its importance, as well as their cooperating in its taking. Certainly, every Canadian should be aware of the fact that while up-to-date information about their society does not guarantee good government, it is an impossibility without it, no matter how good the intentions of the government might be.

REFERENCES

Illing, Wolfgang M.: *Population, Family, Household and Labour Force Growth to 1980.* Staff Study No. 19. Economic Council of Canada, Ottawa, The Queen's Printer, 1967.

Population Research Bureau: "Canada Land of Plenty." *Population Bulletin,* Vol. XIV, No. 3 (May 1958), Washington, D.C.

United Nations: *World Population Prospects as Assessed in 1963.* Population Studies, No. 41. New York, United Nations, 1966.

Zsigmond, Z. E., and C. J. Wenaas: *Enrolment in Educational Institutions by Province, 1951–52 to 1980–81.* Staff Study No. 25, Economic Council of Canada, Ottawa, Queen's Printer, 1970.

FOOTNOTES

[1]Estimates of population based on "medium" fertility trends. United Nations, *World Population Prospects as Assessed in 1963,* Population Studies No. 41, New York, United Nations, 1966, Table A3:2, p. 134.

[2]Kingsley Davis, "Population Policy: Will Current Programs Succeed?" *Science,* 158 (3802), 10 November 1967, pp. 730–739.

[3]Kingsley Davis, "The Urbanization of the Human Population," *Cities,* A Scientific American Book, New York, Alfred A. Knopf, 1965, pp. 3–24.

[4]Dominion Bureau of Statistics, *Estimated Population by Sex and Age Groups for Canada and Provinces, June 1, 1969,* Cat. No. 91-202, Annual, December, 1969.

[5]Dominion Bureau of Statistics, *Population Estimates by Marital Status, Age and Sex, for Canada and Provinces, 1968,* Cat. No. 91-203, April, 1970.

[6]Excluding the Yukon and Northwest Territories.

[7]Dominion Bureau of Statistics, *Estimates of Families in Canada, 1968,* Cat. No. 91-204, December, 1969.

[8]J. F. Kantner, J. D. Allingham, and T. R. Balakrishnan, "Oral Contraception and the Fertility Decline in Canada, 1958–1968. A First Look at a Crucial Component in the Argument." A paper presented at the Annual Meeting of the Population Association of America, Boston, April, 1968, 21 pp.

[9]Dominion Bureau of Statistics, *The Labour Force, May, 1970,* Cat. No. 71-001, Ottawa, The Queen's Printer, Table 2, and Department of Manpower and Immigration, *1968 Immigration Statistics,* Ottawa, The Queen's Printer, Table 2.

[10]W. M. Illing, *Population, Family, Household and Labour Force Growth to 1980,* Staff Study No. 19, Economic Council of Canada, Ottawa, The Queen's Printer, 1967, Chart 4-1.

[11]Economic Council of Canada, *Fifth Annual Review,* Ottawa, The Queen's Printer, 1968, p. 13.

[12]Dominion Bureau of Statistics, *The Labour Force, May, 1970,* Cat. No. 71-001, Ottawa, The Queen's Printer, p. 2.

[13]Economic Council of Canada, *op. cit.,* p. 9.

[14]*Ibid.,* pp. 106–107.

[15]Dominion Bureau of Statistics, *Income Distribution by Size in Canada, 1965,* Ottawa, The Queen's Printer, 1968, p. 9.

[16]*Ibid.*

[17]*Ibid.,* pp. 109–110.

[18]Dominion Bureau of Statistics, *Vital Statistics, 1967,* Ottawa, The Queen's Printer, 1969, Table D4A; and, Economic Council of Canada, *op. cit.,* p. 121 (Erratum).

[19]Economic Council of Canada, *op. cit.,* pp. 112–113.

[20]W. M. Illing, *op. cit.;* and Z. E. Zsigmond and C. J. Wenaas, *Enrolment in Educational Institutions by Province, 1951–52 to 1980–81,* Economic Council of Canada, Staff Study No. 25, Ottawa, The Queen's Printer, January, 1970.

[21]United Nations, *World Population Prospects as Assessed in 1963,* Population Studies No. 41, New York, United Nations, 1966, Table A3:8, pp. 140–144.

[22]W. M. Illing, *op. cit.,* Tables 3-B, 3-2, 3-3, and Chart 3-2.

[23]Z. E. Zsigmond and C. J. Wenaas, *op. cit.,* Tables A-1, A-2, and A-3.

[24]*Ibid.,* Table A-3.

[25]Illing, *op. cit.*

[26]*Ibid.* These female labour force rates are calculated as a proportion of the population 15–64 years of age. Estimates based on the population 14 years of age and over were 32.8 in 1966, and 40.1 per cent in 1980. See Table 4-5.

[27]*Ibid.,* p. 74.

[28]*Ibid.,* Table 4-1.

GLOSSARY

Age-specific birth rate. Number of live births to females in a specific age group (e.g., 20–24) per 1,000 females in that age group at mid-year.

Age-sex specific death rate. Number of deaths in a specific age and sex group per 1,000 individuals in that age group at mid-year.

Child-woman ratio. A ratio of the number of children under five years of age in a population to the total number of women in reproductive ages in that population.

Cohort. A group of persons experiencing a specific event, e.g., birth, marriage, etc., in a given period of time, such as a calendar year.

Crude birth rate. Number of live births occurring in a one year period per 1,000 mid-year population.

Crude death rate. Number of deaths in one year per 1,000 mid-year population. Rates are generally based on place of residence of the deceased rather than place of occurrence.

Dependency ratio. A ratio of the dependent population, usually defined as persons under 15 and over 64 years of age, to the population in the major working or economically active age groups, i.e., the population 15–64 years of age.

General fertility rate. Number of live births in one year per 1,000 females of *childbearing age*.

Gross reproduction rate. The total number of female births that would occur per 1,000 women during their childbearing years if they experienced no mortality and were subject to the age-specific rates of a specified fertility table. This is generally obtained by multiplying the *total fertility rate* by the proportion of births which are female.

Infant mortality rate. Ratio of deaths to children under one year of age in a given year to the number of live births in the same year.

Life expectancy. The average number of years of life remaining to males or females of a specified age under a given set of mortality conditions, i.e., a schedule of age-sex specific death rates.

Gross migration. The total of the number of persons arriving to establish residence in an area (immigrants), and the number leaving to establish residence elsewhere (emigrants).

Net migration. The difference between the number of arriving immigrants and departing emigrants.

Morbidity rate. The proportion of sickness, or of a specific disease, in a defined population.

Population forecast. A projection based on fertility, mortality, and migration assumptions which are regarded as most probable or realistic for a given population.

Population projection. An estimate of future population based on certain assumptions regarding the future course of fertility, mortality, and migration.

Proportion. A ratio indicating the relation in size of a part to a whole.

Rate. A ratio used to indicate the relative frequency of a specified event within a defined population. For examples, see *crude birth rate, infant mortality rate,* etc.

Ratio. A quotient which indicates the relation in size of one number to another. For examples, see *child-woman* or *sex ratio.*

Sex ratio. Number of males per 100 females in a specified population.

Standardized rate. A rate which has been adjusted to permit the comparison of several populations with respect to one variable, e.g., fertility, mortality, or migration, while holding constant the effect of one or several other variables, e.g., age, marital status, etc.

Stable population. A population, closed to migration, which experiences constant age-specific fertility and mortality for a sufficiently long period of time to achieve a constant rate of increase. Under such conditions, the proportion of persons in the different age and sex groups will also remain constant.

Stationary population. A *stable population* with a zero growth rate, i.e., a rate of natural increase equal to zero.

Total fertility rate. The total number of births per 1,000 women that would occur during their childbearing years if they experienced no mortality and were subject to the age-specific fertility rates of a specified fertility schedule.

[1]For a much more complete list and discussion of basic demographic concepts, see the *Multilingual Demographic Dictionary* prepared by the Demographic Dictionary Committee of the International Union for the Scientific Study of Population and published by the Department of Economic and Social Affairs of the United Nations in 1958 (ST/SOA/Ser.A/29. Sales No. :58.XIII.4).

Index